GALATIANS

St. Paul's Epistle to the Galatians is a message of freedom. The peoples of the world are longing for freedom. When so many religious peddlers are selling us alternative ideas which invariably lead us to bondage, it is heartwarming and even merciful that God should bring to us a fresh commentary on this book of freedom called Galatians. I trust no one more with this needed and most central message of the Gospel that my friend, Dr. Terry Johnson. Dr. Johnson's extensive pastoral work, his insights into the Word of God, his demonstrated leadership in preaching, teaching and living the message of the book of Galatians qualifies him as the man for the hour to write this great new commentary. I commend this new Christian Focus commentary by Dr. Johnson to all without hesitation

MICHAEL A. MILTON,
Chancellor/CEO elect,
The James M. Baird Jr. Professor of Pastoral Theology,
Reformed Theological Seminary

I am grateful to Terry Johnson for providing the church with a faithful exposition of Galatians. The fact that Johnson has preached through Galatians gives this book the benefit of strong and insightful application. Johnson clearly explains some of the most difficult passages in Scripture, stalwartly defends evangelical doctrines such "justification by faith alone," and also interacts with newer movements such as Federal Vision Theology and the New Perspective on Paul. This volume will be of help to any pastor or faithful Christian alike.

GREG GILBERT,
Senior Pastor, Third Avenue Baptist Church,
Louisville, Kentucky
Author of *What is the Gospel?*

Remarkably fresh, insightful and faithful to the gospel. Anyone seeking to mine the riches of this essential Pauline letter will benefit enormously from Terry Johnson's exposition. Teachers and preachers will especially be helped by this rich and balanced treatment of Galatians.

RICHARD D. PHILLIPS,
Senior Minister, Second Presbyterian Church,
Greenville, South Carolina

Given current debates over the meaning of law, gospel and justification, a knowledge of Galatians has become essential. Johnson's commentary is essential reading for preachers and lay folk alike.

DEREK THOMAS,
Minister of Preaching and Teaching,
First Presbyterian Church, Columbia, South Carolina

Clear exposition, forceful exhortation, and brazen applications are the hallmarks of Terry Johnson's preaching. Pastor Johnson doesn't tell us about Galatians; he speaks God's Word to our hearts from Galatians.

PETER KEMENY,
Pastor, Good News Presbyterian Church,
Frederick, Maryland

Galatians

A Mentor Expository Commentary

Terry L. Johnson

MENTOR

Terry Johnson is Senior Pastor of the Independent Presbyterian Church in Savannah, Georgia.

ISBN 978-1-84550-689-6

First Published in 2012
in the
Mentor Imprint
by
Christian Focus Publications
Geanies House, Fearn, Ross-shire
IV20 1TW, Scotland
www.christianfocus.com

Cover design by moose77.com
Printed by MPG, Cornwall, England

MIX
Paper from responsible sources
FSC® C018575

Contents

This work is dedicated to the memory of the
Rev. William Still of Aberdeen, Scotland,
whose *Work of the Pastor* persuaded me to
preach the whole Bible that the people of
God might feed upon the whole Christ.

Preface

The Apostle Paul's epistle to the Galatians divides into two unequal parts. The first part, essentially from 1:1 through 5:12, is densely theological, and among the most difficult portions of Scripture to interpret. We have dispersed practical application throughout this section, but there is no denying the biblical and theological complexity of the teaching through which one must wade. We are not complaining, just acknowledging the fact while urging the reader to persevere through the material. Nothing so thrilled my young Christian soul as when I first grasped the meaning of justification by faith alone, the Apostle's burden in 1:1–5:12. This is the heart of the gospel, a message which, in an important sense, believers can't hear too often, especially in the richly textured ways in which the Apostle Paul tells the story.

On the other hand, 5:13–6:18 is among the most practical blocks of teaching to be found in the entire Bible. In this section, we will deal in depth with the relation between grace and license, the deeds of the flesh and the fruit of the Spirit, bearing one another's burdens, and the law of sowing and reaping. The material is rich indeed with immediate and obvious practical application for Christian living.

Though the sections are unequal, the forty chapters in this work, in the end, turn out to be almost equally divided.

1. Galatians 1:1–5:12. Twenty-two 'theological' chapters (with plenty of practical application).
2. Galatians 5:13–6:18. Eighteen 'practical' chapters (with considerable theological content).

All Christians must be theologians, Spurgeon would say, and all theologians must practice Christian living. There is something for everyone in both sections of the Apostle Paul's letter to the Galatians, a feast for both our theological and practical selves.

This book began as Sunday morning sermons in July 1996 through October 1997. They were reworked and taught for a community Bible study in 2006 through 2007. Finally they were edited and readied for publication in 2010.

I should clarify that I seldom use quotations in my sermons. The reason for not doing so is simple; rarely do they enhance the overall effect, or what might be called the rhetorical impact of a message. I have included them and their sources in this work so that readers might see that credible scholars agree with my reading of the text. In other words, I included them so that future interpreters might have confidence that I've gotten the meaning of the text right, not just because I say so, but because my argument makes sense both to me and to other capable interpreters. However, in the normal course of preaching, I don't recommend their inclusion except on a very limited basis.

I thankfully acknowledge the irreplaceable contribution of Debbie Parker, my secretary, who patiently endures miserably illegible handwriting and interminably tedious revisions. I also must acknowledge the congregation of the Independent Presbyterian Church, which granted me a two month sabbatical in the summer of 2010 in order to finish this project, among others.

1

The Grace of Christ

Galatians 1:1–5

Galatians is undoubtedly the most controversial, the most polemical, and the most personal of all of the New Testament books. Because of its vigorous defense of justification by faith and the Christian's freedom from the curse of the law, Galatians has been called the 'Magna Carta of Christian liberty.' Many of the church fathers wrote commentaries on it (e.g. Chrysostom, Augustine, Victorinus, and Jerome). James Montgomery Boice calls it 'the cornerstone of the Protestant Reformation.'[1] Its influence upon Luther was particularly profound. His expositions of Galatians at the University of Wittenburg, begun on October 27, 1516, preceded the publishing of the *Ninety-Five Thesis* which launched the Reformation by one year almost to the day (October 31, 1517). Luther's commentary on it, published in 1519, exerted enormous influence then and repeatedly since. Charles Wesley and others during the Great Awakening were converted while reading it. Luther said of Galatians, 'I am wedded to it,' calling it his 'Katie von Bora.'

Why is it so important? Because in the context of a direct challenge by legalists, the Apostle Paul defends the gospel against the encroachments of its most persistent enemy, the religion of merit. Nowhere in the Bible is it clearer that one can only be saved through faith alone in Christ alone apart from works. Galatians is from beginning to end dealing with the answer to the question, 'What must I do to be saved?' Given that all of us must one day die and stand before God, there can be no more important question, and none on behalf of which we ought to exert ourselves to be sure that we have answered it correctly.

Background

We must begin by looking at the background to this epistle. What issues were the occasion of its writing? The basic issue was *the relation between law and justification*. Around AD 50 the church faced its first doctrinal crisis. More and more the gospel was taking root in Gentile communities around the Mediterranean. As these non-Jews came to believe in Christ and enter what heretofore had been largely a Jewish Christian church, the question naturally arose regarding their relation to customs and traditions of Judaism. Would Gentile believers be required to keep the Law of Moses, particularly its ceremonial aspects, in order to be Christians? The defining issue was circumcision. Some were teaching, as Luke reports, that 'unless you are circumcised according to the custom of Moses, you cannot be saved' (Acts 15:1). Another important question was that of ceremonial cleanliness (2:11 ff.). Could Jewish and Gentile Christians enjoy table fellowship together? Could they share a meal, or would a practicing Jew (though now a Christian) be contaminated by contact with Gentiles, as Jewish traditions taught? Apparently the issue of observing the Jewish sacred calendar also was raised (4:10). 'In short,' says Lightfoot, 'nothing less than submission to the whole ceremonial law seems to have been contemplated by the innovators.'[2] Thus both the unity of the church and the graciousness of the gospel were being threatened. The 'Judaizers,' as they came to be called, were insisting that the Gentile believers also perform the ceremonial rites and observe the religious festivals of Judaism, and be, in effect, practicing Jews as well as Christians. Membership in the community of God's people as well as salvation itself were said to depend upon it.

Please note that no one was denying that Jesus was the Christ, the Messiah. No one was denying that Jesus had been raised from the grave. No one was denying that His commands must be obeyed. No one was denying that He must be believed in if one is to be saved. This was affirmed by all. Indeed the manner in which the Apostle Paul contrasts his call to be an apostle as being 'not sent from men…but through Jesus Christ,' implying as it does that Jesus stands on God's side of the line that separates God and man, assumes agreement even at this point. As Machen points out, 'even the Judaizers, so far as we can see, had no quarrel with the Apostle Paul's lofty view of Christ.' Paul, he notes, 'does not argue about it,' and 'seems to be under no necessity whatever of defending it against attack within the Church.'[3] But they were adding to Christ these ceremonial ordinances as necessary, at least, if mutual fellowship between Jews and Gentiles was to be enjoyed, and probably for salvation as well. As Bruce summarizes, 'even if they demand only a token measure of law-keeping from the Galatians, any such demand involves acceptance of the principle of justification by works of the law.'[4]

The second issue was *the apostleship of Paul*. More clearly and more forcefully than anyone else, the Apostle was teaching that Gentile Christians were free from the ceremonial requirements of Mosaic Law. Consequently, along with this attack on the gospel came an attack on the chief emissary of that gospel, the Apostle Paul himself. It is easy enough to see how the two are related. The Apostle Paul was watering down the gospel, they were saying. He was altering the gospel as the Twelve had preached it in order to make it more appealing to Gentiles. Consequently, they denied that he was authorized to preach such a message. They denied that he was a true apostle at all. Whatever authority he had, they may have said, it was less than that of the Twelve who, in fact, disapproved of his departure from Jewish ancestral traditions. Thus there was a two pronged attack: one against the message, one against the messenger. One denies the sufficiency of grace; the other denies the authority of the Apostle Paul. On these two fronts, Paul will counterattack.

Amongst whom and when were these issues swirling? The Apostle addresses himself to 'the churches of Galatia' (v. 2). Who are they? The term 'Galatia,' can be used to refer to two separate regions in present day Asia Minor or Turkey. The scholars debate whether or not it indicates 'northern' or 'southern' Galatia. The former was the homeland of a migratory Celtic people who also settled in present day France (and later Britain) and were called 'Gauls,' and came to be distinguished from the West-European Gauls by the term 'Gallo-Graecians,' from which the term 'Galatians' was derived. Or it could refer to the 'southern' Galatian region which carried the Roman provincial name of 'Galatia,' and included such cities as Pisidian Antioch, Lystra, Derbe, and Iconium, that is, major cities of the empire to which Paul was inclined to visit, and indeed did visit, as we read in Acts 13 and 14. Most modern scholars take the latter view though the matter cannot be resolved with certainty. Whichever is the case, Paul himself had brought the gospel of grace to the 'churches of Galatia.' He was, in some respects, their 'founding pastor.' He refers in 4:13 ff. to a 'bodily illness' of an especially repulsive nature which detained him in Galatia, leading to his ministry among them. They responded to his proclamation as though Paul were 'an angel of God, as Christ Jesus Himself.' He had a deep affection for them. Consequently, when they began to listen to the Judaizers, he reacted with righteous indignation. 'You foolish Galatians,' he says, 'who has bewitched you?' 'I fear for you,' he complains, 'that perhaps I have labored over you in vain.' 'Would that those who are troubling you would even mutilate themselves' (3:1; 4:11; 5:12). The Apostle sees in their changing views a supreme crisis for the church, one which is undermining the gospel itself. About this he is clear and dogmatic. Those who add works to grace preach 'a different gospel,' they 'distort the gospel of Christ,' and are 'accursed' (1:6–9).

It is difficult to date the precise time of writing. It is fairly certain that it lies between the eve of the Jerusalem Council described in Acts 15, usually dated at AD 48–49, and the Apostle Paul's imprisonment recorded in Acts 21, approximately AD 58. Paul's lengthy stay in Ephesus, about AD 52, is often cited as a likely possibility. F. F. Bruce and R. Y. K. Fung argue for the earlier date. It is typically regarded as the earliest of the New Testament books, indeed the earliest extant Christian document, and therefore provides us with our first glimpse of the primitive church.

Finally, we may broadly outline the epistle as follows.

1:1–10	Salutation and Introduction of Issues
1:11–2:21	Defense of Paul's Apostleship
3:1–5:12	Defense of the Gospel
5:13–6:10	Practical Exhortations

Paul's Apostleship

Paul begins with an introductory defense of his apostleship.

> Paul, an apostle (not sent from men, nor through the agency of man, but through Jesus Christ, and God the Father, who raised Him from the dead). (Gal. 1:1)

This unusual introduction shows Paul's understanding of the *importance of the issues*.

Let us remember that the Apostle Paul is one of the primary authors of the New Testament. He was once a violent persecutor of the church, but was dramatically converted on the Damascus road, was called by Christ to be an apostle, and went on to be the greatest missionary in the history of the Christian Church. Paul's introduction contains all of the usual elements found in the letters of antiquity and his letters to the other churches: the writer's name, the name of those to whom the letter is written, and an expression of good wishes ('grace and peace'). But unlike his other letters, there is no expression of praise for the Galatian churches. Instead, he plunges directly into the matters of concern which will be addressed throughout the letter. Immediately he defends his apostleship and his gospel from those who had attacked it. I am 'Paul,' he says, 'an apostle (not sent from men, nor through the agency of man, but through Jesus Christ, and God the Father.' Compare this, for example with the opening lines of Philippians:

> Paul and Timothy, bond-servants of Christ Jesus, to all the saints in Christ Jesus who are in Philippi, including the overseers and deacons: grace to you and peace from God our Father and the Lord Jesus Christ. I thank my God in all my remembrance of you, always offering prayer with joy in my every prayer for you all, in view of your participation in the gospel from the first day until now. (Phil. 1:1–5)

The tone is entirely different. He is obviously pleased with the Philippian believers. He has deep affection for them. His thanksgiving overflows. There is a complete absence of the defensiveness of Galatians, even as Galatians is devoid of the affectionate and thankful tone of Philippians. Listen to him again with the Ephesians:

> For this reason I too, having heard of the faith in the Lord Jesus which exists among you, and your love for all the saints, do not cease giving thanks for you, while making mention of you in my prayers. (Eph. 1:15–16)

Similarly he says to the Colossians:

> Paul, an apostle of Jesus Christ by the will of God, and Timothy our brother, to the saints and faithful brethren in Christ who are at Colossae: grace to you and peace from God our Father. We give thanks to God, the Father of our Lord Jesus Christ, praying always for you, since we heard of your faith in Christ Jesus and the love which you have for all the saints. (Col. 1:1–4)

With both the Ephesians and the Colossians, he identifies himself, his readers, offers grace and peace, as in all his correspondence. But then he overflows with thanksgiving and praise for them. The same is true for Romans, 1 & 2 Corinthians, and 1 & 2 Thessalonians. But, uniquely, in the letter to the Galatians, there is an urgency that is missing in all the rest of letters. He foregoes the niceties. He gets right down to business. He is urgent, even indignant, and he will not be deflected even for a moment from his task of defending the gospel from those who threaten it. This means initially that he must defend his authority to preach his gospel. This is not personal defensiveness on his part. He defends himself because it is crucial to his defense of the gospel itself. If he is discredited, his gospel is discredited.

In what sense could he claim to be an 'apostle'? An 'apostle,' in the non-technical sense, means a 'sent one,' a messenger, a missionary (Acts 14:14; Rom. 16:7; Luke 11:49; 2 Cor. 8:23; Phil. 2:25). But it is also used in the New Testament in a restrictive sense, designating a special office in the Christian church. The 'Apostles' were those set apart by Christ for the purpose of building the foundation of the church. The first chapter of Acts lays down two requirements for apostles: that they had been eyewitnesses of the ministry of Jesus from the time of His baptism by John, including the resurrection, and that they had been chosen for the office by the risen Lord Himself. These criteria were fulfilled by the original Twelve and others who may have joined their ranks, including Barnabas, James, and Silvanus (1 Cor. 15:7; 1 Thess. 2:7). But the Apostle Paul obviously did not. He is an exception in this, and many other ways. He had not been a witness of Jesus' earthly ministry. As Boice points out, 'undoubtedly he considered his Damascus experience to be the equivalent of this.'[5] He had witnessed Christ and been called by Him only after the resurrection. Yet this was more than enough. No man or group of men had called him to be an apostle. Not even the apostles had asked him to be an apostle. 'Paul, an apostle,' he says, '(not sent from men nor through the agency of men, but through Jesus Christ).' His call was a divine call. His gospel, consequently, was a divine gospel. 'Am I not an apostle?' he will later ask. 'Have I not *seen* the Lord?' (1 Cor. 9:1). We should note that the apostles' authority came to them directly from Christ. It was not given to them by the church. The church was subject to them, not they to the church. The church did not commission them, rather they, through the gospel that Christ gave to them, called the church into existence.

So Paul makes this initial point. He just touches on it in the salutation. He will spend the rest of the first and second chapters elaborating the point. But from the outset he lets them know that he is on to them and defends the legitimacy of his apostleship.

Paul's Gospel

> And all the brethren who are with me, to the churches of Galatia. (Gal. 1:2)

Now Paul begins to introduce his defense of his gospel. First, he *appeals to the brethren*. He does not name who the 'brethren' are who are with him, as he does in his other letters. This may be, as Boice guesses, because he does not want 'to give the impression that his gospel requires additional support.'[6] At the same time, he cites the brethren in order to remind the Galatians that his message was more than a 'Pauline oddity,' but was indeed 'the received doctrine of all the Christian church and its missionaries.'[7] He writes to the 'churches' or 'congregations' of Galatia (*ekklesiai*). Note that first century Christianity assumes that the churches have a collective identity. It is generally recognized that *ekklesia* 'refers primarily to the entire community of believers and only secondarily to the community of believers living in a specific area,' says Fung. 'A corollary of this truth,' he goes on to say, 'is that the Church as the total community is not a mere aggregate of individual congregations; rather the local church is the universal Church in its local manifestation.'[8] The universal or catholic church, what Paul calls 'the church of God' (v. 13), is understood in the New Testament to be divided into local churches, or congregations. The Christian churches in a given region could be referred to collectively by either the plural ('churches') or the singular ('the church'). John Stott sees in this usage 'some biblical warrant for the concept of a regional church, the federation of local churches in a particular area.'[9]

Second, he reminds them of *grace and peace*, the essential elements of the gospel.

> Grace to you and peace from God our Father, and the Lord Jesus Christ. (Gal. 1:3)

'Grace' is the unmerited favor of God to us in Christ Jesus. 'Peace' is the state of well-being we are brought to in our relationship with God, with others, and within our own hearts. These are God's gifts to us.

Third, he *summarizes the message of the cross*.

> Who gave Himself for our sins, that He might deliver us out of this present evil age, according to the will of our God and Father. (Gal. 1:4)

Already the Apostle Paul has mentioned the doctrines of God and Christ, and the reality of the resurrection, grace, and peace. Now he affirms the substitutionary nature of Christ's atonement. Notice the emphasis on the sovereign will of God, implicitly contrasted with the part played by man as imagined by the Judaizers. Christ 'gave Himself for (*hyper*, 'because of' or 'on behalf of') our sins,' he says, 'that *He* might deliver us...according to the *will of our God and Father*.' As Boice comments, 'It is hard to imagine a statement better calculated to oppose any intrusion of the will or supposed merits of man in the matter of attaining salvation.'[10] 'He' delivers us according to His 'will.' He died as our substitute, on our behalf, in our place. He became 'a curse for (*hyper* again) us' (3:13). The message of the cross is packed here in Paul's greeting because he wanted to make the point quickly and firmly. Salvation is the result of God's work, not man's. God willed it, He sent His Son to accomplish it, and by His Spirit He applies it, giving us grace and peace, resulting in our deliverance 'out of this present evil age.' This is the same 'age' to which we are not to be conformed in Romans 12:2. The gospel is a 'rescue' (NEB). The same word is used of Peter's rescue from prison and of Paul's from a lynch mob (Acts 12:11; 23:27). His point is that Christ has set them free, and so they are not to return to the bondage of works religion.

Fourth, he *underscores the great purpose of the gospel.*

> To whom be the glory forevermore. Amen. (Gal. 1:5)

Doxologies are not ordinarily found in the Apostle's introduction. He places one here in order to emphasize the great end which the doctrines of grace serve. It is not to honor man's will and man's works. The gospel of salvation by grace gives all the glory to God.

Thus in these four ways, the Apostle Paul begins the debate even before he completes his salutation. He is so eager to defend the gospel that he's arguing on the envelope. Let's ask ourselves again about why Paul is so urgent. We begin to answer our question when we ask, 'Who is Paul?' The Apostle Paul is the man of all men who knew the insidious, self-deceiving power of self-righteousness. If ever anyone might have succeeded in saving himself through works, it was he. Paul was born in Tarsus, the capital of Cilicia, the son of Jewish ex-patriots. Paul's father was a Roman citizen making Paul a Roman citizen by birth (Acts 22:28). Since they were Roman citizens, his family was likely to be a leading family and, indeed, were substantial enough to send Paul to Jerusalem to be trained. Further, his was a religious family belonging to the strictest sect of Judaism, the Pharisees (Acts 23:6). Because he was reared in a Gentile city, Paul grew up speaking not only the Greek of Tarsus but the Aramaic of Palestine. His training in Jerusalem was under the famed Gamaliel, the leading rabbi of his time. The picture that emerges from the New Testament of Paul's pre-conversion life is that of a sincere, devout, zealous practitioner of first century Judaism. He was, by his own testimony,

> Circumcised the eighth day, of the nation of Israel, of the tribe of Benjamin, a Hebrew of Hebrews; as to the law, a Pharisee; as to zeal, a persecutor of the church; as to the righteousness which is in the law, found blameless. (Phil. 3:5–6)

Paul was an admirable man, even exemplary in many respects. He was a man of impeccable moral character. His religious practice was one of exceptional devotion. No doubt he was always present in worship services, he tithed his money, and he practiced charity. We would have admired and honored the man if we had known him.

If ever a man might have been saved through moral and religious conduct, it was Paul. How many of us can say that we are *blameless* in relation to the requirements of the law? How many of us, in a day of religious zealotry like his, could claim to have advanced beyond our contemporaries '*being more extremely zealous*' for our religious practices than the rest (Gal. 1:14)?

But of what use was his self-attained righteousness? He acknowledges that he had more of a moral leg to stand on than others.

> Although I myself might have confidence even in the flesh. If anyone else has a mind to put confidence in the flesh, I have far more. (Phil. 3:4)

He was a Hebrew! A Pharisee! Blameless! Of what value was it?

> But whatever things were gain to me, those things I have counted as loss for the sake of Christ. More than that, I count all things to be loss in view of the surpassing value of knowing Christ Jesus my Lord, for whom I have suffered the loss of all things, and count them but rubbish in order that I may gain Christ. (Phil. 3:7–8)

What counts is being 'found in Him.'

> And may be found in Him, not having right eousness of my own derived from the Law, but that which is through faith in Christ, the righteousness which comes from God on the basis of faith. (Phil. 3:9)

For Paul to be saved, grace had to overcome monumental barriers to the gospel. It had to overcome his self-righteousness, spiritual pride, and works-based confidence in his good standing with God. It had to overcome his violent hostility to Jesus and his followers. Paul was not just indifferent or uncaring. Neither was he one who is simply ignorant of the truth. He was a ferocious opponent and, humanly speaking, the least likely candidate for conversion in all the world.

Consequently, the Apostle Paul knew what the grace of God was and what it wasn't. He knew the insidiousness of any theology which would reintroduce works as necessary for salvation. He knew how subtle self-righteousness could be, and how blinding.

Is this remote for us today? It is true, we are not dealing with Phariseeism. It's true, we're not battling Judaizers. But do we still struggle with a false gospel of self-righteousness? Are our churches still filled today, nearly 2,000 years after Paul wrote this letter, with those who think that salvation is achieved through human merit? I'm afraid the answer to that question is, 'Yes.' Even today, in the popular mind, it is thought that going to heaven is just a matter of being nice. Typically it is said that just so a person is sincere, just so they do good, just so one tries hard, just so one doesn't hurt anybody else, that's all that matters. These sentiments may sound benign, but they, in fact, shift the ground of our salvation from the grace of Christ to human merit. They undermine the gospel and turn it into a works religion, just like all the rest. They destroy the grace of Christ.

Beyond what we might identify as the widespread thinking of the person in the pew, there are theological challenges to the gospel today arising from the most surprising places. Among conservative Presbyterians there is the 'Federal Vision,' reformulating the doctrine of justification so as to accommodate a greater role for covenant obedience in salvation. Among evangelical scholars the 'New Perspective' theologians (e.g. E. P. Sanders; N. T. Wright; J. D. G. Dunn) are also redefining the Pauline doctrine of justification so as to underscore its corporate dimension, namely membership in the covenant community as the key to a right relationship with God. As unbelievable as it may seem nearly 500 years after the Reformation, the personal, forensic, imputational dimensions of justification are at risk. Today it is as important as it was 2,000 years ago that we understand the gracious nature of Christ's gospel, lest we find ourselves without a gospel to preach. No one will help us more to do so than Paul in this letter to the Galatians.

2

No Other Gospel

Galatians 1:6–10

It is only with great difficulty that we can convince anyone these days that what one believes matters. It is universally acknowledged that it is important *that* one believe. But the content of one's faith, *what* one believes, is largely assumed to be a secondary matter, if it has any importance at all. For example, if I were to describe an individual as a moral man, a religious man, a wonderful father and husband, an exemplary employer in the treatment of his employees, one who lives the golden rule, who loves his neighbor, who helps the poor, who gives generously to charities, and so on, and then lament that he rejected the doctrine of the Trinity and so was headed for hell and would surely end up there if he didn't change his views, I dare say that even in our church among our Sunday morning congregation, there would be a great outcry and some would turn away in disgust. Why? Because we assume that what we believe is virtually irrelevant so long as we do believe. Denominational or doctrinal differences are unimportant. What matters is the presence of true faith, sincerity, and consistency between what we believe and what we practice, whatever that belief might be. The details of doctrine are secondary. It is inconceivable to us that one who was so devout, so sincere, so kind, so loving could be lost. We have a strong bias and therefore distorted preference for practical matters, how one lives, how one treats others. The terms 'doctrine,' 'dogma,' and 'dogmatics' all have a pejorative sense these days.

This diminishing of the importance of the contents of one's beliefs cannot be squared with what the Bible says. We would not for a moment deny that practice is vital. But we do wish to assert that what we *think* is every bit as vital as what we *experience*. What one believes is of critical, even eternal importance. The content of one's theology must be fundamentally correct or one is lost. Deny an essential of the Christian faith, and there is no hope of salvation. Sound tough? This is exactly what Paul teaches in Galatians 1:6–10.

No Other Gospel

First, there is but one gospel.

> I am amazed that you are so quickly deserting Him who called you by the grace of Christ, for a different gospel. (Gal. 1:6)

The Apostle Paul is 'amazed,' or 'astonished,' at what is taking place among the Galatians. As the founding pastor of their churches, he had taught them of the 'grace of Christ.' They had known and received the truth. Yet they were turning from the truth, a circumstance that clearly causes the Apostle considerable pain. The statement that they had turned 'quickly' from Christ recalls some Old Testament language directed at Israel's apostasies (e.g. Exod. 32:8; Judg. 2:17). The word translated 'deserting' (*metatethemi*) has in the middle form, says Longenecker, the special sense of 'change over,' 'turn away from,' 'fall away,' 'desert,' and 'become apostate.' In the world of Greek philosophy it was used to refer to one who left one school of thought for another. Used in the present tense, it indicates that the apostasy of the Galatians was in process. 'They were,' says Burton, 'on the point, or more exactly, in the very act, of turning.'[11] This is confirmed by 4:9–10 and 5:2–4 as well. Remarkably, they were turning away from God Himself, 'Him who called you by the grace of Christ,' in their zeal to be more religious. They were turning to a 'different gospel,' and repeating the apostasies of old Israel. Notice, to turn away from the biblical gospel is to turn away from God. It is not just a matter of adopting a new theology. Theology and Christian experience cannot be separated. To turn away from the gospel of grace is to turn away from the God of grace. This 'gospel,' he says,

> ...is really not another; only there are some who are disturbing you, and want to distort the gospel of Christ. (Gal. 1:7)

This 'different gospel' is not 'another' gospel, he says. If the new preachers were claiming that their work was merely 'in addition to,' and complimentary of Paul's teaching, Paul emphatically denies it. It is 'different' (*hetero*), meaning 'of a different kind,' and not merely 'another' (*allo*), meaning 'another of the same kind.' He did not consider it to be the same with slight differences. Because they were denying the graciousness of the gospel, their teaching could not be called a 'gospel.' These preachers were 'disturbing,' or 'confusing,' them by calling the new teaching a 'gospel.' But this was fundamentally dishonest of them. The verbs are in the present tense indicating 'that these errorists were still in Galatia when Paul was writing this letter, and that he wrote with the intention of stopping them in the very midst of their activities.' The Judaizers were seeking to 'distort,' or 'pervert,' the gospel, a political term (*metastrepho*), says Longenecker, 'having revolutionary action particularly in view.'[12]

What terrible thing were they teaching? Were they denying the resurrection of Christ? No. Were they denying His deity? No. Were they denying that He was the Messiah and Savior? No. Were they denying the necessity of faith in Him? No. As we saw last time, they merely denied that faith was enough. They added to faith in Christ meritorious work of the Law. That's all. No big deal, one might say.

What is implied in this? That there is but one gospel of grace. It is the one which was originally taught by Paul and the apostles. It is unchanging. It cannot be revised. It cannot be modernized. It cannot be added to. It cannot be improved. If it is altered, it is lost. Any 'different gospel' is not a gospel at all. It cannot be changed without being distorted. The gospel which they and we are to believe is the one which was originally preached to them (v. 8), and which, as he tells them, 'you received' (v. 9). Our gospel is fixed in its content. It described as a deposit, or 'treasure,' a 'standard of sound words' with which we have been entrusted and which we must guard (1 Tim. 6:20–21; 2 Tim. 1:13–14). What is the gospel? It is the teaching of 'the grace of Christ.' The gospel 'of Christ' is the gospel which has Christ as both its content ('about Christ') and its source ('from Christ'). It is a gospel of 'grace,' meaning that salvation is not merited or earned by works but given as a gift through faith alone. This gospel was 'once for all delivered to the saints,' and we are to 'contend earnestly' for it (Jude 3).

If only the church had learned this lesson! We would have had no *Book of Mormon,* no revelations of Ellen White, no Mary Baker Eddy's *Key to Science and Scripture*, no extra-biblical traditions upon which to base the practice and doctrines of the church. Our gospel is fixed. It is not to be added to or subtracted from. Our responsibility is to faithfully preach it and to pass it on to the next generation. That doesn't sound very glamorous. We tend to have a certain pride in our creative abilities. We want to revise and reinterpret it for our generation. Often we wish to do so for the best of reasons. Indeed the case can be made that virtually every heresy introduced to the Christian church has been done so in the name of the high motive of evangelism. The Arians wanted to simplify the gospel, so they denied the deity of Christ. The Pelagians wanted to purify the practice of the gospel, so they denied the sovereignty of God and let everything rest on the will of man. Schleiermacher, the father of modern theological liberalism, wanted to commend the gospel to 'its cultured despisers,' so he emptied it of its historical, supernatural, and theological content, which apparently offended enlightened minds, and gave it an entirely subjective reinterpretation. The early Unitarians wanted to liberate the gospel from its alleged Greek rationalism, and so denied the doctrine of the Trinity. The Judaizers were doing much the same sort of thing. They wanted to make the gospel more palatable for a Jewish audience. Jews were inclined to take offense at an adaptation of Judaism (as they saw it) that removed the ceremonial aspects. So the Judaizers put them back in order to appease and appeal to Jews. They wished to avoid the persecution that arises from the offense of the cross (Gal. 6:12; cf. 5:11). No doubt the same thing is being done today. Modern ears don't like the sound of the judgment side of the gospel so doctrines of sin, atonement, and the cross get neglected or reinterpreted in terms of finding self-fulfillment, or peace, or prosperity. Christ the Savior from sin becomes Christ the Key to success. Christ the 'Holy One' becomes Christ the 'friendly One.' Christ the Judge who commands all men everywhere to repent becomes Christ the Therapist who invites all men everywhere to feel good about themselves. This is undeniably how the gospel is being preached today. Is this the gospel of the grace of Christ? We doubt it.

How often the church has been disturbed and divided because it has violated this principle. As Stott points out, 'to tamper with the gospel is always to trouble the Church...Indeed, the Church's greatest troublemakers (now as then) are not those outside who oppose, ridicule and persecute it, but those inside who try to change the gospel.'[13] It cannot be changed without being lost in the process.

Ironically, it doesn't need to be changed. This is what is so remarkable about the revisionists. It doesn't need to be revised for the sake of modern ears anymore than for ancient ears. It is still the 'power of God for salvation' (Rom. 1:16). Even in apostolic times Paul had to warn:

> For the time will come when they will not endure sound doctrine; but wanting to have their ears tickled, they will accumulate for themselves teachers in accordance to their own desires; and will turn away their ears from the truth, and will turn aside to myths. (2 Tim. 4:3–4)

One might argue that people today don't like to hear about sin, judgment, blood atonement at the cross, repentance and faith, and so on. But the fact is, they never did like it. When did the natural man begin to like to be told that he needs a Savior? He likes to think of himself as self-sufficient. He thinks that he is fine the way he is, even virtuous. He resents being told that he isn't. A sinner? Needs saving? Must repent and turn to Christ? Can't be left alone to do whatever he pleases? Of course he doesn't like to hear these things. This has always been the case. So what are we to do? Tickle his ears? Say what he wants to hear? Provide him with entertainment and nice talks? Paul knew the temptation and the answer. He told the Corinthians, who, by the way, wanted him to spiff-up the gospel so that it would appeal to philosophy loving Greek culture, that,

> I determined to know nothing among you except Jesus Christ, and Him crucified. (1 Cor. 2:2)

Far from sugar-coating his message or repackaging his presentation he says,

> And I was with you in weakness and in fear and in much trembling. And my message and my preaching were not in persuasive words of wisdom, but in demonstration of the Spirit and of power, that your faith should not rest on the wisdom of men, but on the power of God. (1 Cor. 2:3–5)

Should Paul adapt the gospel to the desires of the Judaizers? Should he alter it to accommodate the interests of the Greeks? Should he tone down Christian moral teaching when speaking to the libertines? When it comes to non-essentials he will go far in accommodating them. But compromise the simplicity and graciousness of the gospel itself? Never!

No Other Way

Perhaps at this point someone might not be getting the implications of what the Apostle Paul says. He might be thinking, 'Okay, it's not the gospel of grace, but it's another valid expression of faith. It might do some good, too. It exalts Christ. It affirms the resurrection. It teaches the necessity of faith. Those who have adopted the Judaizer's message are good people. They are moral, fine family men, and generous. It's not the best, but it will benefit some.' So the Apostle goes beyond this. He goes on to say,

> But even though we, or an angel from heaven, should preach to you a gospel contrary to that which we have preached to you, let him be accursed. (Gal. 1:8)

The Apostle Paul sees antithesis between His message and that of the Judaizers, where the Galatians were probably seeing compliment. He uses a strong adversative, *alla* ('but') with *kai* ('even'), 'signaling the extreme nature of the supposition to follow,' says Longenecker.[14] Here he identifies his ultimate concern. It is not his apostolic authority, though that is important and he defends it. But by including himself in this theoretical anathema, he clarifies that the graciousness of the gospel is all important, not his status. 'But even though *we*...should preach to you a gospel contrary...' Not even he could alter the gospel as Christ had given it. 'So disinterested is Paul's zeal for the gospel,' says Stott, 'that he even desires the curse of God to fall upon *himself*, should he be guilty of perverting it.'[15] Indeed, if 'an angel from heaven' should preach another gospel it was not to be received. Satan, after all, can disguise Himself as an 'angel of light' (2 Cor. 11:14–15). Not even a heavenly messenger is to be received or believed if he brings a contrary message.

It is likely that the Judaizers were claiming authorization for their changes from the Jerusalem church. They probably claimed to have the support of the Twelve (see 2:6–14). By appealing to the angels, so to speak, Paul makes any reference to credentials irrelevant if the focus or content of the gospel is being altered. Paul is in effect saying, 'It doesn't matter who they are or where they are from; if they change the gospel, they are 'accursed.'' The Greek term *anathema*, means to deliver over to the wrath of God for destruction.

'Missed what I said?' Paul repeats himself:

> As we have said before, so I say again now, if any man is preaching to you a gospel contrary to that which you received, let him be accursed. (Gal. 1:9)

'As we have said before,' probably refers to a previous visit to the churches. If anyone preaches a gospel that differs from that which they had previously 'received,' he falls under the judicial wrath of God. The shift from the subjunctive in verse 8 ('should preach'), to the indicative in verse 9 ('is preaching'), stresses the immediacy of the situation.

Is this curse contrary to the spirit of Christ? Some have argued that it is. If it is, we must face the fact that it is emphatic, deliberate and twice repeated. But in reality, that it is not. Jesus Himself said,

> And whoever causes one of these little ones who believe to stumble, it would be better for him if, with a heavy millstone hung around his neck, he had been cast into the sea. (Mark 9:42)

Why must these things be stated in such extreme terms by both Paul and Jesus? Because those who obscure the gospel threaten the eternal destiny of those whom they confuse. We, after all, are not talking about taking a loss on the stock market. We're not talking about losing a track meet. We're not even talking about activities that threaten the lives of people. This has to do with eternal life and damnation. If one were teaching dietary habits that purported to extend life, but in fact resulted in shaving years off the life span of their practitioners, it would be serious enough. But this has to do with the gaining or losing of one's own soul, in comparison with which even gaining the whole world is insignificant. Consequently the strongest language and strongest measures must be taken.

Does this ring true to modern ears? Probably not. Religious and moral relativism is so deeply ingrained today that anyone who says such things is seen as a bigot, at best, and probably a nut. But we might pause to point out the inconsistency. You say that all is relative, but you buy music as though there were criteria by which one might distinguish the good from the bad. You say that there are no absolutes, and yet you talk as though there were transcendent, universal values such as love and justice, and are quick to denounce what you see as unloving and unjust behavior. If we were to stand on the top of a ten-story building you would acknowledge absolutely the relevance of the laws of gravity. If we were to plunge down deep into the ocean you would entrust your life to engineers who designed an underwater vessel in conformity with the 'laws of nature.' At none of these points would you say, 'The laws of gravity may be true for you but they are not for me,' or 'For me water is the same as air,' or 'For me love and justice can mean hurting innocent people.' No, we all live as though there were universal criteria by which to distinguish types of behavior and by which to live our lives. There are absolutes, if you will. Why should we be surprised to find that the same is true in matters religious? If there is one God, and most will grant this, then there is one truth. One God means one final reality. God is. God is what He is. He is not what He isn't. Therefore all opinions about God cannot be equally valid. Religions cannot say mutually exclusive things about God, as indeed they do, and all be true. It is intellectually dishonest to say that they are all just saying the same thing, when indeed they are saying opposite things. If Jesus Christ is the Prophet of God, then what He says is true and that which contradicts Him is false. If Jesus Christ is the Son of God and God the Son, then what he says, being a revelation of the One true God, is universally true and binding upon humanity. What He does is absolutely unique and universally relevant, that is, relevant for all peoples, and all places, and all times. When He says, 'No one comes to the Father but by Me,' we better pay attention.

It is so much easier to be a relativist. One will have a better time socially if one will say that sincerity is all that matters, and the differences among the religions of the world are external only and largely irrelevant. Everyone will appreciate one's magnanimous spirit if one can agree that we are all on different paths leading to the same mountaintop, that we all worship the same God. There's just one problem with it. It's not true. It doesn't conform to reality. Paul's view of Christ and the Judaizers view cannot both be right. And according to the Bible, your eternal salvation rests on *getting it right*. The Muslim view of Christ and the biblical view cannot both be right. The Hindu view of Christ and the Christian view cannot both be right. One cannot have whatever view of Christ one wishes and be right any more than one can have whatever view of gravity which one wishes and be right. One might counter, 'I don't think that so much should rest on theological or religious views.' The answer is, it doesn't matter what you or I think. It does matter if God says it does. God is. Christ is. This is reality. Gravity applies whether you believe it or not. The One, True, and Living God has spoken and acted through His Son. He sent Him to the cross to bear the sins of the world, and that event is universally and eternally significant. His call goes out to the world through Him. And He is not giving other alternatives, much as modern pluralism wishes that God would conform to its expectations.

These are uncomfortable things to say. Yet the church must say them in this age and in every age if it is to be faithful to the gospel and continue to have a gospel to preach. Paul is driving at this in the last verse of our section,

> For am I now seeking the favor of men, or of God? Or am I striving to please men? If I were still trying to please men, I would not be a bond-servant of Christ. (Gal. 1:10)

Paul seems to have been accused of trimming his message, preaching half a gospel, in order to secure a popular response. They said that he was a 'man-pleaser' (see 1 Cor. 10:33; 1 Thess. 2:4–5). In fact the opposite was the case. Paul's strong language proves that he is no flatterer. He is not against pleasing others per se, but against pleasing them for the sake of one's own advantage. He is willing to be 'all things to all men' when it comes to matters of culture and taste (1 Cor. 9:19–23). But he does not teach and preach as one whose main concern is to please others. One cannot truly be a servant of Christ and do so, and neither can we.

David Wells says that evangelicals have, in the words of the title of his acclaimed book, *No Place For Truth*. Even we are awash in a sea of subjectivity and relativism. But our responsibility is clear. Truth matters. What we think counts forever. The gospel of grace of Christ must be proclaimed and protected, against the world, and for the world.

3

Not According to Man

Galatians 1:11–24

Paul and his gospel are under serious attack. The Judaizers are accusing him of emptying the gospel of a significant portion of its content and thereby compromising its message. He was neglecting to instruct his Gentile converts to keep the ceremonial law. He was teaching that faith alone in Christ alone was all that was necessary for salvation. They maintained that one had to be circumcised to be saved. They challenged Paul's right to preach as he did. Consequently, the faith of the Galatian churches is in jeopardy. What shall he do? Shall he defend his teaching? Or shall he do nothing? Though there is no doubt that there are times when a person should remain passive and allow the Lord to be his defense, this is not one of them. As we have seen, the Apostle Paul counterattacks. He says,

> If any man is preaching to you a gospel contrary to that which you received, let him be accursed. (Gal. 1:9)

How can he say such a thing? How can he be so absolutistic, so dogmatic, so narrow, so sure? The answer is not to be found in some sort of worldly self-confidence. Paul is so strong because his gospel is 'not according to man,' but from God.

It may be that some were saying that the Apostle Paul was the source for his own gospel, that he made it up. Others may have been saying the true gospel had been taught to Paul by the Twelve and that he had deviated from it. So the Apostle sets out to demonstrate the supernatural origins of his gospel and his apostleship to the Gentiles against these kinds of accusations, and in doing so, confirms for us all the divine initiative in our salvation.

Supernatural Origins

> For I would have you know, brethren, that the gospel which was preached by me is not according to man. (Gal. 1:11)

The burden of the Apostle Paul's message from 1:11–2:14 is found in verse 11: his gospel is 'not according to man,' or not 'man devised, of human origin.'[16] It was not 'simply human,' as Longenecker renders it.[17]

This means, *first, that he did not receive it from others.* The accusation of his opponents seems to have been that Paul was dependent upon and subordinate to the Twelve for his gospel and commission to preach it. This he denies.

> For I neither received it from man, nor was I taught it, but I received it through a revelation of Jesus Christ. (Gal. 1:12)

Where did Paul get his gospel? He did not invent it. He did not receive it by human tradition (as handed down by the church). He received it by revelation. He did not receive it from a human source. He was not taught it by any human teacher. He received it 'by means of' (the meaning of the preposition *dia*) a direct 'revelation' from Jesus Christ. This is probably a reference to the Damascus road, where he was converted and first received his call to preach to the Gentiles (Acts 9:1ff.). Though he sometimes refers to his message as 'my gospel' (Rom. 2:16; 16:25), it was not peculiar to him. It did not differ from that which was preached by the Twelve, except perhaps in the clarity with which he understood how the gospel to the Gentiles was to relate to Jewish rituals. They all taught that Gentiles were not required to conform to the Mosaic ceremonial law and cleansing ordinances in order to be saved, or to enjoy equal status in the church with Jews. He can refer to this message as a 'mystery' long 'hidden' and uniquely revealed to him (Rom. 16:25–6; Eph. 3:2–10; Col. 1:26–7), and at the same time acknowledge its Old Testament background and his apostolic predecessors (1 Cor. 11:23–6; 15:3–11; Eph. 3:5; cf. Gal. 2:12). His unique revelation was unique only with respect to the *clarity* with which the application of these principles were given to him, not with respect to *content.*

Second, he further elaborates that his gospel was *not from himself.* In verses 13–24 the Apostle Paul seeks to demonstrate the divine origin of his gospel by references to his own life. He begins in verses 13–14 with his former life in Judaism. He wishes to show that nothing in his pre-conversion experience anticipated the proclamation of a ritual-free, works-free gospel. On the contrary, he invites them to recall his 'manner of life,' or 'behavior' in Judaism. He cites two examples of his zeal: his persecution of the Christian church (v. 13), and his fanaticism for all things Jewish (v. 14).

> For you have heard of my former manner of life in Judaism, how I used to persecute the church of God beyond measure, and tried to destroy it. (Gal. 1:13)

He persecuted the church 'beyond measure,' a word (*huperbolen*) which indicates excess. He tried even to 'destroy' the church. Notice that the 'church of God' is more than a local congregation. He speaks here of the church in its universality or catholicity. He was in 'hearty agreement' with the execution of Stephen (Acts 8:1). He was 'ravaging' the church, a word used of wild animals tearing apart their prey, going 'house to house,' dragging off men and women and putting them into prison (Acts 8:3). He was 'breathing threats and murder against the disciples of the Lord' (Acts 9:1). He sought authorization from the high priest to pursue the disciples of Christ to other cities, asking—

> for the letters from him to the synagogues at Damascus, so that if he found any belonging to the Way, both men and women, he might bring them bound to Jerusalem. (Acts 9:2)

He later referred to himself during this period as 'a blasphemer, a persecutor, and a violent aggressor' (1 Tim. 1:13). He continues,

> And I was advancing in Judaism beyond many of my contemporaries among my countrymen, being more extremely zealous for my ancestral traditions. (Gal. 1:14)

'He was equally fanatical in his enthusiasm for Jewish traditions,' writes Stott.[18] He was 'progressing,' developing morally and spiritually beyond that of his contemporaries. He was 'more extremely zealous' for the 'ancestral traditions,' the traditions of the fathers (*patrikos*). He had lived 'as a Pharisee according to the strictest sect of our religion,' he later said (Acts 26:5). As Longenecker summarizes, 'What Paul is insisting on is that as far as his standing in Judaism is concerned, his credentials are impeccable.'[19] He had nothing to gain by leaving Judaism and everything to lose.

What conclusion does he wish for us to draw from this? That his conversion and subsequent preaching could only be the result of divine intervention. For a mind so set, so biased, so fanatically attached to the ceremonies and consequent culture of holy days and rituals of Judaism to change, a catastrophic event would be required. One who was as rigid as he was could only have been transformed as he had been by a direct revelation from God. To this he brings us in verse 15:

> But when He who had set me apart, even from my mother's womb, and called me through His grace, was pleased to reveal His Son to me, that I might preach Him among the Gentiles. (Gal. 1:15–16a)

The Apostle Paul now identifies the foundation for his ministry: he was 'set apart' or ordained, and 'called' to be an apostle. Like Jeremiah (Jer. 1:5), and the Servant of the Lord (Isa. 49:1–6), Paul was set apart for his preaching mission among the Gentiles 'from my mother's womb.' Why? Because God was 'pleased' to do so. The shift in subject from verses 13–14 and 15–16a is dramatic. 'I used to persecute... [I] tried to destroy it... I was advancing in Judaism... [I was] more extremely zealous for my ancestral traditions.' But the subject of 15–16a is God. 'He set me apart ...(He) called me ...(He) was pleased to reveal His Son.' These are the stages of his salvation. He was 'set apart,' or chosen from the womb; he was 'called' in time, on the Damascus road; and Christ was revealed to him and in him. God had done it all.

His point is clear. It could only have been this way, he is saying. He could not have made this up. One who was so fanatical for the ancestral traditions, including the ceremonial aspects of the Mosaic Law, would never have made up a gospel for the Gentiles that did not include these provisions. Only divine intervention could have convinced him. Left to himself, he would not have neglected them. He loved the gathering of the family on holy days. He loved the annual pilgrimages to Jerusalem. He loved ritual rites of passage through which every Jewish child passed. He was violently opposed to anyone who threatened to undo this culture.

Over the last 150 years, there has been considerable scholarly speculation over where Paul got his 'religion.' Some skeptical theologians have speculated that he derived it from the Greek mystery religions; others have looked to pre-Christian Jewish sources. But as J. G. Machen demonstrated in his *The Origin of Paul's Religion*, those origins are almost impossible. Everyone, friend or foe, agreed that the Apostle Paul was a fanatical Pharisee. He did not have to defend his record. He had a reputation that was well known. 'For you have heard of my former manner of life in Judaism,' he says (v. 13). In Acts, he put it even more strongly.

> So then, all Jews know my manner of life from my youth up, which from the beginning was spent among my own nation and at Jerusalem; since they have known about me for a long time previously, if

> they are willing to testify, that I lived as a Pharisee according to the strictest sect of our religion. (Acts 26:4–5)

No one disputed this. He was not part of a Qumranian cult. It is impossible to attribute to him pagan Greek influences as well. He was an orthodox Jew, a Pharisee of Pharisees. Friend and foe alike acknowledged this. Given that this is so, what finally convinced him? Christ on the Damascus Road! The most reasonable explanation for the change in his views is a revelation from Christ Himself. The Apostle did not create a second form of Christianity. He got his religion from Jesus, the founder of Christianity, the Savior of the World.

The Apostle Paul's case is unique. Our confidence in him as a true messenger of the gospel of Jesus is in part based on his statements here. But there is a secondary sense in which every one of us who believes could say something like this. You know my former manner of life, we might say. Many of us are able to point to past lives which were diametrically opposed to the gospel. We were perhaps self-righteous like Paul, always criticizing and condemning others, never seeing any fault in ourselves. Or perhaps we were sadly fallen into sin, living self-indulgent and morally degrading lives. And so we can say to the world, to our friends and family, you know how I lived. You know what I was like. But now look at me. I've changed. I'm not what I was. Even those brought up in Christian homes, who have no conversion moment to which they can point, have a before and after, though less dramatic. Like Jesus, they have grown in 'wisdom and stature' (Luke 2:52). Through the years they have grown in knowledge, discernment, commitment, and holiness. They can look back on a past of ignorance, immaturity, and foolishness. Out of this they have grown as enabled by the grace of Christ through the power of the Holy Spirit. They, too, are not what they were. How is the change experienced by the adult convert and the covenant child possible? Both would say by the power of God. We didn't just adopt a philosophy. We could never have brought on this transformation by ourselves. Nor could we have ever made up this gospel message. We would not create a religion that makes so much of the problem of sin and the need of atonement. We would not create a gospel that threatens us with judgment. We would not have provided a solution that involves the bloody death of the Son of God. Nor would its primary principle be grace, making it impossible for us to take credit for our salvation. Nor would we require repentance, when we would rather hang on to our sin. We believe all these things, we might say, but we would never have invented it in this way. We often want to say this to our critics, when they castigate us for the 'scandal' of our particularity, for our convictions about sin, and so on. We didn't make this up, we tell them. Your problem is not with us, it is with Jesus. This is in effect what the Apostle Paul is saying. Their problem is with Jesus, not him.

This goes as well for the Apostle's claim as to where Christ's work began in his life. He was converted on the Damascus Road. But that is not when God began to deal with him. He is able to look back over the course of his whole life and say I have been 'set apart, even from my mother's womb' (v. 15). He had been providentially prepared for his missionary task even from birth. Everything he had experienced before conversion had contributed. His rearing in a Greek city, his Roman citizenship, his Jewish zealotry had all been providentially ordained.

There had been no wasted circumstances. God's hand had been upon him from the beginning. Indeed we marvel at divine blending of man and job in Paul the Apostle to the Gentiles. Has anyone ever been more perfectly prepared for a job than he? Again, in a derived and secondary sense we can say the same. Jesus did not become Lord when we confessed Him to be such. He has always been Lord. He has been sovereign over our lives and circumstances from the beginning. He superintended all the factors that led to our conversion and subsequent growth. What others have meant for evil, He meant for good (Gen. 50:20). He has been working all things for good (Rom. 8:28). So in a very profound sense there have been no accidents, and no mistakes. Like the Apostle, we can see tragic failure and sin in our past. But even in these things we can see a bigger reality, that of God using even our foolish errors for our and His ultimate good. It's like the fellow who told me that if his wife had not divorced him he would never have become a Christian. He was too proud and self-sufficient, not to mention self-indulgent. It would have been better for him if he had come to Christ on an easier path. But God had His purposes even in his obstinacy.

This is among the most comforting and healing teachings of the Bible. Look back over your life and marvel at the hand of God. Do you see that He set you apart from the womb? Do you rejoice that He called you by His grace? Do you humbly admit that you know Christ only because God 'was pleased to reveal His Son' in you?

Subsequent Events

> I did not immediately consult with flesh and blood. (Gal. 1:16b)

Christ, says the Apostle Paul, was revealed 'in me.' This points to 'the inward reality of Christian experience,' says Longenecker.[20] Now the Apostle's attention shifts to what happened after his conversion. Maybe his conversion was entirely a work of God, one might agree. But was he then taught by others? No. He says he did not 'consult,' or 'confer,' or 'communicate with' what he calls 'flesh and blood,' defined by Longenecker as 'mankind in its finitude and frailty.'[21]

> Nor did I go up to Jerusalem to those who were apostles before me; but I went away to Arabia, and returned once more to Damascus. (Gal. 1:17)

Paul now presents the first of three alibis proving that he did not spend time in Jerusalem being instructed by the apostles. Those who were 'apostles before me' would include the Twelve, James (v. 19), and perhaps others (cf. 1 Cor. 15:7).

His first is, he 'went away to Arabia,' and remained there for perhaps the better part of the three years (v. 18). This was probably a time of solitude where Paul meditated on the Old Testament Scriptures and the meaning of the gospel. God may have provided this for him to compensate for the three years of ministry Jesus had with the disciples which Paul missed.[22] Then he returned to Damascus briefly on his way to Jerusalem (cf. Acts 9:24–5).

> Then three years later when I went up to Jerusalem to become acquainted with Cephas, and stayed with him fifteen days. (Gal. 1:18)

His second alibi is, he only went up to Jerusalem later, and then only briefly (vv. 18–20; cf. Acts 9:26). The three years away from Jerusalem is meant to contrast with fifteen days with

Peter. Obviously he could not be a disciple of Peter or in any sense dependent upon him. Why did Paul wait so long to return to Jerusalem? It could be that he had a price on his head. After all he had not only failed to carry out the high priest's commission (Acts 9:2) but had gone over to the Christians!

> But I did not see any other of the apostles except James, the Lord's brother. (Gal. 1:19)

James, 'the brother of our Lord,' was not a follower of Jesus during his lifetime but was converted after the resurrection by an appearance of Christ (Mark 3:21, 31–5; 1 Cor. 15:7). He became a prominent member of the Jerusalem church, and was instrumental in the resolving of the issues at the council of Jerusalem (Acts 15:13; cf. 21:18–19; Gal. 2:1–10). He was martyred during the Jewish persecutions of Christians in AD 62.

His third alibi is, he then went off to Syria and Cilicia (vv. 20–24; cf. Acts 9:30). The Apostle Paul puts himself under oath, perhaps in Roman fashion, which signaled to one's opponents that one was ready to go to court to attest to the veracity of one's position.

> (Now in what I am writing to you, I assure you before God that I am not lying.) (Gal. 1:20)

So it is that the Apostle Paul affirms, 'in the strongest manner possible,' says Longenecker, that he is telling the truth and is ready to stand up to any challenge otherwise.[23]

> Then I went into the regions of Syria and Cilicia. (Gal. 1:21)

'Then,' he says, indicating that nothing lies between the Jerusalem visit and what follows. After my short visit in Jerusalem, he is saying, I went straight to Syria and Cilicia.

Finally, he concludes and clinches his argument by pointing out that up to that time he was not known to the Judean churches by face, but only by reputation. This again seems to be a matter about which every one was aware.

> And I was still unknown by sight to the churches of Judea which were in Christ; but only, they kept hearing, 'He who once persecuted us is now preaching the faith which he once tried to destroy.' And they were glorifying God because of me. (Gal. 1:22–4)

The fact that he was 'still unknown by sight' (literally 'by face') to the Judean churches, that is in the province of Judea which included Judea, Samaria, and Galilee (cf. Acts 9:31), means that he had not been serving under the direction and supervision of the Jerusalem apostles. It was not until 14 years after his conversion that he finally had an extended stay in Jerusalem (Gal. 2:1).

Indeed, though they had not yet met Paul, they had rejoiced in his early ministry, and were 'glorifying God' because of him. But now things had changed. 'The dissatisfaction of the Judaizers with Paul is here dramatically contrasted with the satisfaction that the Judean Christians had in his earlier missionary activity,' says Longenecker.[24]

Don't you remember this, he is implying? Everyone is aware of these things. It is a matter of record. Thus the Judaizers reconstruction of events was wrong. Fifteen days with Peter and then James was not sufficient to establish subordination. His ministry thereafter in Syria and Cilicia, when he was virtually unknown to the Judean churches, shows that he could not have been under the supervision of the Jerusalem apostles. His gospel was independent of them, given by direct revelation from Christ.

So where did Paul get his gospel? He got it from Jesus! I know a number of people who claim that they like Jesus but reject Paul. Paul has a different message and especially a different spirit, they say. So they want to follow the Jesus of 'judge not,' and reject the Paul who calls for wifely submission to husbands, forbids sexual acts outside of marriage, and abominates homosexuality. But this won't wash. The Apostle Paul was set apart, called, and taught by Christ Himself! Is he then chauvinistic when he calls down the curse of God upon those who corrupt his gospel? No, because it's not his in origin. It is 'not according to man.' It is Christ's gospel of grace. It is the only way of salvation, which he, and we, accordingly, must guard with the greatest zeal.

4

The Truth of the Gospel—1

Galatians 2:1–10

Back when I was in seminary, a question was posed to our class, 'What is more important, principle or people?' What would you say? Almost without exception the class answered, 'people.' The question was then restated by a student who asked, 'Do you mean to say that your relationships come before the maintenance of the truth? Are you saying that promotion of the well-being of one's neighbor, preserving peace and harmony with one's friends and associates, and preserving unity in the church is a greater priority than the preservation and proclamation of the truth?' His indignation, I believe, was justified. That such a thing could be said by the majority of the students at an evangelical seminary demonstrates the degree to which fuzzy thinking has taken over our culture and even infected the church. We are constantly reminded by our culture of the importance of 'inclusion' and 'tolerance,' as those terms are repeated with mantra-like regularity. A 'big tent' is thought to be mandatory. The problem is that if one's 'big tent' is so big as to accommodate all points of view, then one doesn't need a tent! Isn't the point of a tent to separate oneself from the world? If the world is in the tent, you don't need a tent. You've become the world.

Paul continues his defense of himself and his gospel in 2:1–14. His great burden in this section is with 'the truth of the gospel' (vv. 5, 14). He saw this truth as singular and under attack. The gospel could not be given a dozen different interpretations. It could not be molded to take on whatever shape one might wish. Its meaning was God-given, and therefore fixed and unchanging. Most importantly, its message of free grace cannot be compromised by adding works to it. Yet there were those who were trying to alter its message in order to accommodate the interests of Jewish culture. Their method was to attack both the messenger and the content of his message. Paul was not a full apostle, they said. He has watered down the gospel, they claimed, separating the ceremonial law from it in order to appeal to Gentiles. The Apostle Paul demonstrates in our passage both his unity with the other apostles and the priority of truth, even at the cost of disunity and division.

Apostolic Unity

The gospel that the Apostle Paul preached was affirmed by all the apostles.

> Then after an interval of fourteen years I went up again to Jerusalem with Barnabas, taking Titus along also. (Gal. 2:1)

The Apostle Paul's main emphasis up to this point has been to demonstrate the legitimacy and independence of his apostleship and gospel. What he preached he received 'through a revelation of Jesus Christ' (1:14). He was not dependent upon or subordinate to the other apostles. In 1:16–18 he reminded his readers that immediately following his conversion, he went to Arabia where he remained for three years. Only then did he go for the first time to Jerusalem, and then only for fifteen days. Then he went to Syria (and its chief city Antioch) and Cilicia (and his hometown Tarsus) where he ministered 'for an interval of fourteen years.' Whether he means those fourteen years in a cumulative sense (i.e. three plus eleven years), or as fourteen in addition to the three (for a total of seventeen years), we can't be sure, though the latter is the more natural reading. Whichever he has in mind, his point is that only then, after this extended period of time, did he make a second visit to Jerusalem. What happened at that time? Now he has a new point to make. Having established his authority as independent of the other apostles, he wishes to establish that, even so, they were in agreement with one another respecting the Gentiles and the ceremonial law. The other apostles in fact supported and endorsed Paul's message. This visit should perhaps be identified with the famine visit of Acts 11:30, when the Apostle Paul and Barnabas brought contributions from the Antioch church to the Jerusalem church.

The Apostle mentions 'taking Titus along also.' Titus was one of the Apostle's Gentile converts (Titus 1:4), who as Fung says, 'became his close associate and, on occasions, his personal delegate,' and who, on this occasion, Paul wished to bring along 'as a representative of Gentile Christians.'[25] He will serve as a test case for the issues before the church.

> And it was because of a revelation that I went up; and I submitted to them the gospel which I preach among the Gentiles, but I did so in private to those who were of reputation, for fear that I might be running, or had run, in vain. (Gal. 2:2)

He went to Jerusalem the second time because of a direct 'revelation' which he received. This does not refer to his conversion experience, but some subsequent prophetic insight. Thus this visit was not a response to a summons by the Jerusalem authorities, or even at his own initiative, but by divine direction. His point is that both his message and his movements were independent of the authority of the other apostles. Once there he met 'in private' with 'those who were of reputation,' probably a reference to the apostles and other church leaders. He 'submitted,' or set before (*anatithemai*) them his gospel. In what sense did he do so? Was he seeking their approval? This is hardly likely in light of what he says about the independence of his authority in chapter one. He seems rather to be seeking their acceptance of his Gentile converts, and to avoid the division of the church into Gentile and Jewish factions. His 'fear' was that they might lay some ceremonial burden upon them, and deny them full acceptance until such requirements were fulfilled. If this were to happen, his work might be ruined, his labor, or 'running,' might prove to have been 'in vain.' 'It was not, we may be sure, that he had any personal doubts or misgivings about his gospel and needed the reassurance of the other Jerusalem apostles,' says Stott, '...but rather lest his ministry, past and present, should be rendered fruitless by the Judaizers.'[26]

Note what is being said. Only the true gospel will bear fruit that lasts. Compromise the truth, for whatever high motive, and you in fact hurt people. The superficial view is that it is more 'open,' or 'nice,' or, to use the terms of the week, 'tolerant' and 'inclusive' to permit a variety of points of view. The Apostle Paul's answer is, not when it touches the heart of the gospel. Undermine grace and persuade Christian people to shift the ground of their salvation from faith to works, and you destroy their lives. The Apostle sees this. His preaching would have been 'in vain,' to no effect, fruitless, and his converts, lost.

Admittedly, this is difficult for people to see. It is always easier to be a toleration-loving liberal. It is simple for such to play the 'more compassionate than thou' game. All they have to do is deal with surface issues. The Apostle Paul is so critical of others, one might say. Why must he exclude as he does? Why is he intolerant of others' points of view? Whey can't he be kinder? Why can't he be more accepting of others? At first blush, this is persuasive. But one must, with the Apostle, move beyond the immediate, and plunge below the surface. The reason he must be so narrow is that truth lies on narrow paths. Error ruins lives. Error destroys souls. Error deprives people of God's grace in Christ. This is why principle comes before people and truth before relationships. In other words, the only way to put people first is to put them second, to establish the priority of truth in their lives. The Apostle Paul goes on:

> But not even Titus who was with me, though he was a Greek, was compelled to be circumcised. (Gal. 2:3)

Paul digresses in his description of what did happen in the meeting with the Jerusalem leaders to tell first what didn't happen—Titus, a Gentile, was not compelled to be circumcised. In other words, they agreed with Paul! They did not yoke the Gentiles with Jewish rituals.

> But it was because of the false brethren who had sneaked in to spy out our liberty which we have in Christ Jesus, in order to bring us into bondage. (Gal. 2:4)

Because Paul writes with considerable emotion, we must supply the main clause, telling us to what he refers. The most natural reading is that he means, 'The matter of circumcising Gentiles was first raised by false brethren...' This all came later, he is saying. It was not an issue on my second visit to Jerusalem, or at least not initially. He calls them 'false brethren.' They were probably people who considered themselves Christians, but their beliefs and conduct revealed otherwise. They had 'sneaked in,' or slipped in. They came to 'spy out,' a term which carries the nuance of inquiry without the right of supervision. They were claiming authority which was not rightly theirs. And their goal was to rob Gentile believers of their 'freedom,' which, according to Fung, refers to 'the freedom from the necessity of circumcision for justification before God.'[27]

We note again, what would be the result of toleration of the Judaizing doctrines? Slavery. Bondage. Why? Because the true gospel maintains the right relationship between law and grace. It says that one may only be saved by Christ through faith apart from any kind of meritorious works. The law, in its ceremonial aspects, is fulfilled in Christ. Its moral requirements are to be fulfilled by Christians, but for the purpose of pleasing God, not for earning their salvation. They are *necessary*, but not *meritorious*. But err on either side of this equation, and the result is slavery. The formula for Judaizers was faith and meritorious works. Justification then became a matter of ongoing performance, with no possibility of certainty. One ever thus becomes a slave of doing 'one more thing' in order to be saved. One becomes a slave to fear, tyrannized by the uncertainty, by the impossibility of ever knowing if one has done enough. This is what mobilizes the cults. This is why they are out riding their bikes and knocking on doors. Likewise the Judaizers would have Gentile believers submitting to a perpetual series of Jewish rituals, beginning with circumcision, but continuing with the cleansing rites, the calendar of festivals, and the dietary laws, all so that they might be saved. It's bondage. It's slavery.

On the other hand, deny the moral law any place in the Christian life, and one falls into another form of slavery. Grace becomes cheap grace. Liberty leads to license, and back to slavery, because, as the Apostle Peter says, 'by what a man is overcome, by this he is enslaved' (2 Pet. 2:19). The way of the antinomian and the libertine is equally disastrous. Jesus said, 'everyone who commits sin is the slave of sin' (John 8:34).He also said, 'you shall know the truth, and the truth shall make you free' (John 8:32). Only the truth, the singular, narrow, uncompromised truth, can make us and keep us free.

> But we did not yield in subjection to them for even an hour, so that the truth of the gospel might remain with you. (Gal. 2:5)

They didn't yield to the Judaizers because to do so would have been to compromise the fundamental principle of the gospel and destroy it. Allow even for a moment the principle of works into the gospel, allow it to be combined with faith as the means of our justification, and the gospel is overthrown and slavery enthroned.

> But from those who were of high reputations (what they were makes no difference to me; God shows no partiality)—well, those who were of reputation contributed nothing to me. (Gal. 2:6)

The phrase, 'those who were of high reputation,' used also in verse 2, may be a title that had currency in the early church. Perhaps as Fung suggests, it was 'a title given by the Jerusalem church to its leaders, which Paul uses, possibly with a tinge of irony, in depreciation of the arrogant and extravagant claims which the Judaizers were making for the Jerusalem leaders.'[28] Stott finds balance in the Apostle's intent: 'Paul's words are neither a denial of, nor a mark of, disrespect for their apostolic authority…he accepts their *office* as apostles, he is not overawed by their *person* as it was being inflated by the Judaizers.'[29] These men, Paul says, 'contributed,' or literally, 'added,' nothing to his message. They did not modify it. They did not amplify it. In other words, his gospel was fully endorsed by the other apostles and the leaders of the Jerusalem church. You can see that he is ambivalent about citing their support. The truth stands on its own. It does not need the testimony of those considered to be great men. 'What they were makes no difference to me,' he says. 'God shows no partiality,' and neither should we. I have always been a bit uncomfortable with the evangelical use of star testimonies for the same reason. Why not let a ditch-digger give his testimony at the big crusade rather than a movie-star or athlete? God is not partial! Nevertheless, he does cite them because they did agree with him, contrary to what others had said.

> But on the contrary, seeing that I had been entrusted with the gospel to the uncircumcised, just as Peter had been to the circumcised (for He

> who effectually worked for Peter in his apostleship to the circumcised effectually worked for me also to the Gentiles). (Gal. 2:7–8)

In verses 7–9 Paul gives a positive account of what happened in Jerusalem. First, they recognized that Paul was the apostle to the Gentiles, entrusted with the gospel to them, in the same way that Peter was to the Jews. This is not two different *gospels* but two different *missions*. Of course there would be differences in emphasis as one seeks to be 'all things to all men,' but no differences in substance (1 Cor. 9:22).

> And recognizing the grace that had been given to me, James and Cephas and John, who were reputed to be pillars, gave to me and Barnabas the right hand of fellowship, that we might go to the Gentiles, and they to the circumcised. (Gal. 2:9)

'Grace' here means 'favor,' as in the NIV, the privilege of apostleship. Second, they recognized God's 'grace' to Paul. He is saying a second time, and in a second way, that the apostles recognized that God had given to Paul this mission to the Gentiles. This division of labor between the Apostles Peter and Paul was not absolute, but a matter of emphasis. Paul also preached to Jews and Peter to Gentiles. But they would concentrate their efforts in this way. Third, he tells them that their agreement was confirmed by the 'right hand of fellowship,' that is, with a handshake.

> They only asked us to remember the poor, the very thing I also was eager to do. (Gal. 2:10)

Here is the only request made of Paul by the Jerusalem leaders: remember the 'poor,' probably the Jerusalem poor, a thing that he was not so much 'eager to do,' as already doing, or 'made it my business to do' (NEB margin). He had had a part in the relief effort described in Acts 11:29 ff.. It was already a part of his apostolic policy.

Stott points out that it is fashionable to speak of 'Pauline,' 'Petrine,' and 'Johannine' doctrines as though these three were different from each other, even contradictory. James and Paul are widely regarded as being hopelessly contradictory. But this is not the case according to Paul. The apostles agreed with each other. There may be differences in *style* among them. Paul's Greek is unlike John's. He also tends to write with more emotion, and more autobiographically. There are also differences in *emphasis*. We would expect this because, as Stott points out, 'they were called to different spheres and preached or wrote to different audiences.'[30] But regarding the message, there was total agreement. They preached the same message. The New Testament speaks with one voice. The whole Bible speaks with one voice.

It is important that we realize that the gospel of the Apostles alone has the power to help. Only this gospel bears lasting fruit, as we have seen. It alone has the power to break the bondage of sin. Only this gospel can truly change your heart. Only this gospel truly frees people from the bondage of legalism which denies them their freedom and traps them in a form of slavery. This is a gospel worth fighting for. It is the principle, the truth that must be put first, if we are to serve Christ and be of service to others.

5

The Truth of the Gospel—2

Galatians 2:11–14

Modernity has not been kind to traditional religions. Whether one speaks of orthodox Protestantism, orthodox Catholicism, or orthodox Judaism, the forces of the modern world have presented these groups with perhaps the greatest challenge that they have ever faced. When one considers that virtually all Christians and Jews were of the orthodox, traditional variety in the late nineteenth century, and that about one hundred years later those who remain such are generally viewed as exotic, quaint, or threatening, but definitely not main-stream, one senses the scope of the revolution that has taken place. Around the world those with traditional religious views are labeled 'fundamentalist,' or 'ultra orthodox,' or 'extreme right.' Their once majority views are considered regressive, even oppressive.

There are many explanations for why this is so. Among those I would like for us to consider as we engage our text is the pressure to conform to a secular world view. Specifically, the pressure to fit in, to restrict all religious distinctives to one's private life where they won't be noticed; the pressure for Jews to cut their beards and ignore their Sabbath, for Catholics to ignore their church's teaching on contraception, for Protestants to reject Christian particularism and adopt the civic universalism so frequently expressed by our politicians (God loves everyone, everyone goes to heaven). Our civilization places a premium on conformity/uniformity, not in all areas, but specifically in the areas of religions and morals, because only such, it is thought, will permit the peaceful co-mingling of all the various groups that constitute our world. Pluralism, and its cousin relativism, dominate the religious landscape. One cannot and must not think or say that there is a single religious truth or a single moral standard. To do so is not only impolite, but secular heresy.

What then should we fight for? When, if ever, is it right to draw a line in the sand? When should we, if ever, publicly declare truth and error in religion and morals? Our whole civilization is strongly biased against our *ever* doing so. We tend to maximize verses such as 'love one another' and 'judge not lest you be judged,' and so minimize the claims of truth. After all, we don't want to appear unloving and judgmental. But clearly, there is a time to stand, even if it embarrasses us, and even if it divides the church.

Pressure to Compromise

In the remarkable account that follows, we are introduced to a heated disagreement between the Apostles Peter and Paul over the question of the Gentiles and the ceremonial law. This seems to have been a disagreement not so much over doctrine, as over practice. It was not so much a matter of truth, but tactics. However, the tactics employed by Peter *implied* doctrines that were so contrary to the heart of the gospel that Paul was convinced he had to be confronted.

> But when Cephas came to Antioch, I opposed him to his face, because he stood condemned. (Gal. 2:11)

Let's review where we have come thus far. The first of his arguments for the authenticity of his gospel and apostleship was that nothing in his background anticipated a law-free gospel. He had been a zealot for the Law and a persecutor of the church (1:13–14). Second, he had no opportunity after conversion to be instructed by the Twelve, having spent the immediate three years after the Damascus road in Arabia, then only fifteen days in Jerusalem, followed by at least eleven years and probably fourteen in Syria and Cylicia (1:16–24). Third, on his second visit to Jerusalem, he received the approbation of the Twelve and their endorsement of his mission and message (2:1–10). Now his fourth argument is introduced in verse 11, in which he recalls an incident in Antioch in which the issues came up while the Apostles Peter and Paul were in the presence of each other.

> For prior to the coming of certain men from James, he used to eat with the Gentiles; but when they came, he began to withdraw and hold himself aloof, fearing the party of the circumcision. (Gal. 2:12)

The Apostle Peter had been clearly instructed about fellowship with Gentiles through the thrice repeated vision of Acts 10, the implications of which he had even initially resisted and received further clarification (Acts 10:14 ff.): there is no unclean food and there are no unclean men. Peter knew what was right. He 'used to eat with Gentiles.' We know that he visited and ate with Cornelius and his family (Acts 10:28). He was confronted about this at the time.

> And when Peter came up to Jerusalem, those who were circumcised took issue with him, saying, 'You went to uncircumcised men and ate with them.' (Acts 11:2–3)

Peter answered their objections and defended his doing so (Acts 11:4–18). 'His old Jewish scruples had been overcome,' says Stott. 'He did not consider himself in any way defiled or contaminated by contact with uncircumcised Gentile Christians, as once he would have done.'[31] But when a delegation came 'from James,' Peter 'began to withdraw' from the Gentiles and 'hold himself aloof.' The imperfect tense suggesting, says Bruce, 'that he did not make an abrupt break with his former practice, but proceeded to change it gradually.'[32] If we are to put the most positive construction on this, it could be that word was getting back to Jerusalem that Jewish Christians were no longer observing the Jewish dietary laws. The Jerusalem church would have come under considerable criticism, even persecution from the scribes and Pharisees, if this were so. Remember, these are the years just prior to war with Rome, and there is a rising tide of Jewish nationalism and accompanying hatred for things Gentile. Therefore it may be that James and others saw this step back as necessary in the context of Jewish evangelism. They may not have objected in theory if Gentiles did not observe the dietary laws, but they were sure that Jewish Christians must if they were to have credibility with non-Christian Jews. In fact, even Paul said he was willing to become 'as a Jew' and 'as under the Law,' so he might 'win Jews' (1 Cor. 9:20). He had Timothy, who was half-Greek, circumcised 'because of the Jews,' and himself submitted to Jewish purification rituals (Acts 16:1 ff.; 21:20–7).

Peter's 'fear' may be a fear for the future of the church's mission to Jews. Or it may be fear of criticism or persecution for his free mixing with Gentiles, the latter being the more likely. The Apostle Paul calls their withdrawal from Gentiles 'hypocrisy,' meaning 'play-acting,' a word used to describe the role of a stage actor. It was hypocrisy because their actions contradicted their inner conviction. Stott attributes the Apostle Peter's hypocrisy not to theological conviction, but 'craven fear of a small pressure group.'[33] He also reads 'from James' as meaning that the delegation claimed to have come from James, but that the claim was false, as James later said. 'Some of our number to whom we gave no instructions have disturbed you,' James told the Jerusalem council (Acts 15:24). 'They posed as apostolic delegates,' Stott says.[34] Because of the bad example of Peter, 'the rest of the Jews,' and even Barnabas, were 'carried away' by the hypocrisy and also compromised. The result for Peter and the rest was social separation from the Gentiles. They were saying, in effect, 'Unless you conform to the Jewish way of life we cannot have social relations with you,' as Bruce puts it.[35]

The Apostle Paul's courageous confrontation of the Apostle Peter may have saved the Christian church from a permanent split into Jewish and Gentile wings, 'one Lord, but two Lord's tables,' as one author put it. What had been privately discussed in Jerusalem was now public (the withdrawal must have been public) and so had to be opposed publicly (v. 14). It was not that the Apostle Paul loved a fight, or was hot tempered. The problem was, as Luther put it and Stott quotes him, 'he had here no trifling matter in hand, but the chiefest article of all Christian doctrine.'[36] At stake was nothing less than 'the truth of the gospel' (vv. 5 and 14).

> And the rest of the Jews joined him in hypocrisy, with the result that even Barnabas was carried away by their hypocrisy. (Gal. 2:13)

The rest of the Jewish believers, even Barnabas, joined in with this 'hypocrisy' and broke fellowship with Gentiles, to Paul's dismay.

What we have here is a first century example of our vulnerability to group pressure. Peter knew what was right. So did Barnabas. But then they began to hear other voices. You're not doing that, they asked. How could you? How could you do such? How could you say such? Gradually, they were worn down. This is how it works on us. You believe *that*, they ask. You believe the Bible is *literally* true? You believe that *only* Christians go to heaven? You won't marry that sweet young couple just because one professes Christ and the other doesn't? These sorts of questions bring tremendous pressure to bear upon a religious community. Hasidic Jews, Mennonites, orthodox Presbyterians, and traditional Catholics all feel it. All we want to be is a traditional Presbyterian church. Or so we think. But, frankly, we also want others to think well of us. We want to be accepted. The world won't let us have both. When our friends and associates on the ball field, at the PTA, at the bowling alley, or the country club ask, 'Is it true that at your church...,' and there follows a belief or practice that is thought to be weird or heretical according to the standard of modern pluralism, we become uncomfortable and embarrassed. We don't like it.

Are you aware of how vulnerable we are to social pressure? The clearest examples of this that we have experienced would have to do with marital ethics, broadly speaking. The positions we have taken with respect to two issues, Christians marrying non-Christians, and homosexuality, are those of our *Westminster Confession of Faith*. What we have said is nothing more and nothing less than what Presbyterians have said for 450 years. We have stated our views, and for some that was bad enough. But we have also put our views into practice, and for many that is the unforgivable sin. It was thought to be okay to have convictions about marriage, but then let folks do what they want. Don't let convictions ever effect the real world, where they might hurt feelings. That we would actually carry through on our beliefs and make our *practice* conform to our *convictions* is more than many can bear.

I cite these examples not in order to argue the merits of each case, but to highlight how social pressure works and how vulnerable we are to it. I have seen people who knew better utterly cave in when clear biblical requirements touched their personal circumstances. They couldn't bear the embarrassment of social non-conformity. They felt humiliated. They couldn't stand their neighbor's scorn. They required relief. So they compromise. This is exactly what the Apostle Peter faced and what he bowed to. Be ye warned!

Confronting Serious Error

> But when I saw that they were not straightforward about the truth of the gospel, I said to Cephas in the presence of all, 'If you, being a Jew, live like the Gentiles and not like the Jews, how is it that you compel the Gentiles to live like Jews?' (Gal. 2:14)

Paul sees in Peter's action a compromise of the gospel that is completely unacceptable. Peter, he pointed out, had been eating and living like a Gentile, rightly understanding the freedom of all Christians, Jewish and non-Jewish, from the ceremonial requirements of the law. Since this was so, how could he require of the Gentiles that they conform to Jewish dietary laws, i.e. 'live like a Jew,' in order to enjoy fellowship on equal terms in the Christian church? This was a compromise of nothing less than 'the truth of the gospel.' Why? Because it undermines the graciousness of the gospel. The Apostle Peter's behavior contradicted the gospel of God's free grace in Christ to all who believe apart from meritorious works. This is the point of verses 15–16.

> We are Jews by nature, and not sinners from among the Gentiles; nevertheless knowing that a man is not justified by the works of the Law but through faith in Christ Jesus, even we have believed in Christ Jesus, that we may be justified by faith in Christ, and not by the works of the Law; since by the works of the Law shall no flesh be justified. (Gal. 2:15–16)

We have some important distinctions that we need to make if we are to correctly understand this situation.

First, it was *serious* error that was confronted. Not everything is worthy of confrontation. Love should normally cover a multitude of sins. A more low-keyed approach may have been employed if it had been a secondary issue. But because the Apostle Peter's hypocrisy was an implicit denial of justification by faith, it had to be corrected, even if it meant conflict and division in the church. We do not believe in unity and peace at all costs. Truth takes priority over unity. Why? Because if you do not protect the gospel you will not have a church within which to preserve unity. Compromise the gospel for the sake of 'peace' in the church, remove from it whatever offends anyone in the church, and initially one might enjoy harmony in the church. But one will have so emasculated the gospel in the process and emptied it of its authority, that it will lose its power to convert sinners and build the church. Churches that compromise are empty churches or on their way to being empty. Serious error must be confronted, whoever might be offended in the process. Fail to do so, water down the gospel in order to avoid hurt feelings, and ultimately you destroy the church.

Second, it was confronted *personally*. The Apostle Paul says of the Apostle Peter, 'I opposed him to his face' (v. 11). This means that Paul personally stood face to face with Peter and told him he was wrong. Paul was not content to complain behind Peter's back. Neither did he merely hurry off a letter, which likewise can often be a cowardly way to deal with differences. No, Paul went toe to toe with Peter. He did what Jesus counsels in Matthew 18:15, at least with respect to going personally to an offending party and confronting them. How much more peaceful would the life of the church be if this were universally observed! If only Christians would obey Christ! If only when you take offense at another Christian, or our pastors, or our Session we would deal with them directly! Instead, members get mad at each other and don't even talk about it or attempt to reconcile. They get mad at the Session because of a decision and they don't know the issues, and don't bother to become informed. I've periodically had folks upset with me and I don't know why, and for the life of me can't figure out why. The Apostle Paul has the decency to go directly to the Apostle Peter and confront him face to face.

Third, it was a *public* error. Consequently, it had to be confronted publicly. He rebuked the Apostle Peter 'in the presence of all.' Why? Because it was known to all. Public sins must be rebuked publicly. The circle of discipline or correction must be as broad as the circle of knowledge. Private sins are corrected privately. Public sins are corrected publicly. If not, the error remains uncorrected in the minds of those who were exposed to the error. The Apostle Paul states the principle to Timothy:

> Those who continue in sin, rebuke in the presence of all, so that the rest may be fearful of sinning. (1 Tim. 5:20)

In other words, if they know of the sin and do not see it corrected, they will not 'be fearful of sinning.' They will think that the transgressor got away with it! They may conclude that they may as well. The bad example may be followed. So public offenses must receive public correction.

This is apostolic Christianity, as the Apostle Paul confronts the Apostle Peter over a central principle of the Christian faith, threatening the peace and unity of the church in the process. Why? Because the priority of truth demands it. Because the priority of the truth of the gospel must be preserved. Was it embarrassing to the church to air its dirty linens, so to speak? Was it harmful to have two apostles clashing like this? Perhaps in some ways it was. This incident would not have provided a clear testimony of love or unity to the world, so vital for the gospel's success (John 13:35; 17:22–3). But at this point there was clearly a higher duty, that of preserving the truth. This was more important than unity. Consequently the Apostle Paul did the tough thing and confronted the Apostle Peter. It had to have been painful for him to do. It had to have cost him a great deal. He had no way of knowing ahead of time how it would turn out. Some probably got mad at him. Others may have accused him of being a trouble maker and rocking the boat. But it was the right thing to do. This is not just an argument over 'minor' doctrine or theology. This is the heart of the gospel for which no confrontation can appear too frightening, no sacrifice too great. Our flabby minded and fuzzy thinking culture will never understand why we might do such a thing. We need to understand that they won't, and accept that, and do what is right anyway. The irony of it all is that truth is the only sure foundation upon which unity can be built.

An artificial unity is possible on the basis of superficial ideals of brotherhood and the mutual commitment to avoid doctrine. One could say, 'We will come together on the basis of love and mutual respect.' But such a unity won't last. There is not enough substance to hold people together in the long run. There is not enough there that calls forth the sacrifice and self-denial that makes true and lasting unity possible amongst a people. It would also be possible to unify on the basis of error. One could determine just to go along with whatever the majority believed and to stifle differences in order to preserve the peace and unity of the church. But the apostle Paul says that the church is built upon the foundation of the 'apostles and prophets' (Eph. 2:20). The foundation of the church is apostolic teaching. In the long run, if the gospel is compromised, the church, as we have seen, is going to die.

True unity however is built upon the mutual conviction of the truth of the gospel. This is what brings them together, and this is what keeps them together. The Apostle Paul, in exhorting the Corinthians, urges them to 'all agree.' He says that he wants 'no division amongst them.' But on what basis? He goes on and says, 'but that you should be of the same mind and of the same judgment' (1 Cor. 1:10). Unity then is based upon common thinking, common convictions. Likewise in Philippians 1:27, the Apostle Paul urges them to 'stand firm in one spirit and with one mind, striving together for the faith of the gospel.' Unity then, that is, being of 'one spirit,' is built upon the foundation of single-mindedness as they strive together for 'the faith' of 'the gospel.' The irony then is that in the long run, the true unity and peace and harmony of the church is built upon the very confrontation that the Apostle Paul manifests here. And the reason is, his confrontation produced a higher unity and a greater unity based upon a clearer and purer grasp of the truth of the gospel.

6

Justification by Faith Alone

Galatians 2:15–16

Let us remember that the letter to the Galatians was inspired by the need to defend the gospel from the attacks of the Judaizers, who sought to add to faith the ceremonial requirements of the Law as necessary for salvation. These attacks were directed against both the primary messenger (the Apostle Paul) and the message (the gospel of grace). Having defended his apostleship from 1:5–2:14, Paul now shifts in mid-sentence to his defense of his gospel in 2:15, the theme which shall occupy his mind through 5:12. In this section we have a clear, passionate, defense of the heart of the gospel, justification by faith *alone.* Six times in 2:16 he declares either positively or negatively that we are justified by faith in Christ and not by works. I recently heard a former seminary classmate of mine attacking this doctrine, claim-ing that the Bible nowhere says that we are justified by faith *alone.* He is as wrong about this as is the person who claims that the doctrine of the Trinity is not taught in the Bible because the word 'Trinity' is nowhere to be found. The error in both cases is to demand specific language or vocabulary instead of looking for what Scripture teaches. Does the Bible teach the doctrine of the Trinity? Does it teach justification by faith alone? In both cases the answer is 'yes.' In the latter case, we will even find in verse 16 the phrase 'but through faith,' or 'except through faith,' in substance the same in meaning as the 'by faith alone.' But this is, in one sense, beside the point. What the Bible repeatedly *teaches* is that we are saved by *faith* and not by *works.* Because others have come along and added to faith other requirements the word 'alone' has been added in to clarify what the Bible means. We are saved by faith plus *nothing.*

This, we say with the Apostle Paul, is the heart of the gospel. Calvin described the doctrine of justification by faith alone as 'the principle hinge by which religion is supported.'[37] Luther called it 'the principal article of all Christian doctrine, wherein the knowledge of all godliness consisteth.' He said that it was mandatory that 'we should know this article well, teach it unto others, and beat it into their heads continually.' Lose this, he said, 'then is all true doctrine lost.'[38] Similarly, Cranmer called justification 'the strong rock and foundation of the Christian religion.'[39]

What is justification? It is a term borrowed from the law courts. It is the opposite of condemnation. For example Paul writes,

> Who will bring a charge against God's elect? God is the one who justifies; who is the one who condemns? Christ Jesus is He who died, yes, who was raised. (Rom. 8:33–4a).

To condemn means to declare guilty and so liable to punishment. To justify, then, is the opposite. It means to declare not guilty, or innocent; to pardon or acquit. Stott writes, 'In the Bible it refers to God's act of unmerited favour by which He puts a sinner right with Himself, not only pardoning or acquitting him, but accepting him and treating him as righteous.'[40] Boice defines it as 'the judicial action of God apart from human merit according to which the guilty are pardoned, acquitted, and then reinstated as God's children and as fellow heirs with Jesus Christ.'[41] Fung says it 'means to be declared righteous before God, that is, to enjoy a status or standing of being in a right relationship with God, of being accepted by him.'[42]

Is this legal talk complex and difficult for people? Perhaps. The simpler question to ask might be that of the Philippian jailer: 'What must I do to be saved?' (Acts 16:31). All people are aware, at least subconsciously, that God is righteous and that they are not (see Rom. 1:17 ff.). Our experience tells us that things are not right with God. We are separated from Him. We are under His judgment. He knows our hearts and our hearts are not right. He knows what we say and do, and what we say and do are displeasing to Him. 'How may a man be right before God?' Job asks (9:2; 25:4). It is this question that all the religions of the world address, with their rituals and ceremonies and other requirements. What must we do to appease the deity? How can we satisfy His demands? Here is the formula, they say. Here is the map. Even the non-religious walk about with a sense of unease, of angst, as they suppress what they know and fear about God. It is this fundamental question that is answered in our text.

Not by Works

> We are Jews by nature, and not sinners from among the Gentiles; (Gal. 2:15)

Contrary to what every natural instinct of our fallen nature might tell us, we are not justified by works. 'We,' meaning he and Peter and the other Jewish believers, 'are Jews by nature,' that is, by birth. Consequently, as Jews they had great advantages. They were 'entrusted with the oracles of God' (Rom. 3:2–3). To them 'belongs the adoption as sons and the glory and the covenants and the giving of the Law and the temple service and the promises, whose are the fathers, and from whom is the Christ according to the flesh' (Rom. 9:4–5). They are not 'sinners from among the Gentiles,' that is, pagans who are ignorant of the law and living out of conformity with it. What is the point? 'But even so great advantages as these,' notes Boice, 'are inadequate for achieving a state of righteousness before God.'[43] Or it may be that this verse, set as it is before the next, may indicate that Paul means 'and we (Jews) know that a man is not justified by the works of the Law.' They knew this based on the Old Testament, as Paul will demonstrate in chapter 3.

> Nevertheless knowing that a man is not justified by the works of the Law but through faith in Christ Jesus, even we have believed in Christ Jesus, that we may be justified by faith in Christ, and not by the works of the Law; since by the works of the Law shall no flesh be justified. (Gal. 2:16)

The 'works of the Law' would include all human efforts on behalf of one's salvation. Boice notes that the definite articles are missing, meaning that it is not just the law of Moses that is in view, but 'any system of attempting to please God by good deeds.'[44] It would include conformity to the moral law, keeping the Ten Commandments for example, and conformity to the ceremonial law as well, such as circumcision, the dietary laws, and cleansing ordinances. It would include any system of merit, biblically based or not. This is essentially the religion of the man in the streets, and the religion of the world's religions since the beginning of time. Do enough good things and you go to heaven. Do more bad than good things and you go to hell. Salvation is found in doing the moral things or religious things that the given religion requires. Offer the sacrifices, perform the rituals, keep the holy days, and so on. According to the Apostle Paul, those who approach God in this way are 'seeking to establish their own righteousness' (Rom. 10:4). As a former Pharisee, he himself sought 'a righteousness of my own derived from the Law' (Phil. 3:9). This is self-righteous and we all, more or less, are guilty of it. We want 'a righteousness of our own,' one which we achieve by ourselves. We deceive ourselves into thinking that we are good enough or can make ourselves good enough for God. We attempt to win the favor and approval of God on the basis of our performance. But here we read, 'by the works of the Law shall no flesh be justified.'

Why is this? There is no defect in the Law, is there? No. If the Law were perfectly kept it would result in life. We read in Leviticus,

> So you shall keep My statutes and My judgments, by which a man may live if he does them; I am the Lord. (Lev. 18:5).

The Apostle Paul writes in Romans that the Law is 'holy and righteous and good' (Rom. 7:12). The Law 'was to result in life' (Rom. 7:10). But the standard is too strict, too difficult, too high. It cannot be accomplished. All fall short. Why then do so many mistakenly believe that they can accomplish their own salvation through moral and religious good works? What is their error? We can identify two closely related causes.

First, justification by works is based on a *weak grasp of God's holiness*. Second, it is based on a *high estimate of our own virtue*. The problem with the religions of the world and the man on the streets is that their god is not so holy that he cannot be appeased with a few honest efforts. There is no appreciation for the awesome holiness of the true God. There is no sense of His fearful wrath against what Paul calls 'all ungodliness and unrighteousness of men' (Rom. 1:18). The God of the Bible is 'too pure to look upon evil' (Hab. 1:13). He is 'light, and in Him there is no darkness at all' (1 John 1:5). It is a 'fearful thing' to fall into His hands. He is a 'consuming fire' (Heb. 10:31; 12:29). This holiness manifests itself in His justice. Because God is just, He will not tolerate even one sin. He will 'by no means clear the guilty' (Exod. 34:7). 'The soul that sins, it shall die' (Ezek. 18:4).

As for man, he is seen as basically good, but just a little misled. He is twisted, for sure, but still capable of good. Yes, we fall and fail, but God knows all that, and accepts us just as we are. Just so we are sincere. Just so we do our best. Offer a few sacrifices. Do some good deeds. Participate in the occasional religious ritual. Muddle through. It will all turn out in the end. Why? Because God's standard is not so high and man's performance is not so low. This is the fatal flaw. On the contrary, the Bible teaches that if we keep the whole law and stumble at one point we are guilty of all (James 2:10). The Apostle Paul says in this letter,

> For as many as are of the works of the Law are under a curse; for it is written, 'Cursed is everyone who does not abide by all things written in the book of the law, to perform them. (Gal. 3:10).

At the heart of our problem is pride. We think that we are good. We think that we are nice, respectable, big-hearted people. We fail to understand how completely unacceptable we are to the God who is there. He is offended at us and our feeble efforts. He is offended at our self-deluding self-sufficiency. He is angered by our self-righteousness. He is offended by our mutual self-congratulations as we pat each other on the back for our virtues. He is insulted by our poisoned efforts at appeasing Him. All our righteousness is as filthy rags to Him (Isa. 64:6). Getting right with God on this approach is utterly futile and impossible. Do you appreciate this? I often think of the very well-heeled and well-mannered lady who has never done a thing wrong in her whole life, and the potential for self-deluding self-righteousness on her part. Like the Apostle Paul, she is 'blameless' (Phil. 3:6). How easily she is blinded to her pride, her selfishness, her covetousness, and other sins of the heart. I think of the outstanding man, the accomplished man, who has always done the right thing in the honorable way, excelling in school, in business, in his contribution to the community, and so on. Yet he does not love God with all his heart, mind, soul, and strength. He does not love his neighbor as himself. He does not seek in all things the glory of God (1 Cor. 10:31). The law requires these things of him. Yet he fails, and so along with the drug dealer, the pimp, the child molester, the embezzler, he is a transgressor of the law, in some ways worse because of his inflated self-assessment, his pride, arrogance, self-righteousness, and will-to-power. One cannot get right with God on this approach. It is impossible. It is hopeless. 'By the works of the *law* shall *no flesh*,' that is, no one without exception, 'be justified.'

Faith alone

Justification can be found nowhere 'but,' or 'except' (*ean me*) or 'only' 'through faith in Jesus Christ.' The preposition supplies the means—through faith. As Paul moves from the universal to the personal and back to the universal again, he repeats six times that justification is not by works but by faith in Christ.

1. 'a man is not justified by the works of the Law;'
2. 'but through faith in Christ Jesus;'
3. 'even we have believed in Christ Jesus;'
4. 'that we may be justified by faith in Christ;'
5. 'and not by the works of the Law;'
6. 'since by the works of the Law shall no flesh be justified.'

He asserts this truth both by dogmatic affirmation as well as personal experience—'we have believed in Christ Jesus, that we may be justified by faith in Christ.' The final clause of verse 16 is probably a citation of Psalm 143:2, which says,

> And do not enter into judgment with Thy servant, for in Thy sight no man living is righteous.

'No flesh' is a universal. It allows for no exceptions. Faith is the only way because Christ is the only way. All fall short through works. No one does well enough. 'There is none righteous, not even one …There is none who does good, there is not even one' (Rom. 3:10–12). Some do better than others, true enough. But all fall short. Because it is true that 'by the works of the Law no flesh will be justified in His sight,' every mouth is closed, and 'all the world [has] become accountable to God' (Rom. 3:19–20). Righteousness must come through another means, 'apart from the Law' and the works of the Law. Righteousness must come from God as a gift 'through faith in Jesus Christ for all those who believe' (Rom. 3:21–2). We need to clarify what is meant by faith.

First, he does not mean *mere assent to doctrine*. 'We have believed *into* Christ,' he literally says in verse 16, implying says Boice, 'an act of personal commitment, not just assenting to the facts concerning Christ, but actually running to him for refuge and seeking mercy.'[45] Faith is not just a matter of saying the Creed. As James says, 'the demons believe and tremble' (James 2:19). Faith means receiving Jesus Christ as Savior and Lord. It means turning from sin in repentance (Mark 1:15; Acts 3:19; 20:21; 2 Pet. 3:9) and turning to Christ (2 Cor. 3:16). It means receiving the whole Christ, the One who died on the cross and who now sits upon the throne (John 1:14).

Second, he does not mean *faith in faith*. Often it is said that one only needs faith. 'Just so you have faith,' they say. It doesn't matter what you believe. The content of one's faith is irrelevant. Doctrine is irrelevant. Such sentiments reveal a faith in faith. But this is not biblical faith. It is not what the Apostle Paul has in mind. Faith itself is of no value. It is only as good as its object. In one sense we all live according to faith. Every time I sit down in a chair, I have faith in the strength of that chair. Every time I walk into a house, I have faith in the builder of the house and its continuing structural integrity. But if a given chair or house are weak and unable to stand under the pressure exerted on them, then one's faith or confidence in them is worthless. I may believe that a chair can hold me. But if it can't, then my faith is useless. I will crash to the floor, or in the other case, the house will crash on me. Faith has no inherent power. It has no ability to save. It is only as good as the thing or one in whom I place my faith. Faith in 'the force,' or an idol of wood or stone, or Krishna or Mohammed's Allah, is of no value whatsoever. Why? Because they are false gods. They are not the God who is there. They are figments of someone's imagination. Paul says the Gentiles sacrifice to demons and not to God (1 Cor. 10:20). Isaiah delivers scathing rebukes of idolaters who cut from one tree a block of wood to burn and warm their bread and another to fashion into a god, to which they cry out, 'Deliver me, for thou art my god' (Isa. 44:9–20). Such 'faith' is worthless and foolish. Faith is only as good as the one in whom I am placing my faith. These other so-called gods are fantasies. They cannot hear your prayers. They cannot deliver you from trouble. They cannot reward your obedience. Faith does not even do the saving when it is placed in Christ. Properly speaking, faith does not save, Christ saves. The question that faith answers is the one of how I receive the benefit of what Christ has done. The answer is not by jumping through the requisite moral and religious hoops, but by simple trust. Jump through hoops all the day long and you will never do enough to be rewarded with the salvation that Christ has won. It must be received by faith, by empty-handed faith. Faith in itself is not an end. We do not seek faith. We seek Christ. It is not true that all one needs is faith. All one needs is Christ. Don't be fooled by thinking that because you have 'faith' that you are saved. Faith must be placed in the proper One for it to be effective.

Third, he does not mean *faith in God generally*. One will often hear people say before they get onto an airplane, 'I'm trusting in God to get me there safely.' It is sometimes amazing to me how generally diffused this outlook is. Even in the midst of tragedy people will say, 'We believe that there is a purpose in this.' People widely share this outlook. They trust God that 'it will all work out.' There are no atheists in the foxhole, it is sometimes said. Many, many people claim that they believe in God, even that they are trusting in God. They cry out to God in their trials. They even want to please God and obey God. Is this saving faith? Is this justifying faith? No. We're not there yet.

Fourth, he does not mean *faith in the church*. Neither can we say that justifying faith is trusting the church's teaching (the 'implicit' faith of Roman Catholicism), nor to trust the church's membership roll (the New Perspective, understanding justification as being rightly related to God through membership in the covenant community).

What then is the faith that saves? Saving faith is personal, focused, and specific. It is particularly trust in Jesus Christ, not just in God generally, and not in the church. We cannot come to God or trust in God or receive the blessings of God apart from the mediation of Christ. He is the only mediator between God and man (1 Tim. 2:5). All the blessings of God are ours in Christ and only in Christ. Jesus said,

> ...I am the way, and the truth, and the life; no one comes to the Father, but through Me. (John 14:6)

There are scores of people who talk about God but never get around to Jesus. It is impossible to believe in God and not approach Him through His Son. Saving faith is, specifically, trust in Jesus Christ, in His sin-bearing death on the cross for my sin. It is not merely belief in God's existence. Remember, as James says, the demons believe and tremble (James 2:19). It is not even trust in God generally. It is specifically trust in and commitment to Christ. It is the whole person trusting in the whole Christ. It is the whole person with mind, will and emotions; it is the whole person agreeing with God's word, turning our will away from sin to Christ, and grieving our sin and rejoicing in our salvation, as we surrender to Him as Savior and Lord. Those who so turn are justified, declared to be not guilty, counted as righteous in His sight, acquitted in the heavenly court, forgiven for their sins.

The moment that we believe, it is done. The instant that we trust, we are forgiven. Not when we first get our lives straightened out. Not when we first clean up our act. But then, *at that moment* of trust, we are saved. We are, said Luther, at once, *simul Justus et peccator*, at once just and a sinner, justified but still a sinner, a sinner, yet justified.

True, the quality of our faith will then, over time, be demonstrated by works. But the works flow from the one justified, they do not justify. This is the glory of the gospel. Christ has done it all. Salvation is offered and granted to all who will place their complete trust in Him. We do not have to be good enough. Indeed, we cannot be. The offer is extended to the so-called saint and sinner alike. The harlot, the drug dealer, the corrupt businessman, the Pharisee, the persecutor of the church, even the chief of sinners, the foremost of sinners, may find forgiveness and life eternal through this gospel of grace.

Finally, let us return to 1:8–9.

> But even though we, or an angel from heaven, should preach to you a gospel contrary to that which we have preached to you, let him be accursed. As we have said before, so I say again now, if any man is preaching to you a gospel contrary to that which you received, let him be accursed.

Is there another gospel? Can we preach works and still be a true disciple of Christ? Can you combine faith and merit and still be faithful to Christ? Those who add to faith the works of the Law; those who add to grace a system of merit; those who obscure or undermine the gospel of free grace are anathematized by the Apostle Paul himself. It is a heinous, soul destroying error, from which we all must flee, as individuals, and as a church.

Come then to Christ Jesus. Look to His cross. Believe that through the shedding of His blood you may have the remission of your sins (Heb. 9:22). Embrace this truth in your heart, and you shall be saved.

7

Union with Christ

Galatians 2:17–20

The Apostle Paul has just emphatically and repeatedly stated in verse 16 that we are justified by faith in Christ and not by the works of the Law, or by any other system of merit. Now he shifts his attention to the typical and oft repeated charge that the gospel of grace promotes carnality. It is obvious from his writings that he frequently faced this accusation (Rom. 6:1, 15; Gal. 5:13–26). If one can be saved without doing good works, then what motive remains for doing what is right? Will the gospel not become a license for sin? Will not Christians become passive or indifferent to holiness?

This charge has been leveled against the gospel of grace ever since. Indeed it can be said that one sign that one is truly preaching the gospel is that the accusation arises. Grace should receive such a clear emphasis in our proclamation that we are open to the charge of moral indifference. Of course the charge would be false, even as it was in the Apostle Paul's ministry. Free grace does not lead to carnality. The whole 'free grace' tradition, from Calvin to the Puritans to the Wesleys and into the present, demonstrates this. But there should be enough grace in our ministry that some get confused and wrongly think that we are encouraging sin.

What is the answer to the charge? The Apostle Paul's answer is that by faith we are united to Christ, both in His death to sin and His resurrection to new life. The same faith in Christ that saves us also unites us to Christ, bringing us into a relationship with Him that cannot leave us unchanged.

Crucified with Christ

> But if, while seeking to be justified in Christ, we ourselves have also been found sinners, is Christ then a minister of sin? May it never be! (Gal. 2:17)

Verses 17–19 are difficult and are open to a variety of interpretations. He seems to be answering the charges of his Judaizing opponents. They seem to have been saying that since being justified 'in Christ' means abandoning the Law, then are not such 'found sinners,' that is, have they not become like the Gentile sinners (v. 15) who do not have the law? If one is no longer looking to the law for salvation, then one is no better than the Gentiles. Consequently, has not the gospel as the Apostle Paul preached it made Christ 'a minister of sin'? Is Christ an agent of sin since he separates people from the law? No, never, he answers.

For if I rebuild what I have once destroyed, I prove myself to be a transgressor. (Gal. 2:18)

On the contrary, Paul writes, if I 'rebuild' the law as a means of justification after having destroyed it already through faith in Christ, then I become a 'transgressor.' 'If I start building up again a system which I have pulled down,' the NIV renders it, 'I prove that I am a lawbreaker.' This is what Peter had done. He in effect sought to 'rebuild' what he had already 'destroyed' when he resubmitted to Jewish ceremonial distinctions and rejected table fellowship with Gentiles. The system of separation elsewhere called a 'wall of partition,' the 'barrier of the dividing wall,' which Christ 'broke down,' was not to be rebuilt (Eph. 2:14). To do so, the thought seems to be, is to become a true transgressor of the law, not just a 'sinner' as considered by the ceremonial distinctions between Jew and Gentile (vv. 15, 17). To reinstitute the law as the basis of justification was an offense against God and His gospel. It also meant that one necessarily must become a transgressor of the law and be condemned by it, since no one is able to keep it perfectly. If one is to place oneself under it, one must live by it.[46] This is his meaning in 5:3:

And I testify again to every man who receives circumcision, that he is under obligation to keep the whole Law. (Gal. 5:3)

Now comes his main point;

'For through the Law I died to the Law, that I might live to God.' (Gal. 2:19)

We should probably see in verse 19 a capsule version of what Paul teaches in Romans 7. It was 'through the Law,' that is, through the Law's condemnation of the transgressor, that Paul saw all hope of salvation on the basis of Law destroyed. In this sense, he 'died to the Law.' He died to it as a means of justification. He says there,

And this commandment, which was to result in life, proved to result in death for me; for sin, taking opportunity through the commandment, deceived me, and through it killed me. (Rom. 7:10–11)

But through this death he came to life, because it demonstrated that salvation could only come through the gracious provision of God. Thus *through the Law's* condemnation he died *to the Law* as a way of salvation, and awakened to faith in Christ as the true way of life. This faith by which he was justified also united him to Christ in His death and resurrection. Paul continues,

I have been crucified with Christ; and it is no longer I who live, but Christ lives in me; and the life which I now live in the flesh I live by faith in the Son of God, who loved me, and delivered Himself up for me. (Gal. 2:20)

As Stott points out, justification 'is not a legal fiction, in which a man's status is changed, while his character is left untouched.'[47] Through faith we are united to Christ. 'We have believed *into* Christ,' he literally says in verse 16, implying as we saw earlier from Boice, 'an act of personal commitment, not just assenting to the facts concerning Christ, but actually running to him for refuge and seeking mercy.'[48] We are justified 'in Christ,' that is, by a faith that unites us to Christ (v. 17). 'And someone who is united to Christ,' Stott continues, 'is never the same person again...he is changed...radically, permanently changed...He has become a new creation and begun a new life.'[49] Because we are united with

Christ, we die with him and are raised to new life with him. We share in both His death and resurrection. This is the point of verses 19 and 20. We die to the law and to our old way of life. 'This is because the death and resurrection of Christ are not only historical events…but events in which through faith-union with Him His people have come to share,' explains Stott.[50]

So why is Christ not a minister of sin? Because those who are justified by faith are united to Him in his death. Through the condemnation of the law they die to law as a means of justification. They die with Christ a death to the old way of life, life based on self-righteousness and self-indulgence. They 'die to sin,' as the Apostle Paul puts it in another text in which he is addressing the charge of carnality (Rom. 6:1–2). We have been 'baptized into His death.' We have been 'buried with Him through baptism into death.' We have 'become united with Him in the likeness of His death.' Moreover, 'our old self was crucified with Him, that our body of sin might be done away with, that we should no longer be slaves to sin; for he who has died is freed from sin.' What is the conclusion? 'Even so consider yourselves to be dead to sin' (Rom. 6:3–11). Why does the gospel of grace not encourage sin? Because we have been united to Christ in His death. Consequently we have died to ourselves and our old ways.

> Now those who belong to Christ Jesus have crucified the flesh with its passions and desires. (Gal. 5:24)

Now, 'it is no longer I who live.'

This is a fundamental fact of the Christian and the first principle of the Christian life. Through union with Christ we have died to self and sin. We have died to the old ways. What were the old ways? I was proud. I was always tooting my own horn. I could never admit error or weakness or need. I maintained a facade of religiosity, all the while I was self-righteous and hypocritical. I was *selfish*. I was always looking out for #1. All the world revolved around me and my interests and desires. And I made sure that those needs were met, at whatever cost and no matter who was hurt. But now I've died to this. My insatiable appetite for material goods has been crucified. My obsessive concern for sensual pleasure has been crucified. My quest for power and position has been crucified. I can no longer live in the old way. We have been 'crucified with Christ.' We 'no longer live.' The Apostle writes elsewhere, 'one died for all, therefore all died,' with the ethical point being,

> And He died for all, that they who live should no longer live for themselves, but for Him who died and rose again on their behalf. (2 Cor. 2:15)

It is not just a death to *sin*, but a death to *self*. Our great ambition in life no longer has to do with our own advancement or pleasure. It is simply 'to be pleasing to Him' (2 Cor. 5:9). You say, I have these needs. I have these desires. Jesus says, it is not your life any longer. When you came to me I said, 'Deny yourself, take up your cross and follow me.' I said,

> For whoever wishes to save his life shall lose it; but whoever loses his life for My sake shall find it. (Matt. 16:25)

When you come to Me, he says, you die to self-righteousness and self-indulgence. You deny your material covetousness. You deny your sensual lusts. You deny your self-centered ambition. You say no to self and yes to God and to others.

You become a servant of God and of others, and you do so joyfully because you no longer live. You have no more private ambitions. You have no more independent personal quests. You surrender your secret dreams. 'You are not your own,' as Paul says elsewhere (1 Cor. 6:19). You no longer say, I can't do this or that because it would cost me too much. You no longer calculate how much you can do and still preserve your comforts and convenience. You have died to self. This is true of everyone from the Christian *mother* to the Christian *martyr*. The Christian mother, who would rather be doing something more glamorous or fun or fulfilling, 1,000 times a day dies to herself as she changes diapers, reads to her children, corrects the same behavior a hundred times over, and cleans up behind them all day long. 'I die daily,' she says with Paul (1 Cor. 15:31). Likewise the martyr who would rather have enjoyed a comfortable, middle-class life, enters the ministry, heads for the mission field, places himself in harm's way, suffers persecution, and is finally murdered for the gospel. Why is he willing to do it? Because he died years before. He has been crucified with Christ. Didn't he have a *right* to a personal fulfillment, to a family, and a home? No, he had no rights because he had no life. 'When Jesus bids a man come,' said Bonhoeffer, 'He bids him come and die.'

So it is that Christians are the most selfless, other-oriented, self-sacrificing people in the world. Do the doctrines of grace promote carnality? No, they create a kingdom of servants, foregoing much that the world assumes is our 'right,' in the way of material well-being and comfort. Denying ourselves, as we serve our families, our community, and our church. Off we go to the mission field, into the inner-cities, defending the unborn, and into a thousand other worthwhile projects, as we die to sin, and live to God.

New Life

We look now at the positive side of the equation. Not only have we died with Christ, but we have also been raised with Him. The Apostle Paul continues,

> I have been crucified with Christ; and it is no longer I who live, but Christ lives in me; and the life I now live in the flesh I live by faith in the Son of God, who loved me, and delivered Himself up for me. (Gal. 2:20)

Negatively stated, we die to sin and law. Positively stated, we are 'alive to God' (2:19). Though I no longer live, yet 'Christ lives in me.' The life I now live 'I live by faith in the son of God.' Why? Because He 'loved me, and delivered Himself up for me.' This is among the most appealing aspects of the Christian faith. My old life of rebellion, of selfishness and pride, that life that I had made such a mess of for myself and others, has been buried. I now have a new life, a new beginning, a fresh start in Christ. Let's elaborate as best we can on what he says.

First, this new life is characterized by a *new nature and new power*. Much is packed into the next phrase, 'but Christ lives in me.' This is another way of speaking of spiritual rebirth and the indwelling of the Spirit of Christ. Faith unites us to the regenerating and empowering Holy Spirit of Christ. Paul doesn't elaborate this theme until 5:16 ff., but it is here in seminal form. 'Therefore if any man is *in Christ*,' that is, united to Christ, 'he is a new creature; the old things passed away; behold, new things have come,' he told the Corinthians (2 Cor. 5:17). Union with Christ results in our transformation. One cannot be united with Him without being radically changed. I become 'a new creature.' This is the dynamic that makes the Christian life possible. Christianity is no mere religion. It is no mere system of morals or philosophy. If it were Christians *would* live just like everybody else. Christians would remain in bondage to sin and consequently would continue to sin in the same proportion as they always did. The same weakness would remain. The same inability would remain. The same selfishness and pride and lust would remain. The 'deeds of the flesh' would remain: immorality, impurity, sensuality, idolatry, sorcery, enmities, strife, jealousy, outbursts of anger, disputes, dissensions, factions, envying, drunkenness, carousing, and things like these (5:19–21). This is the old life and the old way. But with the indwelling of the Spirit comes the 'fruit of the Spirit' and the transformation of behavior: love, joy, peace, patience, kindness, goodness, faithfulness, gentleness, self-control (5:22–3). Thus the Christian is not led by the flesh, by selfishness, pride, lust, but by the Spirit (5:18). The Christian does not walk by the flesh or live by the flesh, but by the Spirit (5:16, 25). He has a new life. He has a new nature. Christ lives in him.

Someone might say, 'I've never experienced this. I've been a 'Christian' all my life and I've never sensed that transformation or power of which you speak.' My life is the same as it's always been. I have all the same motives and conduct myself in all the same ways. If this is so, then ask yourself, have you been united to Christ by faith? Have you truly trusted Him, committed yourself to Him, turning from sin to Him without qualification or reservation? All who have are utterly transformed, new creations in Christ Jesus. Why then do the doctrines of grace not result in carnality? Because we have a new power in our life through the Spirit of Christ.

Second, this life is characterized by a *new approach to living*. Look now at the next phrase. He writes, 'and the life which I now live in the flesh I live *by faith* in the Son of God' (my emphasis). Our new life is lived 'by faith in the Son of God.' Some have made the mistake of over-interpreting Paul, as if he literally meant that he 'no longer' lived, and the self were somehow obliterated. Some have devised a whole approach to Christian living that imagines that we do not live that life at all. We are passive, even dead, they say. Christ lives the Christian life through us. Even as we have nothing to do with the justification, we have nothing to do with sanctification. Our task then, they go on to say, is to get out of the way. What we must do is let Christ live His life through us. Some even went so far as to press the meaning of the KJV translation, 'the faith of the Son of God,' as meaning that we don't even exercise faith, that it is Christ's faith, not ours. We live by His faith. This was thought to be the key to a 'higher life,' or 'victorious life.' Let Christ trust through us. Let Christ live through us. We do well to pay attention to the personal pronouns. He says 'the life which *I* now live *I* live by faith.' The phrase 'in the Son of God' should be seen as the proper translation ('in' not 'of') as in all the modern translations. I am still 'in the flesh,' he says, in this world and in this body. But the life that I now live I live by faith. What does he mean? He means that even as faith inaugurates the Christian life, so it also characterizes it. By faith I believe everything that Christ has to say. It 'does not mean some kind of mystical depersonalization,' says Fung, 'but a life of believing dependence.'[51] We 'walk by faith and not by sight' (2 Cor. 5:7). To 'walk by faith' means that I live according to what Christ has promised and commanded. It means living not for the temporal, the here and now, but for the eternal.

> While we look not at the things which are seen, but at the things which are not seen; for the things

> which are seen are temporal, but the things which are not seen are eternal. (2 Cor. 4:18)

This means that I must frequently ignore my natural feelings, appetites, and desires, and 'by faith' do what Christ commands. Many if not most people in our day are slaves of their feelings. They are absolutely driven by passions and instincts into ungodliness. To walk by faith means that I must frequently ignore my natural cowardice, fears, and anxiety, and 'by faith' do what Christ wants. Like Joseph in Potiphar's household, by faith I must say 'no' to my natural passions and flee from the opportunity of sin in order to say 'yes' to holiness. Like Moses in Pharaoh's court, by faith, I must say 'no' to the 'passing pleasures' of sin, 'no' to the 'treasures of Egypt,' in order to say 'yes' to God's people and 'yes' to the 'reproach of Christ.' Like Joshua, I must by faith say 'no' to my natural cowardice, receive the frequently repeated exhortation of God to 'be strong and courageous,' and lead the people of God into battle. Like Abraham, by faith I say 'no' to home and to family and to their comforts in order to say 'yes' to the 'heavenly country' whose 'builder and architect is God.' Like Noah, by faith I must say 'no' to social respectability and accept the mockery of the world in order to build an ark through which the people of God will be saved. Again, in spite of all of our alleged freedom to do whatever we want in our culture, most of us are governed by the opinions of others. We want to be respected and admired by our neighbors, and at least, thought to be normal. What a curse it is to be unusual, weird, different! Solzhenitsyn has said a number of perceptive things about how Americans are slaves of fashion, of fashionable dress, speech, arts, and thoughts. We have a moronic, oppressive uniformity in this country, which is cruel to all manner of political, social, and religious incorrectness. How do we manage in the midst of this environment to do what Christ commands? By faith! We do it because we are convinced that He is Lord, this world is temporary and passing away, and eternity is long and incomparably glorious. So John says,

> Do not love the world, nor the things in the world. If anyone loves the world, the love of the Father is not in him. For all that is in the world, the lust of the flesh and the lust of the eyes and the boastful pride of life, is not from the Father, but is from the world. And the world is passing away, and also its lusts; but the one who does the will of God abides forever. (1 John 2:15–17)

It takes faith to believe that all of those appealing things are 'passing away,' and that only those who do the will of God abide forever. It is not obvious that this is so. It is not apparent in this world. Yet it is so and we live accordingly 'by faith.' As Paul says with regards to suffering,

> For I consider that the sufferings of this present time are not worthy to be compared with the glory that is to be revealed to us. (Rom. 8:18)

How can he say that? Has he been there? Of course not. It has to be accepted by faith, and life conformed to accordingly. As the writer to the Hebrews says,

> And without faith it is impossible to please Him, for he who comes to God must believe that He is, and that He is a rewarder of those who seek Him. (Heb. 11:6)

Third, this new life is characterized by a *new motive*. Why do 'I live by faith in the son of God?' Because the next phrase tells us, He 'loved me, and delivered Himself up for me.' This sentence was not just stuck on to the end of the verse. It gives the context within which all the rest takes place. Here is what makes the Christian life possible. Here is the foundation. Here is where it all began. Here is what enables and motivates the life of faith. Believers have found these words to be among the most precious in the Bible ever since Paul first wrote them. He speaks of Christ's death as *voluntary*. He 'delivered *Himself*' up for us. He was not a victim. He was not forced to die against His will. He went to the cross by conscious choice. He also indicates that it was *substitutionary*. He 'delivered Himself up *for* me,' that is, on my behalf or in my place. He died '*for* our sins' (1:4). He 'bore *our* sins,' says Peter (1 Pet. 2:24). Thus also, he speaks of Christ's death as *particular* and *personal*. Christ 'delivered Himself up for *me*.' Look at how personally the Apostle Paul speaks. When Christ died on the cross, when he was 'delivered' up for sins, it was not just for all the world indiscriminately. He did not die for everyone in general and for no one in particular. No, Paul says, He 'loved *me*, and delivered Himself up for *me*.' Love for Paul personally and individually motivated Christ on the cross. Jesus had Paul in mind as He bled. Jesus contemplated Paul's salvation as He suffered. This is also true of every other sinner predestined to salvation through the cross. He knew His sheep 'by name' (John 10:3). He lays down His life 'for the sheep' (John 10:11, 15). He 'knows His own' (John 10:14). He calls them 'my sheep.' They are given to Him by His Father, and He gives eternal life to them (John 10:26–8). Realizing this, the Apostle Paul and all Christians with him respond with overwhelming gratitude. This is the 'amazing grace' of which we sing. It saves lost and blind wretches like us. We are amazed by it. It is almost too much to grasp. The church has often had to resort to poetry and song to give expression to the wonder of this love. We sing,

> Alas! and did my Savior bleed,
> And did my Sovereign die!
> Would he devote that sacred head
> For such a worm as I!

Would He? For me? That 'sacred head' for a 'worm' such as I?

> Was it for crimes that I had done
> He groaned upon the tree!
> Amazing pity! Grace unknown!
> And love beyond degree!

This shatters all the categories. What pity! What incalculable grace. What immeasurable love, that He should groan on that tree for 'crimes that *I* had done.' In the words of Charles Wesley,

> And can it be that I should gain
> An int'rest in the Savior's blood?
> Died he for me, who caused his pain?
> For me, who him to death pursued?
> Amazing love! How can it be
> That thou, my God shouldst die for me?

Would He die 'for me,' the one 'who caused His pain,' who 'pursued' Him to death? This is amazing! How can it be that the 'blood of God' should be shed for me?

Or back to Watts,

> While all our hearts and all our songs
> Join to admire the feast,
> Each of us cries, with thankful tongue,
> 'Lord, why was I a guest?

Why me, Lord? I am not worthy. Why me?

Why was I made to hear your voice,
And enter while there's room,
When thousands make a wretched choice,
And rather starve than come?

Given this personal, particular love of Christ for us, a love that was extended to us 2000 years ago on the cross and continues even to this day, how can we not respond in grateful service? Do the doctrines of grace promote carnality? No. They overwhelm us with positive incentive to please our gracious God. We're not driven into obedience by slavish fear. Gratitude motivates us. The doctrine of grace, far from removing the incentive for holiness, provides one far deeper than any mere legal approach could. We want to please our Maker and Savior for what He has done for us. How can we not die to sin and live to righteousness? How can I not 'live by faith in the son of God, who loved me, and delivered Himself up for *me*?'

8

Did Christ Die Needlessly?

Galatians 2:21

The Bible's starting point is the Genesis account of the creation and fall of man. We were created by God and for God, but we have rebelled against His purposes, refusing to honor or obey Him, and so have fallen under His condemnation. The Bible's starting point is also the starting point for each and every one of us. We are rebels. We are separated from God and far from Him. Indeed, that is the way that we want it. We are 'lovers of darkness' who 'hate the light,' said Jesus (John 3:19–21). We are under God's curse, and yet not inclined to do what is necessary to escape from it.

How may a person be saved from the damning judgment of God upon their sins? The Bible's answer is, through faith in Jesus Christ and not by the works of the Law (2:16). The righteousness that God requires of a person cannot be achieved through meritorious works. No amount of religious works or moral works can raise us to that status. Righteousness is a gift that God gives 'through faith in Jesus Christ for all those who believe' (Rom. 3:22–4). Saving righteousness is a status, not a condition. That is, it is a standing with God that He declares or confers, not a description of performance. He declares all who believe in Jesus Christ as Savior and Lord, who believe in the sufficiency of His sin bearing death, to be righteous, or 'not guilty.' Their sins are forgiven and they are given the 'free gift' of eternal life (Rom. 6:23).

But perhaps some might be tempted to explore other options. Are there other ways by which one might be judged righteous by God? Are there other beliefs that one might have? Are there other approaches which might prove beneficial? Perhaps one might even grant that Christ is the *primary* way to God, and even the *best* way. But may there not be other ways as well, perhaps in combination with Christ?

These types of questions raise a larger issue. Of course you want to be broad minded. You don't want to seem narrow or exclusive. It would be nice if one could answer yes to the above questions, and say indeed there are other alternatives. But if you do, then you must follow through on the logic of your statement. If there are other ways to a right standing with God, then you have pulled out the rug from under the necessity of the cross itself. Why then did Christ die? The specific issue in verse 21 is that of righteousness 'through the Law.' If one can be made right with God through performing the works of the Law, 'then Christ died needlessly.' What is true of the 'works of the

Law' would be true of every other alternative as well. Since this is so, then why did Christ die? The inescapable conclusion is, if there are other ways to get right with God, ways in addition to faith alone in Christ alone, then Christ died needlessly. This we shall explore in detail.

The Death of Christ

> I do not nullify the grace of God; for if righteousness comes through the Law, then Christ died needlessly. (Gal. 2:21)

No one wants to say that 'Christ died needlessly.' Then why did He die? As we mentioned briefly last time, the consistent teaching of the New Testament is that the death of Christ was substitutionary, voluntary and necessary. Simply, He 'delivered Himself up for me' (2:20). It was *substitutionary* in that He stood in our place and bore our sin and punishment. He 'gave Himself *for our sins*' (1:3). He 'was pierced through *for our transgressions*, He was crushed *for our iniquities*' (Isa. 53:5–6). He 'gave His life a ransom *for many*' (Mark 10:45). He 'bore *our sins* in His body on the cross' (1 Pet. 2:24). He is 'the propitiation *for our sins*' (1 John 2:1–2). In each of these texts, what He did 'for' us was 'on our behalf' or 'in our place.' We note again the pronouns. What He did He did for *us* personally, to deliver us from *our* sins. He was in other words our *penal substitute*, bearing our guilt and receiving our judgment.

It was also *voluntary*. He 'delivered *Himself* up' (2:20). No one took Jesus' life from Him. He is the Good Shepherd who 'lays down His life for the sheep' (John 10:11, 15, 17). He said, 'I lay it down on My own initiative. I have authority to lay it down, and I have authority to take it up again' (John 10:18). Death was not forced upon Him. Events did not tragically spin out of control and overwhelm Him. He came to die. His death was planned. He willingly submitted to it.

In addition, it was *necessary*. Throughout the New Testament we encounter the language of divine necessity. 'The Son of man *must* suffer many things,' we read (Mark 8:31; Matt. 16:21; Luke 9:22; cf. Luke 17:25). Jesus refused to call upon legions of angels to deliver Him because 'it *must* happen this way' (Matt. 26:54). He '*must* be delivered into the hands of sinful men' (Luke 24:7). What was written of Christ 'must be fulfilled' (Luke 22:37). Jesus said, 'the son of Man is to go, just as it is written of Him' (Mark 14:21). He said, 'Was it not *necessary* for the Christ to suffer these things?' (Luke 24:26). He said, 'Thus it is written, that the Christ should suffer...' (Luke 24:46). In John's Gospel we read of Him saying,

> And as Moses lifted up the serpent in the wilderness, even so must the Son of Man be lifted up. (John 3:14; cf.12:34)

We read of the Apostle Paul's missionary work in Thessalonica that he was,

> Explaining and giving evidence that the Christ had to suffer and rise again from the dead, and saying, 'This Jesus whom I am proclaiming to you is the Christ.' (Acts 17:3)

This 'necessity' is both a matter of what Scripture predicted (and therefore must happen because God's word was at stake), and also what one might say was in the nature of things. In other words, if a holy God was to forgive sinners, there had to be a *sufficient* sacrifice for their sins. He is not one to wink at sin. Forgiveness only comes at a cost. But it could not be an arbitrary cost, but one suited to the offense and thus, a *suitable* sacrifice. For God to forgive man, a man had to be punished. For God to forgive the infinite weight of sin, an infinite sacrifice had to be offered. The Medieval theologians debated whether or not God could have atoned for the sins of the world through the sacrifice of a donkey. The answer is no, He could not. 'It is impossible for the blood of bulls and goats to put away sin,' says the writer to the Hebrews (Heb. 10:4). Animal blood is both *unsuitable* and *insufficient*. Only man can die for man and only God can die for all men. Only a God-Man could to the job, so to speak. It was necessary that the savior be truly God and truly Man. 'He had to be made like His brethren in all things' if He were to be a 'merciful and faithful high priest' and 'make propitiation for the sins of the people' (Heb. 2:17–18; cf. Heb. 4:14–16).

Nowhere is this necessity seen more clearly than in the Garden of Gethsemane. There Jesus prayed three times for 'this cup,' the bitter cup of death, to 'pass' from Him. The gospel accounts tell us that He was in 'agony,' and was praying 'very fervently,' even His sweat 'became like drops of blood' (Luke 22:39–46). What was Jesus praying? For an alternative. He was looking for another way to accomplish the will of His Father even as He prayed, 'Not my will but Thy will be done.' He was pleading, in effect, 'If there is some other way to save sinners, let us do it that way.' We can be sure that the Father heard that prayer. We can be sure that if it were possible for His holiness not to be compromised and sinners still be forgiven through some other means, it would have been discovered. The infinite knowledge of God would have searched every corner of the universe to find an alternative. No rock would have been left unturned. No possibility would have been left unexplored. But there was no other way. The answer that came back to Jesus from the infinitely wise Father who loved His beloved Son with infinite love was 'no.' We can know with certainty if there would have been any alternative, the cup would have passed and Jesus spared. But it didn't, and He wasn't. Only He could die in our place, bearing our sins. This He willingly did.

Another Righteousness?

If then the point of Jesus' substitutionary, voluntary, death on our behalf was to provide us with a righteousness not our own, a right standing with God which we could not achieve for ourselves, then what becomes of attempts to substitute a righteousness that 'comes through the Law?' They make the cross unnecessary. If I or anyone else could make myself right with God by fulfilling the 'works of the Law,' then Christ need not have died. Indeed, He need not have come! The whole incarnation and atonement become a needless extravagance. If morality was enough; if decency and sincerity were enough; if religion and devotion were enough, then there was never any need of the cross. God could have spared Himself a lot of trouble. In the American South we say, 'If it ain't broke, don't fix it.' Leave well enough alone. Let people continue to come to heaven on the basis of their moral performance. Let God be the divine calculator, adding up good works and subtracting bad ones. Let the good save themselves and the bad condemn themselves.

It makes sense, doesn't it? The problem is that that system never was in effect. It has never been possible to merit eternal life. It has never been possible to earn a right standing with God on the basis of good works. Why? Because the good are never good enough. Because it never has been possible, Christ came and died. That was the whole point. We were lost. We were helpless and hopeless. Our good was never good enough. It never can be. If it could, then 'Christ died needlessly.' If it could, then humanity did not need a Savior. It may have needed a Teacher. It may have needed an Example. It may have needed a Helper. But it didn't need a Savior.

Remember this when you are tempted to say of the fine, moral, sincere agnostic that surely he will be in heaven. Remember if that is possible, then Christianity is ruined. You, however innocently, have destroyed the need for the centerpiece of the Christian religion, the cross, and with the cross, the One who died upon it.

Another religion?

Well what about other religions? What about those who have never heard of Christ, who live on the outskirts of civilization, who 'sincerely' practice their local religions? Can't they be saved? Or, for that matter, what about those who 'sincerely' practice one of the great religions? Perhaps they've been reared in a culture dominated by that religion, one in which other religions are illegal and persecuted. We can't expect them to be Christians, can we?

Let's begin with the last question. Phrased that way, 'We can't expect them to be Christians, can we?', or worse yet, 'Do you mean that everyone has to become a Christian in order to go to heaven?', biases the answer. Why? Because it sounds like bigotry. Why? Because it sounds like we are comparing a party or team called 'Christians' with other groups with other names and demanding that they all become like us—like saying only Americans go to heaven. Of course it sounds narrow and bigoted. So we would rather phrase it in another way. We would rather answer the question with a question—Are you saying that one can get right with God apart from the mediation of Christ? Let's begin with the ancient religions. Were the religions of antiquity sufficient to confer the forgiveness of sins and eternal life? Paul doesn't think so. He says of the Gentiles,

> Therefore remember, that formerly you, the Gentiles in the flesh, who are called 'Uncircumcision' by the so-called 'Circumcision,' which is performed in the flesh by human hands—remember that you were at the same time separate from Christ, excluded from the commonwealth of Israel, and strangers to the covenant of promise, having no hope and without God in the world. (Eph. 2:11–12)

If the religions of antiquity were adequate to make a man right with God, then Christ died needlessly. He need never have come.

What about the many local, tribal religions found all over the world? Can they make a person right with God? If they can, then Christ died needlessly. What if I make up my own religion? Can it be adequate to get me to heaven? If it could, then Christ died needlessly. Then what about the world religions, the great religions of the East and Middle East? Can they confer the forgiveness of sins and eternal life upon their sincere, devout adherents? If they could, then Jesus would have gotten a different answer in the Garden of Gethsemane. God would have put into effect 'Plan B' at that point, and redeemed humanity through a different means. Perhaps He would have selected eastern meditation, or religious austerity, or self-deprivation, or moral purity. But He didn't because it couldn't be done. God would not have it any other way. Again, we must realize the implications of our words. If for the sake of being seen as broad-minded, tolerant, and so on, you allow for salvation through other religions, then you destroy Christianity. You remove the necessity of the cross, and with it the necessity of the incarnation, and the Christian religion at that point collapses. 'Christ died needlessly,' if salvation can be conferred and received through some other means.

So Jesus and the Apostles preached a religious particularism. They preached 'one way.' Jesus said,

> …I am the way, and the truth, and the life; no one comes to the Father, but through Me. (John 14:6)

Peter preached,

> And there is salvation in no one else; for there is no other name under heaven that has been given among men, by which we must be saved. (Acts 4:12)

Paul wrote,

> For there is one God, and one mediator between God and men, the man Christ Jesus. (1 Tim. 2:5)

John wrote,

> And the witness is this, that God has given us eternal life, and this life is in His Son. He who has the Son has the life; he who does not have the Son of God does not have the life. (1 John 5:11–12)

The apostles believed that Jesus was the unique Son of God and that His death was of universal significance. Its application was not limited to a few people here and there, but for all people in all places and all times. What He did, He did for the sake of the whole world. Thus they went with the gospel to all the world. They never concluded that because a people had a religion of their own that they should be left alone. Quite the contrary. Their particularism produced a true universalism! In the context of Jewish evangelism today, it is sometimes questioned whether we should evangelize Jews at all. To fail to do so, to exclude Jews or any other religious or ethnic group, we maintain, would be bigotry. Our absolutism about Christ creates a true universalism—He is the Savior of the whole world and died for all peoples, excluding none!

Foreign missions are drying-up in our 'mainline' denominations. The once mighty mission force of the Southern Presbyterian church is now smaller, in the combined Northern and Southern Presbyterian churches (the PCUSA) than in the PCA, which has 1/10th of the membership base as they have to support it. Why the decline? Because they no longer believe that 'no one comes to the Father but by [Christ].' Since they don't, since they believe that virtuous or religious non-Christians go to heaven, why should they send missionaries? In fact, if the argument is that those who are ignorant are not held accountable, then the preaching of the gospel becomes the surest means of sending people to hell ever devised. If apart from Christ they could be saved, and it is only through hearing of Christ and consciously rejecting Him that we are condemned, then I better not go! Let them alone in their blissful ignorance!

Someone might say, 'I've been a Presbyterian all my life. I've never heard this before.' Then listen, if you will, to your *Westminster Larger Catechism*:

> Q 60: Can they who have never heard the gospel, and so know not Jesus Christ, nor believe in him, be saved by their living according to the light of nature?

> A: They who, having never heard the gospel, know not Jesus Christ, and believe not in him, cannot be saved, be they never so diligent to frame their lives according to the light of nature, or the laws of that religion which they profess; neither is there salvation in any other, but in Christ alone, who is the Savior only of his body the church.

The *Westminster Confession of Faith* adds 'to assert and maintain that they may, is very pernicious, and to be detested' (10:4). The old confession says this because the Bible says it, and all Christians believed it until the twentieth century when some began to lose their nerve. Our gracious God has provided a way. But it's His way and one way—faith in His Son and no other. Look no further! If you would know God; if you would enjoy the forgiveness of your sins; if you would know peace with God and confidence as you face eternity, then come to Jesus, who alone is the Savior of the world.

9

You Foolish Galatians

Galatians 3:1–5

We are in the midst of the Apostle Paul's defense of the gospel of grace, which extends from 2:15–5:12. In chapters 3–4 Paul writes particularly concerning the Christian view of the law as it relates to justification. Up to this point he has been defending his gospel in light of his own experience. Now he begins to appeal to their experience by asking a series of what Morris calls 'indignant questions.'[52] Essentially what he wants to know is this: did they receive the benefits of the gospel by the works of the Law or by faith in Christ? Were those benefits a result of their meritorious efforts or the work of the Spirit? 'Their own experience should have taught them,' summarizes Morris, 'that God grants wonderful gifts to believers and does it out of sheer grace, not as a reward for merit.'[53] His argument is based on three inter-related reasons—the message of the gospel they first heard, their initial experience of the gospel, and their subsequent experience of the Christian life.

The Galatian Foolishness

> You foolish Galatians, who has bewitched you, before whose eyes Jesus Christ was publicly portrayed as crucified? (Gal. 3:1)

'You' is actually 'O,' a Greek vocative that indicates great emotion, even anger. 'Foolish' (*anoetos*), literally 'mindless,' indicates not so much a lack of intelligence as a failure to use the intelligence one has. If Paul had meant to indicate mental deficiency, he had available the word *moros*, as in the 'foolish man' who builds his house upon the sand (Matt. 7:26; cf. Matt. 5:22; 25:2ff.). This word, however, indicates 'a lack of spiritual perception,' says Morris.[54] Christ used it of the two he met on the Emmaus Road (Luke 24:25). Phillips rendered it, 'O you dear idiots of Galatia,' and the Revised English Bible, 'You stupid Galatians!' It is not so much that they have weighed two alternatives and made a decision. Rather they have been mindless. They have failed to think consistently, logically, and biblically. They have embraced a doctrine of salvation that makes the cross of Christ unnecessary, as was demonstrated at the end of chapter two. To do so was irrational. 'They were being intellectually inconsistent, self-contradictory,' says Boice.[55] So much is this the case that he wonders if they have been 'bewitched.' 'Who put a spell on you?' (GNB) or 'who has hypnotized you?'[56] They could not have come to such conclusions on the basis of a rational process of thinking. 'What other reasons can there be for his converts to come to such a wild conclusion as to hold that adherence to the law was more important than salvation by grace?' Morris asks.[57] The devil himself must have tricked them.

What are we to think of this strong language employed by the Apostle? He is getting rather personal, isn't he? Yes, and he is getting rather *pastoral* as well. This is the key to understanding the strong rebuke. These are his people. He founded this church. He sees them falling into soul-threatening heresy. He understands the foolishness of it. So what does he do? He calls their revised views what they are. He may be using 'greater forcefulness than tact,' as Morris puts it.[58] But that is what it is. He calls a spade a spade. Foolishness! You know better than this! It was 'before' your very 'eyes' that 'Jesus Christ was publicly portrayed as crucified.' You were taught the truth. You've been over this before. For you to adopt this view, for you to embrace this concept is foolishness! Paul writes as a profoundly concerned pastor.

There are times when such things must be said. Parents sometimes have to tell their children that the things that they are thinking or doing are foolish. Sometimes spouses have to use strong language with their spouses, and friends with friends. Such language at times is appropriate when a situation is serious and a loved one's perception for one reason or another is warped, when he or she has taken a completely distorted view of things. The same can be said of the church. Congregations can get way off base. Colson writes in his book, *The Body*, of a Sunday morning worship service in which a fist-fight broke out, culminating in a right hook to the jaw of the pastor. Foolishness! Churches can become obsessed with obscure and irrelevant things. Members can sometimes worry about problems that don't exist, or don't exist in anything like the proportion of concern given to them. Leaders can propose the adoption of programs that are counter-productive or just plain silly. Churches can lose the forest of the gospel in the trees of what the old theologians called (in Latin) *adiaphora*, or things which ultimately are indifferent or unnecessary. In so doing, they get sidetracked and harm their witness.

The medieval theologians debated endlessly about how many angels could dance on the head of a pin. Our equivalents today are such matters as the nursery, how the facilities are to be decorated, the various personalities in the church, and the choir. Thankfully the last of these items has never been a problem at this church. I think this has a lot to do with the fact that the choir sings in the back and so they are anonymous. No one sings in the choir in order to be seen. What ought to be said about the petty and indifferent matters which occupy churches these days? I once had a man come into my office all worked up over what he considered to be the neglect of the church archives. He actually said, 'The archives are what the church is all about.' I'm not saying that such things are irrelevant. They have their place. But to allow that to rob you of your joy and sow discord in the church is foolish. Why do you worry about matters that are relatively trivial and unimportant things when the eternal destiny of souls is at stake?

The Galatian Experience

Now Paul begins reminding them of the specifics of *their* experience, contrasting it with their current convictions. First, he reminds them of *the preaching that led to their conversions*. Christ was 'publicly portrayed,' a vivid way of speaking of the power and clarity of Paul's preaching. That word was used for public notices or proclamations, as well as pictures. He was so portrayed 'before' their 'eyes.' Machen says, 'It was as though a great picture of Christ on the cross were being held up before your eyes, or…as though a great placard were being held up before you with the words on it, 'Jesus Christ crucified.''[59] It is rendered by Morris as 'placarded.' He was portrayed 'as crucified,' the perfect tense pointing not only to the historic event, but also to its ongoing meaning and efficacy. He is the crucified One even now, whose death is sufficient for our sins in the present. His benefits are 'for ever fresh, valid and available,' says Stott.[60] Since this is so, there can be no room for human merit in addition to or along side of the cross. Why then be so foolish as to make room? Why trade grace for works? Why alter the original message which you received and believed and by which you were saved?

This, by the way, has a great deal to say about both the content and sufficiency of the ordinary means of grace. Voices everywhere are prophesying the demise of traditional ministry as outmoded in an age of visual media. Lectures cannot 'cut it' in our pictographic age, they say. But preaching is not a lecture. There is a supernatural dynamic to it, sometimes not understood. Preaching *is* a picture. It is a portrayal of Christ and the cross. Even the sacraments are to be understood as a form of preaching, a 'visible word,' as Augustine (354–430) defined it. Drama and the visual arts have nothing to add to our proclamation. The message of the cross preached and administered in the sacraments paint a vivid picture of the crucifixion that can be seen and understood by all. This is what they had received. Paul had proclaimed the cross. His preaching was clear and powerful and engaged the senses, as it were. Christ was 'public portrayed' as 'crucified' before their 'eyes.' Its focus was 'nothing but Jesus Christ and Him crucified' (1 Cor. 2:3). The content of the message was that of His satisfaction for sin; of the sufficiency of His death; of the free offer of salvation to all who believe; of the forgiveness of sins and eternal life that results. This was what they heard proclaimed and further illustrated in the sacraments. All the benefits of the cross were offered and promised through word and sacrament apart from meritorious works.

The point then seems to be that they should know better. Having heard and seen so clearly the message of the cross and its implications, they should never have been so foolish as to trade it for a message that implies that 'Christ died needlessly,' as Paul has just told them (2:21). It was foolish of them! Why would the Galatians give up grace in order to embrace law? It is foolishness! Why would they abandon salvation by grace in order to put in its place salvation by human merit? Why would they accept doctrines that void the cross and make the death of Christ unnecessary? The answer is, they are being irrational, illogical, and unreasonable. Not only are they committing religious treason (1:6), but they are behaving foolishly. Realize that the same is true when we say that so-called 'good' people go to heaven. If they do, as we saw last time, then Christ died needlessly. We repeat ourselves: If we say that only those who consciously reject Christ go to hell and all the rest are judged on the basis of the light that they have, then we better not send missionaries, but instead leave them blissfully ignorant. Indeed, as was pointed out to me last week, if this is true, then the best thing that we could do to ensure the salvation of mankind would be to burn all of our Bibles and close our churches and silence our preachers, so that all might remain ignorant of the truth and so remain guiltless and go on to heaven. This is foolishness and those who hold to such views need to be honest about where their convictions lead. It is this kind of work that the Apostle Paul is doing. He is jarring them. He is demanding their attention. He is waking them up.

The same would be true of all doctrinal errors. Every deviation from truth involves an element of foolishness. When the Trinity is denied; when the dual nature of Christ is denied; when Scripture's authority is compromised; when the problem of sin is minimized; when the sufficiency of Christ's death is challenged; when the demands of discipleship are softened; when the return of Christ is doubted; all this is ultimately contrary to reality and so contrary to reason. It is foolish to abandon historic, orthodox Christian teaching. Likewise we must say to those today who are apart from Christ: How could you neglect the cross? How could you prefer the world? How could you pass up grace? Why do you resist His call? Why do you trust self-righteousness? Nothing could be more unreasonable. Sometimes strong words are needed to wake folks from their slumbers. Don't be so foolish!

Second, he reminds them of *the benefits of the gospel they initially received.* Now he moves from the preaching of the atonement to their response.

> This is the only thing I want to find out from you: did you receive the Spirit by the works of the Law, or by hearing with faith? (Gal. 3:2)

'Tell me this one thing,' the Apostle says. Did you receive the Spirit by works or by faith? They knew from experience that the Spirit had been working in their individual lives and in their life together. How had this come about? Did they not 'receive' the Spirit, a word that implies that the Spirit was given to them as opposed to being earned by them? Did they not 'receive' the Spirit 'by hearing with faith,' and not 'by the works of the Law?' The meaning of 'hearing with faith' is disputed, though most commentators indicate it means a hearing that results in believing. To ask this question as Paul does, is to answer it. Was the Spirit given because you responded to the gospel with faith or because you performed the works of the law? There could only be one answer, and they all knew it. It is implied, as Bruce points out, 'that there could be no higher privilege for mortal men and women than the gift of the Spirit.'[61] The Spirit was not given because of one's obedience to the Law, moral accomplishments, or works. He came to indwell the Galatian believers because of God's grace and their faith. 'The superiority and sufficiency of the gospel called for no further demonstration,' concludes Bruce.[62]

Third, he reminds them of their subsequent *experience of the Christian life.*

> Are you so foolish? Having begun by the Spirit, are you now being perfected by the flesh? (Gal. 3:3)

'Are you so foolish?' he says again. Relentlessly he demonstrates the senselessness of their new views. He pounds away at them. You inaugurated the Christian life by faith, receiving the Spirit. What happened since then? Morris sees in the phrase, 'having begun in the Spirit,' a pointer to 'the truth that from their first embracing of the gospel they had accepted the truth that they could not serve God acceptably in their own strength. They had come to see that they must look to the Holy Spirit for the wisdom and the strength they needed to live out their Christian faith.'[63] The expectation then would be that they would continue to look to the Spirit for that wisdom and strength. Why then would they shift from dependence on the Spirit to dependence on the 'flesh,' on their own unaided efforts and accomplishments? Is this the way to be 'perfected' or 'completed'? Or more precisely, would they shift the ground of their relationship with God from faith to works? Would they begin the Christian life trusting in Christ alone for salvation, and then subsequently throw in the law as an additional requirement for salvation?

> Did you suffer so many things in vain—if indeed it was in vain? (Gal. 3:4)

He reminds them of the things that they have 'suffered,' or perhaps more generally, 'experienced,' as Morris and Zerwick suggest. They had become Christians. They had received the Holy Spirit. They had undergone a multitude of experiences. Had that been 'in vain'? Note, the Apostle's concern is still with justification. He has not moved on to sanctification as many popular writers claim. Paul's labor would have been 'in vain' if they were no longer trusting in salvation by grace and were now trusting in salvation through law. They would be lost, not merely confused. These two alternatives, faith and law, spirit and flesh, are incompatible. They are mutually exclusive. A friend of mine recounts a conversation with the late John Gerstner (1914–96) in which that old Presbyterian war horse warned him that if he now believed that salvation was to be found in a system combining faith and works, and if he were denying justification by faith alone, he was damned. I found the remark startling and sobering. The Apostle Paul says no less. If they were trusting in works, all was 'in vain.' The qualification, 'if indeed it was in vain,' is meant to leave the door open to the possibility that in spite of all that he has heard, they may not have yet entirely embraced the legalistic 'gospel' of works.

> Does He then, who provides you with the Spirit and works miracles among you, do it by the works of the Law, or by hearing with faith? (Gal. 3:5)

The word translated 'provides' conveys the thought of generosity. He speaks of God doing two things: giving the Spirit and working miracles. How are these things done, he asks? Is it by faith or by law? How do we continue in Christ? How are we preserved in Christ? Is conversion a matter of grace but continuation of works? How is the Christian life to be lived? How are miracles in his day, including miracles such as healing, and in our day, consisting mainly of conversion, to be done? Does God do these works on the basis of works? Do we first go out and perform and then He responds? Or must the Christian life be lived in constant dependence upon the grace of Christ?

The temptation to which they had succumbed, and which they and we must resist, is that of shifting the ground of our relationship to Christ from that of faith to works. How were you converted? By faith. How did you receive the Holy Spirit? By faith. How does the work of Christ move forward? By faith. The whole of the Christian life is a life of dependence upon Christ, for justification and sanctification, from beginning to end. We are not saved by faith and then completed by works. There is an inner consistency to the Christian life. It is all of faith. Do we merit God's favor at the inauguration of the Christian life? No. Do we keep God's favor by meritorious works once in the Christian life? No. It is all of Christ, all of grace, and all of faith.

Do we want to be Christians? Then we must give up our pretended self-sufficiency and trust in Christ. Do we want to continue as Christians to the end? Then we must not be so 'foolish' as to move post-conversion from Christ to law, from grace to merit, from faith to works. That would be a disaster. It would be to run 'in vain.' We are Christians, in Christ, beginning and ending, only by the grace of God, through faith.

10

The True Sons of Abraham

Galatians 3:6–14

Paul is defending himself and his gospel against people known to history as 'Judaizers,' that is, those who were attempting to combine the grace of the gospel with the works of the Law. He has argued on the basis of his experience (2:15–21), and then on the basis of their experience (3:1–5), that we are justified by faith alone in Christ alone apart from the works of the law (or any other sort of meritorious works).

Now the apostle will turn to the Old Testament Scripture, which one might have thought of as their 'turf.' One might have thought that while the gospel surely does teach justification by faith, the Judaizers were right about the Old Testament. The Old Testament, they might have argued, teaches salvation through keeping the law. The Old Testament requires circumcision, ceremonial cleansing, and the observance of the high holy days, as well as conformity to the moral law, if one is to be saved. Could you then, on that basis, repudiate the New Testament revelation as the Pharisees continued to do, or require some combination of grace and law as the Judaizers were arguing? The Apostle Paul would have none of it. Not only experience but that which transcends experience, the infallible and authoritative word of God, even in the Old Testament, proves that one may be made right with God only by faith in the Redeemer. Paul takes them back to the Patriarch Abraham, and cites the Old Testament six times in these nine verses to demonstrate that justification has always been received on the basis of faith.

The Example of Abraham

> Even so Abraham believed God, and it was reckoned to him as righteousness. (Gal. 3:6)

Abraham was recognized by both sides as the father of the people of God. The pattern found in him is crucial for all who follow him. The Apostle Paul says, 'Abraham believed God!' How then was he saved? He was saved by faith!

The rabbis of Paul's day often had a very different view of Abraham than that expressed by the Apostle Paul here. They revered him as one who kept the provisions of the Law of God that would later be delivered in detail through Moses. They emphasized his 'virtues and deeds,' says Morris (98). However the biblical record says little of Abraham's works. He heard the call of God in Genesis 12, the promises of Genesis 12 and 15, and responded with faith.

Recall the circumstances. Abraham was childless, and advanced in years. God led him outside, told him to look up at the stars of heaven, promising him, 'So shall your descendants be' (Gen 15:5). In what Stott calls a 'master-stroke' (72), Paul quotes Genesis 15:6:

> Then he believed in the Lord; and He reckoned it to him as righteousness.

Because Abraham believed God, he was just-ified. He was 'reckoned' as righteous, a word (*logizomai*) that means to 'calculate' or to 'credit to one's account.' He had not done good works. He had not been circumcised. The law had not yet been given. He simply had believed God, and God, in response, credited to his account a righteousness that he had not earned or merited. Thus 'righteousness' is not an ethical quality, but a verdict, a legal standing. The righteous are 'those who get the verdict when they stand before God,' says Morris.[64] It indicates not a change in character, but in status. Abraham does not *become* righteous, but is *considered* as righteous.

> Therefore, be sure that it is those who are of faith who are sons of Abraham. (Gal. 3:7)

If Abraham was justified by faith, then what conclusion ought to be drawn regarding his children? 'Therefore,' he says. 'Follow the logic,' he is saying. The word translated 'be sure,' literally 'know,' is in the imperative. Paul commands them to realize this truth. Learn this, he is saying, 'that it is those who are of faith,' meaning, says Morris, 'not that they sometimes have an impulse to believe, but rather that believing is their constant attitude; faith is characteristic of them,' 'who are the sons of Abraham.'[65] The Judaizers would have argued that those who conform to the Law are the sons of Abraham. The Apostle Paul identifies faith as of prime importance. Since Abraham was justified by faith, then his true children are those who likewise are justified by faith.

The claim to be the true sons of Abraham is vital to his argument. Proof of authentic descent from Abraham is crucial to determining religious legitimacy. Who are the rightful heirs of Abraham, those who are of faith, or of law? Who may rightfully claim to be his sons, those who are his physical seed, or those who follow in his faith?

If this kind of question sounds remote, consider the parallel in American politics. Every player in our political arena today, as indeed has been the case since the eighteenth century, has attempted to legitimize his or her political agenda by an appeal to the Founding Fathers. It is crucial even today for the sake of political survival that one be able to show that one is embodying the principles first established by our founders. Who best represents their concepts of justice? of freedom? of the 'common good?' of the separation of church and state? Conservatives, liberals, even the American Communist party, even the American Nazi party of the 1930s, present or presented themselves as the true heirs of the Founding Fathers. In the latter case, you may have seen pictures of their Madison Square Gardens rally where pictures of George Washington and Swastikas were featured side by side. 'If George were alive today, he would be one of us,' they were saying. Our point is that even they had to demonstrate succession from the Founding Fathers in order to have any hearing at all. Incredibly, even pornographers and abortionists appeal to the First Amendment and 'the principles upon which this country was founded.'

The same appeal to the Fathers can be seen in the church. The Presbyterians, the Baptists, the Charismatics, the Roman Catholics, the

Episcopalians, indeed virtually every Christian group, attempts to demonstrate that they are the true heirs of the apostles. We all claim apostolic succession in one form or another. Our legitimacy rests on our ability to demonstrate that our polity, doctrine, worship, and mission are those first established by the early church. Similarly, we would argue in both the political and ecclesiastical realms that the true successors of the Founders or Fathers are not those who can trace their bloodlines to the Mayflower, or to the Apostles, but those who believe and live as they did, whether one's family immigrated 400 years ago or yesterday.

In a similar manner, the early Christians attempted to demonstrate that they were the true successors of the Patriarchs, particularly Abraham. The true sons of Abraham are not those with bloodlines or physical descent, but those who share Abraham's convictions and conduct. His true children are those who believe and live as he did. Paul therefore is arguing that he, not the Judaizers, represents the faith of the Fathers. He goes on:

> And the Scripture, foreseeing that God would justify the Gentiles by faith, preached the gospel beforehand to Abraham, saying, 'All the nations shall be blessed in you.' (Gal. 3:8)

Abraham not only believed God, but he believed the 'gospel'!

The Apostle Paul now quotes Genesis 12:3, citing the promise of God, that Abraham would inherit land, that his descendants would form a great nation, and that all the nations would be blessed through him. This is the foundational text of the covenant with Abraham, and subsequently with Israel. Genesis does not specify of what the blessing of the nations will consist. But surely the tenor of the whole Bible would lead us to believe that the blessing promised was primarily spiritual, not physical descendants and real estate. As the writer to the Hebrews says of Abraham,

> He was looking for the city which has foundations, whose architect and builder is God. (Heb. 11:10)

Paul identifies justification, the greatest of all blessings, as indicated by this promise. Indeed, the Apostle says the Scripture 'preached the gospel beforehand' (*proseuangelomai*) to Abraham. The message to Abraham was a pre-preaching of the gospel. His point is that the message to Abraham and the message preached by Paul were essentially the same (cf. Acts 13:22; Heb. 4:2). The response of Abraham and the response Paul called for were the same. Abraham saw in the promises of God the promise of a Redeemer and of the blessings of justification. The 'gospel' preached in the promise of blessing to the nations is 'that God would justify the Gentiles by faith.' Jesus said,

> Your father Abraham rejoiced to see My day, and he saw it and was glad. (John 8:56)

How would Christians receive this blessing of justification? By faith, even as Abraham did. The Judaizers may have argued that one became a son of Abraham by circumcision. But as the Apostle Paul asks in Romans 4 of the righteousness reckoned to Abraham, 'How then was it reckoned? While he was circumcised or uncircumcised?' (4:10). Abraham was 'reckoned' as righteous while uncircumcised. He continues,

> And he [Abraham] received the sign of circumcision, a seal of the righteousness of the faith which he had while uncircumcised, that he might be the

> father of all who believe without being circumcised, that righteousness might be reckoned to them, and the father of circumcision to those who not only are of the circumcision, but who also follow in the steps of the faith of our father Abraham which he had while uncircumcised. For the promise to Abraham or to his descendants that he would be heir of the world was not through the Law, but through the righteousness of faith. (Rom. 4:11–13)

Gentile believers follow directly 'in the steps of the faith of our father Abraham, which he had while uncircumcised.' Even as Abraham was justified while uncircumcised, so also are all who believe. Abraham is 'the father of us all,' both Jew and Gentile, both circumcised and uncircumcised. Morris cites Lenski: 'While Abraham is the forefather of the Jews, when he received this promise he was as much a Gentile as the Gentile Galatians themselves. He was still uncircumcised…'[66]

> So then those who are of faith are blessed with Abraham, the believer. (Gal. 3:9)

'So then' implies a logical connection with what preceded. 'Given what Scripture says, it necessarily follows that….' What? The blessings of God are to be found in following the example of the 'believing Abraham.' Abraham heard the gospel, believed, was reckoned righteous, and blessed, all apart from the law and works. So likewise shall Christians be.

The Impossibility of Works

Paul next demonstrates from the Old Testament that it is impossible to be justified by obedience to the Law of God. He will do so by citing the Law itself, quoting Deuteronomy 27:26, Leviticus 18:5, and Deuteronomy 21:23 (plus Habakkuk 2:4).

> For as many as are of the works of the Law are under a curse; for it is written, 'Cursed is everyone who does not abide by all things written in the book of the law, to perform them.' (Gal. 3:10)

Having shown that Abraham was justified by faith, he goes on to demonstrate the impossibility of the opposite, justification by law-keeping. 'For' ties what follows with what preceded. Morris renders 'works of the law' as 'law-workers.' 'For as many as are works of the law,' or 'For as many as are law-workers,' that is, those for whom law-keeping is the means of justification, 'are under a curse.' Then he cites Deuteronomy 27:26. 'Cursed is every one who does not abide by *all things* written in the book of the law….' To 'abide,' or 'continue,' means that 'small lapses now and then are not to be overlooked, as does the specification *all the things*,' says Morris.[67] No one, Paul is emphasizing, can keep the law, that is, the whole law. This is indisputable. They may be devoted to the law. They may profess to keep it. But it is the whole law which must be considered, not selective parts of the law. 'The law is not a collection of stray and miscellaneous parts, some of which may conveniently be disregarded' says Boice. 'It is a whole, and must be kept in all its parts if it is to be considered kept at all.'[68] Had the Galatians considered this when they submitted to circumcision? You may not chop up the Law. You may not pick and choose. No detail may be overlooked and no lapses allowed. If you go under the Law, it must be the whole Law, and if you fail at any single point, you fall under God's curse. James says the same.

> For whoever keeps the whole law and yet stumbles in one point, he has become guilty of all. (James 2:10)

On these terms, 'no one is justified by the Law'.

> Now that no one is justified by the Law before God is evident; for 'The righteous man shall live by faith.' (Gal. 3:11)

He again calls upon biblical support, citing Habakkuk 2:4. This makes it 'evident' or 'clear' that 'no one is justified by the Law before God.' After all, Habakkuk 2:4 says, in the context of the imminent Babylonian invasions, 'the righteous man shall live by faith.' The life of which he speaks is not the life of faith, but the life that comes by faith, that is, 'the way the sinner receives salvation, not the way he lives out the implications of his salvation.'[69] Only by faith can one be right with God, Habakkuk said so long ago. Life, eternal life, is ours only by faith.

Perhaps someone might be tempted to claim that one is justified by some combination of faith and works. This Paul denies in verse 12. Faith and works are incompatible.

> However, the Law is not of faith; on the contrary, 'He who practices them shall live by them.' (Gal. 3:12)

He says, 'the Law is not of faith.' These are two contrary things. Law and faith cannot be mixed. 'Conformity to the law is not a matter of trust, of belief; it is a matter of achievement,' says Morris.[70] Paul cites Leviticus 18:5 which says, 'He who practices them shall live by them.' Faith has to do with believing. Law has to do with doing. They cannot be reconciled as grounds of justification. They are incompatible. Either one trusts in Christ or one trusts in works, but one cannot do both. Notice he holds out at least the theoretical possibility of life through the law. The problem is that no one keeps it. Consequently everyone who tries to do so is cursed. If there is to be salvation for man, it must come through Christ. Indeed, the very thing that Christ came to do, and we could not do for ourselves, was to deliver us from the curse (just mentioned in verse 10) under which we have come because of our failure to keep the law.

> Christ redeemed us from the curse of the Law, having become a curse for us, for it is written, 'Cursed is everyone who hangs on a tree.' (Gal. 3:13)

Christ's Apostle now introduces a new term to describe the work of Christ. He 'redeemed us,' he says. 'Redemption,' says Morris, 'points to the payment of a price that sets sinners free.'[71] During times of warfare it was not uncommon for the captives of the vanquished side to be ransomed, or bought back, by the people back at home. Those thus bought and liberated were said to have been 'redeemed.' Similarly a slave might accumulate earnings and be able to purchase his freedom, and thus 'redeem' himself. It was also used of those under a sentence of death who were delivered on the payment of a price. Paul's use of it highlights the sinner's enslaved condition and the great price of our freedom. Elsewhere the Apostles speak of Christ 'purchasing' us with His blood (1 Pet. 1:18–19; Acts 20:28). This He did 'for us.' He was 'cursed' on our behalf, Paul citing Deuteronomy 21:23 and the curse of hanging on a 'tree,' which is identified with the cross. He was cursed with our curse, delivering us from it by bearing it Himself. For the fourth time in verse 10–14 Paul has cited the Old Testament to prove his point, the sixth time since verse 6.

> In order that in Christ Jesus the blessing of Abraham might come to the Gentiles, so that we might receive the promise of the Spirit through faith. (Gal. 3:14)

Here then is the purpose of it all. Christ was cursed for us, thereby redeeming us, 'in order that in Christ Jesus the blessing of Abraham,' referring to Genesis 12, 'might come to the Gentiles.' This blessing he, in this instance, identifies with 'the promise of the Spirit,' or 'the promised Spirit,' which we 'receive...through faith.' Thus he speaks of a three-fold blessing: justification, eternal life, and the indwelling of the Spirit. How are they received? The same way Abraham received the blessings of the gospel, through faith. The Apostle has set before them two ways and two destinies—law or faith, death or life, curse or blessing. As God spoke through Moses,

> I call heaven and earth to witness against you today, that I have set before you life and death, the blessing and the curse. So choose life in order that you may live, you and your descendants. (Deut. 30:19)

Stott says, 'The challenge of this passage is straightforward. We must renounce the proud folly of supposing that we can establish our own righteousness or make ourselves acceptable to God.'[72] Abraham couldn't be justified by law. It is impossible to be justified by law. Let us then forever repudiate any claims of personal merit. Let us then forever repudiate any claims of self-righteousness. Let us 'get right' with God only in Christ Jesus through faith, and rest upon the gifts of justification and the Spirit which He gives.

11

Law and Promise

Galatians 3:15–22

Paul has been boldly demonstrating that justification by faith is taught in the Old Testament as well as in the New Testament. Remember, this is not supposed to be the Apostle's turf. The Pharisees, reputed to be experts, reject Christianity because they are convinced that the Old Testament teaches salvation through the works of the law. The Judaizers, who profess faith in Christ, are so certain of the same that they teach salvation through a combination of faith plus the works of the law. Even within the Christian community today there are those who see two ways of salvation in the Bible, a New Testament way of faith and grace, and an Old Testament way of law and merit. They have sometimes argued vehemently for their views. Paul refutes any such dichotomy. There is but one way of salvation in the Scriptures, and it is the way of faith and grace. He argued in verses 5–14 as follows:

1. Abraham was justified by faith, being 'reckoned' righteous because he believed, as described in Genesis 15:6.
2. Scripture promised that the Gentiles would be justified by faith in Genesis 12:3. (This foundational covenantal text promises that the Gentiles will be blessed in Abraham. This blessing, and indeed the whole covenant, must be understood primarily spiritually. Since Abraham's chief blessing was that of being 'reckoned as righteous' because he 'believed God,' then it follows that the blessing of the Gentiles will also come through the same means, faith.) Remarkably, Paul calls the promise of Genesis 12:3 'the gospel beforehand.'
3. It is impossible to be justified by works, as shown by Deuteronomy 27:26, Leviticus 18:5.
4. All those who are justified (saved) are so by faith, as taught by Habakkuk 2:4.

If what the Apostle argues is true then it raises a question. What is to be made of Moses and the covenant made at Sinai? If the law did not teach salvation by performance of the works of the law, then what was its purpose? If the law didn't establish a different principle than that of grace (as in God's dealings with Abraham), then what was the point of the law? Why did God give the law at all? The Apostle answers this by demonstrating the permanence of the

Abrahamic promises, and (as we see in the next chapter) the true purpose of the law.

The Permanence of the Promise

Paul demonstrates in verses 15–17 the permanence of the promises that God made to Abraham. God made promises to Abraham in Genesis 12, 15, 17, and so on. He did not attach conditions to those promises, except to believe them. He did not say, 'Go and do thus and so and you will be blessed.' Rather, the promises were unilateral. 'I will bless you,' God said, 'and I will multiply you and give you this land.' Of course, the foremost of all promised blessings was that of justification. What was required of Abraham? Faith. The law, when it was given centuries after Abraham, did not overthrow the promise! God did not allow conditions to be attached to His promises. Having granted the blessing by faith, He would not later require something other than faith. God is consistent. God is faithful. He would never have introduced a new way of salvation, or an altered way, once having promised it another way.

> Brethren, I speak in terms of human relations: even though it is only a man's covenant, yet when it has been ratified, no one sets it aside or adds conditions to it. (Gal. 3:15)

The word 'covenant' in Greek usage indicates a last will or testament. But Paul is likely following the LXX[73] which uses *diatheke* to translate the Hebrew word *berith*, covenant. In our terms, think of a contract. He is pointing out that even in 'human relations,' a covenant is a binding obligation. Once 'ratified,' it may not be set aside, nor may new 'conditions' be added to it, except by mutual consent. The point is that one does not complete a contract or agreement and unilaterally pencil in changes in the terms of the contract. You may not, for example, complete your mortgage agreement, return home from the lawyer's office, and pencil in changes and impose those changes on the other parties. Once established it is binding. This is true 'though it is only a man's covenant.' How much more must this be the case when the covenant is made by God?

> Now the promises were spoken to Abraham and to his seed. He does not say, 'And to seeds,' referring to many, but rather to one, 'And to your seed,' that is, Christ. (Gal. 3:16)

Paul now points out that the covenant was made not just with Abraham, but with his descendants. Genesis 13:15–16, 17:7–8, and 24:7 all refer to the blessings that will come to the 'seed' or 'descendant' of Abraham. It was to Abraham and to his seed, that is, his descendants, that the promise was made. His true descendants inherit the promise. Notice however, the point that it was his seed, not seeds, that the promises were given. The singular, he is saying, is significant. While it is true that the singular 'seed' can be used in collective sense, referring to all Abraham's descendants, Paul sees a greater purpose behind it. Abraham had two sons, Ishmael and Isaac, yet the promise was transmitted only to one of them, Isaac. In the next generation there were two sons again, Jacob and Esau, but the promise was transmitted only through Jacob. Thus 'seed' does indicate selectivity. The promise is made not to all Abraham's descendants, but to the elect seed, culminating in Christ, *the* seed. His point is that the parties in this covenant are God on one side, and Abraham and the seed, Christ, on the other. Thus the terms of the covenant extend through the centuries to the present. No alteration in this covenant with the true descendants of Abraham, ratified in Christ, could be made.

> What I am saying is this: the Law, which came four hundred and thirty years later, does not invalidate a covenant previously ratified by God, so as to nullify the promise. (Gal. 3:17)

Remember some of the history referred to here. God made his covenant with Abraham around 2000 BC. To Abraham was born Isaac, to Isaac was born Jacob, to Jacob was born his twelve sons who followed Joseph into Egypt, where they remained for 400 plus years. The twelve sons became twelve tribes, and a threat to the Egyptians who enslaved them. Then came Moses, the Exodus, Mount Sinai and the Law. But this was over 400 years after the covenant with Abraham. The precise number, 430 years, probably refers to the time of the sojourn in Egypt indicated in Exodus 12:40. Paul may be dating from the time of the confirmation of the Abrahamic covenant to Jacob (Gen. 28:14). When the law was given 430 years after the covenant with Abraham, it did not annul the promises of that covenant.

The law does not supersede or annul or 'invalidate' grace. It does not 'nullify the promise.' What promise? The promise of salvation and blessing made to Abraham in Genesis 12, 13, 15, 17, and 24. Abraham received these blessings by way of a promise, not as a reward for works. It was a matter of grace. When the law was added 430 years later it did not overthrow grace and put works-righteousness in its place. With respect to justification, the principle of grace was permanently established in the Abrahamic covenant, a covenant ratified by God and so inviolable. 'Paul is not denying the validity of the law,' says Morris. 'But,' he goes on, 'he is saying quite firmly that those provisions did not provide a path by which they could merit salvation.'[74] The law, in other words, has nothing to do with justification.

> For if the inheritance is based on law, it is no longer based on promise; but God has granted it to Abraham by means of a promise. (Gal. 3:18)

The Judaizers stressed the Law. Christ's Apostle reminds them of the promise, the provisions of which precede and do not depend on the Law. If inheriting the blessings of Abraham (chief of which is justification) is based on law, then the promise is broken, and that's impossible. The blessings can come by law or by promise, but not by both. If law, then the promise is nullified and the covenant overthrown. 'But,' the Apostle says, 'God has granted it to Abraham by means of a promise.' The 'inheritance,' or the blessings of the covenant to future generations, came not by law-keeping, but by promise, meaning by this, by the unmerited gift of God. Remember there was no law at the time of the promise. Inheritance could not have been based on law because there was none. As Stott writes, 'There were no works to do, no laws to obey, no merit to establish, no conditions to fulfill. God simply said, 'I will give you a seed. To your seed I will give the land, and in your seed all the nations of the earth will be blessed."'[75]

This concludes the Apostle Paul's argument for the permanent validity of the Abrahamic covenant and the promises of blessing to his heirs through faith. The bedrock upon which his argument rests clearly is the nature of God. God, as we have seen, is consistent. He is unchanging, or to use the theological term, immutable. 'I, the

Lord, do not change' (Mal. 3:6). This is why He can be depended upon. In a world of change, where nothing remains the same, where people are fickle, where institutions are unreliable, here is unchanging reality. God's ways don't change. God's words don't change. God's promises don't change. He can be trusted. He can be relied upon. As Jeremiah wrote:

> The Lord's lovingkindesses indeed never cease, for His compassions never fail. They are new every morning; great is Thy faithfulness. (Lam. 3:22–3)

He promises to save you from your sins in Christ, and He will do it. He promises never to leave or forsake us, and He will do it. He promises to hear our prayers, and He will. Even when it seems that He doesn't, He does! Even when our world seems dark, and we feel alone and abandoned, even then we can rest confident in His unchanging and everlasting love.

The Unity of the Bible

Closely related to the principle of permanence, we should understand the Bible is one book. God is One. He is the same, Old Testament and New Testament. His principles and promises don't change. He has always saved by faith, by grace, by Christ.

Those who continue to divide Scripture push us perilously near to the errors of the Judaizers. Law did not and does not abolish promise. Yes, there are differences in *administration* from the Old Testament and New Testament. We might refer to these as *external* differences. Passover gives way to the Lord's Supper, circumcision to baptism, priests to pastors, altars to tables, and so on. But the fundamental principles are the same. All the Bible is about God's dealing with His covenant people on the basis of grace. This requires what some have disparagingly referred to as 'spiritualizing' the Bible, but this is exactly what the Apostle Paul does. The 'seed' of Abraham is spiritualized—it is Christ and all who are in Christ by faith. The land of Canaan, the heart of the promise of Abraham, is not even mentioned. Paul interprets the 'blessing' exclusively as justification. In Romans 4:13, he writes,

> For the promise to Abraham or to his descendants that he would be heir of the world was not through the Law, but through the righteousness of faith.

The inheritance is not of the land, but the world, through faith! Abraham desires 'a better country, that is a heavenly one' (Heb. 11:6). Stott writes, 'Paul realized that both the 'land' which was promised and the 'seed' to whom it was promised were ultimately spiritual. God's purpose was not just to give the land of Canaan to the Jews, but to give salvation (a spiritual inheritance) to believers who are in Christ.'[76]

This is why we can read the Old Testament with meaning, and could not otherwise. Their experience parallels ours. Paul assumes this as he writes,

> For I do not want you to be unaware, brethren, that our fathers were all under the cloud, and all passed through the sea; and all were baptized into Moses in the cloud and in the sea; and all ate the same spiritual food; and all drank from the same spiritual drink, for they were drinking from a spiritual rock which followed them; and the rock was Christ. (1 Cor. 10:1–4)

They were baptized, so to speak; they ate and drank spiritual food, as we do, and they followed a spiritual rock, who was Christ, no less! We can learn directly from them because they followed

Christ! I remember a friend once commenting to me about some of the Psalms of lament, that one can tell that they didn't have the light of the Holy Spirit or else they wouldn't have gotten so discouraged! No, no, this is a serious misreading of the Bible. They did have the Spirit. They couldn't have believed God and certainly couldn't have written Scripture if they didn't. If there are fundamentally different principles at work, say if the Old Testament is law, and New Testament is grace, all grace, then basically, we have nothing to learn from the Old Testament. There would be no continuity between their lives and our own. But the fact is, they are 'an example …for our instruction,' precisely because their experience does overlap our own (1 Cor. 10:11). The Psalms speak to our hearts so profoundly precisely for this reason. In the midst of the terrible suffering of sickness, persecution, and death, the Holy Spirit spoke through them. We can learn by studying the lives of Moses, David, and Elijah and all the rest, because though they lived in the shadows, though they did not see with the clarity with which we see, they were men of 'like passions,' with 'a nature like ours' (James 5:17).

God does not contradict Himself. He has been doing the same things and saying the same things to us over and over in the Bible. And that message, in both deed and word, has been the message of grace. Abraham was justified by faith. The law, given 430 years later did not overthrow grace. No less than the faithfulness of God Himself guarantees that this is so and will always be so. 'God has granted it to Abraham by means of a promise,' and nothing in heaven or earth can ever alter His word.

12

The Purpose of the Law

Galatians 3:19–25

The Apostle Paul is giving us a lesson in Bible history and theology. He has taken us back to Abraham and the original arrangements by which he became the father of the people of Israel. The covenant with Abraham was based on promises, not law; grace, not merit; Christ, not works. The central promise was that of salvation, which Abraham received by faith (Gen. 15:6). The message that Abraham believed was the gospel (3:8). The law, which came 430 years later, did not overthrow the promise. Salvation for all the descendants of Abraham continued to be by way of promise, not law (3:17–18). This then raises a question we introduced last time, and to which we now return. What then was the purpose of the law (3:19)? If the law was not given for the purpose of providing a works-based system of salvation, then what was its purpose? If the law was not given to provide the path whereby I become a member of the people of God, then why was it given? Paul gives a three-fold answer.

1. It was given to deal with the 'transgressions.'
2. It was not given to impart life, but to condemn.
3. It was given to lead us to Christ.

Transgressions

> Why the Law then? It was added because of transgressions, having been ordained through angels by the agency of a mediator, until the seed should come to whom the promise had been made. (Gal. 3:19)

'Why the law then,' he asks? What is the place and function of the law? It was 'added,' says Paul, indicating that it was not a substitute for the promise. It was given *in addition to* the promise, not to replace it. 'The expression indicates that the promise was the primary thing; the law was simply a supplement to the promise,' says Morris.[77] Completing his phrase, 'it was added *because of transgressions*,' a phrase that the Apostle never explains. What does he mean 'because of transgressions?' He must mean that it was in some sense given to deal with our sins. How does it do this? We may identify three ways.

First, the law *defines* our sins as transgressions. It was given 'to make wrongdoing a legal offense,' says Fung.[78] Boice adds the thought, from Romans 4:15 and 5:20, that 'the law turns sin into transgression,' by defining sin as a violation of the law of God.[79] This it did through its moral commandments. Sin then is not merely wrongdoing, but law-breaking, a legal offense against the lawgiver.

Second, law *provides* for transgressions through the sacrificial system. 'Because of transgressions' a means of atonement was established whereby the sins of God's people might be forgiven.

Third, law provides for sin on a *temporary basis*. Considered as a whole, the law as a system that defined sin and then provided for the sins thus defined was temporary. It was to function in this way, the Apostle Paul goes on, 'until the seed (that, is Christ, as in v. 16) should come (in His incarnation) to whom the promise had been made.' Why was it temporary? The Apostle does not spell that out here. But the basic reason was that it was inadequate. The blood of bulls and goats cannot put away sin (Heb. 10:4). A greater sacrifice was necessary, and the more thoughtful of God's people would come to see this. Hebrews 10 develops this theme in some detail, urging the reader to see in its yearly repetition of sacrifices evidences of its inadequacy.

> For the Law, since it has only a shadow of the good things to come and not the very form of things, can never by the same sacrifices year by year, which they offer continually, make perfect those who draw near. (Heb. 10:1)

The law is just a 'shadow' of Christ and 'can never by the same sacrifices year after year' deal adequately with sin. Again he says,

> For it is impossible for the blood of bulls and goats to take away sins. (Heb. 10:4)

The priest, who offers 'time after time' the same sacrifices 'can never take away sins' (Heb. 10:11).

> But He, having offered one sacrifice for sins for all time, sat down at the right hand of God. (Heb. 10:12)

The need of yearly repetition of the law's sacrifices prove that the law's provision for sin was temporary and inadequate, covering sin only until a perfect sacrifice could be made by Abraham's Seed. Morris believes that it is implicit in verse 16 'that the central function of the law was that it pointed to Christ, to who He was and what He would do.'[80] Once Christ would come, His atoning sacrifice would eliminate the need for this system as a whole. Setting aside for a moment the question of whether or not it will thereafter continue to define sin (i.e. apart from a sacrificial system), the Judaizers have missed the point of the law. 'The law was never meant to be a permanent guide to the people of God showing them the way of salvation. It was there to point people to the Son of God.'[81] He is not demeaning the law. It was 'ordained through angels by the agency of a mediator.' The role of angels in the giving of the law is referred to several times in Scripture (Deut. 33:2, LXX; Ps. 68:17; Acts 7:38; Heb. 2:2). The 'mediator' referred to is probably Moses. The point of these references probably is that the law is more remote than the promise, being twice removed from God Himself because of intermediaries such as angels and men. This underscores its temporary nature. 'The function of the law,' summarizes Stott, 'was not to bestow salvation, however, but to convince men of their need of it.' How? We repeat ourselves. By defining our sin as transgressions of God's law (and therefore against Him), and then providing a system of atonement that must be repeated, is inadequate, and temporary. Stott quotes Andrew Jukes, 'Satan would have us to prove ourselves holy by the law, which God gave to prove us sinners.'[82] Paul says similarly elsewhere, 'through the law comes the knowledge of sin' (Rom. 3:20; cf. 7:7). It convinces us that we are in trouble, but then makes a temporary and ultimately inadequate provision for sin.

> Now a mediator is not for one party only; whereas God is only one. (Gal. 3:20)

There is no consensus on the meaning of this verse, the commentators pointing out that there are 300 different interpretations of it. Morris suggests that the meaning is that when mediation is going on, there are at least two parties involved. The law was mediated, thus it is conditional and inferior, whereas the promise was unilateral, unconditional, and therefore superior. Thus the NASV: 'a mediator is not for one party only.' But, he goes on to say, 'God is only one,' thus in the promise we are dealing only with God, whose promises are unilateral and unchanging.

Let me summarize. The law was given 'because of transgressions,' to define them and make temporary provision for them until permanent provision could be made, 'until the seed' who fulfills the promise should come. It was never God's intention that the Mosaic sacrificial system should be permanent. The Apostle Paul is excluding from continuing use the *ceremonial* aspects of the law. The Christian should contemplate no revival of the ceremonial. We do not return to ceremonial washings. We do not erect altars and offer sacrifices. We do not create 'holy days,' all of which are connected in some way with the sacrificial system, or observe what Paul calls 'days and months and seasons and years' (4:10). These shadowy, temporary, inadequate forms are fulfilled in Christ, and any religion calling itself Christian that apes these Old Testament forms misses the whole point of His sacrifice. Their use was only intended until Christ should come and fulfill that which they imperfectly anticipated.

Condemns

The Apostle Paul demonstrates that while the law has a legitimate function, it is not designed to impart life. Positively, it was given to deal with transgression. Negatively, it was not given as a path to eternal life, but rather to condemn us.

> Is the Law then contrary to the promise of God? May it never be! For if a law had been given which was able to impart life, then righteousness would indeed have been based on law. (Gal. 3:21)

'Is the Law then contrary to the promise of God?' No, it is not. Law and promise are not cross-purposes. There can be no final contradiction between the promises of God and the law of God. Ultimately, law and gospel, law and grace, law and promise are not inconsistent with each other. The Law is not 'contrary' to or 'against' (*kata*) the promises of God. They have their differing realms or functions. Law does not abolish promise, and one might add, promise does not abolish law (Matt. 5:17). But the law was never intended to 'impart life.' It is not able to do so. If it were, then righteousness could have come through the law. But the Law has no such power. It cannot impart life. It cannot make one right with God. 'The law can keep telling them to do what is right but it cannot give them the power to do this … it cannot give them the power to overcome the temptations to do evil,' notes Morris[83] What is its role then? It can only condemn.

> But the Scripture has shut up all men under sin, that the promise by faith in Jesus Christ might be given to those who believe. (Gal. 3:22)

'But,' he says, using a strong adversative, indicating that what follows is the actual reality over against the false ideas of the Judaizers. They sought life through the law. But the fact is that the law, indeed all of Scripture (probably used here synonymously with 'law'), condemns mankind as sinners. It 'has shut up all men under sin.' As Calvin says, it not only does not impart righteousness, it in fact takes away righteousness through its verdict. All mankind is 'shut up,' a word used of confinement or imprisonment. The confinement is 'under sin,' that is, under sin's condemnation (see the parallel in v. 23 'under law'), from which the law could provide no escape. It defines us as transgressors. It condemns us as such. But it does not provide a way out. It only deals with our sin temporarily, leaving us still under the curse. He says the same again in verse 23:

> But before faith came, we were kept in custody under the law, being shut up to the faith which was later revealed. (Gal. 3:23)

The law kept us 'in custody.' We were 'shut up.' Five times in two verses he speaks of the law's role in trapping us 'under' the law's condemnation of sin and of its inability to set us free. It could not make us righteous. It could not give us life. It kept us in bondage with no way of escape. The law does this to us 'that,' or 'so that' (*hina*), indicating purpose. For what purpose does the law condemn us? So that 'the promise by faith in Jesus Christ might be given to those who believe.' The law through condemning us drives us to Christ so that we might receive salvation. How do we receive it? It is 'by faith …to those who believe.' Salvation comes to those who are convicted by the law that they are sinners and repent and turn to Christ. Notice the grace words: promise, faith, given, believe. The promise is received by faith! The connection between faith and salvation could hardly be made more clear. The word 'by,' or 'through,' 'points to the truth that faith is not a merit which of itself brings the blessing; it is no more than the channel *through* which the blessing comes,' notes Morris.[84]

We see that not every function of the law was temporary. Law and promise are complimentary. The law, through its condemning voice, continues to 'shut up,' to imprison, to keep 'custody,' and thus reinforce the need of the promise through which we are liberated. The law drives us to Christ, as we shall soon elaborate. But once we come to Christ, the Christian experiences complete freedom from the *condemnation* of the law. We have in Christ the complete assurance of the forgiveness of our sins. The once for all sacrifice of Christ is sufficient for all my sin. 'There is now no condemnation for those who are in Christ Jesus' (Rom. 8:1).

> Therefore having been justified by faith, we have peace with God through our Lord Jesus Christ. (Rom. 5:1)

We have hope that 'does not disappoint' because the love of God has been 'shed abroad' in our hearts through the Holy Spirit (Rom. 5:6). Thus we have both *objective* peace with God and *subjective* peace in our hearts. The law can no longer threaten and curse us. We have a 'peace that passes comprehension' and a 'joy that is inexpressible and full of glory.'

Leads to Christ

This, then, leads to our third point, already twice introduced. The purpose of the law was to lead to Christ. At this point we will make a distinction which may clarify our discussion. The purpose of the *moral* law was to condemn and point out the need of a Savior. The purpose of the *ceremonial* law was to illustrate the work that Christ would do. The sacrificial system with its priests and altars and lambs all pointed to the great High Priest, the cross, and the Lamb of God who would take away the sin of the world. The holy days and various ceremonies all revolved around this typology-rich system.

As we have seen, the system however could not impart righteousness. We return to verse 23.

> But before faith came, we were kept in custody under the law, being shut up to the faith which was later to be revealed. (Gal. 3:23)

The words 'before faith' refer to the time before faith could be placed in Christ. Literally it says 'the faith,' which Boice understands to mean 'the Christian faith.'[85] He doesn't mean that no one before Christ had faith, just that their faith was not specifically in Jesus. Prior to the coming of Christ, all 'were kept in custody under the law.' We were imprisoned, so to speak, kept under guard, by the law's condemnation and threats. There we were 'shut up,' a word used of fish trapped in a net. The law is a jailor. The only way out of jail was 'the faith which was later to be revealed' in Christ, meaning the salvation that was to be found through faith in Christ. Is the Apostle now speaking experientially, as opposed to principally? 'Yes,' says Stott; 'No,' says Boice. Stott (we think rightly) sees in the progression from promise through law to faith not only a historical fact of redemptive history, but also 'the biography of every man,' or at least of every Christian man. We are all either under the law's condemnation or we have found faith and freedom in Christ. The use of the personal pronoun here may point in that direction. 'We were kept in custody,' he says.

> Therefore the Law has become our tutor to lead us to Christ, that we may be justified by faith. (Gal. 3:24)

'Therefore' points to results. The result of our imprisonment was a situation in which the law functioned as our 'tutor.' The 'tutor,' *paidagogos*, 'schoolmaster' (KJV), 'guardian' (ESV), was not a teacher but a slave whose job it was to look after a child, a custodian. He supervised his education, monitored his behavior, and oversaw his activities from the ages of approximately 7–17. He was responsible for the disciplining of the child and could be severe. The law is not a teacher, but a leader. Through its threats, rebukes, punishments, and provisions it *leads* us to Christ. It leads us to Christ 'that' (*hina*), 'we may be justified by faith.' Thus the law does not confer salvation, but points to the need of salvation. This is its divinely appointed role. How does it do this? Calvin, in an extended passage, explains,

> But it may be asked in what the instruction of training by this schoolmaster consisted. First, the law, by displaying the righteousness of God, convinced them of their own unrighteousness. For in the commandments of God, as in a mirror, they could see how far they were from true righteousness. And so they were reminded that

> righteousness must be sought elsewhere. The promises of the law served the same purpose, for their meaning was this, 'If you cannot obtain life by works or by fulfilling the law, some new and different method must be sought. Your weakness will never allow you to reach it. However much you may desire and strive, you will fall far short of the aim.' On the other hand, the threatenings urged and pressed them to seek refuge from the wrath and curse of God. Indeed, it gave them no rest till they were constrained to seek the grace of Christ. This was the aim of all the ceremonies; for why were there sacrifices and washing except that men might continually consider their pollution and condemnation? When a man sees his uncleanness before his eyes, and the innocent animal is held out as the image of his own death, how can he indulge in sleep? How can he fail to be roused and desire a remedy? And certainly ceremonies had the power not only of alarming and humbling consciences, but of exciting them to faith in the coming Redeemer. In the whole solemnity of the ceremonial everything that was presented to the eye had impressed on it, as it were, the mark of Christ. The whole law, in short, was nothing but a manifold variety of exercises in which the worshippers were led by the hand to Christ.[86]

> But now that faith has come, we are no longer under a tutor. (Gal. 3:25)

'But now that faith has come,' meaning, now that Christ has come and we have put our faith in Him, 'we are no longer under a tutor.' Note that prior to coming to faith in Christ, we still are under the tutor. It condemns us and leads us to Christ. But once we've come to Christ, there is no longer any reason to crawl back under the law's supervision and threats and condemnation and inadequate provision. The law as a system that identified us as sinners, condemned us, and made temporary atonement for us, is no longer needed. We don't need its sacrificial system. We don't need its ceremonies. We are not 'under' its obligations or condemnation. Christ has delivered us from all of that. He has made permanent provision for our sin and delivered us from the law's curse.

On the balance then, what are we to conclude about the purpose of the law? Sometimes in Paul's polemic against the Judaizers he states things very one-sidedly in order to make a point. He employs hyperbole, as Jesus and all the prophets sometimes do. Yet as we have seen the law still has its place in leading us to Christ. This is hinted at in verse 23, as we've seen. Verse 25 sees us 'no longer under a tutor' only when we come to faith in Christ.

Our visitors are sometimes surprised to see us using the Ten Commandments as much as we do. We recite them prior to each morning communion service, and nearly every Sunday evening. One could point as well to the extended expositions of the law found in our Larger and Shorter Catechisms. Why do we do give to the law such prominence? The implication of the question is that we are in an era of grace. Why use the law? The reason is that the law has an important role to play both in the history of redemption and in each of our lives. The law was given to condemn Israel and drive it to its knees, and sensing the inadequacy of its ceremonies, to plead for a savior. But the same is true in each of our lives. The law was added alongside of the promises 'because of transgressions,' that is, to show us our transgressions against God (v. 19). It is not 'contrary to the promises of God,' but compatible with them (v. 21). It 'shut(s) up all men under sin' so that they might be given 'the promise by faith in Jesus Christ' (v. 22). One could make the case that one reason for the carnality and triviality of the church today is its negligence of what the Puritans called 'law-work.' Orthodox Protestantism has always understood that the law precedes the gospel both historically and experientially. Paul said,

> I would not have come to know sin except through the Law; for I would not have known about coveting if the Law had not said, 'You shall not covet.' (Rom. 7:7b)

Let's put it this way. How can a person become a Christian, receiving Jesus as Savior and Lord, unless he is first convinced that he is in need of being saved? A person needs to know that he is a sinner, a transgressor of God's commands, under his condemnation, under his curse, headed for hell, if he is ever to come to Christ. The law can never nullify the promise. But that doesn't mean that it doesn't have a vital role to play. It brings conviction. It shows us our sin. It demonstrates to us our need of a Savior. As I measure myself against others I may look okay. I'm not as bad as many or most. I do good things. I'm a pretty good guy. But when I measure myself against the standard of God's law, an altogether different picture emerges. I see my conduct in its true colors. My pride is brought to light. My jealousies and envies are drawn into the open. My lust emerges. My wretched selfishness is exposed. I begin to hate my sin and to seek deliverance from all that it deserves.

But today we have a different situation. People are coming to Christ because of promise without law. They want the benefits of the gospel but have never faced their sin. So they come to Christ not as Savior but as Santa. They are attracted by what they think he might be able to do for them. They come not to be His slave but to make Him their servant. They never face their sins. They never repent. So they continue in the patterns and the same conduct, to which they have added 'fire-insurance.' The results are predictable and observable. Widespread carnality followed by widespread defections from the faith. They try Christ for a while. He doesn't deliver in the proportions demanded. So they go back full time to the sins that they have clung to in the meantime.

Law does not nullify promise, but neither does promise (or grace or Christ) nullify law's proper role. It is vital that we keep these things in their biblical place and proportion. Grace (or promise) is a permanent principle in God's dealing with man. The principles of the Abrahamic covenant may never be revoked. God always saves by faith, by grace, by Christ. The law was 'added' not to overthrow grace, but to bring sinners to a sense of their need of grace. This too is a valid and necessary function of the law which we neglect to our peril in our day.

13

All One in Christ

Galatians 3:26–29

When God sent His Son to die an atoning death for the sins of the world, He did not then envision the salvation of countless isolated individuals. In calling sinners to Christ, He called them out of the world and into the church. God created a new community, a new society to which all those united to Christ would be united to one another. This of necessity meant that the old divisions of race, ethnicity, class, and gender would be superseded by the new reality of belonging to one another. Those separated by the world's categories would be united in Christ, by belonging to His family, His church.

This is the point that the Apostle Paul drives home in verses 26–9, as he clinches his argument that the law, particularly the ceremonial aspects of the law, can no longer divide Jew and Gentile in the Christian church. So far his argument has been primarily negative. He has labored to demonstrate the impossibility of justification by law (2:15–21); that salvation was always by faith not by law (3:1–18); and that the law was given to condemn and lead to Christ (3:18–25). It has then a temporary function both in the *historia salutis* (history of redemption) and the *ordo salutis* (the application of redemption to the individual). Considered as a system that defined sin and made atonement for it through the sacrificial system, it was provisional. The blood of bulls and goats could only temporarily provide for sin, until the Lamb of God should come (Heb. 10:4). Even considered as a system that continues to condemn sin and thereby leads sinners to God's permanent provision in Christ, it also is temporary, in that believers no longer have the status of children, but of heirs. Believers do not remain under its condemnation (even if they do continue to look to it for moral instruction). The sum is, this temporary system cannot be the basis for distinctions in the Christian community. No longer can Christians think in terms of the circumcised and the uncircumcised. No longer can rank or status in the church be determined by one's fidelity to the ceremonial requirements of the law, such as laws of cleansing, observance of holy days, and other ritual observances. We are no longer under the law as a harsh 'tutor,' whose discipline and supervision lead us to Christ in the time of our immaturity. We no longer have the status of children, but of heirs.

Now the Apostle moves on from his critique of the Judaizer's false views of and use of the law, to positive principles of unity which are inherent to the gospel. Negatively, the law cannot divide us, because the law's categories are no longer relevant (e.g. clean/unclean; circumcised/uncircumcised). Positively, the gospel demands unity, because of our adoption into a common family, God's family; because of our union with Christ; and because of our union with the saints of old.

Sonship

> For you are all sons of God through faith in Christ Jesus. (Gal. 3:26)

The emphasis of verse 26 is on 'all.' All are sons of God through faith in Christ. Adoption, or sonship, is not ours by nature, but by 'faith in Christ.' It is a great misconception to think that we are God's children merely as a fact of creation. While there is a sense that we are all God's offspring (Acts 17:28), the full meaning of sonship, with all that it implies in the way of fatherly love and care, can only be received in Christ. We are not children of God by birth, but by rebirth. We are born 'children of wrath' (Eph. 2:3). We become children of God by adoption in Christ Jesus. Of those who have faith in Christ Jesus, 'all' are 'sons' or 'children' of God. The gospel will allow for no distinction between the circumcised and the uncircumcised. Gentiles and Jews both are members of the heavenly family. Indeed, they are 'sons,' suggesting as Lenski points out 'the idea of standing, independent standing, that is free from any mentor such as children would have' (i.e. as in the 'tutor' of vv. 24–5; quoted in Morris, 120). By faith we have passed into a new relationship with God that was not possible under the law. We were under the curse of the law. Now we are under grace. To Israel belonged 'the adoption as sons' (Rom. 9:4). Gentiles were 'excluded from the commonwealth of Israel, and strangers to the covenants of promise, having no hope and without God in the world' (Eph. 2:12). Now we have all been adopted into the family of God and we all have the privileges of sonship. Notice even the Judaizers are included in this description, even as defective as their understanding was.

The implications of sonship are obvious. If I am a son of God and you are a son of God, then we are brothers and sisters in Christ. We extend to one another the love and care that normally is given only to blood relatives. I can't treat you as one unclean. I can't treat you with condescension. I can't even treat you with indifference! We are members of the same family, and so owe to one another filial affection and care.

Union with Christ

Not only are we sons of God, but we have all been united to Christ. He uses the word 'all' again.

> For all of you who were baptized into Christ have clothed yourselves with Christ. (Gal. 3:27)

All who have been baptized have been baptized both 'into' Christ and have 'clothed' themselves with Christ. His meaning is that their faith in Christ, culminating with their baptisms, united them to Christ. They were baptized (literally) 'into' (*eis*) Christ, and have (literally) 'put on' Christ. We can discern two dimensions of this union. The internal dimension is their union with Christ represented and sealed through baptism. The external dimension is their being 'clothed' with Christ, which speaks of 'habitual association and identification with Christ.'[87] 'If Paul is thinking of the theatre, where this word was employed,' says Boice, 'he means that one is identified with Christ on the world stage.'[88]

Baptism has both these internal and external dimensions. It represents and effects internal grace. It represents and confirms external commitment. His point: both this baptism into and putting on of Christ occurred apart from circumcision and the ceremonial law. We have become sons of God through faith in Christ. We have been baptized into Christ and have clothed ourselves with Christ. All this has happened apart from the law. How then could law-based divisions be introduced into the Christian church? Indeed, how could *any* divisions be introduced into the Christian church? If there is in Christ such fundamental unity, such shared experience in Him, how could we divide up over Mosaic or worldly criteria? This, then, is his next point:

> There is neither Jew nor Greek, there is neither slave nor free man, there is neither male nor female; for you are all one in Christ Jesus. (Gal. 3:28)

Paul now broadens the principle of unity in Christ beyond the circumcised and uncircumcised to include all categories by which we include and exclude. He introduces a sample of racial, social, and gender distinctions in addition to those of circumcision and uncircumcision. 'Jew' and 'Greek' despised each other. The 'freeman' looked condescendingly toward the 'slave.' Women were universally considered inferior, even chattel, in the ancient world. Jewish men, for example, gave thanks each morning that God had not made them Gentiles, slaves or women. Every society in every era of human society has had divisions of this sort. We divide on the basis of race. All over the world one will find bigotry on the basis of *race* or *ethnicity*. The English mock the Irish, the Swedes, the Norwegians, the Germans, the Poles, and so on. We divide on the basis of *rank*. As Stott points out, 'Nearly every society in the history of the world has developed its class or caste system. Circumstances of birth, wealth, privilege and education have divided men and women from one another.'[89] We divide on the basis of *gender*. All over the world women are oppressed, denied fundamental human (and God-given) rights, and mistreated. These divisions separating Jew and Greek, slave and free, male and female are meaningless in Christ. One does not have a superior status before God on the basis of these sorts of distinctions. Because I am an American or an Asian or an African I am not uniquely favored by God. I am not spiritually superior. God doesn't look upon me more kindly than He does upon others. Consequently, when it comes to spiritual status, culture is irrelevant. Race and ethnicity and gender are irrelevant. We stand on level ground at the foot of the cross. Jews do not need to become Greeks, or vice versa. The slave is not inferior to the freemen nor is the freeman to the slave. Men are not superior to women or women to men. We are all equally baptized, united to Christ, justified, and adopted. We cannot assign an inferior status, or perpetuate social distinctions of inclusion or exclusion in the church. 'In Christ snobbery is prohibited and class distinctions are rendered void,' says Stott.[90] We are to treat each other as brothers in Christ.

Let me ask us all to examine our own attitudes towards those of differing races and ethnic groups, differing rank, or the opposite sex. Do we see the black Christian as a brother in Christ? Do we see the Latin woman as a sister in Christ? Do we love them with the same love as we love those of our own group, whatever our group might be? This is a sensitive issue to raise in the South (USA) because of the legacy of slavery and segregation. There have been times when fellow Christians were made to feel as though they were second-class citizens, even within the context of the church. There were times when those of another race were not welcome through the doors of the church. Bigoted racial attitudes which would perpetuate the second class status of other races still lurk in the dark places of the heart. This is wrong.

There are also the rich who won't extend Christian fellowship with the poor, viewing all such as 'white trash.' Countering this is the 'reverse snobbery' of the poorer element directed against the perceived worldliness of those with means. Sometimes those who have are tried and condemned by the 'have nots,' for allegedly being worldly, materialistic, and so on, without a bit of evidence.

Some try to divide up the church on the basis of gender as well. How do they do so? By highlighting 'women's issues' as though they were somehow different from 'Christian issues.' Of course there are some concerns that are distinctive to women. But there is not a fundamentally different perspective of 'women' that is distinctive from that of 'men' and Christians generally. We live in a day of revived 'class' warfare. Young are pitted against old, women against men, rich against poor, black against white. There are even regional tensions such as north against south, and east against west. Lots of folks in the south were brought up not knowing that 'damn' and 'Yankee' were two different words. Sometimes the church mimics the tactics of the world and permits the same divisions to be perpetuated in the church. The Apostle Paul makes it clear here, it must not be so. We are all one in Christ. The superficial, worldly distinctions of race, rank, and gender have no place in the church.

We note as well that this also means that Christ does not obliterate cultural or social distinctions. This is a subtle and difficult point to harmonize with what we've just said. Nevertheless, the Jew remains a Jew and the Greek a Greek. The slave remains a slave and the freeman free. The male remains a male and the female a female. Women do not become men and men do not become women. Gender distinctions remain. This verse has sometimes been interpreted to mean that we are required to leave all such distinctions at the door of the church, and adopt some kind of neutered ethnic and gender identity. Just the opposite is meant. The black man remains a black man when he becomes a Christian, and the white man a white man. Neither is required to abandon his culture in favor of the other. Each is to sanctify and cleanse his culture through the influence of the gospel. It is permissible, and at some points (such as language) desirable, for a Dutch church to be a Dutch church, a Brazilian church to be Brazilian. There is not a single superior culture, or even a decultured ideal, to which we all must conform. We remain what we are. The point is that in so remaining, we are equal in Christ.

In a similar manner, one should not attempt to overturn all gender distinctions, and on the basis of this text deny creation-based, gender-based roles. Some have tried to argue for an androgynous ideal on the basis of Galatians 3:28, advocating egalitarian marriage and opening church offices to women. But this is to read into the Apostle Paul's words a meaning that is contrary to his own interpretations of the implications of our unity in Christ. He repeatedly maintains male headship in the Christian home (Eph. 5:22f., Col. 3:18) and in the church (1 Cor. 11:3–16; 14:34–7; 1 Tim. 2:9–15). Men remain men and women remain women, though in Christ we are equally justified, adopted, and united to Christ. The Apostle's words no more mean that women ought to preach than that men should have babies.

Sons of Abraham

Perhaps most surprising of all, we become sons of Abraham (and heirs of the covenant) not by following the law, but by following Abraham's faith. The Apostle Paul has already said,

> Therefore, be sure that it is those who are of faith who are sons of Abraham. (Gal. 3:7)

Now he adds,

> And if you belong to Christ, then you are Abraham's offspring, heirs according to promise. (Gal. 3:29)

Trace his logic. How does one come to 'belong to Christ?' By faith. If we 'belong to Christ,' then we are 'Abraham's offspring,' or Abraham's 'seed.' Then we are the 'heirs' of the promise made to Abraham. By faith we become heirs of the promises of the covenant made to Abraham. The same faith which unites us to Christ, also unites us to the Abrahamic promise and the Abrahamic community formed by that power. The 'promise' (singular) must be understood as the promise of salvation, which, as we have seen (3:7), was the primary promise made to Abraham and that to which all God's dealings with him ultimately pointed (Gen. 15:6; Heb. 11:8 ff.). Those who are the spiritual descendants of Abraham are just as much his 'seed' as were his physical descendants. In fact, more so. Physical descent alone did not make one a descendant of Abraham. One only is a true son of Abraham if one belongs to Christ through faith, as did Abraham. Abraham believed the promise of a Messiah to come, and was justified by faith (Gen. 15:6). We believe in the Messiah who has come, and we are justified by faith. This makes us his true children.

Let us use a secular analogy to illustrate. Imagine, on the one hand, a direct descendent of James Madison, architect and signer of the U. S. Constitution, who is a member of the Communist party, and, on the other hand, a recent immigrant from Poland who fully embraces the U. S. Constitution. Which of the two is the truer American, the one who shares belief in Madison's system or the one who, though a direct descendant, wishes to overthrow it? Of course it would be the former, not the latter.

So also by faith we receive the Spirit (3:2–5), are justified (3:7 ff.), adopted (3:26), and united to Christ (3:27–8), thereby becoming true sons and heirs of Abraham. All this we share by faith. And if we share all this, what can be left of our pitiful worldly distinctions? What unity ought to characterize the church! What care ought we to show to one another! Our wealth of common identity in Christ, our justification, adoption, union with Christ, and possession of the Spirit ought to overcome every remaining vestige of racial bigotry, class envy, snobbery and bias.

As Stott points out, those who are in Christ 'find their place in eternity (related first and foremost to God as His sons and daughters), in society (related to each other as brothers and sisters in the same family) and in history (related also to the succession of God's people down the ages).'[91] This identity overwhelms whatever temporal identity we may have had when we came to Christ. Sons of God, sons of Abraham, heirs of the covenant, members of the Covenant community, disciples of Christ: these are our primary identity.

14

The Fullness of the Time

Galatians 4:1–7

The text before us is one that often has been read and preached during the Christmas season. The Apostle Paul says, 'When the fullness of the time came, God sent forth His Son.' This has everything to do with Christmas, discussing as it does the timing and purpose of the incarnation. At the time which He planned and purposed, at just the right time, God sent His preexisting and eternal Son to be 'born of a woman,' in a manger in Bethlehem, that through Him He might 'redeem' and adopt a people to be His own.

This then is a very instructive text for us at Christmas time, when there are so many competing voices claiming to know the 'true meaning' of Christmas. What does the Bible say about the matter? What is the true meaning of the incarnation? We are given the answers here. When did the incarnation occur? In the 'fullness of the time.' What happened? 'God sent forth His Son.' Why? So that 'He might redeem,' and that 'we might receive the adoption as sons.' This cosmic sized event, conceived in the eternal counsels of God, executed by the three persons of the Trinity with omniscient timing, has as its end both our status of sonship and the experience of God's fatherly love and care (v. 6).

The Divine Plan

> Now I say, as long as the heir is a child, he does not differ at all from a slave although he is owner of everything, but he is under guardians and managers until the date set by the father. (Gal. 4:1–2)

Let us remind ourselves of the flow of Paul's argument in Galatians. In chapter 3 he has just explained two thousand years of biblical history, highlighting its three central personalities: Abraham, Moses, and Christ. The promise of salvation was given to Abraham; the law which was given through Moses did not nullify the promise, but rather made it more urgent by pointing out our sins; and Christ fulfilled the promise, so that, as Stott points out, 'everyone whom the law drives to Christ inherits the promise which God made to Abraham.'[92] Now he will explain how the law had a limited, specific, historic role to play according to the plan of God until Christ came in the 'fullness of the time,' and how this is true for Gentile religion as well.

First, verses 1–2 explain how it was *the 'fullness of the time' in relation to Israel.* Time was 'up,' or 'full,' in that the role which the law had played for the people of God was completed when God sent His Son. Paul explains this by way of a human analogy. The situation he envisioned is either that of a man who has died leaving his estate to his young son, or perhaps more generally that of a young man's passage from childhood to adulthood. During the time of his minority, a 'child' (*nepios*, infant) does not have the capacity to manage the estate, and remains under the orders of 'guardians' and 'managers' until his preparation is completed. In this respect he is like a 'slave,' receiving the orders rather than giving them, though everyone knows that he is 'owner of everything,' and will one day be in charge.

Israel then is being likened to this 'child,' under the law which functions like the child's 'guardians' or 'managers.' Paired together like this, these two terms refer in the first case to those responsible for the training of the boy, and in the second case to those responsible for running the estate. This was to continue for a specified time, 'until the date set by the father,' or literally, 'the term previously appointed' (*prothesmias*). In other words, the law was given to Israel for a specific, limited time only, until 'the date set by the father,' until 'the fullness of the time.'

Second, verse 3 explains that it was also *the 'fullness of time' in relation to the Gentiles.*

> So also we, while we were children, were held in bondage under the elemental things of the world. (Gal. 4:3)

'So also we' refers to the Galatian Gentile Christians as well as Jews. There is a similarity between the status of Jews as immature heirs under the law and Gentile Christians with their pagan religions. Of course their experience was not parallel in every respect. The Jews had the 'oracles of God' (Rom. 3:2; cf. Rom. 9:4–5). The Gentiles were without hope and without God in their religious darkness (Eph. 2:12; Isa. 9:2). But there is a true sense in which both 'were held in bondage' by their religions. Both were enslaved by what the master Paul calls 'the elemental things of the world.' The term 'elemental things' (*stoicheion*) is difficult. It is used of basic units, such as the ABC's or the basic elements out of which the world is composed. Commentators take it variously to refer to 'basic principles of the world' (NIV), meaning in this context basic religious principles, elementary (but incomplete) teachings; or to 'the elemental spirits of the universe' (RSV), meaning demonic forces; or the literal and uninterpreted 'elemental things of the world' (NASV). Here it probably refers to the elementary principles of religion, which Jews learned through the law (and corrupted!), and the Gentiles learned through nature. But both Jews and Gentiles were enslaved by these principles and were unable to transcend them. Paul identifies the 'elemental things' with the observance of days and months and seasons and years in verses 9–10, and with submitting to 'decrees' such as 'do not handle, do not taste, do not touch' in Colossians 2:20 (cf. 2:8).

He seems to have in mind religious systems which encourage salvation through religious works, particularly participation in religious ceremony, 'self-made religion and self-abasement and severe treatment of the body' (Col. 2:23). In other words, corrupt Judaism (as opposed to the true content of the Old Testament, explained in Galatians 3) and paganism both enslaved their practitioners in a system of salvation through ritual and asceticism. Judaism and paganism were alike in this respect. They were both systems of religion in which one could put one's trust and, consequently, by which one could become enslaved. Both could be seen as providing salvation through works. Both could be seen as providing reconciliation with God through visible ritual and ceremony. These are the common-place things of religions throughout the world. And both, by the time of the incarnation of Christ, could be seen as total failures. The law had not prevented the pre-exilic polytheism and decadence that had led to the destruction of Israel and then Judah. Following the restoration, the law had not prevented the hypocrisy and legalism that had been characteristic of even the best in Israel. It had failed. Its time was up. The point of the failure was to point to the need of Christ (3:21ff.). So also with the Gentiles, their religions had run their course, and there was widespread dissatisfaction. Stott notes that 'the old mythological gods of Greece and Rome were losing their hold on the common people, so that the hearts and minds of men everywhere were hungry for a religion that was real and satisfying.'[93] Morris cites Hamann, who notes 'the bankruptcy of paganism as seen in the multiplication of cults and the degeneracy of the old religions of Greece and Rome.'[94] Boice speaks of a world that had 'sunk in a moral abyss so low that even the pagans cried out against it and that spiritual hunger was everywhere evident.'[95]

What are we saying then?

First, it was the 'fullness of time' in the *religious realm*. The universal sense of failure and dissatisfaction pointed to the need of a Savior. People in Judah sensed that the time had come for the fulfillment of the promises made long before through the prophets. Palestine was rife with Messianic expectation, as is evident in the gospels. One false Christ after another appeared on the scene (Acts 5:35–6; Matt. 24:23–4). When John the Baptist began his public ministry, 'the people were in a state of expectation and all were wondering in their hearts about John, as to whether he might be the Christ' (Luke 3:15). This was typical. The people were in a heightened state of expectation.

Second, in the *cultural realm*, in 330 BC Alexander the Great crushed the Persian Empire, completing his conquest of the known civilized world. He carried with him a vision of a Hellenized world, a world enlightened with the glories of Greek culture. The result was that, by the time of Christ, Greek culture had given to the world a measure of social cohesion, as well as a common language, Greek being the *lingua franca* of its day. 'For while each province still had its own tongue or dialect, everywhere the people were bilingual and all knew Greek,' noted James Stewart in his book *The Life and Teaching of Jesus Christ*.[96] Everywhere the early Christian missionaries went they could preach in Greek and be understood.

Third in the *political realm*, the Roman army united an empire of 100 million souls under the umbrella of the *Pax Romana*, the peace of Rome, and tied it together through a network of roads (built for the rapid movement of the armies that maintained the peace) not equaled in Europe until the nineteenth century. James Stewart stated it this way:

> If Christ had come a century earlier, his gospel would have been blocked at every turn, blocked on the land by closed national frontiers, blocked on the ocean by the pirates who made the high seas impossible. Or of he had come a few centuries later, he would have found civilization too preoccupied with its terrible struggle against the barbarian hordes from the North to have any ear for the gospel. But Christ came to a generation when the Roman peace held the world, held it no doubt with an iron hand, but held it sure and far-flung and unbroken; and men could hear the Bethlehem angels sing.[97]

In addition, the Jewish *diaspora,* following the Maccabean wars, had resulted in the establishment of synagogues throughout the Mediterranean world, which became the initial preaching points of the early Christian missionaries, and the source of the initial converts, especially Gentile converts. A hundred or so years before, and the *diaspora* would not have taken place. A hundred years later, the Jews would have lost their protected status as an approved religion and contacts with the synagogues would have been much more difficult. In sum it was, says Boice, 'a perfect time for the coming of Christ and for the early expansion of the Christian gospel.'[97] Greek language and culture, Roman peace and roads, Jewish synagogues, and a pervasive religious dissatisfaction signaled that the time was ripe for Christ to come. James Stewart sums up the situation with these elegant words:

> Search the pages of history up and down, and in all the tales of the centuries you will not find any generation in which Christ could better have come than just the generation in which he did come. 'There is a tide,' says Shakespeare, 'in the affairs of men.' We can go beyond that and say that there is a tide in the affairs of God; and it is when that tide reaches the flood, when all the preparatory work is done and world conditions are clamoring for it and human souls are open, it is then, at the flood-tide hour of history, that God launches his new adventure. So it was when Luther sent his 'Ein feste Burg' ringing and singing along the roads of Europe. So it was when Scotland heard the rugged voice of John Knox. So it was supremely when upon the whole Greco Roman world there burst suddenly out of Galilee, with the shouts of saints and the trumpetings of angels, the sound of a new name, the name of Jesus. It was the fullness of the time, said Paul—it was the hour foreordained in the divine wisdom—when God sent forth his Son. Jesus came at the very point in history at which all the conditions were ripe for his coming.[98]

The Divine Initiative

> But when the fullness of the time, God sent forth His Son, born of a woman, born under the Law. (Gal. 4:4)

So what did God do in the fullness of time? He 'sent forth His Son,' that's what. When did He do so? 'The fullness of the time' means not only that it was exactly the right time, but that He came according to plan. Whose plan? God's plan. The coming of Christ was not a chance matter. Nor was it something entered into suddenly or on impulse. Redemption had been planned from eternity. Looking down the halls of history, God selected just the right time for the incarnation of the Son of God. It was not too late. It was not too soon. It was, 'when world conditions were exactly ripe for it that God's supreme revelation in history came,' says James Stewart, again.[99]

'But...God,' says Paul (see Eph. 2:1ff.). Here is the turning point in human history. 'We should not miss the emphasis on the divine act,' urges Morris. 'Paul is not saying that Jesus decided to start a new religious movement. He is saying that God acted in Christ.'[100] The expression, 'the fullness of time' is found only here in the New Testament (though see Eph. 1:10). Christ was sent at just the right moment. He came when the time was ripe. The Apostle means, says Morris, 'that God has been working his purpose out through history, and it was only when the right time came that he *sent his Son.* Paul is not talking about a more or less casual happening: *God,* no less, *sent his Son,* no less.'[101] Behind the word 'sent' lies the fact of Christ's preexistence in eternity with the Father (Phil. 2:5ff.; John 1:1ff.). Yet, this is not an angelic visitation. This Son of God was 'born of a woman,' indicating the genuineness of his humanity, 'born under the law,' indicating that he was born at a certain stage in redemptive history. He had a Jewish mother and was born into the Jewish nation which had been promised a Jewish savior. Thus He was perfectly qualified to be the Savior, being both truly divine and truly human, truly Jewish and truly righteous as well. At the perfect time God sent a perfect Savior. Who sent? God sent! What did God send? God sent His Son! For whom? For us! Wonder of wonders.

Now we are getting at the true meaning of Christmas. I have written in the past, somewhat tongue-in-cheek, about whether Christmas is about giving or getting. It is not about giving but getting! Christmas is about what God gives to us. We have good intentions when we teach our children otherwise. We do not want them to be obsessed with what others are going to be giving them. We want them to be imitators of God and to give as He gave. But the larger reality not to be obscured is that God gives His Son and demands nothing in return, but that we receive His gift.

The Divine Purpose

> In order that He might redeem those who were under the Law, that we might receive the adoption as sons. (Gal. 4:5)

The Apostle Paul says, 'in order that.' Here then is the purpose behind Christmas. Here is the reason for the incarnation of Jesus Christ. First, it was '*in order that He might redeem...*' Having spoken of slavery to sin (see 3:22–3; 4:3), the Apostle speaks of salvation as a redemption. To 'redeem' means to buy out of slavery, to purchase one's freedom. The Son was sent so that He might redeem us from our slavery to sin. A price had to be paid, and it was at the cross, resulting in freedom. Those 'under the law' literally says 'under law.' The absence of the article (also in v. 4) indicates a broader application, indicating, says Morris, 'all those who come under condemnation from whatever law they serve; they will be without any hope of saving themselves.'[102] All such must be 'redeemed.' The law cannot save any of them. Or another way of looking at it is, if even those under the Mosaic law must be redeemed, how much more so everyone else! Because this is so, it is not necessary for Gentiles to go under the law. If even Jews who are under the law must be redeemed, then there is nothing to be gained by Gentiles going under the law.

Then he adds a second reason, '*that we might receive the adoption as sons.*' He goes on to say,

> And because you are sons, God has sent forth the Spirit of His Son into our hearts, crying, 'Abba Father!' (Gal. 4:6)

Notice the Trinitarian activity. God sends the Spirit, which is the Spirit of His Son. The Spirit is sent 'into our hearts,' that is, into our innermost beings, and is not, as Morris puts it, 'a minor disturbance on the surface of life.'[103] The evidence of the presence of the Spirit in our lives is 'not by some spectacular gift or sign,' notes Stott, 'but by the quiet inward witness of the Spirit as we pray.'[104] Thus there is added to the *status* of sons the *experience* of sonship as well. It comes not because the believer works after it, but because he is a son.

> Therefore you are no longer a slave, but a son; and if a son, then an heir through God. (Gal. 4:7).

The Apostle Paul now uses the 'you,' singular, as though he is speaking to each one of his readers individually. You were slaves, but now you are not. You are not working to become sons, but are sons, and heirs.

The purpose of the incarnation of Christ, and the purpose of Christmas, is that we might be redeemed, adopted as children into the family of God, and finally indwelt by the Holy Spirit, through whom we receive the experiential confirmation of our sonship. God awaited the perfect moment to provide the perfect Savior that we might be made Sons of God, and might know it in our hearts, crying out with confidence to God our Father, and being certain of his fatherly oversight and care. Not only is this the key to the incarnation, it is the key to the whole Christian life as well. We understand everything by way of sonship. Why do we have assurance of our salvation? Because God's Spirit bears witness with our spirit that we are the sons of God (Rom. 8:16). Why do we have confidence in prayer? Because God is a good father who won't give his children stones when they ask for bread (Matt. 7:9 ff.). How are we to understand adversity? As the discipline of our loving father (Heb. 12:5 ff.). What is to be our motivation in obedience? To please our Father in heaven and bring him glory (Matt. 5:16). And why should we live holy lives? So that we might bear the family image, being imitators of God as beloved children (Eph. 5:1). The celebration of Christmas is the celebration of the whole work of redemption, from the eternal decree and plan of God, to the appointed time of the incarnation, to the cross, to the resurrection, to Pentecost, to the creation of the church, to the salvation of sinners like us. This is what happened in the 'the fullness of time.' This is the true meaning of Christmas, and in this we rejoice in our celebration in December of each year.

15

The Folly of Turning Back

Galatians 4:8–11

There is a widespread dissatisfaction with 'religion' today that parallels the first century setting into which Christ came. Religion is widely perceived to have failed to provide credible answers to the big questions of life, death, eternity, and God. Opinions are given here and there on spiritual matters, but religion is treated subjectively, as though certainty were impossible. Amongst mainline liberals there is an almost official kind of agnosticism on major theological and moral questions. People rightly ask, 'What good is religion if it can't provide us with answers?' In addition, there is a sense that religion has failed to change lives. History has had its Inquisitions and its Wars of Religion. Even today Protestant fights Roman Catholics in some parts of the world, Christian fights Muslim in Africa, Jew fights Muslim in the Middle East, Hindu and Muslim battle in India. Religious hypocrisy has bred cynicism on a large scale, especially as regards organized religion. Some in the West have fled to exotic eastern and new age cults. Many more have adopted 'stay-homeism' as their creed. Voting with their feet, our contemporaries are staying home in droves.

We saw last time that Christ came 'in the fullness of the time' (4:4). At just the right time, at the time when Messianic expectations were at a fevered pitch among the Jews, and a sense of dissatisfaction at the failure of religion was rife among the Gentiles, 'God…sent forth His Son…in order that He might redeem….' (4:5–6). In Christ the bondage of the old religions was broken. Before Christ came, he said,

> we were children, were held in bondage under the elemental things of the world. (Gal. 4:3)

The 'elemental things,' the old religious principles, were a form of 'bondage.' But in Christ we were redeemed, adopted, and given the Spirit of adoption. 'Therefore,' he said, 'you are no longer a slave, but a son; and if a son, then an heir through God' (4:7).

Yet for one reason or another, a number of those who seem to come to Christ ultimately fall back into the old failed religions. They have been 'enlightened,' they have 'tasted of the heavenly gift,' and have been made 'partakers of the Holy Spirit' (Heb. 6:4–5). Yet they fall away. Why does it happen? Just as importantly, how are we to prevent it from happening? The Apostle Paul is concerned enough to say in verse 11,

> I fear for you, that perhaps I have labored over you in vain. (Gal. 4:11)

He sees them being seduced by the old religions and he is concerned. And so to arm them against future defections, he reminds them of errors out of which they have been saved, and contrasts them with the blessings that they enjoy in Christ.

The Failure of Religion

He begins by reminding them of the failure of religion. We mean by religion a man-made system of ritual and practice whereby one is made right with God. Such man-made systems, found the world over, are a total failure. They promise much, but deliver nothing.

First, he speaks of *the failure of Gentile religion.*

> However at that time, when you did not know God, you were slaves to those which by nature are no gods. (Gal. 4:8)

The Apostle Paul reminds them of their pre-Christian religious condition. He provides us with insight into the biblical view of non-Christian religions. Back then, he says, 'you did not know God.' Elsewhere he tells the Gentiles, you were 'without God in the world' (Eph. 2:12). You were 'excluded from the life of God' (Eph. 4:18). This is not the same as saying that they were not religious. They seemed to have been religious enough. He said to the Athenians, 'I observe that you are very religious in all respects' (Acts 17:22). But they didn't know or serve the true God in their religions. And it doesn't seem to matter which religion they belonged to. Whichever it was, they did not know God. They were instead 'slaves to those which by nature are no gods.' The phrase, 'no gods,' may recall Jeremiah 5:7, and sums up the biblical view. The gods of the nations are not gods at all, but idols or demons. This is consistently the biblical view. Listen to the Apostle Paul:

> Therefore concerning the eating of things sacrificed to idols, we know that there is no such thing as an idol in the world, and that there is no God but one. (1 Cor. 8:4)

Again:

> No, but I say that the things which the Gentiles sacrifice, they sacrifice to demons, and not to God; and I do not want you to become sharers in demons. (1 Cor. 10:20)

There are no idols, there are no gods. But neither does that mean that religion may be regarded as a 'useful fiction,' as some intellectuals have said. 'Of course it's all myth,' they would say. 'But it is an important myth. Belief in a god results in better behavior as well as providing comfort and hope,' they may maintain, with no small degree of condescension. It is the opiate of the people as Marx said. But the Bible doesn't share this benign view of religion. Behind the religions of the world are demons, misleading the multitudes. You didn't know God, Paul tells them, and you were a slave to demons. That is the Apostle's assessment of Gentile religion.

Second, he speaks of *the failure of the Judaizer's religion.*

> But now that you have come to know God, or rather to be known by God, how is it that you turn back again to the weak and worthless elemental things, to which you desire to be enslaved all over again? (Gal. 4:9)

'But now' contrasts sharply with what preceded. You were slaves of demons, 'but now that you have come to know God,' the situation is entirely different. Look at what you now have! Now you know the true God, or more importantly have come, 'to be known by God.' He quickly reminds them that the initiative in knowing God rests with God. Boice says Paul wishes 'not to leave the impression that it is possible for any man to come to know God by his own efforts.'[105] You know God at God's initiative and apart from religious or moral works. He uses the language of personal intimacy and communion. You know God and are known by Him. You enjoy personal communion with Him.

All this is leading to his big question. Since they have come from slavery to demons to a true knowledge of the true God, how can they 'turn back again to the weak and worthless elemental things' (*stoichia*), to be 'enslaved all over again'? This is the same word as was used in verse 3, meaning basic religious principles. For them, as Gentiles, to embrace the teachings of the Judaizers did not mark advance in the Christian faith, as they probably supposed, but rather reversion to the bondage of paganism. It is not that Judaism and paganism are equally false. They are not. But they share with all the religions of the world excepting Christianity the principle of salvation through works and law. Therefore to revert either to a Judaized Christianity, with its necessary ritual and ceremony, or to pagan idolatry, is one and the same. Abandon justification by faith alone and one returns to the 'elemental' principles. He calls this a reversion to 'weak and worthless' principles. Both the law and paganism are weak and ultimately worthless. Speaking of the law Barclay says, 'It can define sin; it can show a man when he is sinning; it can convict him of sin; but it can neither find for him forgiveness for past sin nor strength to conquer future sin. The law's basic and inherent weakness always was, and is, that it can diagnose the disease but it cannot produce a cure.'[106] Paganism could do even less than biblical law, having no clear definition of sin. How could you 'desire to be enslaved all over again?' he asks them. Your pre-Christian religion was slavery. Your Judaized Christianity is slavery as well. Not only is it 'a different gospel; which is really not another,' and so heresy, but it is also experientially a disaster (1:6–7). It is a return to slavery.

How is this so? Think of the joyless efforts of those who go from house to house knocking on doors, hoping that they are doing enough to get into heaven, but fearing they aren't. They are in bondage. So it is the world over. Witch-doctors and medicine men, priests and holy men, prey upon the ignorance and fears of the people, demanding that they perform the requisite rites and rituals if they are to have any hope of salvation. It is bondage. It provides no hope. They can never be sure if they've done enough. But in Christ we know God and are known by God. This came about not because we did all the right religious works, but by the free grace of God through faith. We were redeemed from this slavery. We were adopted and made sons. We were given the spirit of adoption and now cry out to God as our Father.

The Appeal of Religion

This raises a question. Why would anyone be tempted to go back to that? Is the problem that they don't recognize it as slavery, or does slavery have its own attractions? My guess is both\and. Slavery has attractions that obscure its nature as slavery. Remember the children of Israel longed to return to the 'leaks and melons' of Egypt. Many of the Exodus generation preferred slavery. Slavery provides womb to the tomb security. Slavery is safe. Freedom is difficult. We see the same thing happening today in the former Iron Curtain nations. Despite the legacy of brutal oppression under communism many wish to return to its security. At least we had jobs then, some lament. Religious freedom, the freedom of grace can also be difficult. Slavery to rules and rituals provides answers and directions, rules for how to live, rituals for how to do religion. One merely works the system. One does what one is told. Decisions don't need to be made. Self-examination and deep heart change can be avoided. This is very appealing for many people. They like a religion in which they can remain their same old selfish selves, and yet operate the machinery of religion to their advantage. They like to observe the ritual and obey the rules without the discussion turning to heart and motive. Religion may remain *external* and *superficial* if it consists wholly of rules and ritual. Let's outline what we mean.

First, religion fulfills the *desire for rules*, especially in the area of decision making. Many people want a rule for every ethical and interpersonal situation. Then they don't have to think. Ironically, one doesn't have to deal with God either. One just keeps the rules. Pride and selfishness remain untouched. Religion remains external. But as such it is manageable. They want rules such as, 'do not handle, do not taste, do not touch,' called by Paul these same 'elemental principles' in Colossians 2:20. If faced with having to marry persons 'A,' 'B,' or 'C,' they can't bear the thought that in Christ they are free to marry 'in the Lord' whomever they wish. They want rules that will eliminate options. Freedom can be frightening. They fear making a mistake. This is the appeal of the cults. They provide a word for every decision. Amongst the young couples one of the big issues is where and how to educate one's children. Some want an absolute rule: only in a Christian school, or only in a home school, or even only in the public school. But there is no absolute rule. In Christ we are free to make the best choice that we are able to make in light of a myriad of factors as we are led by the Holy Spirit. Amongst liberal Christian churches, the same desire has led to moralism and moralizing, especially in adopting politically correct opinions and attitudes.

The Christian faith is wonderfully balanced. On the left, there are those who say there are no rules at all (excepting tolerance, of course). Do whatever you want, even if that means promiscuity, adultery, abortion, and so on. Clearly that is wrong. There are rules. The Ten Commandments are not Ten Suggestions. But the other extreme is to think that there is a rule for everything. This first error is that of the *libertines*. The second is that of the *legalists*. In Christ there is always a balance between the word and Spirit. If we had only the word, if we had a word for everything, we wouldn't need the Spirit. On the other hand, if Christ had only given us the Spirit, we would have no guidelines, or means of checking our subjective understanding of what the Spirit was leading us to do. It takes both together. We have been called to freedom (5:1, 13). Morris comments, 'The life of faith is a wonderful life, but it involves living as free people with all the demands that makes (as well as all the privileges it brings).'[107]

Second, religion fulfills the *desire for rituals*. If Colossians 2:20 addresses the 'elemental rules,' Galatians 4:10 addresses the '*elemental rituals*.'

> You observe days and months and seasons and years. (Gal. 4:10)

Paul is referring to Jewish holy 'days,' 'months' are new moon observances (Num. 28:11–15), 'seasons' refer to seasonal feasts such as Tabernacles and Passover which last more than a day, and 'years,' to events such as the Sabbath year (Lev. 25:4–5) and the year of Jubilee (Lev. 25:8 ff.). 'In this enumeration, Paul apparently intends to say that the Galatians had taken over the entire Jewish system of religious observances,' says Fung.[108] Unlike the Old Testament, the New Testament does not mandate the observance of any holy days excepting the weekly Lord's Day. Not even one—not Christmas, not Easter. To require the observance of holy days represents another form of bondage. The appeal of a calendar of ceremonies, and more broadly a ritual of approach to God, is also the appeal of *external observance* without *internal conformity*. If I do such and such things, I make myself right with God, whatever the condition of my heart. People like to feel like they are doing religious things. They like to take on the vows of lent or advent, and feel like they are doing something for God and earn His appreciation. They especially are drawn to such a system if it remains external and does not deal with matters of heart and motive. If they can do so and their pride, selfishness, covetousness, idolatry, and lust remain untouched, all the better. Ceremonies and rituals please us, and so we assume that they please God as well. 'In other words, your religion has degenerated into an external formalism,' says Stott.[109] But as Paul told the Colossians,

> These are matters which have, to be sure, the appearance of wisdom in self-made religion and self-abasement and severe treatment of the body, but are of no value against fleshly indulgence. (Col. 2:23)

Do this, do that, and God will be pleased, the world thinks. This in combination with an exhaustive list of dos and don'ts regulating behavior in every circumstance of life, all the while allowing the idols and lusts of the heart to remain unchallenged, is of the essence of legalism and of all the religions of the world, including Judaized Christianity. They have 'the appearance of wisdom.' They appeal to our pride and self-righteousness. We like to think that we can save ourselves. We like to boast in our holiness and religiosity. But it is of 'no value,' Paul says. They cannot change the heart. They cannot transform the sinner. We can keep the rules and do the rituals, but only the gospel can change us from within.

Religion's Destructive End

> I fear for you, that perhaps I have labored over you in vain. (Gal. 4:11)

Trade grace for works and one has lost any hope for salvation. The Apostle Paul is saying this of those of whom it was true that they would have plucked out their eyes for Paul, so great was their devotion to Him and His gospel (v. 15). But now they were wavering. They were being pressured by the Judaizers. Works, no doubt, was appealing to their flesh, their pride. But Paul says, if you go back to law and works, then I will have 'labored over you in vain.' It will have all been for nothing because you will be lost!

These are the stakes, and this is why we must resist the inroads of 'works' religion. We cannot reduce Christianity to rules and ceremonies rightly done. These are not the means by which we are made right with God. We are only made right through faith in Jesus Christ. The appeal of slavery is very strong. Many would like to deal with God superficially through a ritual. There is something twisted within us that would like a set of rules which we could mindlessly follow and thereby avoid the painful process of spiritual maturation. But such is slavery, and ultimately it costs us our soul. Do not turn to religion, turn to a person, Jesus Christ, and in Him find the answers to all the religious questions. Granted there is a cost—the hard process of sanctification. But in Christ find redemption. In Him find forgiveness. In Him find true knowledge of God. In Him find a filial relationship with God. In Him find the certainty of eternal life.

16

The Perplexed Apostle

Galatians 4:12–20

Up to this point in his letter to the Galatians, Paul has been presenting a theological argument against the teaching of the Judaizers. Roughly he has argued as follows:

1. Chapters 1–2:14. Paul defends his *apostleship* and his right to preach authoritatively;
2. Chapters 2:15–5:12. Paul defends his *gospel* of justification by faith on the basis of:
   - i) *experience (2:15–3:5)*
     - a. his (2:15–21)
     - b. theirs (3:1–5)
   - ii) *the teaching of the Old Testament (3:6–25)*
     - a. the example of Abraham (3:6–9)
     - b. Old Testament teaching re. the impossibility of works (3:10–14)
     - c. the permanence of the Abrahamic covenant (3:15–18)
     - d. the purpose of the law (3:19–25)
   - iii) *the implications of the gospel (3:26–4:11)*
     - a. unity in Christ (3:26–9)
     - b. sonship and freedom in Christ (4:1–11)

Now he will again appeal to the Galatians to remain faithful to the gospel, this time on the basis of his personal relationship and dealings with them. In verses 12–15 he reminds them of their prior devotion to him, and he to them. There was a time when they would have done most anything for him. Yet things had changed. They now regarded him as their enemy (v. 16). Why? How could this have happened? Because outsiders with false motives had come in and poisoned his work, perverting his gospel, and undermining his relationship with his converts. We have often observed it only takes one person to stir up trouble and upset a good work. At a local church which we have been helping get back on its feet we spent months in turmoil, essentially because of one man. 'A little leaven,' the Apostle Paul told the Corinthians, 'leavens the whole lump' (1 Cor. 5:6). The leavening agent among the Galatians was not just one man, but a whole group, known to history as Judaizers. Throughout verses 12–20 he deals with the Galatians in a way that demonstrates unmistakably his continuing love and devotion for them. As Stott says, 'we have been listening to Paul the apostle, Paul the theologian, Paul the defender of the faith; but now we are hearing Paul the man, Paul the pastor, Paul the passionate lover of souls.'[110] As a consequence we may learn much about the relationship of pastors and their people, as Paul models pastoral concern for his Galatian converts.

> I beg of you, brethren, become as I am, for I also have become as you are. (Gal. 4:12a)

Paul is pleading with his converts. 'I beg of you,' he says. This is the language of a pastor who loves his people. 'Become as I am,' is an exhortation to the Galatians to 'become Christians in the same sense as Paul is a Christian, one who is not bound by the Jewish law,' says Morris.[111] He adds, 'for I also have become as you are,' that is, I have thrown off the ceremonial requirements of the Old Testament as developed by Judaism, I have rejected the requirement of circumcision, the laws of cleansing, the dietary laws, the observance of holy days, and become like a Gentile, 'as you are.' Do not seek to become like Jews by adopting these practices, he is telling them. Reject the teaching that says that this is required, or even desirable, in addition to faith in Christ. 'Become as I am' is a bold, almost arrogant and yet typical Christian aspiration, as Paul calls the Galatians from the joyless world of legalism. There is a sense in which we should all be able to say this to the unbelievers around us. We should be able to say 'that we are so satisfied with Jesus Christ, with His freedom, joy and salvation, that we want other people to become like us,' says Stott.[112] We can see this in Apostle Paul as he stood before King Agrippa. The King said, 'In a short time you think to make me a Christian!'

> And Paul said, 'I would to God, that whether in a short or long time, not only you, but also all who hear me this day, might become such as I am, except for these chains.' (Acts 26:29)

Imagine Paul in chains saying that to a king! 'Become such as I am,' he says. What I have in Christ is better than all your kingly powers and privileges. We may not be rich. We may not be the most powerful people in the world. We may not be socially popular, or great intellectuals. But we do know Christ and are so grateful for what we have in Him that we wish that *all* could be as we are. We can say this to the great icons of our age: the athletes, the entertainers, the media personalities, the rich and famous. 'If only you knew what I know or had what I have!' We would not trade the knowledge of Christ for anything. This conviction fuels the evangelism of the church. Real Christians have an infectious enthusiasm. They have found the greatest thing in the world, and they want to share it with all.

But part of the process of others becoming 'as we are' is our becoming like them. He says, 'I also have become as you are.' He becomes all things to all men that by all means he may save some (1 Cor. 9:22). In this case, he has in mind particularly the necessity of dropping any hint of legal requirements for salvation. But more broadly, he dropped Jewish cultural practices which he might have retained as a cultural preference for the sake of evangelizing those who were different. This attitude of sacrifice for the sake of the lost bore great fruit for Paul, as we will now see.

The Galatians' Outlook

So he begins to try to persuade them to return to the real gospel. He does so in very personal terms. First, *he reminds them of their former willingness to follow him.*

> You have done me no wrong; but you know that it was because of a bodily illness that I preached the gospel to you the first time; (Gal. 4:12b–13)

'You have done me no wrong' has puzzled interpreters. He may mean that, 'You have wronged Christ, not me.' Or, 'You did not wrong me when I first preached to you, and even now you have not yet wronged me since you are still teetering between truth and error.' Apparently Paul had not intended to come to Galatia, but some 'bodily illness' about which we know nothing, made it necessary for him to change his plans and to convalesce in Galatia. There has been a great deal of speculation about his sickness, that it was malaria, or a disease of the eyes, but there is no way of knowing for sure. Regardless, despite his sickness, he preached the gospel to the Galatians, leading to their conversions and the founding of the Galatian congregations.

> And that which was a trial to you in my bodily condition you did not despise or loathe, but you received me as an angel of God, as Christ Jesus Himself. (Gal. 4:14)

Paul seems to imply that there was something repulsive in his appearance as a result of his affliction. Or it could be that he speaks of the tendency to see 'misfortune' as a sign of God's displeasure with a person, and as a result reject their message. He may very well be saying both things, thanking them that they did not 'despise' his message or 'loathe' his appearance. Instead they received him and his message as 'an angel of God,' or it could be rendered a 'messenger' of God, but the former is the more likely. Even more, they received him as 'Christ Jesus Himself.' Their reception of Paul could not possibly receive higher praise than this. They had received Paul and his gospel absolutely and unconditionally.

> Where then is that sense of blessing you had? For I bear you witness, that if possible, you would have plucked out your eyes and given them to me. (Gal. 4:15)

What, then, has become of 'that sense of blessing you had?' he asks. The word he uses, *makarismos*, may be rendered 'joy' (NIV), or 'happiness' (REB). The joy of grace has been lost as they have slid back into legalism. 'For I bear you witness' underscores the urgency and affection with which he writes. Remember this, he is telling them. Remember how things were. The fact is that 'you would have plucked out your eyes and given them to me,' he tells them. They were ready to do anything for him. Their devotion had been total, and apparently completely appropriate. This is very strong language—an 'angel of God,' 'Christ Jesus Himself,' and 'plucked out your eyes.' Yet, he doesn't rebuke them for their overwhelming commitment to and devotion for the Apostle. Why not? Certainly love for the pastor can become hero-worship, even idolatry. When the people of Lystra responded to Paul's ministry by attributing deity to him and attempting to worship him, he responded with a sharp rebuke (Acts 14:8 ff.). But that doesn't mean that there shouldn't be a powerful, yet appropriate bond between pastors and the people. Those who preach the gospel are in a true sense messengers of God. Because of the dynamic of the gospel, changing hearts, bringing the assurance of peace with God, making one a part of the family of God, the hearts of people and pastors are often wonderfully knit together. I often encounter in new members and potential new members a powerful tie between them and their former pastors, especially if that pastor led them to Christ. Everything in connection with that man and ministry is ideal to them, so much so that they cannot let go of the ways of doing things that were characteristic of the old church. This can even become a problem. No church will ever be the same for them. I was talking to a man at our noon service a few months back, and we began to talk of a PCA minister, and he said, 'He changed my life.' Nothing more needed to be said. He was completely devoted to the ministry of that church. He would have plucked out his eyes for that man. One can easily imagine that there are any number of potential problems with this kind of devotion to a pastor. But the Apostle Paul doesn't even hint at the negatives. He writes of it entirely approving of their reception of him and regard for him.

Second, he *points out the change in their attitude*. They had been devoted to him. But then something went wrong:

> Have I therefore become your enemy by telling you the truth? (Gal. 4:16)

This rhetorical question is really asking, what have I done to become your enemy? All I have been doing from the beginning is speaking the truth, a truth which led to the salvation of your soul by God's grace in Christ Jesus. The Apostle is forcing them to face what they are doing. They are punishing him for telling the truth. 'His frankness in telling the truth does not mean that the apostle has ceased to care for his converts and becomes their enemy,' says Morris.[113] 'Enemy' is put at the front of the sentence for emphasis. 'Your *enemy* did I become because of speaking the truth?'

Astonishingly, their once great devotion had gone sour. Those who received him initially as an angel, who would have plucked out their eyes for him, now regarded him as an enemy. Why? You can be absolutely sure that they had what they considered to be good reasons. Undoubtedly they could justify their conduct. They could explain their animosity. But the fact was, they didn't want to hear the truth. Why would that be? Remember that the problem with Galatia was legalism. Legalism substitutes self-righteousness for Christ's righteousness. Paul's gospel truth would have constantly reminded them of their hypocrisy. When they became comfortable and self-satisfied, Paul would have hammered them back down again. The gospel themes of sin, judgment, the impossibility of righteousness through works, the need of faith alone in Christ alone are all very humbling. Hearts filled with pride in self tire of hearing of it. By way of contrast, a truly converted heart never tires of hearing of it. We love to hear the same old gospel themes over and over again. But the unconverted heart, or a temporarily hardened believing heart, tires and resists it. It hates to be reminded of its sin; of its pride; of its self righteousness and hypocrisy; of its twisted motives and blackened heart; of the futility of its attempts at righteousness through religious observance and ceremony; and so on. So the preacher becomes the enemy. The point of question is this: Is your change of attitude justified? Does it make sense? Is this what I deserve? Or should you be ashamed of yourself for persecuting me just because I'm preaching the truth? Should you not wake up and see that you are abandoning the truths that you once so eagerly accepted?

The Apostle's Response

Paul now demonstrates his continuing devotion to the Galatians. He does so, first, by pointing out the *ill motives of the Judaizers*. Look at the people that you've begun to follow!

> They eagerly seek you, not commendably, but they wish to shut you out, in order that you may seek them. (Gal. 4:17)

The Apostle Paul concedes the zeal of the Judaizers. 'They eagerly seek you,' he admits. They desperately wish to win you to their cause. They are courting you. But as Morris notes, 'Throughout history there have been many earnest people whose zeal for their cause has far exceeded their grasp of reality.'[114] They have zeal (*zelousin*), but 'not commendably,' not in any good sense. Their efforts would only harm, not help, the Galatians. 'They wish to shut you out,' or isolate you from Paul himself and from the rest of the Christian church which, as a matter of fact, concurs with Paul's gospel over against the Judaizing distortions (1:7–10). Thus isolated, the Galatians would look only to the Judaizers for instruction and fellowship. They seek 'to shut you out, in order that you may seek them.' Paul repeats the word 'eagerly seek,' or 'zealous' again. They want you to be zealous for them even as they are zealous for you. This is a classic description of a cult! When Christ is the focus there is freedom from men and the commandments of men. The conscience is not bound by man-made rules. This can be universalized as a test of a true movement of the gospel. Where the gospel is, the people are not brought into bondage to rules and regulations, and the interpreters of those rules and regulations, the teachers and leaders of the movement. It is typical of the cults that they bring people into bondage to their peculiar rules and under the excessive authority of their leaders. A friend in college married a man because the 'elders' of her 'church' told her she must. It was a disaster for her and her family. This is typical. The cults go beyond the appropriate mutual affection that we've just seen, even where the teacher is received as an angel of God, and where the people would pluck out their eyes on his behalf. That is considerable devotion already. But the Judaizers, and the cults, go beyond this. Their leaders become authoritarian, demanding obedience and undermining Christian freedom.

> But it is good always to be eagerly sought in a commendable manner, and not only when I am present with you. (Gal. 4:18)

It is not that Paul is against zeal. He clarifies, 'But it is good always to be eagerly sought in a commendable manner…' 'Eagerly sought' is the word 'zeal' again. Zeal is crucial, but it must be zeal for the truth, or for what is good. Zeal must be 'in accordance with knowledge' (Rom. 10:4). The problem with the Judaizers, and potentially with the Galatians, is that their zeal was misplaced. At the same time their zeal for the true gospel was temporary, lasting only as long as Paul was present. Proper zeal for truth will 'always' be present, 'not only when I am present with you.' You've made a bad trade, he's telling them. You gave up the truth for this bondage.

Second, he *points out his own proper motives.* He does this not directly, not by talking about it, but by demonstrating his love through words.

> My children, with whom I am again in labor until Christ is formed in you. (Gal. 4:19)

The Apostle Paul is full of emotion as he writes. 'My children' is a form of address used nowhere else in the New Testament. Paul can speak of himself as a father of his converts (1 Cor. 4:15), as a nurse (1 Thess. 2:7), and now as a mother 'in labor.' Note the irony. He is their mother. He calls them his 'children.' But because of their flirtations with apostasy he finds himself 'again in labor until Christ is formed in you –' They had been through this before. He had already been in labor with them. 'Labor' indicates a painful process. They had been converted. They had died to self and been united to Christ. But then they had reverted, making rebirth necessary. Notice what is the aim of the Apostle's work. The Judaizers were being driven by selfish ambition. The Apostle Paul's focus is Christ. They are being urged to accept not Paul, but Christ. He describes this as Christ being 'formed' in a person. This points to the inward transformation of the believer into the image of Christ. The Galatians were not making progress by moving in the direction of the Judaizers. They instead were 'in danger of needing to start all over again,' says Morris.[115]

> But I could wish to be present with you now and to change my tone, for I am perplexed about you. (Gal. 4:20)

The Apostle would like to be with them to talk. 'I could wish to be present with you now.' Face-to-face dialogue would be better. Then, he says, I could 'change my tone.' Then they could hear his voice inflections, see the look on his face, and better understand his intent. Communication is often more difficult in print. Words committed to print, as it is often said, can take on a life of their own. He is 'perplexed,' he admits. He cannot understand why those who had been converted by the grace of the gospel would be tempted to run off into a form of legalism. He is confused by their behavior. He is hurt that they now regard his as an enemy. 'Why?' he says. One of the commentators points out that Paul practices 1 Corinthians 13 throughout this letter. They have failed Christ's Apostle, but he responds with a love that never fails, that is longsuffering, that is kind, and even at this point hopes all things.

Sometimes relations between pastors and people sour. Jonathan Edwards, after 20 years at the Northampton church, was fired by the congregation. In his case, as in the Apostle Paul's, it was for no good reason. After twenty years! 'Does this make sense?' he is asking. After such devotion to both the messenger and the message, does it make sense that you now abandon both for this blind, enslaving zealotry? If you can't think about this theologically, then at least think about it in terms of interpersonal relations. Surely even on these terms, this makes no sense at all.

Come back to grace, he is arguing. Come back to faith, back to Christ, and back to me, as Christ's Apostle.

17

Children of Promise

Galatians 4:21–31

Paul seeks to clinch his argument with the Judaizers by making allegorical use of the story of Hagar and Sarah. This is undoubtedly the most difficult passage in Galatians. It assumes a knowledge of the Old Testament that few have. It requires an ability to follow a rabbinic allegorical argument, which even fewer possess. But the importance of the passage is obvious from the first verse.

> Tell me, you who want to be under law, do you not listen to the law? (Gal. 4:21)

He addresses those who wish to be 'under the law.' This was a problem in the Apostle Paul's day, and has been one ever since. There have always been those both inside and outside of the church who imagine that the way to God is the way of rules and regulations rightly observed. They prefer law to gospel. They fail to understand grace, and think instead that through good works one can get right with God. When I was in a fraternity at the University of Southern California, there was a night when both Zeffirelli's 'Jesus of Nazareth' and Cecil DeMille's 'Ten Commandments' were on television at the same time. The room in which 'Ten Commandments' was showing was packed, and the Jesus room was nearly empty. The Christians in the fraternity saw symbolic significance in this beyond preference for Charlton Heston. We saw a preference for law and discomfort with gospel. So the basic problem is ever contemporary. Hardly an 'Inquirers' Class' goes by when someone doesn't answer the question, 'How do you hope to get to heaven?' with the answer, 'By being the best person that I can be,' that is by works. Hardly a Sunday School class is conducted when some adult or child doesn't betray a legalistic understanding of salvation. To all such he asks, 'Do you not listen to the law?'

> Tell me, you who want to be under law, do you not listen to the law? (Gal. 4:21)

Are you really listening to what the law actually says? Do you really understand it? Do you really know what it demands? And here is the real question: Do you understand the distinctions that the law makes? Not all the sons of Abraham are sons of promise. Not all sons of Abraham are saved. Physical descent is not enough. There is a problem of selectively reading the Bible. We all tend to pick and choose what we want to read. Read the whole law, he is telling them, and you will find this crucial distinction, which Paul strives to demonstrate as he takes us back to Abraham, Sarah, Hagar, and the children born to them. Stott helps us to identify the three stages in the Apostle's argument. The first is *historical* (22–3), the second is *allegorical* (24–7), the third is *personal* (28–31).

Historical Background

> For it is written that Abraham had two sons, one by the bondwoman and one by the free woman. (Gal. 4:22)

Paul says 'it is written,' but doesn't cite a specific text. Instead, he summarizes scriptural teaching found in Genesis 16–21. Go back to Abraham. How many sons did he have? This is an historical question. The Judaizers knew the answer, but had failed to recognize the significance. Abraham had two sons, one of which he had by the slave, the 'bondwoman' Hagar, and the other by the 'free woman' Sarah. This is a highly pertinent reference because physical descent was such a source of pride for the Jews. So he reminds them that Abraham had two sons. 'From which of them do you really descend?' he is asking. One mother was a slave, the other was free. Consequently one of the children was born a slave, and the other, free.

> But the son by the bondwoman was born according to the flesh, and the son by the free woman through the promise. (Gal. 4:23)

'But,' is a 'strong adversative,' says Morris.[116] Even more important than the *social* status of the mothers was the *spiritual* status of the births of their respective children. Ishmael was born 'according to the flesh,' Isaac 'through the promise.' Ishmael was born through human contriving, as Sarah gave her maid, Hagar, to her husband that he might father a child through her. Isaac was born when Abraham was a hundred years old and Sarah was ninety, by a miracle of God according to the promise of God (Gen. 16:1ff.; 17:15ff.). Later he will contrast these births as 'according to the flesh' and 'according to the Spirit' (v. 29). Thus the main point is made. Physical descent is not enough. There are two lines of descent from Abraham. One is physical, the other is spiritual. One results in slavery, one in freedom. One is based on the works of man, one on the power of God. One is of human origin, one of divine. Religious claims made on the basis of physical descent alone will be inadequate. If he were speaking to us today he would be warning us not to rely on a pious ancestry. Don't think you're going to heaven just because you had a godly grandmother or godly father. He might say, 'Remember Uncle Charlie.' Every family has an Uncle Charlie. Every family has a black sheep. Remember, he too is a descendant of your godly grandmother. A family pew dating back one hundred years means nothing. It always comes back to personal faith in Christ. In the end that is all that counts.

Allegorical Interpretation

The Apostle Paul then interprets the historical facts allegorically.

> This is allegorically speaking: for these women are two covenants, one proceeding from Mount Sinai bearing children who are to be slaves; she is Hagar. (Gal. 4:24)

These events may be understood 'allegorically,' or 'figuratively' (NIV), or perhaps even what we mean by 'typologically.' This does not mean that the stories are not factual. But it does mean that an allegory or illustration will be drawn from the passage. The Jews made much of the Sarah–Hagar story, and Paul can assume considerable knowledge on their part, so much indeed, that he doesn't name two of the most important players in the story, Sarah and Ishmael. His basic argument is that the Jews, though they are Sarah's offspring, are actually the children of Hagar, since they, like Ishmael, possess physical descent only and not faith. Christians, however, are children of Sarah because they, like Isaac, are descendants by way of promise. Paul is dealing with people who made generous use of allegory in interpreting the Scriptures, and no doubt had such an interpretation of this passage. So he is 'responding in kind,' Morris says.[117] He is attempting to beat them at their own game. There are two covenants represented by these two women: one is Hagar, Sinai, and slavery. The other is Sarah, Calvary (implied), and freedom. Whereas the Judaizers would have seen themselves as descendants of Sarah the free woman and Gentiles as descendants of Hagar the slave, Paul says the opposite is the case.

> Now this Hagar is Mount Sinai in Arabia, and corresponds to the present Jerusalem, for she is in slavery with her children. (Gal. 4:25)

Sinai, the mountain on which the law was given, is in Arabia, as are Hagar's descendants, and as the Apostle sees it, is a land of slaves. It is not the holy land that God gave to Israel. Then he says, corresponding to Sinai/Arabia today is Jerusalem. Such an interpretation would have shocked the Judaizers. But because Jerusalem was the center from which 'Sinaitic' teaching or legalism was emanating in the present, this was the case. Hagar–Ishmael–physical descent–Sinai–slavery from long ago corresponds to Judaizers–physical descent–Sinai–Jerusalem–slavery in the present. Hagar and her 'children,' meaning the Judaizers, are 'in slavery,' he says. Their additions to faith as the basis for justification, their requirement that all submit to the ceremonial regulations of the Old Testament was a form of slavery.

> But the Jerusalem above is free; she is our mother. (Gal. 4:26)

Continuing the allegory, or what is more precisely typology, Jerusalem is not merely the capital of the Jewish state, but represents the heavenly Jerusalem. Jerusalem below is under Roman domination, but Jerusalem above, where God dwells, is free from all forms of bondage. The heavenly Jerusalem, he says, is our 'mother,' or as in some manuscripts, 'the mother of us all' (KJV). From her we draw life and spiritual sustenance. And she is a spiritual entity. The law cannot give life or sustain life. It has no such life-generating powers. Only the Spirit does.

If you go the way of law, if you seek to get right with God through keeping rules and regulations, then you are a child of Hagar and the result is slavery. You will be in bondage to rules. Freedom is only to be found in Christ. Rule-keeping cannot make you right with God or bring about freedom from sin. Only as you turn to Christ and are spiritually regenerated and transformed will you find God and true freedom.

> For it is written, 'Rejoice, barren woman who does not bear; break forth and shout, you who are not in labor; for more are the children of the desolate than of the one who has a husband.' (Gal. 4:27)

The Apostle Paul quotes Isaiah 54:1, words which seem to be directed to Jerusalem at the time of the exile. She was at that time 'a barren woman who does not bear.' The people had been carried off to Babylon and she was empty. Yet she is to 'rejoice… break forth and shout.' Why? Because once more Jerusalem would be filled with people, more even than she had before the exile. Paul takes this to mean that in time those who follow the way of faith will outnumber those who follow the way of the Judaizers. Sarah's spiritual children will come to outnumber Hagar's physical children. Indeed it was soon the case, and, as Morris says, 'in due course Gentile believers would considerably outnumber Jews.'[118] The way of law is on the wrong side of history. Stay there and you will not be where the Holy Spirit is going. Ultimately it loses, and you lose.

Personal Application

> And you brethren, like Isaac, are children of promise. (Gal. 4:28)

Finally, Paul makes *personal application to the Galatians*, and also to us. Galatian Gentile believers are 'brethren,' and are 'like Isaac,' and as such are 'children of promise.' In Christ Jesus they are of divine origin. They are spiritual children of Abraham and Sarah. One becomes a child of promise, a descendant of Abraham like Isaac, not through birth, but rebirth; not by law, but by promise; not by works, but by faith. 'If you belong to Christ,' Paul wrote, 'then you are Abraham's offspring, heirs according to promise' (Gal. 3:29).

But if we are like Isaac, then we can expect to be treated like Isaac.

> But as at that time he who was born according to the flesh persecuted him who was born according to the Spirit, so it is now also. (Gal. 4:29)

In the first instance being 'like Isaac' means *persecution*. The one born 'according to the flesh *persecuted* him who was born according to the Spirit.' Paul is probably referring to the 'mocking' of Isaac by Ishmael recorded in Genesis 21:9. At that time Ishmael was probably seventeen, and Isaac, being just weaned, was about three. Isaac was subject to the scorn and derision of Ishmael. Ishmael was 'born of the flesh,' that is, through human devising, whereas Isaac was 'born according to the Spirit.' This mocking by Ishmael of Isaac corresponds to the persecution of believers by those ensnared in legalism. 'So it is now also,' Paul says. One commentator observes that legalistic religion is always a persecuting religion because it cannot survive unless its regulations are enforced. This explains why in the early years of the church Judaism persecuted Christianity and why so often the persecution of the church arises from within the church. It is often the case that Christians are persecuted 'by their half-brothers—the unbelieving but religious people in the nominal church,' says Boice.[119] Stott writes,

> It has always been so. The Lord Jesus was bitterly opposed, rejected, mocked and condemned by His own nation. The fiercest opponents of the apostle Paul, who dogged his footsteps and stirred up strife against him, were the official church, the Jews. The monolithic structure of the medieval papacy persecuted all Protestant minorities with ruthless, unremitting ferocity.[120]

Even though this is universally observable as being true, the shock of the reality is something that the people of God never get accustomed to. I can only think of one time in twenty years that our congregation has suffered persecution, either fierce or mild, from outside the organized, visible church. But from within? I can hardly think of anything good that hasn't been resisted, often fiercely. On a personal level, Christian people typically suffer far more at the hands of fellow professing Christians than worldlings. Remember Ishmael was a part of the visible church. The longer I am in the ministry, the more I am astonished at how cruel Christian people can be to one another, all under the guise of righteousness as well. This is in part because we are a family in the church. As a family we become familiar with each other and begin to take liberties. But it is also because there are wolves in sheep's clothing. I have a friend in the ministry serving the PCA in South Carolina who is a young, experienced, gifted pastor, but because he is not sufficiently 'dynamic' to suit some, has been told some of the cruelest things imaginable. He faithfully conducts a fine, reverent worship service, he competently preaches verse-by-verse sermons, he is godly, humble, an excellent father and husband, yet they want to drive him off. Their pretense is concern for the welfare of the church, which has seen some drop in attendance. Their actions, however, are self-righteous and cruel.

Think of your own wounds and scars of recent years. Who has inflicted them? Who has criticized your priorities? Who has criticized your choices? Who has discouraged and defeated you? Has not most of this come to you from within the visible church? As it has sometimes been said, the church is the only army that shoots its wounded. Why? Because the besetting sin of zealous Christians is Pharisaic self-righteousness. We all seem to have our lists of things to which everyone else must conform. I don't mean biblical things like keeping the Ten Commandments, tithing, witnessing, loving one's neighbor, and so on. Of course we must all do those things. I mean extra-biblical expectations regarding ways of doing things and saying things, and matters of judgment not principle, about taking the left fork not the right fork. We can become Pharisees about food and drink, about child-rearing and education, about fashion and finances. Take care about what you say, when you say, and how you say it! Take care lest unwittingly you become a persecutor of the saints.

But second, being like Isaac means *separation*. What should be done about this conflict between law and grace? Paul cites the precedent of Genesis 21:10, in which Hagar and Ishmael are 'cast out' and not given an inheritance with Isaac. He probably means that both legalism and the legalists are to be thrown out of the church.

> But what does the Scripture say? 'Cast out the bondwoman and her son, for the son of the bondwoman shall not be an heir with the son of the free woman.' (Gal. 4:30)

Finally, there must be a separation. The persecutor of the church from within cannot be allowed to continue forever. There must be relief, and though 'cast out' doesn't sound very nice, there comes a point where vigorous action must be taken. A few years back we had a member of our church regularly mailing out to other members attacks aimed at the leadership of the church. They were tolerated for a while. But these mailings were keeping the church in a state of turmoil. Action was necessary and rightly taken by the Session.

Genesis 21:10 was interpreted by the Jews as God's rejection of the Gentiles. Paul gives it the opposite interpretation. It is God excluding unbelieving Jews. The point of it all is that the promises of the Old Testament are inherited not by physical descent, but by faith. We are the inheritors of the promises of God, through the Spirit, by faith.

> So then, brethren, we are not children of a bond-woman, but of the free woman. (Gal. 4:31)

'So then,' he says, my point has been made. We are children of Sarah, 'the free woman,' and because we are we live by faith, free from the bondage of ceremonial law and justification by works, and in the rich pleasure of the grace of God.

18

Freedom or Slavery?

Galatians 5:1–4

In verse 4, Paul provides for us a wonderfully convenient summary of the Galatian problem. False teachers, known to history as 'Judaizers,' had come into the Galatian assemblies, and had taught the Gentile Christians there that they had to be 'justified by law.' How is one made right with Christ? By faith in Christ plus the keeping of the law, they said, particularly its ceremonial aspects. 'Unless you are circumcised according to the custom of Moses, you cannot be saved,' they taught (Acts 15:1). They urged the observing of 'days and months and seasons and years,' that is, of religious holidays (4:10). They borrowed from Moses or made up their own rules restricting enjoyment of Christ's creation, saying 'do not handle, do not taste, do not touch' (Col. 2:21). In other words, one is saved by the keeping of rules and rituals. There are *moral rules* requiring that one do this and not do that. If they are followed, one may be saved. There are *religious rituals* of cleansing, for observing holy days, for pilgrimages, for presenting sacrifices, and so on. Follow them, and one may be saved. Follow the rules, observe the rituals and do all the right things. This is what it means to be 'justified by law,' and it is the essence of all the religions of the world. The Apostle Paul calls this 'a yoke of slavery'. He calls it 'a different gospel; which is really not another' (1:6–7). Twice he repeats,

> As we have said before, so I say again now, if any man is preaching to you a gospel contrary to that which you received, let him be accursed. (Gal. 1:9, cf. 1:8)

He sets before the Galatians two options: freedom or slavery. Freedom is to be found in the gospel of grace, slavery in every other alternative, even in those which merely add small requirements to faith in Christ. He permits no compromise. While we might search for some middle ground where the tension between the two opposites might be relieved, he will permit none. The tension remains. He will not allow us to blur the distinction between the two choices. We have two choices and only two choices: freedom in Christ or slavery in legalism.

The yoke of slavery

> It was for freedom that Christ set us free; therefore keep standing firm and do not be subject again to a yoke of slavery. (Gal. 5:1)

Why is it that seeking to be justified by law is a 'yoke of slavery'? We can provide two reasons.

First, law means the oppression of works. As we have seen, justification by law means justification by works, by obeying the rules and performing the rituals of that law. This means slavery. One is required to infallibly perform the works of the law when one rises up in the morning, all throughout the day, and when one is at sleep at night. Do right. Do good. Obey the rules. Perform the rituals. Keep at it. Never stop. Inevitably it raises the unanswerable question: when will I have done enough? And the answer is, never. There is always another day, another task, another performance. One can never relax. One can never slow down. The law is a tremendous burden for one to carry. Its exhausted practitioners are never able to escape from its requirements. They live in fear. They are always asking the question, have we done enough? Are our works adequate? Have we fallen short? Will we make it? One carries an enormous burden of guilt. One is always asking, could I have done better? Should I have done better? Should I have done more? The yoke of justification by law is a yoke of slavery. It yokes us to a system of unceasing works as the means by which we must be made right with God but never can.

Second, law means demands without assistance. Can I make myself righteous through the law? The law with its rules and rituals can show us our sin and define our sin and convict us of sin. It may also in a positive sense show us what we are supposed to do. But it cannot forgive our sins. It cannot deal with existing guilt. Even with all its rules and rituals, its sacrifices and ceremonies, it cannot propitiate guilt. Neither can it empower us to fulfill the requirements of the law. If I must make myself righteous, then I am in trouble. When we place ourselves under law as a means of justification, we find ourselves hopelessly condemned. We are condemned by the law for what we've already done and powerless to fulfill what it requires. The law, as Paul said in Galatians 3:21, cannot 'impart life.' It places us in 'custody,' as he said in Galatians 3:23. It locks us up and imprisons us. Indeed we are like prisoners, burdened by the guilt and anxiety and depression and fear of those who are condemned. So the apostle Paul writes, 'do not be subject,' that is, do not be 'loaded down' or 'burdened' (NIV). He envisions a beast that has been yoked to a heavy and unbearable burden. This is what it means to seek to be justified by law. It means the slavery of works and the slavery of self-righteousness. It means being yoked to a burden that we cannot bear. It means being imprisoned by requirements that we cannot fulfill.

Christian Freedom

The Apostle Paul literally calls Christian freedom *the* freedom, using the definite article. He is speaking of Christian freedom specifically. 'Christ set us free,' he says, that we might enjoy 'freedom.' This may seem obvious, even a tautology. But he is making a point. We were not freed by Christ only to go back to slavery. There are many ways to look at salvation. One might emphasize being justified, or adopted, or rescued. Here the emphasis is on freedom. It was for the sake of freedom that Christ saved us. 'Therefore keep standing firm,' he tells them with great emphasis. They should 'resist any attempt to bring them into bondage of any sort,' says Morris.[121] Do not be 'subject again, to a yoke of slavery.' What then, is Christian freedom? What is the freedom for which Christ has set us free?

First, it means freedom from the law's obligations.

We are free from the rules and the rituals of the law because we are justified not by law but by faith. Consequently we are no longer under the great burden of the law. We are not required to perform, to gain the approval of God. We are not required to approach God on the basis of works. We are not exhausted by the necessity of always doing more, and more, and more in order to secure His favor. We don't live under the fear that we may have performed inadequately or fallen short or failed to 'make it.' We don't live with the guilt of knowing that we could've done better, or should've done better. Why? Because Christ has fulfilled the righteousness for us. We have been justified. We have been adopted. We are free from the obligation to fulfill the rules and rituals of the law in order to be saved.

Second, it means freedom free from the law's condemnations. 'There is therefore no condemnation for those who are in Christ Jesus,' says the apostle Paul (Rom. 8:1). We are no longer subject to the law's curses and threats. Why? Because the condemnation has been removed, the law has been fulfilled. We are no longer prisoners of the guilt and anxiety and depression and fear of those who are under the curse of the law. As Paul writes in Romans, 'having been justified by faith we have peace with God' (Rom. 5:1). We don't live with guilt any longer. We aren't burdened with anxiety any longer. We no longer live with the fear of failing to perform. The condemnation has been removed, the law has been fulfilled.

In addition, the power of sin has been broken. As Paul writes in Romans 6:6, the old self was crucified, the body of sin was done away, we are no longer slaves of sin. He writes in Romans 8:3,

> For what the Law could not do, weak as it was through the flesh, God did: sending His own Son in the likeness of sinful flesh and as an offering for sin, He condemned sin in the flesh,

The law was not able to 'condemn sin in the flesh.' It was too 'weak.' But what the law was not able to do, 'God did' in 'sending His own son.' The result? Sin shall no longer 'be master over [us] for [we] are no longer under law but under grace' (Rom. 6:14). We are now 'new creations' in Christ Jesus (2 Cor. 5:17). The law lacks the dynamic, but the gospel has it! The gospel is the power of God unto salvation (Rom. 1:6). Jesus Christ gives us His Holy Spirit who enables and empowers us to live free from the tyrannical and oppressive power of the law.

Third, it means freedom to enjoy and please God. We have been justified. That means that our sins are forgiven and we have been given the gift of eternal life. As a result, we are able to rejoice, and even beyond rejoicing, we are able to 'exult in the hope of the glory of God' as the Apostle Paul puts it (Rom. 5:2). We have been adopted into the family of God. God is now my Father. I am no longer motivated by fear and anxiety and by the need to perform for a God who is condemning me. Instead, we are motivated as sons to please our Father who is in heaven. As he writes in Romans 8:15,

> For you have not received a spirit of slavery leading to fear again, but you have received a spirit of adoption as sons by which we cry out, 'Abba! Father!'

We were once in slavery to the law, works righteousness, and the guilt that accompanies such a system. We once participated in the 'dreadful struggle to keep the law, with a view to winning the favor of God,' says Stott.[122] This was something to which they and we as Gentiles could be subject 'again' because the principle of works righteousness is characteristic of all the religions of the world (see 4:9). The Pharisees found 613 commandments in the Law. Just to remember them was a burden. To keep them was impossible. The conscience was bound by the obligation to do so. One carried the burden of imperfect conformity. One carried the burden of having never done enough, of always needing to do more. Christ has liberated us from this burden. Therefore we are to stand up and 'keep standing,' and not bow over and 'be subject again to a yoke of slavery'.

Our Choice

Is it difficult to avoid this yoke? Yes it is. This is why he must exhort them, 'do not be subject again to a yoke of slavery' (cf 4:9–10). We are all tempted to return to a form of religion which depends on rule-keeping to make us right with God. Why? Primarily because of pride. We want to think that we are contributing to our salvation. Look into the heart of the natural man and you will find either a Pharisee or a libertine. The Pharisee thinks that he is in favor with God because he keeps God's rules. He earns his salvation. He is proud of his accomplishment. It feeds his pride. He boasts of his righteousness. He sneers at the corruption of others. The libertine thinks that he is in favor with God not because he keeps the rules, but because God has no rules, or at least no rules that he fails to fulfill. So even if he is a philanderer, a thief, and a liar, he is confident because he is not as bad as the murderer. The murderer is confident of heaven because he is not as bad as the mass-murderer. The mass-murderer is not as bad as Hitler. And so it goes. Ironically, the libertine stands upon the same foundation as the Pharisee. They have different conceptions of God and of God's standards. But they both think that they fulfill the standards, be they high or low, and are in that sense self-righteous, self-deceived, and enslaved. The Pharisee is enslaved by his religion. The libertine is enslaved by his sin. Both are in bondage.

The emphasis in Galatia was certainly on Phariseeism/Judaizing. Yet we merely note that Christian people can fall into either error if they are not careful. Those tempted to excess can turn their freedom into 'an opportunity for the flesh' (Gal 5:13), and find themselves out of control (v. 17). Jesus said, 'Whoever sins is a slave of sin' (John 8:34). Peter said, 'By what a man is overcome, by this he is enslaved' (2 Pet. 2:19). On the other hand (and the more immediate concern addressed in this epistle), those tempted by Phariseeism can fall back into a works mentality, either Mosaic or man-made. They can begin to settle for the righteousness of rules or rituals. They begin to settle for relating to God on the basis of external criteria. One begins to say of oneself and others that we have the favor of God because we keep certain rules or perform certain rituals. Remember, the Galatians had already begun to 'observe days and months and seasons and years' (4:10). Paul sees this as 'weak and worthless elemental things' by which they might be again 'enslaved.' Why? Because it was introducing the principle of works. Similarly he asked the Colossians,

> If you have died with Christ to the elementary principles of the world, why, as if you were living in the world, do you submit yourself to decrees, such as, 'Do not handle, do not taste, do not touch!' (Col. 2:20–1)

These, he said, are 'the commandments and teachings of men,' which have 'the appearance of wisdom in self-made religion and self-abasement and severe treatment of the body' (Col. 2:23). This is not to say that the law has no ongoing role in the life of the people of God. It does. The moral law is still the rule of life for us. 'Do we nullify the Law through faith?' Paul asks. 'May it never be! On the contrary, we establish the Law' (Rom. 3:31). But as we have seen, we are freed from the law's condemning voice. Christ has removed our condemnation (Rom. 8:1). We have peace with God (Rom. 5:1). We have no more guilt, and no guilt feelings. We are freed from the futile attempt to be justified by keeping the law. And we are free from the extra-biblical commands of men.

The specific issue which represents the return to slavery was circumcision.

> Behold I, Paul, say to you that if you receive circumcision, Christ will be of no benefit to you. (Gal. 5:2)

In itself, circumcision is of no theological importance. But at that time it had become a 'theological symbol,' as Stott calls it, representing 'salvation by good works in obedience to the law.'[123] They were teaching, let us remember, that 'unless you are circumcised and keep the law, you cannot be saved' (Acts 15:1, 5). Faith in Christ is insufficient. 'Behold I, Paul, say to you,' adds great emphasis to what follows. He warns them that Gentile circumcision renders Christ of no value or 'benefit.' He accepted circumcision for the sons of Jewish believers, presumably as an expression of Jewish culture (Acts 21:20–4). As a cultural ritual, he was not opposed to it. But when Gentiles did it at the insistence of the Judaizing brethren, it took on religious significance. They would be doing so not as a means of adopting Jewish cultural distinctives, but as a religious work in fulfillment of the law. To do so is to depart from grace as the principle of salvation and to adopt works. Once that step is taken, Christ can no longer be of any value. As Stott puts it, 'It is impossible to receive Christ, thereby acknowledging that you cannot save yourself, and then receive circumcision, thereby claiming that you can.'[124]

> And I testify again to every man who receives circumcision, that he is under obligation to keep the whole Law. (Gal. 5:3)

Again the Apostle Paul speaks emphatically. 'And I testify again,' he says, 'to every man,' admitting no exceptions, that anyone who has come to Christ and then submits to circumcision has left Christ and gone under the law and therefore must 'keep the whole law.' Circumcision as a rite of initiation initiated one into a whole way of life. That way was the way of law. The Judaizers may have been only suggesting the observing of certain portions of the law, perhaps religious holidays (4:10), cleansing ordinances, and circumcision. Paul makes it clear that to accept circumcision as a requirement for salvation meant accepting the principle of salvation by law-keeping, which necessarily implies salvation by keeping the whole law.

> You have been severed from Christ, you who are seeking to be justified by law; you have fallen from grace.(Gal. 5:4)

Now he hits the nail right on the head. They were trying to be 'justified by law.' To do so is to reject the only true way of justification, which is in Christ. To turn to law is to turn away from, even to be 'severed from,' Christ. He also describes this spiritual disaster as a fall from grace, a falling away from the central principle of Christianity.

This phrase has been loaded up with meaning that it doesn't carry by those who wish to prove that one can lose one's salvation. The Apostle Paul is saying no such thing. What he is saying is that they have fallen from the principle of salvation by grace into legalism. He is saying no more than we would mean when we say of someone that they've 'fallen into a bad crowd,' or 'fallen on hard times,' or even 'fallen into a cult.' They have fallen into legalism and fallen from grace, he is saying.

There can be no middle road. One either finds freedom in Christ, or one remains in slavery to sin and the law. One cannot say that salvation is found in Christ plus something. One cannot teach that being a Christian means trusting in Christ plus something. The Galatians may have thought that observing the religious holidays was harmless enough. But it was sliding the church in the direction of ritual. They may have thought that receiving circumcision was no compromise of the gospel. But when made obligatory, when made a religious test, it contradicted grace and undermined the gospel. They may have thought that submitting to man-made rules such as 'do not handle, do not taste, do not touch,' was an advanced form of Christian piety, but the reality was a legalism which destroys the gospel.

Let me close by asking a very important question, 'What are you trusting in?' Evangelism Explosion teaches it workers to ask the question, 'Why should God let you in to heaven?' Let me ask you that question. Why should God let you into heaven? Is it because you are doing good and right things? Is it because you go to church or help in the Sunday school? Why do you think He's going to let you in? If your answer is anything other than 'because I am trusting in the finished work of the Lord Jesus Christ and in His righteousness alone,' then you are seeking to be justified by law. What are you trusting in?

Let me ask several additional questions of those of us who know the right answer theologically, but may be missing the boat experientially. We well know that our hearts are deceitful. Let me then ask these questions for the sake of self-examination, which may help provide some insight into what exactly we are trusting in, whether it be works or Christ.

First, are you *defeated*? Is there no joy in your life? Is there no peace? Are you discouraged? Are you depressed? Could it be that you are living as though you are under God's condemnation? Are you still trying to earn His favor? Are you still performing for Him? One who has been justified by faith is not doing these things. One who has been justified by faith in Christ understands that he is not condemned and he already has God's favor and it doesn't need to be earned. He understands that it is not secured on the basis of performance. We have 'joy,' we have 'peace,' we have 'no condemnation' in Christ. If you are constantly defeated and discouraged, if you are striving to secure God's favor through rules and rituals, through performance, it may be a sign that you are trusting in your own works and have not yet trusted Christ alone.

Second, are you *defensive*? Can you accept no criticism? Must you always be right? It may be that if this is true of you that you are trusting in your performance. Maybe you can't bear to fail or be wrong. Why can't you? Is it because this would destroy your whole identity and your whole relationship with God? So you're very defensive. One single crack in the dike will bring the whole wall of self-righteousness crashing down. Isn't this what it amounts to? If you are defensive in this way it may reveal a heart that has never truly dealt with its own sin. Perhaps you have never truly acknowledged your need of Christ. An extreme sort of defensiveness may indicate a heart that has never truly acknowledged its sin and need of a Savior, a heart still self-righteous.

Third, are you *critical*? All hyper-critics have one thing in common—pride. They are confident of their superiority. They are sure of their superior wisdom and righteousness. Are you proud and self-righteous and so condemning and censorious of others? Those who are such are typically unaware of their own weakness. They condemn others because they don't realize the way in which they themselves have failed. They censure others because they are unaware of the way in which the commandments of God censure them. Moreover, they criticize and condemn others in order to pump up themselves in relation to others, so that they might seem more righteous than the rest, more holy, more godly. Does your critical spirit indicate a self-righteousness of which you perhaps have never repented? Does it indicate that you have never seen your own sin and need of Christ and so are still trusting in your own moral and religious performance? Have you heard the words of Jesus, 'blessed are the merciful, for they shall receive mercy' (Matt. 5:7). Have you heard his warning,

> Do not judge lest you be judged. For in the way you judge, you will be judged; and by your standard of measure, it will be measured to you. (Matt. 7:1)

Those who have been justified by faith have seen their own sin, and have been humbled by the sight. They hear this warning and are sobered. The self-righteous rush in where fools dare to tread (cf. James 2:12–13; 1 Cor. 4:5).

These are important questions for us to look at. There is still a great deal of Pharisaism in the church today. There is still a great deal of judgmentalism, which indicates a self-righteousness and a pride that is contrary to the whole spirit of justification by faith. There are only two choices that we can make in this life. We can either seek to be justified by self, by works, by law, or we can turn to Christ for justification, and in Him find freedom from defeat, freedom from condemnation, and freedom from sin.

19

The Simple Gospel

Galatians 5:5

Pilgrim's Progress concludes with Christian observing, 'Then I saw that there was a way to hell, even from the gates of heaven…' So it is with the doctrine of justification. One can get very close, but in the end miss it because of self-righteousness. How may a person get right with God? Paul's epistle to the Galatians is as emphatic as emphatic can be. We are saved by faith alone in Christ alone. To His finished work on the cross on our behalf nothing can be added. Remember, the Judaizers preached Christ. But they found a way to hell even from this gate to heaven. They believed that He was the Savior. But they wanted to add to Him ceremonial requirements such as circumcision, cleansing ordinances, and Jewish religious festivals as necessary for salvation. They taught Christ *plus*. This cannot be, never, not ever. Christ plus is always Christ *minus*. The moment one does add even the slightest personal merit to faith in Christ, one is 'severed from Christ' and has 'fallen from grace.' If I add my moral and religious works to God's grace in Christ, then Christ can be of 'no benefit' (5:2–4). There can be no mingling of Christ and law, of faith and works, of grace and merit. The moment they intersect the gospel is overthrown.

We ask again, what are you trusting in? We ask it of those who have never truly come to Christ with empty hands and surrendered to Him. Perhaps some have never heard these truths before. We invite, we urge you to come to the Lord Jesus Christ by faith, drop all claims of self-righteousness, quit all attempts to commend yourself to God on the basis of your morality, integrity, community service, niceness, kindness, or goodness, and receive salvation as a gift of His grace. We also ask it of those who are doctrinally orthodox, who know and believe the doctrine of justification by faith alone, and affirm it with the best of them. What are you trusting in? We ask it because we suspect that there are some numbered among us who, though they profess *sola fides* with their mouths, in their hearts are like the Judaizers, 'seeking to be justified by law' (5:4). Their righteousness is not that which Christ has imputed to them, but *self*-righteousness. We suggested that some guilt-ridden, joyless, anxious, assurance-lacking Christians may be such because they are still trying to *earn* God's good favor through their works, which of course they fail to do because it cannot be done. The whole gospel assumes that it cannot be done. That's why we need a Savior. But the attempt destroys their peace and joy. We also suggested that some hyper-defensive, or on the opposite end, some hyper-critical Christians are as they are because they are still dominated by a 'works' mentality. They have such pride, and are so self-righteous that they, on the one hand, cannot admit error, cannot receive correction, and cannot be taught anything. Their whole identity before God and man is wrapped up in their performance, which is perfect, and profoundly threatened by the suggestion that they may have something wrong. On the other hand, they dish-out criticism unceasingly, judging and condemning others as though they never sinned, or at least (and more likely!), have never faced their sin. Are you among those who, though they profess with their mouths justification by faith alone, are in their *practice* and *experience* living as though their righteousness were self-earned and self-preserved? These are ways to hell that may be found 'even from the gates of heaven.'

If these are ways to be avoided, then what is the right way to heaven? The Apostle Paul provides for us another convenient summary in 5:5:

> For we through the Spirit, by faith, are waiting for the hope of righteousness. (Gal. 5:5)

'We' is emphatic. 'We Christians as opposed to what others may be saying, believe three things about salvation.' They are, first, salvation is 'through the Spirit.' Second, it is 'by faith.' Third, it requires patient 'hope.' This is the 'simple gospel.' It is this that we shall look at together now.

Through the Spirit

'For we through the Spirit,' says the Apostle. Salvation is not by human striving or by the human will. We are saved by the supernatural work of the Spirit, changing our hearts, renewing our wills, and leading us to Christ. No one ever became a Christian by his own efforts. No one ever determined in his own strength to turn from his sins to Christ. We are too blind and too weak to do so. Indeed, we are by nature utterly disinclined to do so. No one has to convince me not to climb Mount Everest. I have no interest in climbing it. I am too weak to climb it. I can't see the value in climbing it. The human heart is this way toward God. Our nature is evil. We love our darkness. We have no interest in God's light, in fact, we hate it (John 3:19–20). 'No one seeks for God,' says Paul (Rom. 3:11). No one removes themselves from the darkness and steps into the light of their own initiative. We have no more interest in God or ability to turn to God than do most of us have an interest in or ability to climb Mount Everest.

During the fourth century a British monk named Pelegius taught that man has the ability to take the initial steps toward salvation by his own efforts apart from the grace of God. His views were vigorously opposed by Augustine, and ultimately condemned by the Council of Ephesus in 431 AD. The Council maintained, and the Christian church has always taught, that it takes a miracle of grace to make a Christian. The Holy Spirit must change our hearts if we are to believe the gospel. We must be 'born again' if we are to see the Kingdom of God, said Jesus (John 3:3, 5–7). When we are born again it happens 'not of blood, nor of the will of the flesh, nor of the will of man, but of God' (John 1:13). God does it. 'No one can say 'Jesus is Lord,' except by the Holy Spirit,' said the Apostle Paul (1 Cor. 12:3). We are too weak, too blind, and utterly disinclined to believe and obey God without the prompting and enabling of the Holy Spirit. Our righteousness is 'through the Spirit,' Paul is saying to the Galatians and against the Judaizers. Our salvation is not through our moral and religious efforts. It is not through trying real hard to be good. It is not through law and works, but through the Spirit who enables us. We love only because He first loved us (1 John 4:19). It is only 'by His doing' that we 'are in Christ Jesus' (1 Cor. 1:30).

All of this is to say that Christianity is not a natural religion. It is not merely the acceptance of a doctrine or a creed. It is not even merely a decision to follow a Person. There has been too much talk about 'making a decision' for Christ, so much, that people have perhaps begun to believe in decisional salvation, that I save myself by making a decision. People don't become Christians by autonomously weighing the evidence for Christ, evaluating the benefits of Christ, and then making a rational decision. I was saved because I walked an aisle, signed a card, raised my hand, or prayed a prayer, people sometimes think *I* made a decision! But the fact is that they are not capable of a rational decision apart from the light of the Holy Spirit. The sons of Adam will forever choose and irrationally choose darkness. We do not have the strength, wisdom, or desire to come to Christ. Christianity is not a *natural* but a *supernatural* religion. It is only 'through the Spirit' that we become Christians. Let all Judaizers and legalists take note. You did not choose Christ. He chose you (John 15:16). When Jesus said this to His disciples He was not denying the reality of their decision to follow Him. But He was denying that their decision was of primary importance. The critical decision was not their's to follow Him, but His to have them. It was His decision that made their decision possible. We are saved not through our own efforts and ingenuity and energy, but 'through the Spirit.'

By Faith

Second, Paul affirms that we are saved 'by faith.' Not only are we not saved by our own strength, but neither are we saved by merit or as a reward for religious and moral works. Faith is the empty-handed response of one who knows that he cannot earn salvation, and so turns to Christ and pleads for mercy. He tells those who are 'seeking to be justified by law' that justification is by faith alone. This has been the theme of his writing since 2:16. He has been hammering away at them repeating over and over that positively we are saved by faith, and negatively we are not saved by works, by keeping the law. Between 2:16 and the end of chapter 3 he uses the word 'faith' or 'believe' nineteen times! He uses the word 'promise' in contrast to 'law' another seven times in the same section. His kickoff verse is amazing enough, with its six-fold assertion that we are saved by faith, not works:

> nevertheless knowing that a man is not justified by the works of the Law but through faith in Christ Jesus, even we have believed in Christ Jesus, that we may be justified by faith in Christ, and not by the works of the Law; since by the works of the Law shall no flesh be justified. (Gal. 2:16)

But he also goes on to say,

> 'I do not nullify the grace of God; for if righteousness comes through the Law, then Christ died needlessly.' (Gal. 2:21)

And,

> Therefore, be sure that it is those who are of faith who are sons of Abraham. (Gal. 3:7)

And,

> Now that no one is justified by the Law before God is evident; for, 'the righteous man shall live by faith.' (Gal. 3:11)

Christ redeemed us, he said,

> in order that in Christ Jesus the blessing of Abraham might come to the Gentiles, so that we might receive the promise of the Spirit through faith. (Gal. 3:14)

Again,

> But the Scripture has shut up all men under sin, that the promise by faith in Jesus Christ might be given to those who believe. (Gal. 3:22)

And again,

> Therefore the Law has become our tutor to lead us to Christ, that we may be justified by faith. (Gal. 3:24)

Can his meaning be mistaken? Let's make sure that it is not.

First, He is utterly and absolutely denying that our religious or moral accomplishments play any part in our salvation. They contribute nothing. We are saved only by faith in Christ.

Second, the faith of which he speaks is faith *in Christ*. Do not make the mistake of identifying the means with the end. As we saw in chapter 6, faith has no saving efficacy of its own. One may sometimes hear people speaking of faith as though faith *itself* saved. They will say in the context of denying the significance of the differences between religions that 'what is important is that one have faith.' Faith is equated with sincerity. 'Just so one is sincere,' they will say, 'it doesn't matter what you believe.' Similarly they will say in the midst of tragedy or trial, 'You just have to trust that it will all turn out all right. That's what will get you through the tough times.' Faith, in this case, is virtually identical with positive thinking. In both cases faith is an end in itself, a thing which of itself has value, even saving power. The one or ones in whom one places one's faith are seen as secondary. One may have faith in Jesus, in Buddha, or for that matter, in nothing at all. The object of one's faith, in this view, is of no consequence. The content of one's faith is irrelevant. One is saved by sincerity or a positive, upbeat outlook. This is tragically wrong and yet pervasive today. So often we have to say the obvious, yet God help us if we ever tire of saying it. Faith is only as good as its object in which it is placed. Faith in the ability of this pulpit to hold up the preacher is only as good as the wood out of which it is made. My positive thoughts about the pulpit's capacity to do so have no impact on its actual capacity to do so. Faith in Christ saves only because Christ is able to deliver the goods. Faith in a false god is as worthless as faith in a faulty pulpit.

How am I to get right with God? Not by vague notions of believing, but by coming to the Lord Jesus Christ, who in space and time, who in real history, died on the cross as a sacrifice for our sins. You must turn to Jesus. He is the Savior. Faith in Christ saves because Christ is the Savior. You must believe what He says about Himself. You must trust in what He accomplished on the cross. You must humble yourself before Him, confess your sin, and surrender to Him. Christianity means dealing with a person. It is not merely the acceptance of the Creed, or the adopting of Christian ethics, or of a Christian philosophy of life. Finally, you are dealing with a person. You must turn to Him. You must believe in Him. We often distinguish between knowledge, assent, and trust as the three elements of faith. One must know the truth. But knowledge is not enough. One must also assent to the truth, or believe the truth. But even this is not saving faith. Thus far we have only risen to the level of the demons, who know the truth, who even 'believe, and tremble' (James 2:19). One must also *trust*. I am saved by trusting in Jesus. I must come to Him, surrender to Him, and trust in Him.

You may say the Creed. Perhaps you memorized the Creed when you were very young. But have you dealt with the Christ of whom the Creed speaks? Do you pray to Him, confess your sin to Him, and trust in Him as Savior and Lord? You will not be saved by being a good boy or girl. However good you are you are not good enough. Only Jesus can save you. The same is true for adults. You will not be saved by religious and moral works. You will not be saved by high standards of morality or a high level of religious performance. You must come to Christ and trust in Him, and Him alone.

In Hope

We 'are waiting,' Paul says, not working. We anticipate 'the hope of righteousness.' Paul is conceding a very important point making a very important clarification. Christians claim to be righteous in Christ through faith (2:21; 3:6; 3:11, 3:21; cf. Rom. 3:21ff.). But they don't appear to be so. The accusation might be leveled that the Apostle Paul and his followers *claimed* to be righteous but, in fact, as experienced by all who came in contact with them, they were not. Whatever the claim, the *reality* was ongoing sin. One could observe pride among them. And selfishness. And bitterness. And jealousy, envy, covetousness, and lust. This might be thought to discredit the gospel message. You say that you have been made righteous by Christ, but we can see no evidence of it. So the Apostle says, 'we are waiting for the hope of righteousness.' We have not yet arrived. We live between the 'already' and the 'not yet.' We are righteous in Christ, but that righteousness is not yet completed, though it will be in eternity. 'The whole of the Christian life,' says Morris, 'is the present possession of blessings which will be realized in fuller measure in the life to come.'[125]

We will not be perfected in this life. We will always wrestle with sin. Neither will we be protected from all trial and temptation in this life. We will face tragedy. 'In the world you will have tribulation,' said Jesus (John 16:33). Our salvation does not shield us from sin or suffering. This comes as a great surprise to some people. Both some enemies and friends of the gospel expect Christians to be perfect and perfectly free of pain. The enemies of Christ cry, 'hypocrite,' when Christians sin. They roll their eyes and shake their heads and point their fingers, utterly disillusioned when the disciples of Christ fall. But why should they? No one ever said that Christians were sinless. Where do these perfectionist expectations come from? We concede the point—Christians sin. We will not be completed until eternity. We don't thereby excuse the sin or grow complacent about it. But we are *realists*. We are *already* righteous in Christ, but that righteousness is *not yet* completed.

But there are also the *friends* of the gospel who expect salvation to be complete in this world. Back when I was waiting on tables to work my way through college, a young dreamy-eyed couple announced to unsuspecting me that they would never be sick again. 'By His stripes we are healed,' they said. If Christians would just believe, they don't have to be sick. Even my spiritually immature self wondered at that point who would pick up the pieces when that fantasy came crashing down. 'Do you plan on dying some day?' I asked. 'Yes,' they said. Well? Don't you get it? Of course you sin, of course you'll die, and of course you'll get sick in the process. Those who comment on the ecclesiastical scene call this the 'health and wealth' gospel. Their error is that of expecting the life of heaven right now. We hope for that life. We anticipate that life. We confidently expect it. But like the Apostle Paul, we admit that we have not yet obtained it.

> Not that I have already obtained it, or have already become perfect, but I press on in order that I may lay hold of that for which also I was laid hold of by Christ Jesus. Brethren, I do not regard myself as having laid hold of it yet; but one thing I do: forgetting what lies behind and reaching forward to what lies ahead, I press on toward the goal for the prize of the upward call of God in Christ Jesus. (Phil. 3:12–14)

The fast track to total disillusionment is to expect perfection in this life, whether spiritually or physically. If we go there, we will be in a padded cell before we know it. In heaven we will be without sin, sickness, sorrow, or suffering. But not before. Now we grow in holiness and Christlikeness. But like the Apostle, we 'press on' until God takes us into His kingdom.

What does it take to make a Christian? How may a person be saved? We are saved only by the Holy Spirit, who leads us to Christ whom we receive by faith, and who enables us to patiently anticipate the completion of our redemption. How then are we to avoid the 'way to hell' that is present 'even from the gates of heaven'? By trusting in Christ, and Christ alone.

20

Faith Works

Galatians 5:6–10a

Having argued passionately from 2:16–5:5 that one is justified by faith in Christ alone, faith apart from works, apart from obedience to the Law, apart from personal merit, Paul now describes further the nature of the faith that justifies. Granted, we are not justified by works. Yet, is there a positive relation between faith and works? Yes there is. Faith produces works that are done in love. Faith always results in good works. Faith always leads to love, perseverance, and obedience.

Faith Works

> For in Christ Jesus neither circumcision nor uncircumcision means anything, but faith working through love. (Gal. 5:6)

The true Christian is described as being 'in Christ Jesus,' a phrase which 'emphasizes the importance of vital fellowship with the Savior,' says Morris.[126] The real Christian is one who 'does not merely stand 'for' him or 'by' him, but is really 'in' him, surrounded by him.'[127] For those who are such, neither being circumcised nor being uncircumcised amounts to anything. If one is 'in Christ Jesus' it doesn't matter if one is circumcised or not. It has no religious significance at all. He tells the Corinthians,

> Was any man called already circumcised? Let him not become uncircumcised. Has anyone been called in uncircumcision? Let him not be circumcised. (1 Cor. 7:18)

Circumcision had religious significance in the Old Testament. It was commanded by God and necessary for inclusion in the covenant community. It was a sacrament of the old covenant. God warned Abraham,

> But an uncircumcised male who is not circumcised in the flesh of his foreskin, that person shall be cut off from his people; he has broken My covenant. (Gen. 17:14)

Circumcision for them corresponds to baptism for us (Col. 2:11). It was necessary, but not meritorious. But in the New Testament, it is not even necessary. It is utterly devoid of religious significance. The same would be true today of uncommanded religious ceremonies. It is of no consequence if we keep religious 'holy days' or not. We cannot be required to observe Christmas or Easter or Lent or Advent. You may, but the church may not require it. Whether we do or not is of no religious significance. External, formal, ritual, ceremonial, physical ordinances of the old covenant, as well as those created by men and imposed on the church, have no inherent spiritual value at all.

What then does matter? The only thing that counts in relation to Christ is 'faith working through love,' or, as in the NIV, 'faith expressing itself through love.' Faith is 'active in love,' Fung renders it.[128] Other commentators render it as faith 'operating through love,' and manifesting itself 'by means of love.' In this way he sums up the proper balance of the Christian life. We are saved by faith, and only by faith, apart from works. We are forgiven, we are justified, we are acquitted by faith alone. But that faith results in change. When is this so? He has told us already. The same faith that justifies also receives the Spirit. We receive the Spirit not by 'the works of the Law,' but 'by hearing with faith' (3:1–6). We now have a new life which we live 'by faith.' 'Christ lives in me,' he says (2:20). Those who are justified are also adopted, and because they are now sons, God sends 'the Spirit of His Son into our hearts, crying, 'Abba! Father!' (4:6). This new life brings a change in conduct. The Spirit of Christ now lives in us. He transforms our hearts. We are new people in Christ. The old things pass away and all things become new (2 Cor. 5:21). Love is the fruit of the Spirit's presence in our lives. Thus, true faith results in good works. The change in our hearts wrought by the Spirit of Christ always results in a change in our behavior. We cannot live the same way anymore. We have new perspectives and new priorities in Christ Jesus. Thus true faith always works. It is not idle.

At this point we need to clarify. Roman Catholic commentators have argued on the basis of this verse that what the Apostle Paul really meant all along is that we are justified by the works of faith. Love, in this view, precedes both faith and works, generates them, on the basis of them one is (eventually) justified. Love perfects faith, and only perfected faith justifies. In other words they stand the whole letter to the Galatians on its head on the basis of this one verse. Through the works of faith, they say, we are justified. We would argue that this view is not possible after the argument of 2:16–5:13. The works of verse 6 are the *effects* of justification, not the *cause*. Moreover, it is not the best reading of even this verse. The Apostle Paul is addressing the nature of true faith, of justifying faith. The faith that justifies, he is saying, manifests itself to be genuine through works of love.

Faith Loves

Faith, in addition, always results in *active expressions of love*. People of true faith become loving people, people of love. 'That is to say the believer loves, not because he or she has found people worthy of being loved, but because she or he has become a loving person.' 'As Christians,' continues Morris, 'we love because of what we have become when we believe, not because of the attractiveness of the people we meet. Saving faith inevitably issues in love.'[129]

This then points to the central motive in the Christian life. The works of the Christian are not motivated by fear. We do good works out of love, love to God and love for others. Perhaps once we were motivated by the threats of the law. There may have been a time when its curses drove our behavior. But not any more. 'Our ambition,' as the Apostle Paul says, is 'to be pleasing to Him' (2 Cor. 5:9). We work as motivated by grateful love. We want to honor God. We want to serve Him. We want to glorify Him. Our motive is love for God. We also are motivated by love for others. We work not for divine approval, but because God has placed in our hearts genuine love for our neighbor. We care about that neighbor who is lost and needs Christ. We also care about that neighbor who is physically sick, impoverished, lonely, or grieving. Our faith works by means of, or as motivated by, love.

Are our lives characterized by love? A harsh, cruel, unloving Christian is a contradiction in terms. Do we love our spouses? Do we love the brethren? Do we love our enemies? Is this, the first of the fruit of the Spirit, evident in our lives? It will be if the love of God has been 'shed abroad' in our hearts through the Holy Spirit (Rom. 5:5).

Jesus taught us that the world would know that we were His disciples if we would love one another (John 13:35). It is a hard, tough, loveless world out there. People are hungry for genuine love. They are looking for real community where people care about one another. If we preach the truth but do not live it, we will have no credibility in the world. They will not believe us. Our faith must and will result in love if it is genuine. True faith loves.

Faith Runs

> You were running well; who hindered you from obeying the truth? (Gal. 5:7)

Faith is not passive. Its love is not merely a sentiment. 'You were running well,' he says. The Christian life is likened to a race here, as well as in 1 Corinthians 9:24–7 and 1 Timothy 2:5. In the former he asks us,

> Do you not know that those who run in a race all run, but only one receives the prize? Run in such a way that you may win. (1 Cor. 9:24)

We have a race to run. The Christian life is like athletic competition. We have opponents to overcome. We have goals to reach. We have enemies to defeat. We have to run and run hard. This means discipline. This means self-control. Paul writes,

> And everyone who competes in the games exercises self-control in all things. They then do it to receive a perishable wreath, but we an imperishable. (1 Cor. 9:25)

As is the case in so many things, the Christian life requires this finely balanced tension between grace and discipline. He's been telling them about nothing but grace for three chapters. Now he reminds them of the discipline required to live the Christian life. There is always the danger that one will take the disciplines and make a 'legalistic practice' out of them, a basis for self-righteousness and self-justification. We cannot deny, and must be vigilant regarding, the danger of bondage to forms and rituals. But the fear of that danger can't be allowed to silence our voice on the importance of discipline. This is why we urge such practices as twice Sunday public worship, observance of the Sabbath, daily family worship, and daily personal devotions. Is it hard to maintain these disciplines? Of course it is. It is like a race. One trains hard. One gets tired, even exhausted. But in the end, the disciplines bring great benefit to your soul. 'Discipline yourself for the sake of godliness,' the Apostle says elsewhere (1 Tim. 4:7). Of course one must not substitute the discipline for faith in Christ. One must not begin to trust in the disciplines or in one's self. We are at all times seeking Christ in our disciplines. Yet they do require commitment, sacrifice, self-control. They are not easy. There is much to overcome. This is the Apostle Paul's meaning as he writes. You were running. You were in the race. You were training hard, demonstrating discipline, showing self-control.

'Running' may even point to 'rapid progress,' says Morris.[130] Then someone threw up a barrier. 'Who hindered you?' he asks. There are obstacles to progress that we encounter in the Christian life. True faith leaps over the obstacles. It overcomes the barriers. The world is going to throw obstacles such as the *seductive alternative*, as in something better to do than go to church on Sunday. Go ahead and golf, the world will say. We may encounter the obstacle of *ridicule*. We may encounter the obstacle of *hostility*. We may be tempted to compromise certain articles of faith, as were the Galatians, in order to avoid such persecution. We may encounter the obstacle of *busyness* and *exhaustion*, such as crowds out personal and family devotions. Faith keeps running the race. Faith overcomes the hindrances. Faith fights the good fight (1 Tim. 1:18). Faith suffers hardship as a good soldier of Christ Jesus. It doesn't become entangled in the 'affairs of everyday life.' Faith competes like the athlete aiming for the prize. Faith labors like the 'hard working farmer' (2 Tim. 2:6). Faith runs. True faith is not slowed by hindrances.

Faith Obeys

Fourth, faith obeys. 'Who hindered you,' he asks, 'from obeying the truth?' Notice that he can speak of the basic Christian commitment, which up to this point has been called 'faith,' as 'obeying the truth.' Elsewhere he calls it 'the obedience of faith' (Rom. 1:5; cf. Rom. 15:18; 16:26). The writer to the Hebrews can speak of Christ saving 'all those who obey Him' (Heb. 5:9), Peter of God judging those 'who do not obey the gospel of God' (1 Pet. 5:17), and of God giving the Holy Spirit 'to those who obey Him' (Acts 5:32). Faith is in one sense obedience to the command of God to repent and submit to Christ (Acts 17:30).

Faith invariably results in obedience. Faith works. Paul teaches the same principle as James: faith without works is dead (2:14ff.). Real faith produces works. Obedience is the fruit of faith. Where there is true faith one will also find obedience. John Bunyan illustrates this beautifully in his literary and religious classic, *Pilgrim's Progress*. While on his pilgrimage 'Faithful' gets into a conversation with 'Talkative,' a hypocrite from whom the Christian faith is all talk. As Faithful is about to be deceived, Christian gets a hold of him and straightens him out, beautifully addressing the place of works in the Christian faith. Christian says,

> The soul of religion is the practical part: pure religion and undefiled, before God and the Father, is this, to visit the fatherless and widows in their affliction, and to keep himself unspotted from the world. This Talkative is not aware of; he thinks that hearing and saying will make a good Christian, and thus he deceiveth his own soul. Hearing is but as the sowing of the seed; talking is not sufficient to prove that fruit is indeed in the heart and life; and let us assure ourselves, that at the day of doom men shall be judged according to their fruits. It will not be said then, Did you believe? but, Were you doers, or talkers only? And accordingly shall they be judged. The end of the world is compared to our harvest; and you know men at harvest regard nothing but fruit. Not that anything can be accepted that is not of faith, but I speak this to shew you how insignificant the profession of Talkative will be at that day.

Faithful, then goes on to say to Talkative,

> Yea, if a man have all knowledge, he may yet be nothing, and so consequently be no child of God. When Christ said, Do you know all these things? And the disciples had answered, Yes; he addeth, Blessed are ye if ye do them. He doth not lay the blessing in the knowing of them, but in the doing of them. For there is a knowledge that is not attended with doing: He that knoweth his master's will, and doeth it not. A man may know like an angel, and yet be no Christian, therefore, your sign of it is not true. Indeed, to know is a thing that pleaseth talkers and boasters; but to do is that which pleaseth God. Not that the heart can be good without knowledge; for without that, the heart is naught. There is, therefore, knowledge and knowledge. Knowledge that resteth in the bare speculation of things; and knowledge that is accompanied with the grace of faith and love; which puts a man upon doing even the will of God from the heart: the first of these will serve the talker; but without the other the true Christian is not content. Give me understanding, and I shall keep thy law; yea, I shall observe it with my whole heart.

Real faith is more than talk. It results in love, discipline, and obedience. One could almost say that the whole book of 1 John teaches this theme (1:6, 8, 10; 2:3–6, 9, 15–17, 29; 3:4, 14–24,). 'How do we know if we have come to know God?' the Apostle John asks. Because we keep the commandments and love the brethren. So also did Jesus teach this when he warned of those who would say, 'Lord, Lord,' claiming great works in His name, and yet He would say in return,

> I never knew you; depart from me, you who practice lawlessness. (Matt. 7:23)

Who will enter heaven? The one who *does* the will of the Father (Matt. 7:21). Faith works. Faith produces love, discipline, and obedience. One is not justified because of love, discipline, and obedience, rather they are the fruit of justification. On two other occasions the Apostle Paul uses the formula 'neither is circumcision nor uncircumcision anything,' with different but instructive and ultimately harmonious answers. We'll list the three in succession.

> For in Christ Jesus neither circumcision nor uncircumcision means anything, but faith working through love. (Gal. 5:6)

> Circumcision is nothing, and uncircumcision is nothing, but what matters is the keeping of the commandments of God. (1 Cor. 7:19)

> For neither is circumcision anything, nor uncircumcision, but a new creation. (Gal. 6:15)

Being a 'new creation,' 'faith working through love,' and 'keeping the commandments of God' are three certain fruits of the Spirit's work in our lives. Because we are a 'new creation,' our faith works through love, and we keep the commandments of God. Ultimately they are compatible. Ultimately they are necessary. Ultimately they are inevitable.

21

Faith Believes

Galatians 5:8–12

Faith is essentially trust in a person, the Lord Jesus Christ, and confidence in what He accomplished on the cross in bearing our sins. True faith issues in works motivated by and giving expression to love as we saw last time. But true faith also involves the acceptance of certain doctrines, the denial of which damns the soul. Take the case of the Judaizers. They 'accepted Christ' we might say. They believed in Him and could claim, using current terminology, a 'personal relationship' with Him. If that were all that were necessary for salvation, they had experienced enough. They knew Christ. They had repented of their sins in His name. They believed that he was the Messiah. That they added works to Christ might be seen as regrettable, but not as fundamentally upsetting their 'relationship' with Christ. These are just points of doctrine about which theologians argue, one might say. The important thing is knowing and loving Christ. But this is not how the Apostles treated these errors. The content of your faith matters. Err respecting the person of Christ or the doctrine of justification, and you are lost! God cares about what we believe. We must persist in orthodox beliefs, despite the views of others, and despite persecution.

Despite Other Views

Faith believes the biblical and apostolic views over against other views. This is evident in verses 8–10a.

> This persuasion did not come from Him who calls you. (Gal. 5:8)

'This persuasion,' that is, the teaching of the Judaizers, did not come from Jesus who calls you to Himself. Implicitly, there is another 'persuasion' or teaching that does come from Christ, and must be believed. But these denials of justification by faith alone described in verses 2–5 are from another source. They do not originate with Christ. Not everything which claims to be Christian is. There are other doctrines from other sources, and their presence in the church is a dangerous thing.

> A little leaven leavens the whole lump of dough. (Gal. 5:9)

Leaven is a piece of fermented dough left over from a previous baking. When added to fresh dough, it quickly permeates the whole 'lump.' Paul is warning of the corrupting influence of the

Judaizing theology. He is 'warning that although the new teaching had apparently been accepted by only a very small number of people, unless it was vigorously repudiated, it would in time affect the whole church,' says Morris.[131] Thus not only are Christian views to be maintained, but other views are to be vigorously opposed. We'd like to be 'nice guys' and leave it to positively affirming our beliefs and remaining silent respecting others. But we can't. Error spreads like leaven. Error races around the world by the time truth gets its boots on, said Spurgeon. We are responsible to both 'exhort in sound doctrine and to refute those who contradict' (Titus 1:9).

> I have confidence in you in the Lord, that you will adopt no other view; but the one who is disturbing you shall bear his judgment, whoever he is. (Gal. 5:10)

'I' is emphatic. Whatever others may think, *I* am confident that you will reject the Judaizers and remain true to the gospel as I preached it, and 'adopt no other view.' But the one who teaches a false gospel, thereby 'disturbing' the faith of genuine believers, will 'bear his judgment,' whatever might be his reputation or status in the community, 'whoever he is.'

When we receive the gospel, we receive 'the truth' (v. 7), a 'persuasion,' and a 'view.' Any other so-called truth, persuasion, or view would be in error. The Apostle Paul can refer to the gospel as 'a form of teaching' to which one is committed (Rom. 6:17), as 'the words of *the* faith and of *the* sound doctrine which you have been following' (1 Tim. 4:4). As for other views he says,

> If anyone advocates a different doctrine, and does not agree with sound words, those of our Lord Jesus Christ, and with the doctrine conforming to godliness, he is conceited and understands nothing; but he has a morbid interest in controversial questions and disputes about words, out of which arise envy, strife, abusive language, and evil suspicions. (1 Tim. 6:3–4)

He goes on to speak of it as 'the standard of sound words' and 'the treasure' with which we have been entrusted and which we are to 'guard' (2 Tim. 1:13–14). Jude tells us to 'contend earnestly,' not just for Christ but 'for the faith which was once for all delivered to the saints' (Jude 3). Let me understate the case for a moment. Doctrine counts for something. Doctrine is important. God cares both about *who* we believe in and *what* we believe. He is concerned that we personally know Christ and that we know the doctrines *about* Christ. There is no room for flippancy about doctrine. There is not room for casual ignorance, or worse yet, casual error. What we believe matters. John warns of those who deny the true humanity of Christ:

> For many deceivers have gone out into the world, those who do not acknowledge Jesus Christ as coming in the flesh. This is the deceiver and the antichrist … Anyone who goes too far and does not abide in the teaching of Christ, does not have God; the one who abides in the teaching, he has both the Father and the Son. (2 John 7–9)

Remember he is describing the views of those who claimed to be Christian. Their views, he sums up, are wrong, to put it mildly. Those who hold to such teaching do not know God! The Apostle Paul has already warned that those who teach another, or 'different,' or 'contrary' gospel are 'accursed' (Gal. 1:7–9). We have the responsibility to both *proclaim* truth and *oppose* error.

There is a beautiful balance to the Christian life, isn't there? As we saw last time, we need to guard ourselves from certain polarized points of view. Many times the truth is 'both/and' rather than 'either/or.' We are justified by faith and not works. That equation is properly polarized. But as we saw, that faith which justifies produces works of love, discipline, and obedience. The Christian life, that is, the life of one who is already 'in Christ,' already justified by faith, is not one of faith or works, but faith and works. It is not love or law, but love and law. Likewise, our salvation involves a personal commitment to and relationship with Jesus Christ. But it also involves commitment to a body of truth, to biblical teaching regarding God, man, sin, Christ, salvation, the Christian life, the church, and the end. Don't be trapped into saying that I'm committed to Christ, not doctrine. It is not either/or but both/and. Neither let yourself say that I am committed to proclaiming the truth but not to opposing error. This is not an either/or, but a both/and. Christ calls us to trust in Him, but in doing so to believe certain things about Him and oppose the opposite.

Despite Persecution

Faith believes in the truth even when other views are forcefully presented. But second, it also believes even when persecuted.

> But I, brethren, if I still preach circumcision, why am I still persecuted? Then the stumbling block of the cross has been abolished. (Gal. 5:11)

Warmly he addresses them as 'brethren,' and asks to our surprise, 'If I still preach circumcision, why am I still persecuted?' When did the Apostle Paul, of all people, preach circumcision? Does this refer to his pre-Christian convictions? Probably not. It could refer to his circumcision of Timothy, which he accepted as necessary for the sake of conforming to Jewish tradition, but not as necessary for salvation (Acts 16:3). This may have led to the accusation that he preached circumcision. Whichever, he totally repudiates that he 'still' preaches 'circumcision.' If he did, he wouldn't be persecuted by the Judaizers. The 'stumbling block of the cross,' that is, that which causes offense or arouses opposition (*skandalon* from which we get our word 'scandal'), is the message of the cross, the message that we are saved only through the work that Christ did on the cross, apart from the works of the law. The identification of the salvation of the world with the Man hanging on that cross 2000 years ago is what offends. If he had preached the cross plus the law, for example, plus circumcision, then the offense would have been removed. He would have escaped persecution. But the gospel would have been 'abolished,' or nullified. The two ways of salvation are mutually exclusive. To add works to the cross is to destroy the gospel. To preach the gospel of grace is to exclude the possibility of works.

The cross has always been either a 'stumbling block' or 'scandal' to religious people, or 'foolishness' to the educated classes (1 Cor. 1:23). Religious people stumble, or are offended because of what it says about them. The cross is a constant reminder of failure, moral and religious failure. It reminds us that despite our efforts, despite our charm, despite our moral and religious good works, despite it all, God is not pleased. We do not measure up. We still needed a Savior. This is insulting to people. They like to believe about themselves that they're good people. They figure that since all their friends like them, God must too. After all, they're fine people. They're *nice* people. Why wouldn't God be pleased with them? They're not criminals. The gospel insults them. It lumps them together with the common herd and says '*All* have sinned and fall short of the glory of God' (Rom. 3:23). It says 'all we like sheep have gone astray' (Isa. 53:6). It says, 'There is none righteous, *no not one*' (Rom. 3:10). This is insulting.

At my wife Emily's father's funeral, the preacher said, 'Jim Billings was a sinner.' The family appreciated the comment. Though a godly man, Emily understood that her father was not a saint and should not be falsely portrayed as one. He was a sinner saved only by the grace of Christ. Others, however, failed to grasp the concept and took offense at what, for the family, was normal gospel language. The gospel humbles us. Add to the foregoing Jesus saying, 'No one comes to the Father but by Me' (John 14:6). Or this, 'No one can come to me unless the Father draws him' (John 6:44). Not only am I a sinner, but now you say that I am weak and cannot help myself. The proud man objects. But you don't understand, he says, I am a self-made man. I pulled myself up by my bootstraps. I've always achieved what I've set out to achieve. Now what are you saying? I can't please God? I can't make myself acceptable to God? I can't make myself right with God? This religion is demeaning. It is insulting. It hurts my self-image. It hurts my pride. I am offended!

Then there is another group, the Greeks, the philosophers, the intellectually proud, for which the gospel is foolishness. They hear stories of Noah and the flood, the parting of the Red Sea, Jonah and the 'whale,' creation itself for that matter, healing miracles, and above all the resurrection, and then scoff. These are myths, they say. These are fairy tales. Who could believe this stuff? For them the gospel lacks subtlety. It lacks the sophistication of philosophy. It is not intellectually credible for them. They mock believers as uneducated and ignorant. Christianity is 'unscientific.'

Against both kinds of skeptics, the religious and the 'intellectual,' the Christian stands fast. Though he may suffer ridicule, and sometimes more, sometimes physical suffering and even loss of life, he stands firm. Paul acknowledges that he could compromise and escape. In his case, if he preached circumcision and compromised grace, he would remove the offense. He would escape persecution. But he'd abolish the cross in process. The world always wants us to alter our messages to suit the idols of the day. During the 1920s many churches made the message more respectable by intellectualizing it, by toning down the sin and redemption themes, by quietly ignoring the miracles, and reducing Christianity to the Sermon on the Mount, that is, a system of ethics. Now in the twenty-first century Americans want the ethics removed. Liberals want social justice and a bit of mysticism. They definitely don't want personal sexual morals. Conservatives want a religion that is uplifting and encouraging, with excitement thrown in as well. This is why 'health and wealth' Pentecostalism is so popular today. It is religion for the twenty-first century. It makes me feel good about myself, and it can be exciting. Both, in my mind, are much worse than 1920s Liberalism, which at least had high ideals. This new religion makes me feel good about myself *just as I am*. What is this but removing the offense of the cross—the bloody, sin-soaked, wrath-seared cross of Christ. Without sin who needs a cross? Without guilt who needs a Savior? Remove it and you'll fit in the twenty-first century. No one will get offended. The message of sin, of the wrath of God against sin, of our need of a savior, of the universal claims of Christ, the call to repentance and discipleship, all will be silenced. All that will be left is a happy message about a God who accepts me just as I am and who is there to meet my needs. It's a great message! What fun!

But preach the gospel, and offense will be taken. We cannot avoid offending the world and still be a faithful church. The gospel offends! Where are those who are willing to be fools for Christ's sake (1 Cor. 4:10)? I don't mean just be fools. A few years ago a preacher in Savannah tried to attract visitors to his church by promising to sit on the roof if a given number in attendance were reached. It did and he did. Certainly he was being foolish. It's doubtful if it was for Christ's sake. Granted, we do need to make extraordinary efforts to love the world. The command to love our neighbor precedes the command to evangelize. We need to make sure that we are not the ones who offend, as Peter cautions (1 Pet. 4:15). But we don't have to be foolish or offensive, and the gospel *still* offends. Sometimes we are offensive, but we don't have to be to annoy the world. The pure, simple gospel offends all by itself. Get used to it. Someone said to me the other day at a civic club meeting, 'I haven't seen you in the papers lately.' I said, 'Yea, I guess we've gone soft.' We can't avoid notoriety for long though. One of the nearly fatal weaknesses of the Christian witness today is this unwillingness to offend. Christian people don't want to stand out. They don't want to be thought strange, or weird. They want to fit in at the club, or at the bowling alley, or at the ball field. The price that they have to pay is that of adopting mainstream views, ideas, priorities and perspectives. For heaven's sake, don't make waves! As a consequence, the gospel is emasculated. It is stripped of its distinctives and power. If you must deny 'Christ alone' to avoid offending those of other religions, and deny the Ten Commandments to avoid offending the adulterers and homosexuals, and must wink at drunkenness and divorce, and materialism, then what is left? Civil, generic, mayonnaise religion, that's all. The cross is a 'stumbling block.' The real gospel is an offense to the world.

Importance

Finally Paul writes,

> Would that those who are troubling you would even mutilate themselves. (Gal. 5:12)

The word rendered 'mutilate' in the NASV is translated 'emasculate' in the NIV, and literally means 'to castrate.' Zerwick renders the whole, noting that the particle 'would that' *(ophelon)* introduces a wish not likely to be realized. 'This was a dreadful thing to wish,' notes Morris, 'but then the teaching was a dreadful thing to inflict on young Christians.'[132] Castration was a form of service to the deity among pagan priests, and would have been known by the Galatians. The Apostle Paul is putting their insistence upon circumcision on the same level with that sort of despicable paganism which seeks acceptance with its god on the basis of self-mutilation.

How important is doctrine? It is important enough that Paul uses this extreme imagery to seek to silence them. Wake up, he is saying! Change your thinking! Repent! To say it again, what we believe matters. There is one truth. There is one way. We can't alter our views because the gods of relativism and pluralism are offended. We can and must shout out all the more.

22

Liberty or License?

Galatians 5:13–18

What happens when the free grace of God in Christ is proclaimed? I can think of two things. First, people get saved. The fact that there was a Galatian church is proof of that. Paul preached salvation through the cross of Christ Jesus and people believed and were united to Christ and His church. Preach Christ, and people come to Christ. Preach sin, and people repent. Preach faith, and people give up their works. Preach grace and people will experience in Christ freedom from bondage to sin and law, and enjoy the glorious liberty of the children of God. It happened then and it happens now.

But second, others will get confused. Some will become *critics*, and will hurl accusations at the gospel of free grace, primarily that it leads to license. The Apostles faced this and answered it repeatedly. For example, the Apostle Paul writes,

> And why not say (as we are slanderously reported and as some affirm that we say), 'Let us do evil that good may come?' Their condemnation is just. (Rom. 3:8).

And again,

> What shall we say then? Are we to continue in sin that grace might increase? (Rom. 6:1)

I can remember encountering this repeatedly when witnessing to those who were reared in religious homes. We would tell them that 'the free gift of God is eternal life in Christ Jesus our Lord' (Rom. 6:23). We would cite Ephesians 2:8–9 and argue that salvation is 'not according to works, lest any man should boast.' 'Are you saying salvation is a gift?' they would ask. 'Oh, yes,' we would answer. 'Are you saying that it is free?' 'Yes.' 'I don't have to do anything?' 'Not a thing.' 'Nothing?' 'Nothing.' Then they would almost always say, 'Then I guess a person could claim salvation and then go out and do whatever they wanted—murder, steal, lie,' and so on, they would say. Our doctrine, they would say, would lead inevitably to carnality! 'What motive would remain for obedience?' they would ask, sure that in the asking they had disproved the doctrine. That one might be motivated by love and gratitude rather than fear and self-interest seemed not to occur to them.

In addition to the critics, there are the *exploiters* of the doctrines of grace. The Apostle Paul answers the critics by saying, 'May it never be!' The thought is unthinkable. However, the exploiters imagine that they see the same loophole in grace that the critics see, and respond by saying, 'Oh boy.' They see the gospel as 'fire insurance,' promising salvation which allows them to do what they want. They sing,

> Free from the Law, O blessed condition;
> I can sin all I want and still have remission.

Free grace for them is cheap grace. They think that since salvation is free, and since one cannot lose it once it is truly possessed, then they can do whatever they want, and fully intend to do so. They relax about obedience. A little sin here and there is no big deal, they think. They're not uptight about holiness. After all, they can always just ask for forgiveness if they blow it!

However, it doesn't quite work that way. Scripture warns sharply against such an outlook. Jude writes of 'ungodly persons who turn the grace of our God into licentiousness and deny our only Master and Lord, Jesus Christ' (Jude 4). Peter warns us not to use our freedom 'as a covering for evil' (1 Pet. 2:16). Here, Paul writes,

> For you were called to freedom, brethren; only do not turn your freedom into an opportunity for the flesh… (Gal. 5:13a)

Grace is not cheap grace. Justification by faith is not easy believism. Christian liberty is not license. It is freedom *from* sin, not freedom *to* sin. It is not the right to do whatever I *please*, but the ability to do what I *ought*.

The Apostle returns to the theme of Galatians 5:1. 'You were called to freedom, brethren,' he says. When we were saved by Christ, when He called us to Himself, we were delivered from bondage to sin to the freedom of righteousness; from bondage to law and guilt to the freedom of grace and forgiveness. No longer are we imprisoned by an oppressive religious system (whether Jewish or Gentile) in which we slave away in a futile attempt to make ourselves right with God. In Christ our guilt is forgiven and the power of sin is broken. But the problem that arises is that some might misunderstand their newfound freedom, and use it as 'an opportunity for the flesh.' They might conclude that freedom means for them the right to do whatever they want, including the right to indulge the flesh in sinful activity. The word 'opportunity' is 'used in military contexts for a place from which an offensive is launched, a base of operations,' Stott points out.[133] Does grace provide for me a justification for carnality? Does it present me with theological reasons for indulging the flesh? Three reasons are given for why it does not: license is contrary to love, contrary to law, and contrary to the Spirit.

License and Love

> …only do not turn your freedom into an opportunity for the flesh, but through love serve one another. (Gal. 5:13b)

Christian liberty is to issue in loving service. 'Through love,' he says, 'serve one another.' The word 'serve' is the verbal form of the word 'slave.' We are not to be slaves of sin or law, but we are to be slaves of one another. Christian freedom is the freedom to serve. 'Temper your liberty with this bondage,' says Lightfoot, 'and it will not degenerate into license.'[134] We are 'freed-up,' as the current phrase is used, to serve. Christ has freed us from the bondage to self-interest and selfishness that is characteristic of the natural man. He pours His love into our hearts, enabling us to rise above our own interests and to see the interests of others. To use this freedom, this liberty from the bondage of pride and selfishness, to then indulge ourselves, and in the process either use or neglect others, is contrary to everything that Christ has done for us. True Christian liberty functions within the boundaries of love.

License and Law

License is also *contrary to the law.*

> For the whole Law is fulfilled in one word, in the statement, 'You shall love your neighbor as yourself.' (Gal. 5:14)

'The whole Law,' that is, the Law as a whole, and therefore the spirit and intent of the Law, is either 'fulfilled' (*peplerotai*) or 'summarized' by Leviticus 19:18, as Jesus taught (Matt. 22:39; Luke 10:25–8). It is fulfilled 'in one word,' 'in the observance of one maxim or precept,' says Lightfoot.[135] That one word is, 'You shall love your neighbor as yourself.' The Bible is both summarized (this is what it is all about) and fulfilled (this is what it requires of us) in one word—love. The whole Bible is about love. Ultimately, love and law are about the same thing. What is meant by love is elaborated by the two greatest commandments, to love God and love our neighbor. They are further elaborated by the Ten Commandments, the first table of which deals with love to God, and the second with love to my neighbor. The rest of the Bible may be seen as a further elaboration of the Ten. It is all about love. This, by the way, demonstrates that Paul ultimately sees a place for the law in the lives of Christians. While we are not justified by law, it does teach us how to love (Rom. 13:8–10).

What does the Bible mean when it commands us to love our neighbor *as ourself*? It does not teach us to love ourselves, nor especially that we must learn to love ourselves before we can learn to love others, as pop-psychology masquerading as biblical teaching would have us believe. Rather, this verse assumes that we already do love ourselves. This is true even if we don't like ourselves very much. In fact, it is even true of the person who commits suicide. Loving ourselves has nothing to do with feeling good about ourselves, and everything to do with serving ourselves. The Bible is urging us to show the same care and concern for others as we naturally do for ourselves. We feed ourselves, clothe ourselves, house ourselves, rest ourselves, bathe ourselves, entertain ourselves, and so on. There is a sense in which even those with what the gurus of psychology call 'low self-esteem' indulge themselves with pity. Similarly, what could be more self-centered than to take one's life, leaving the rest of the world to pick up the pieces? *The loving of oneself is not a command to follow but a problem to correct.* Paul warns of the difficult last days when men will be 'lovers of self' (2 Tim. 3:2). The aim of the command is to get selfish, self-serving, self-loving people to love and serve others to the same degree as they love themselves. The law and the gospel agree that this is an important element of God's will for His people. We were called by Christ to love one another, and we are called by the Law to love our neighbor. Who is my neighbor? Funny you should ask. Our neighbor, as the Parable of the Good Samaritan shows, is whoever crosses our path (Luke 10:30 ff.). We are commanded not so much to love our neighbor as be a neighbor, or behave in a neighborly manner towards whomever we encounter.

If, however, I interpret the doctrines of grace as providing 'an opportunity for the flesh,' it will lead inevitably to the destruction of the fellowship of the church. Why? Because I (and others) will be living life governed by selfish principles. In the thousands of choices that life presents, I will be giving preference to self at the expense of others. I will neglect them when they are in need. I will use them when I am in need. This is a formula for warfare in a community. This is why the Apostle Paul warns,

> But if you bite and devour one another, take care lest you be consumed by one another. (Gal. 5:15)

The verbs that he uses, 'bite,' 'devour,' 'consume,' all 'suggest wild animals engaged in deadly struggle,' says Burton.[136] You can love one another or destroy one another. Why not enjoy the liberty we have in Christ to escape the pitiful selfish nature with which all of us are born? Jesus has broken the power of sin. He has freed us from the poisoning, oppressive influence of pride and self. His grace can liberate us to enjoy a life of service of others. But if you abuse that liberty; if you make grace an excuse for continued self-indulgence, then you will return to bondage. For you, it will be back to the rat race of pride, self-gratification, lust and consuming self-interest. For the church, it will mean the destruction of its community. We will begin to look like Washington D.C., with competing interests tearing each other apart, each trying to get ahead of the other. *License is contrary to love!*

This, by the way, points out the basic problem in most church fights. There are divisions in congregations because of selfishness. This is what it all basically comes down to. I want power. I want my way. I want recognition. I want what I want and I am against anyone who opposes me. During the early years of my ministry I learned a valuable lesson. I found that most of the problems in the church were driven not by doctrinal division, not by ethical breeches, but by a 'will to power,' as the philosophers would put it. Even in this most doctrinal of letters dealing with doctrinal divisions, he warns them that if they indulge the flesh they will soon resemble wild animals tearing each other apart. The basic human desire is not for wealth or fame or self-gratification. It is for power. It is, to use another word, it is for *control*. Wealth and fame are a means to the end of power. I want my way! The solution? Love.

> Do nothing from selfishness or empty conceit, but with humility of mind let each of you regard one another as more important than himself; do not merely look out for your own personal interests, but also for the interests of others. (Phil. 2:3–4)

Isn't this what Jesus taught and showed us?

> Have this attitude in yourselves which was also in Christ Jesus, who, although He existed in the form of God, did not regard equality with God a thing to be grasped, but emptied Himself, taking the form of a bond-servant, and being made in the likeness of men. And being found in appearance as a man, He humbled Himself by becoming obedient to the point of death, even death on a cross. (Phil. 2:5–8)

The key to the harmony, peace, and unity of the church is love.

License and the Spirit

License is also contrary to the work and ways of the Spirit. It is not as though one must generate attitudes and acts of love from within oneself. They are only possible as we are under the influence of the Spirit.

> But I say, walk by the Spirit, and you will not carry out the desire of the flesh. (Gal. 5:16)

'Walk by the Spirit,' he says, 'and you will not carry out the desire,' or the 'lust' (*epithumia*) 'of the flesh.' 'Walk' is a Hebraism for 'conduct oneself' or 'live.' The Holy Spirit is given to all those who believe in Christ. The Spirit transforms the heart of the believer, renewing its desires and goals and ambitions, and empowering it for holy living. Live by the direction, control, and guidance of the Spirit, and you will not go anywhere near the 'lusts of the flesh.' These are opposites. The Spirit and the flesh (fallen sinful nature) are found in opposite directions. They are contrary to each other. They are incompatible. They cannot co-exist. The key to living a God-pleasing Christian life is walking by the Spirit. The only way that it is possible to obey God is to be under the control of and empowered by the Spirit. We cannot live the Christian life in our own strength. We are too weak and we inevitably will fail and fall. If I approach life with the attitude that I have within myself the ability to please God; if I am self-confident; if I am self-sufficient; I will fall. The key to victory over sin is dependence on the Spirit. He is our Helper. He is 'Spirit of Truth' who abides with us and is in us, who teaches us all things, and leads us into all truth (John 14:16–17, 25; 16:13). Godly character and conduct is the fruit of the Spirit's work in us (Gal. 5:22 ff.).

> For the flesh sets its desire against the Spirit, and the Spirit against the flesh; for these are in opposition to one another, so that you may not do the things that you please. (Gal. 5:17)

We have understated the case thus far. The flesh 'sets its desire,' or again 'lusts,' against the Spirit, and the Spirit against the flesh. They are 'in opposition.' They are at war with each other because they have opposite desires and longings. They are engaged in 'an interminable, deadly feud,' says Lightfoot.[137]

Why then can't you use Christian liberty as 'an opportunity for the flesh?' Because the flesh and the Spirit are opposites. Either the flesh will destroy the Spirit or the Spirit the flesh. Either the desires of the flesh will prevail, banishing as they do the desires of the Spirit, or the desires of the Spirit will prevail, banishing the desires of the flesh. Someone might think, well I just want to indulge my little pet sins. Or, I just have this one vice, just this one habit, just one lust. I know I shouldn't, but I'll ask for forgiveness. Can it be safely indulged? Can it be tolerated? No, not for a moment. It would be like an army allowing just a few enemy soldiers behind the lines to roam about at will. Can you allow just a little poison into your food? How about just one noose around your neck? Flesh and Spirit are incompatible. The one overwhelms and destroys the other. They are mortal enemies. Submit to the flesh and you will find yourself once again a slave of the flesh. You 'may not do the things that you please,' he tells them (Gal. 5:17). Remember what Jesus warned: 'Every one who commits sin is the slave of sin' (John 8:34). Peter warned, 'For by what a man is overcome, by this he is enslaved' (2 Pet. 2:19). Toy with sin and you may find yourself out of control. Paul can use strong language of his own struggle with sin. He says of the power of the flesh,

> For we know that the Law is spiritual; but I am of flesh, sold into bondage to sin. (Rom. 7:14)

He says of the consequences for him,

> For that which I am doing, I do not understand; for I am not practicing what I would like to do, but I am doing the very thing I hate. (Rom. 7:15)

Is this freedom? You who boast of your freedom to indulge the flesh by overdrinking, overeating, filling your mind with the smut and filth of pop music and media, do you think that this is freedom? Do you think that lust, materialism, gossip, and pride can be safely indulged? Beware! Is the drunk free? Is the smoker free? Is the adulterer free? Is the selfish consumer free? No, all these things become compulsive and lead to bondage and the destruction of the Christian life. Freedom for us means not walking wherever we wish, but walking according to the will and wishes of the Spirit.

Christians are more like trains on a track or cars on a road than like all-terrain vehicles. 'Freedom' for the train is found not in jumping off the track for a ride in the woods, but in following the will of the engineers. We know of men whose self-destruction began with indulging pornographic films. They were doing what they wanted! But they were feeding the flesh. Their lust then graduated to live strip shows, and then to prostitutes. Their lives are in ruins. They are slaves. We know of others whose downward spiral began with taking a few dollars from the cash register. But it developed into full-blown embezzlement, conviction, and imprisonment. For us to be free we must stay on the tracks. Our freedom is found in following the Spirit. Only then do we truly live. Only then do we find ourselves, and in so doing find true freedom. This is self-evidentially true, and yet we miss it. I am not free because I can do whatever I want.

Would I experience freedom if I were to train for the next five years to play professional baseball? No, it would be bondage. I can't play baseball at that level. The effort of trying to do so would be full of frustration. I was not made to perform athletically at that level. Surely you have found yourself at one time or another as a round peg trying to fit into a square hole. You may want to be a square peg with all your heart. But you're not. The attempt to be such is difficult and painful. Those who find themselves in such situations will sometimes speak of the freedom that they found when once they left that situation. They will speak of a great burden being lifted off of their shoulders. True freedom is found in doing the things we were designed to do. It is found in loving our neighbor, keeping the moral law of God, in walking by the Spirit, and by following the leading of the Spirit:

> But if you are led by the Spirit, you are not under the Law. (Gal. 5:18)

Walking and being led are practically synonymous, the difference, as Burton points out, is that 'walk' 'makes prominent the conformity of conduct to the guidance of the Spirit,' whereas 'led' (*agesthe*) 'emphasizes the voluntary subjection of the will to the Spirit.'[138] True freedom for the Christian is found in saying to the Spirit, 'I will learn whatever You teach, I will follow wherever you lead, I will obey whatever you command.' By the leading of the Spirit he has in mind not primarily whether to wear the blue socks or the black, but receiving the truth that the Spirit illuminates from God's word and submitting to it.

What then does the Apostle Paul mean when he says that those who are 'led by the Spirit' are 'not under the Law'? He is merely reminding them that by citing the law in verse 14 he is not reverting to legalism. *Nomos* in verse 18 refers to 'that legalistic system from which it is the apostle's aim to keep his readers free,' says Burton, and is not meant in its ethical sense as in verse 14.[139] They are not required to keep the law in any respect as a means of justification. Yet they are required to keep the ethical teaching of the Bible, whether this is denoted by exhortations to love, walk in the Spirit, be led by the Spirit, or obey the commandments. When it comes to living the Christian life and pleasing our heavenly Father, law and grace is not an either/or. As Paul asks and answers,

> Do we then nullify the Law through faith? May it never be! On the contrary, we establish the Law. (Rom. 3:31)

Walking in the Spirit leads to conformity with the Law. 'He condemned sin in the flesh,' says Paul,

> in order that the requirement of the Law might be fulfilled in us, who do not walk according to the flesh, but according to the Spirit. (Rom. 8:4)

This then is our freedom. We are free, but our liberty is not license. We are free from the law as a means of justification. But having been justified, we gladly return to the law in order to know the will of God for us. With the Psalmist we can say, 'Oh how I love Thy law! It is my meditation all the day.' His precepts are 'more desirable than gold, yes, than much fine gold; sweeter also than honey and the drippings of the honeycomb' (Pss. 119:97; 19:10). Our liberty is truly found when we submit to the commands of Scripture to love, and to submit to the will and direction of God's Holy Spirit.

23

The Deeds of the Flesh—1

Galatians 5:19–21

Is it bondage for chess players to play by the rules and within the confines of the chess board, or is it within that framework that the liberty to play is found? Is it bondage for basketball players to play by the rules and within the borders of the court, or do the rules and stripes prevent chaos and make play possible? Do roads and traffic laws restrict your movement or make movement possible? Do the scales and bars of music restrict artistic expression, or provide the framework within which musical expression takes place? In each of these cases, and in all of life, true freedom, freedom that avoids chaos and/or bondage, requires form. Freedom requires a restrictive framework within which it is exercised. Liberty can only be truly experienced in the context of discipline.

As we discuss our freedom in Christ, we do so today in a context in which 'freedom' is popularly understood as the right to do whatever I want. There have always been those who will abuse freedom, who in the name of liberty shed all restraints and indulge license. We see this daily in the political realm, where the purveyors of sleaze invoke the First Amendment to justify their trash (free 'speech'), pro-choicers to defend their murder ('A woman's right to choose'), and moral deviants to excuse their perverted lifestyles, as though pornography, abortion, and sodomy were what James Madison and the Founding Fathers had in mind. Freedom for many today means the right to do or be whatever they wish. The Bible and common sense both see this not as freedom but bondage. Those who kill the unborn become slaves of self interest and a guilty conscience. Those who cannot control their impulses and appetites become slaves of those impulses and appetites. The promiscuous experience the worst sort of bondage, are tormented by both guilt and their inability to restrain their passions. The drunk is not 'free' to drink whenever he wishes, but is a slave of his inability to stop. Those without self-control will not untypically destroy their marriages and families in order to feed their lusts and appetites. They may lose their jobs as well. Freedom as the world defines freedom is bondage.

When the Bible speaks of freedom it warns of the bondage that will result if liberty becomes license. Paul warns the Galatians not to turn their freedom into 'an opportunity for the flesh' (5:13). Because we are justified (or saved) by faith and not by works or law, it is possible to conclude that grace provides a license for sin.

True Christian freedom, Paul argues, may only be enjoyed within the framework provided by love, law, and the work of the Spirit. He argued (as we reorganize his argument):

1. Moral license is contrary to *the nature of true freedom*. True freedom is found not in doing whatever I *please*, but in what I *ought*. Human beings made in the image of God experience true freedom not when they do whatever they feel like doing, but when they live the life for which God designed them. License leads not to liberty but bondage; 'you may not do the things that you please' (5:7).
2. Moral license is contrary to *love*. Christ has called us not to indulge the flesh, and in so doing *use* some in pursuit of self-gratification, and *neglect* others who need my help, but 'through love serve one another' (5:13).
3. Moral license is contrary to *law*. The law commands us to 'love (our) neighbor as (ourselves)' (5:14).
4. Moral license is contrary to the *Spirit*. Spirit and flesh are incompatible. They are 'against' each other and 'in opposition' to one another (v. 17). We who have the Spirit are to 'walk in the Spirit,' and having such, we will be 'led by the Spirit' in paths utterly contrary to the flesh.

If one is still unpersuaded, Paul adds a final argument against moral license. If one is not persuaded by what he says about true freedom, love, law, and the Spirit, that the indulgence of the flesh is not an option for a Christian, then he issues one final and utterly persuasive argument. Those who indulge the desires of the flesh 'shall not inherit the Kingdom of God' (v. 21). They are excluded from the kingdom of God. Here is the flow of his argument:

> Now the deeds of the flesh are evident . . . (Gal. 5:19a)

The Apostle Paul speaks of the 'deeds of the flesh' which are 'evident,' or 'obvious' (NIV), and contrasts them with the 'fruit of the Spirit.' He provides concrete examples of the kinds of behavior that are characteristic of those who are 'in the flesh' and those who are 'in the Spirit.' 'Would you ascertain whether you are walking by the Spirit? Then apply the plain practical test,' says Lightfoot.[140] The difference between a Christian and a non-Christian is plain and evident for all to see. His list of fleshly behavior seems to divide into four classes of sin.

1. Sensual passions (3 words)
2. Religious sins (2 words)
3. Relational sins (8 words)
4. Drunkenness and its accompaniments (2 words)

He warns them solemnly, 'that those who practice such things shall not inherit the kingdom of God' (v. 21). Have you developed a kind of flippant attitude toward sin? Are you casually indulging the flesh and then claiming 'liberty,' or maybe easy forgiveness as a basis for doing so? Then beware. Let us examine the four categories of sins and his final warning.

Sensual Sins

> which are: immorality, impurity, sensuality. (Gal. 5:19)

The first category is that of sensual passions. He speaks of 'immorality' (*porneia*), from which we get our word pornography, it is a general term for sexual immorality, which includes most forms of sexual conduct outside of marriage. Elsewhere Paul tells us to 'flee' and 'abstain from' immorality (1 Cor. 6:18; 1 Thess. 4:3; cf. Eph. 5:3). The second word is 'impurity' or uncleanliness *(akatharsia),* a still more general term which according to Hendrickson 'includes not only uncleanliness in deeds, but also in words, thought, and desires of the heart.'[141] The third term *(aselges)* is translated 'sensuality,' 'licentiousness' (RSV), 'lewdness' (NKJV), and 'debauchery' (NIV), and defined by Morris as 'a disregarding of accepted rules.'[142] Whereas 'impurity' may be hidden and private, 'sensuality' is open, it 'shocks public decency,' says Lightfoot.[143] It is brazen, wanton and unrestrained. It involves 'an open and reckless contempt of propriety.'[144] It is, says Bruce, 'vice paraded with blatant impudence and insolence, without regard for self-respect, for the rights and feelings of others, or for public decency.'[145]

The early church encountered a world that was so utterly degraded, so corrupt and twisted, that even pagan authors were disgusted. Once heterosexual monogamous norms are abandoned, sensual sin never stops with fornication or adultery. It bursts those bounds and races into polygamy, paedophilia, homosexuality, bestiality, and all manner of deviancy. All of these were rampant in the ancient world. The church converted and sanctified the pagan world, and biblical norms were predominant in Christendom until the twentieth century. In the 1960s the preachers of 'free love' (there's 'freedom' again) arrived on the scene, sensual norms collapsed, and we are awash in perversion in the West as we have not been for a millennium. The Christian community now confronts a constant barrage of enticements to sensual sin from nearly every billboard as we drive down the street, every movie in the theaters, every show and commercial on the television. The barrage has resulted in many, many casualties. Christian young people have lost their virtue, Christian families have been shaken by teen pregnancies, illegitimacy, and abortion, and Christian marriages have been shattered by adultery and adulterous divorce. The Apostle Paul's warning is emphatic and unmistakable—'those who practice such things shall not inherit the Kingdom of God.' This is not a game. God has a purpose in sexual intimacy. He designed it. He created it. He created it to be pleasurable. But he created it to operate only within boundaries, the boundaries of the permanence and security of marriage. It is like a fire. What is more beautiful than a roaring fire in a fireplace? We enjoy its heat and light. Even its movement is aesthetically pleasing. But let a log roll out of the fireplace and into the middle of the living room, and it becomes a very destructive thing. In its place it is wonderful. Out of its place it destroys. Within the permanent, lifelong, loving marriage of one man and one woman, physical intimacy is wonderful. Outside of that God-ordained and God-designed environment it destroys.

Christian people should exercise utmost caution with respect to what they *wear, say*, and *view*. Does God care about what I wear? Yes he does. We are to 'adorn' ourselves with 'proper clothing, modestly and discretely' (1 Tim. 2:9). One should never dress in a way that is immodest or improper, in a way that is calculated to appeal to the opposite sex's sensual drives. One's manner of dress should underscore inner qualities, not external, should highlight 'the hidden person of the heart,' not the external shape and desirability of the body (1 Pet. 3:4). We cannot blindly embrace the latest fashion trends. We may often have to be 'out of style.'

Be careful with what you *say*. One should never indulge 'filthiness and silly talk, or coarse jesting, which are not fitting' (Eph. 5:4). Office talk, suggestive comments, cute off-color jokes are completely out of line. We are commanded to 'make no provision for the flesh in regard to its lusts' (Rom. 13:14). Be careful as well with what you *see*. Pay attention to both what you see and how you look. There are many seductive images that we cannot avoid. But we can train our eyes not to look. As Luther said, we cannot prevent the birds from flying overhead but we can prevent them from building a nest in our hair. We are to let our minds 'dwell' only on the things that are 'honorable ...right ...pure ... lovely ...of good repute' (Phil. 4:8). Stay away from what used to be called dirty movies and dirty television. In summary, 'flee immorality' (1 Cor. 6:18). 'Every other sin that a man commits is outside the body,' Paul warns. But this sin is unique. 'But the immoral man sins against his own body' (1 Cor. 6:18). A line may be drawn, and all the sins in the world may be placed on one side of the line. Sexual sin then may be placed by itself on the other side of the line. It is unique in its destructive effects. Do not toy with sensual sin. Do not flirt with immorality. 'Do not let immorality or impurity or greed even be named among you,' the Apostle tells the Ephesians (5:3). And his reason there as well as here:

> For this you know with certainty, that no immoral or impure person or covetous man, who is an idolater, has an inheritance in the kingdom of Christ and God. (Eph. 5:5)

Religious Sins

The second category is that of religious sins.

> ...idolatry, sorcery ...(Gal. 5:20a)

He mentions *eidololatria*, idolatry, and *pharmakeia*, from which we get our word pharmacy, translated 'sorcery.' The first term refers to the worship of visible representations of God, and is used by the Apostle Paul to denote all the religions of the world excepting Judaism (1 Thess. 1:9; Rom. 1:25), and can even indicate anything 'which usurps the rightful place of God,' says Fung (Col. 3:5).[146]

The second term originally referred to the medical use of drugs, later the abuse of drugs, and finally it came to mean witchcraft or sorcery. Both false religions and the occult, we note, are listed as manifestations of the flesh. False religions should not be seen as the highest thoughts of sincere but mistaken people, but as manifestations of rebellion against God. False religion finds its roots in the rejection of God's self-revelation in nature and the deliberate choosing of one's own wisdom over God's. Though God through nature has made his 'invisible attributes, His eternal power and divine nature' clear for all to see, man has 'suppressed the truth.' The Apostle writes,

> For even though they knew God, they did not honor him as God, or give thanks; but they became futile in their speculations, and their foolish heart was darkened. Professing to be wise, they became fools, and exchanged the glory of the incorruptible God for an image in the form of corruptible man and of birds and four-footed animals and crawling creatures. (Rom. 1:21–3)

He repeats himself again,

> For they exchanged the truth of God for a lie, and worshiped and served the creature rather than the Creator, who is blessed forever. Amen. (Rom. 1:25)

The 'flesh,' fallen human nature, will not submit to the true God. It fashions an idol to its own liking. Moreover it likes to dabble in the powers of the invisible world. It pursues the thrills of astrology, Ouija boards, séances, and other forms of the occult. Again, our culture is awash in this sort of thing. As it has been said, when people stop believing in God, they don't then believe in *nothing*, they rather believe in *anything*. Jim Jones, David Koresh, the 'Heaven's Gate' are just a few of the more recent, crazier manifestations of the 'flesh' in religious form. It is arguable that people have never been more interested in spiritual things than is evident right now. The so-called 'New Age' movement is an example of this. Mysticism is rampant. Biblical Orthodoxy, however, is in decline. Man is incurably religious. There has never been a shortage of religion. But little of it corresponds to the will of God. It is idolatry and witchcraft. It is created by man and feeds the ego of man.

The question that we must face is, are my beliefs those which God has taught me through his word? Remember the human heart is a 'factory of idols,' as Calvin put it. Have I settled upon or insisted upon beliefs solely because they appeal to me or make sense to me? This is the essence of idolatry. We ought only believe about God, man, Christ, salvation, the church, the end times, and so on, what God declares is true in his word.

Let me ask of Christian people, how do you come to have the opinions that you do? I can guarantee that if you are not consciously and deliberately submitting your mind to the teaching of Scripture, then you will be infected by the relativism, universalism, and sentimentalism of the world. If you are not being transformed by the renewing of your mind through the Word and Spirit, you are being conformed to the standards and convictions of this world (Rom. 12:1–2). Of course you'll drift toward universalism. Our age has no stomach for judgment and hell. It has no place for a God of wrath. Of course you'll drift toward relativism. The unforgivable sin today is that of saying that there are true and false religions, and right and wrong systems of ethics. Of course you'll want to 'accept' everybody and every opinion and every point of view. Of course you'll cringe when the preacher makes distinctions, and especially when he names names! When he says 'X' is right or 'Y' is wrong, oh do some people become uncomfortable! Why? Why, when no one would have been uncomfortable just 40 years ago? Because for so many the Christian faith has been reduced to sentimental, empty, contentless feelings. All that is left is pious posturing. The Christian faith has been reduced to thinking nice thoughts about other people, calling it 'love,' condemning anyone who thinks otherwise, all the while letting them go to hell. This is the flesh, not the work of the Spirit. Sure it can be wrapped up in very pious sounding language. It can even sound convincing. 'We need to love everyone,' they'll say. Of course we do, but does that mean we accept all points of view as equally plausible?

'Judge not, lest you be judged,' they quote, by which they mean, don't ever, ever imply that someone is wrong. That would be judgmental. Except that the same Jesus goes on in the same text to warn us not to cast our pearls before swine, which requires judgment about both pearls and swine (Matt. 7:1–6). We've seen the Apostle Paul anathematize the Judaizers in Galatians. This mushy sentimentalism is not biblical religion. It is not of the Spirit but of the flesh. Insofar as I fall back upon my own concepts, I refuse to submit to God and so manifest the flesh. Will I receive what God reveals of his wrath as well as his love? His law as well as Christian liberty? Repentance as well as forgiveness? Church discipline as well as fellowship? The whole truth? The whole counsel of God?

What then is Christian freedom? It is not the freedom to indulge whatever sensual pleasure I may want, or to indulge whatever exotic belief system I may want. I am not free to *do* what I want or *believe* what I want. That freedom would not be freedom at all, but bondage to sin and error. I only find true freedom as I express my sensual desires in the environment in which God approves in His Word. I only find true freedom as I believe about God and all matters religious and spiritual what he teaches in His Word. All other options are not freedom but flesh, not liberty but license, not reality but unreality, and bondage to error. Only as I follow His will with regard to sensual pleasure and religious beliefs and practices do I find the framework within which true freedom may be enjoyed.

24

The Deeds of the Flesh—2

Galatians 5:19–21

The gospel teaches that we are saved by faith in Jesus Christ and not by religious and moral works. Salvation is a gift that we cannot earn and cannot lose. Because this is so, some have concluded that Christians can do whatever they want without consequences. 'Since we are saved no matter what we do, then we can sin with impunity,' they think. Grace for them is a license for sin. Paul argues forcefully against this perversion of the gospel, citing examples of sinful conduct and warning that 'those who practice such things shall not inherit the Kingdom of God' (5:21).

We have looked at the first two categories of the 'deeds of the flesh,' sensual sins ('immorality, impurity, sensuality') and religious sins ('idolatry, sorcery'). We note that both wrong *actions* and wrong *beliefs* are manifestations of the flesh. We are not permitted to say, I have orthodox doctrines, and thereby excuse our immoral conduct. Neither are we permitted to boast of our moral purity and excuse doctrinal heterodoxy. God cares about both our moral conduct and our doctrinal convictions. The work of the Spirit results in both *moral* and *doctrinal* purity.

Relational Sins

The third category is that of relational sins. The same God who cares about our moral conduct and our doctrinal beliefs, cares about how we treat people. We cannot console ourselves with being as moral and orthodox as the Pharisees and then fail to love one another. Here also, indeed perhaps here *primarily,* the flesh is manifested.

> …enmities, strife, jealousy, outbursts of anger, disputes, dissensions, factions. (Gal. 5:20b)

He lists 'enmities,' or 'hostility' or 'hatred' (NIV), the opposite of love; 'strife' or 'discord' (NIV), that divides and disrupts the church; 'jealousy' (*zelos*), defined by Burton as 'the unfriendly feeling excited by another's, possession of a good.'[147] It is a 'self-centered zeal' says Fung, 'which resents the good which another enjoys but is denied to oneself …and may actively seek to harm the other person.'[148] The fourth term is *thumos*, 'outbursts of anger' or 'fits of rage' (NEB); the fifth is 'disputes' (*eritheiai*), defined by Burton as 'selfish devotion to one's own interest,'[149] rendered 'selfish-ambition' by the NIV.

Then he mentions 'dissensions' or 'divisions,' and *hairesees*, heresies or 'factions.' The first word indicates temporary divisions, the second, permanent. Together they indicate a 'state of affairs in which men are divided and feuds flourish,' says Boice.[150]

> ...envying, drunkenness, carousing, and things like these, of which I forewarn you just as I have forewarned you that those who practice such things shall not inherit the kingdom of God. (Gal. 5:21)

The final word in this category is 'envyings,' which goes beyond jealousy, according to Lightfoot, in wishing 'to deprive another of what he has.'[151] Remember these eight words describe the 'deeds of the flesh,' which exclude one from the kingdom of God. Where there is division, conflict, bitterness, and hatred, the flesh is present. We can perhaps look at these relational sins in two ways.

1. What kind of person do I tend to be? What tends to be the disposition of my own heart? Am I typically filled with hatred, bitterness, and anger? Is my instinctive response to anything new or unanticipated or contrary to my own wishes to gripe and complain? Do I have a critical spirit? Is my immediate reaction to virtually everything to criticize—if they say 'X,' I say it should have been 'Y.' If they say 'Y,' I say now it should be 'Z.' If they jump three feet, I say it should have been four? Are you one of those people for whom no matter what decision has been made, no matter how trivial or how monumental, it is always wrong, and you know what is right? This embittered, complaining, criticizing attitude is a manifestation of the flesh. Ironically this sort of person can often be popular. They typically employ heavy doses of humors and sarcasm as they cut and slash the enemy. In this way, they build themselves up as they tear others down. They are funny and fun to be with. But this attitude is no joke. It is a sign of an unconverted heart. Paul cites the example of Israel in its wilderness wanderings and warns the Corinthians,

> And do not be idolaters, as some of them were; as it is written, 'The people sat down to eat and drink, and stood up to play.' Nor let us act immorally, as some of them did, and twenty-three thousand fell in one day. Nor let us try the Lord, as some of them did, and were destroyed by the serpents. Nor grumble, as some of them did, and were destroyed by the destroyer. (1 Cor. 10:7–10)

He lists together the idolatrous and the immoral along with grumblers! He warns the Philippians,

> Do all things without grumbling or disputing.(2:14)

Add to these the problems those of 'jealousy' and 'envyings.' As a young minister I was shocked to find out how much conflict in the church could be traced to jealousy, or worse, envy. First there were those who just didn't like each other because of jealousy. They don't like her because she is rich or beautiful or thin or has a happy marriage or accomplished children. They don't like him because he's rich and powerful and influential. It sounds unbelievably petty and ridiculous, but there it was and there it remains. Worse yet, there was jealousy manifested in what one might call 'turf-consciousness.' There are folks who are more concerned with protecting and extending their personal, or their group's, power and control of the church than in the welfare of the church. Ask yourself, am I that sort of person? The Bible commands us to 'rejoice with those who rejoice' (Rom. 12:18). Are you able to rejoice with the success and happiness of others, or do you become envious, embittered against them, and angry with God? Does my heart burn with jealousy when that Christian brother or sister receives some good thing? When he gets that new house or job, or when he receives significant worldly recognition, or is given important churchly responsibility, do you seethe with envy, or rejoice with them? What kind of person am I? What is the condition of my heart? The embittered, criticizing, complaining, jealous, envying individual is a miserable person. But he doesn't have to be. Amazingly some people seem not to be happy unless they are miserable! What I mean is that they are not content unless they have something to be upset about. Their soul feeds on misery. They seem to have a psychological need to be inflamed about something, and so live in a constant and unending state of agitation. What is this but the flesh? Those who 'practice such things,' Paul warns, 'shall not inherit the kingdom of God.'

2. What kind of effect do I have on the church? He mentions 'strife,' 'disputes,' 'dissensions,' and 'factions.' Am I one around whom there is always swirling a controversy, relational or otherwise? Am I hard to get along with? Do others feel as though they must walk on eggshells around me? Must they carefully watch not just their words, but their tone of voice, body language, and so on, lest I misinterpret them? Is the fellowship of the church constantly being disrupted because I am *always* crossing swords with someone else? Do I then take it beyond the interpersonal and force others to take sides? This is the classic move by a divisive person. He can't stand to be alone in his conflicts, so he forces his issues upon others and insists they side with him. He poisons the views of others towards his adversaries. He gathers a group around him and his pet themes. He divides and disrupts the church. He assembles a faction, which together with him sits on the perimeter of the church and throws stones at the leadership, or a group within the church, or those doing the things which they oppose. There are people who are given to this kind of behavior. They are constantly disrupting the peace and unity of the church. This is the flesh, though ironically they will often clothe their flesh in high sounding language. They will seize the high moral ground, and claim to be defending truth or love or the church or the traditions of the church. Sometimes this is sincerely believed, but typically it is a smokescreen for ego and pride. They are like Diotrephes, 'who loves to be preeminent' (3 John 9), or like those who preached Christ 'from envy and strife,' 'out of selfish ambition' and 'in pretense' rather than 'in truth' (Phil. 1:15–18).

One of the great ironies of the ministry is that typically the most critical and divisive people are those who complain that we don't love each other enough. Pastors can sometimes look out over their happy and unified churches, see a wealth of acts of love and care going on within the congregation, care for the sick, care for the bereaved, care for those struggling financially, care for the elderly, care for college students, and so on. Then he can look over in the corner there and see a little group complaining that we don't love enough and are too judgmental! And for their part they do 'nothing for nobody!' They complain about the lack of love and do absolutely nothing to contribute to the life of the church!

The Scripture demands unity and peace in the church. The Apostle writes,

> Now I exhort you, brethren, by the name of our Lord Jesus Christ, that you all agree, and there be no divisions among you, but you be made complete in the same mind and in the same judgment. (1 Cor. 1:10)

He tells the Philippians that he wishes to hear that they are

> ...standing firm in one spirit, with one mind striving together for the faith of the gospel. (Phil. 1:27)

Again he tells them,

> make my joy complete by being of the same mind, maintaining the same love, united in spirit, intent on one purpose. (Phil. 2:2)

Jesus prayed fervently,

> that they may be one, just as We are one; I in them, and Thou in Me, that they may be perfected in unity, that the world may know that Thou didst send Me, and didst love them, even as Thou didst love Me. (John 17:22b–3)

Unity is essential. The Spirit brings unity to the church because He works love and peace in the hearts of believers. It is not an artificial unity. It is not unity wrought through coercion. The Spirit changes our hearts and gives us in common 'the mind of Christ' (1 Cor. 2:16). We all together come to see things from Christ's perspective. The 'wisdom' that is worldly manifests 'jealousy and selfish ambition' and results in 'disorder and every evil thing.' Wisdom from above however is 'first pure, then peaceable' (James 3:14–17). Paul urges the Ephesians to be diligent to preserve the 'unity of the Spirit in the bond of peace' (Eph. 4:3). On the other hand, Titus is instructed to,

> Reject a factious man after a first and second warning, knowing that such a man is perverted and is sinning, being self-condemned. (Titus 3:10–11)

Am I typically and habitually a disputing, dissenting, factious person? Do I regularly disrupt and divide the church? We are being warned that such a pattern indicates an unconverted heart. 'Those who practice such things,' he warns, 'shall not inherit the kingdom of God'.

These relational sins are not the fruit or products of the Spirit's work. They come from our fallen human nature, from the flesh, from a heart still dominated by sin. Love should be characteristic of me, not enmity; peace not strife; joy not jealousy; self-control, not outbursts of anger. Notice that whereas he lists only two or three sins in the other categories, in the relational he lists eight. If nothing else, it indicates the seriousness with which we ought to take these sins which poison relationships and disrupt the fellowship of the church. I certainly cannot hide behind my moral purity and doctrinal orthodoxy. I cannot be self-righteous and proud, as I fear many are, like little Pharisees, because I believe the right things and live an upright life, all the while my relationships are disastrous. I cannot say, 'I'm not like the liberals and the Arminians and the libertines; I believe in inerrancy; I believe in the 'Five Points of Calvinism;' I believe in the Ten Commandments;' and yet constantly hurt and hate people. I cannot boast like the Rich Young Ruler that 'I've never murdered;' 'I've never committed adultery;' 'I've never stolen;' and then consistently divide and disrupt the peace and unity of the church. I can't say 'two out of three aren't bad,' either. This isn't baseball.

Do I want to change? Some may be saying to themselves, 'I don't want to be the way that I am. I don't want to be bitter and divisive.' Good, but we can't change by ourselves. The Holy Spirit must change us. We are able to love only as Christ dwells in us (2:20), and we walk according to the Spirit, are led by the Spirit, and He bears His fruit in us (5:16, 18, 22). I cannot make myself good. But I can look to Christ, plead for help, and he promises to transform and empower me for godly, selfless living (2 Cor. 5:17).

25

The Deeds of the Flesh—3

Galatians 5:19–21

The 'flesh,' that is our fallen, anti-God human nature, is identified as manifesting itself in the three categories we have examined thus far. They are:

- Sensual sins: immorality, impurity, sensuality
- Religious sins: idolatry, sorcery
- Relational sins: enmities, strife, jealousy, outbursts of anger, disputes, dissensions, factions, envyings

Abuse of alcohol

The final category of sin is that related to the abuse of alcoholic beverages:

> ...drunkenness, carrousings...(5:21)

He mentions 'drunkenness', which we note is treated as a sin for which one is responsible just like all the rest, not a disease of which one is a victim (cf. Rom. 13:13; 1 Cor. 5:11; 6:10), and he mentions 'carousing' (cf. Rom. 13:13, 1 Pet. 4:3), also rendered 'reveling' (RSV) and 'orgies' (NEB and NIV). These two are associated because the one tends to lead to the other. Drunkenness is itself a sin. But it also leads to all manner of excess and abominations that might not otherwise have been contemplated. The Bible does not forbid the moderate consumption of alcoholic beverages. Indeed it commends them for health reasons, Paul urging Timothy,

> No longer drink water exclusively, but use a little wine for the sake of your stomach and your frequent ailments. (1 Tim. 5:23)

It also is commended as one of God's good gifts that He has given to be enjoyed. It 'makes the heart glad' (Ps. 104:15), and is used as a symbol of God's bounty (Prov. 3:10), even that which will be enjoyed in the Messianic Kingdom, 'when the mountains will drip with sweet wine'(Amos 9:13). After all, Jesus turned the water into 'good wine,' wine of the sort, we note in passing, whose alcohol deadens the taste buds thereby permitting a cheaper variety to be served later when the difference would be indiscernible (John 2:1–11). The argument that Jesus turned the water into grape juice is just plain silly. It was an alcoholic beverage.

But some have taken this freedom as a license to abuse alcohol and to indulge intoxication. This too is a manifestation of the flesh and is wrong. This spirit too is condemned and is characteristic only of those who 'shall not enter the kingdom of God.' Drunkenness is not cute. It is always wrong to surrender self-control to the controlling influence of alcohol. When it is done regularly or repeatedly, when it is done flippantly or casually, when it is thought to be cute or funny, or becomes the thing to do in order to have a 'good time,' it is wrong, it is the spirit of the world and of the flesh, and it receives the strongest condemnation. We are commanded not to even 'associate' with one who claims to be a Christian yet is immoral, or an idolater, or covetous, or a 'drunkard.' We're not even 'to eat with such a one' (1 Cor. 5:11). Drunks are lumped together with fornicators and thieves, among others, in 1 Corinthians 6:9–10. Drunkenness is listed with the sexual promiscuity, strife, and jealousy and other 'deeds of darkness' in Romans 13:13. 'Do not get drunk with wine,' he tells the Ephesians, 'for that is dissipation, but be filled with the Spirit' (Eph. 5:18).

The Christian's freedom to drink alcoholic beverages has been subject to considerable abuse in recent years. Alcohol consumption has risen significantly in the last several decades. Indeed per-capita consumption did not reach the pre-Prohibition levels until the 1970s. Attitudes toward drink have correspondingly softened, and even Christians are less careful. People who ought to know better have consumed alcohol to excess, come 'under the influence,' and behaved foolishly. This is being done with alarming frequency, and with an alarmingly casual attitude, as though it were no big deal. The Apostle Paul says that 'those who practice such things shall not inherit the kingdom of God.' If I became intoxicated even one time I believe that I would allow at least five years to pass before I'd touch another drop, if ever again. I believe that this kind of severity is warranted whether one is talking about a problem with drinking too much at home alone, or drinking too much socially, with friends, at parties or in restaurants. We must be above reproach in this. We live in a culture where abuse of alcohol is rampant and destructive. How many jobs have been lost because of the excess consumption of alcohol? How many children have been abused because of drunkenness? How many marriages have been destroyed because of alcoholism? How many people have been killed on the road and elsewhere because of intoxicated drivers? More human misery is caused each year because of alcoholic beverages than perhaps from any other single external cause. We are not commanded to abstain, but we are commanded to be moderate. In our moderation we are strongly warned. 'Wine is a mocker, strong drink a brawler, and whoever is intoxicated by it is not wise' (Prov. 20:1). Heavy drinking leads to poverty (Prov. 23:20–1), it impairs judgment (Prov. 31:4–7, Isa. 28:7–8) leads to relational conflict, physical harm, hallucination, habitual drinking and all manner of trouble. Do not underestimate these problems. Listen to this pathetic description.

> Who has woe? Who has sorrow? Who has had contentions? Who has complaining? Who has wounds without cause? Who has redness of eyes? Those who linger long over wine, those who go to taste mixed wine. Do not look on the wine when it is red, when it sparkles in the cup, when it goes down smoothly; at the last it bites like a serpent, and stings like a viper. Your eyes will see strange things, and your mind will utter perverse things. And you will be like one who lies down in the middle of the sea, or like one who lies down on the top of a mast. 'They struck me, but I did not become ill; they beat me, but I did not know it. When shall I awake? I will seek another drink.' (Prov. 23:29–35)

If we can't be moderate, then we must abstain totally. Are you struggling in this area? By the Spirit of Christ you can and will gain victory over it. Indeed, you must. Those who have the Spirit do not 'practice drunkenness.'

> ...and things like these ...(v. 21)

Is anyone breathing a sigh of relief? Don't. Lest you think that none of your sins have been named and you've escaped the censure of the apostle, he goes on to add, 'and things like these.' This is not an exhaustive list but merely suggestive. There are many similar sins of the flesh that he might have listed. For example, he might have added unrighteousness, wickedness, greed, deceit, malice, and gossip; or noted those who are slanderers, haters of God, insolent, arrogant, boastful, inventors of evil, disobedient to parents, without understanding, untrustworthy, unloving, and unmerciful, as he does in Romans 1:29–32 (see also Rom. 13:13; 1 Cor. 5:10 f.; 6:9 f.; 2 Cor. 12:20 ff.; Eph. 4:25–31; 5:3 ff.; Col. 3:5; 1 Tim. 1:9 ff.; 2 Tim. 3:2–5). His meaning is that any habitual practice of sin, and sinful practice that is typical or characteristic, is inconsistent with the work of the Spirit and excludes one from the Kingdom of God.

The Warning

> ...of which I forewarn you just as I have forewarned you that those who practice such things shall not inherit the kingdom of God. (Gal. 5:21b)

Paul reminds them that he has already warned them of the seriousness of these matters, even as he is warning them again. 'I forewarn you just as I have forewarned you.' We've been over this before, he is saying. What is the warning? That 'those who *practice* such things shall not inherit the kingdom of God.' The kingdom that he has in view is the eschatological kingdom. By 'inherit the kingdom of God' he means 'go to heaven.' Those who shall not go to heaven are those who 'practice' these and similar sins, the present tense according to Boice, indicating 'a habitual continuation in fleshly sins rather than an isolated lapse.' The Apostle's point then is not, says Boice, 'that if a Christian falls into sin through getting drunk, or some such thing, he thereby loses his salvation,' but 'that those who continually practice such sins give evidence of having never received God's Spirit.'[152] The additional thought may be that those who never submit to God's rule (i.e., kingdom) in this world will have no part in God's kingdom and rule in the future world. The question is not, 'Do I sin or not?' All Christians sin. In fact, 'if we say we have no sin' we are deceived (1 John 1:8–9). We all sin, we all fall, we all fail. The question being raised is, what is characteristic? What is typical? What is habitual? Further, what is my outlook on my lapses? If any of these sins are characteristic or typical of us, and if, especially, I am unconcerned or flippant about it, claiming Christian freedom or easy grace, then something is seriously amiss. Is immorality characteristic? Is idolatry? Is jealousy? Is dissension? Is carousing? If so, it is unlikely that the Spirit is present in your life or that you have submitted to God's rule. This is consistently the Bible's point of view. As we've already seen Paul says the same thing to the Corinthians. He asks them,

> Or do you not know that the unrighteous shall not inherit the kingdom of God? (1 Cor. 6:9a)

'Do not be deceived,' he warns them. He then lists a similar group of sins and warns again that they 'shall not inherit the kingdom of God' (1 Cor. 6:10). John writes in much the same way throughout his first epistle.

> And by this we know that we have come to know him, if we keep his commandments. The one who says 'I have come to know him,' and does not keep his commandments, is a liar, and the truth is not in him. (1 John 2:3–4)

The present tenses carry the same meaning for John as for Paul. What is characteristic of your behavior? Do you typically (though imperfectly) 'keep his commandments'? Or do you typically fail to keep them? Wherever the Spirit is present, conformity to the will of God will be the result for in all areas of life, whether we speak of moral, religious, or relational terms.

Realizing these things, how could we ever consciously indulge in sin? How could we ever take sin lightly? How could we ever relax our zeal for holiness? Whenever the love of God and Spirit of God are present in a person's heart, he will be led away from these sins and into conformity with the will of God. This is true, as we have seen, on a broad front, not just a narrow area or two, but in all of life. We will not practice immorality, but will practice moral purity, in what we wear, what we say, what we view and read, and what we do. We will not practice idolatry, but will submit to and believe all that is in God's Word, respecting God's being, His works, and His worship. We will not spread enmity and strife in the church, but will be unifying influences, peacemakers. Finally, we will practice moderation with alcoholic beverages and with respect to all things. These are the effects of the work of the Spirit of God. He banishes not one or two of these sins, but all of them. We cannot say, 'I'm doing pretty well in the religious and relational areas but failing in the moral area.' One cannot settle for three out of four. The Spirit's work is holistic, working all these things at the same time. Yes we may struggle more in one area than another. Nevertheless, transformation must take place in all areas and will, so that it cannot be said of us that we 'practice such things.'

'But aren't we justified by faith and not by works? This sounds like works!' one may object. No, the good works in mind here are not those which justify, but those which give *evidence* of justification. The question here is not what one must do in order to be saved, but rather how behavior is affected by salvation. Inevitably and invariably the Spirit puts an end to the deeds of the flesh and produces the fruit of the Spirit. Those who use grace to excuse license are self-deceived. They are unconverted. This is his point. He is attempting to awaken them from their tragic complacency and unwarranted presumption. I have talked to people who are living lives utterly contrary to the word of God, and yet believe they are Christians because they walked an aisle or prayed a prayer. If you are such, the Scripture seeks to wake you up. You are not a Christian! Wake-up! You are fooling yourself. You show no evidence of a new heart. You show no evidence that Christ is in you (Gal. 2:20; 3:23). Whatever you experienced in the past was a counterfeit of the real thing. Wake up so that you might truly be saved, experience true transformation, true freedom, and be delivered from the damning 'deeds of the flesh.'

You might have noticed that throughout our study of this list we've not said much about how you can improve in any area of weakness. We've not said, 'If you habitually are guilty of ____ (fill in the blank with immorality, jealousy, divisiveness, drunkenness, etc) here is what you can do, first 'a,' then 'b,' and finally 'c.' The reason is, to do so would be to imply that you can improve merely by following rules and procedures. This is not the point. We *can't* improve by merely enrolling in a new program. The problem is more fundamental than that. Years ago I found myself dealing with a person who was chronically causing dissension in the church. I had hopes that if he learned better interpersonal skills he'd improve. At one point I finally figured out that he would not change. I found myself with a powerful urge to tell him *not* 'here are the how-to's to better relationships,' but 'you must be born again!' This I believe is the point. Those who are indwelt by the Spirit of Christ (2:20; 4:6), who 'walk by the Spirit' and are 'led by the Spirit' (5:16, 18) do not practice these things. They do not flirt with immorality or impurity or sensuality, they flee from them. Their thinking is not conformed to this world's. They aren't jealous or envious of other's blessings, but rejoice with those who rejoice. They do not disrupt and divide the church. They are peacemakers. They do not indulge alcoholic beverages to excess, but are careful to remain within the bounds of moderation. They have a zeal for God's kingdom that is evident in their hatred for all forms of sin, (sensual, religious, relational, and social), and in their love of righteousness. When this Spirit-wrought outlook and attitude is not present, the obvious conclusion to draw is that the Spirit is not present. The solution is not 'Ten steps to a new you,' but 'you must be born again.' The solution is not more effort on your part, but supernatural transformation by the Spirit of Christ.

Have you been born again? Has your 'old self' been crucified with Christ, your 'body of sin' done away, so that you are 'no longer a slave of sin' (Rom. 6:6)? Do you 'belong to Christ,' and so have 'crucified the flesh with its passions and desires' (Gal. 5:24)? Are you a 'new creature' in Christ? Have the 'old things,' the old lusts, the old opinions, the old sour disposition, the old dependence upon drink, the old party spirit 'passed away?' Have 'new things' come to take their place (2 Cor. 5:17)? Are you a new person? Do you have a new outlook on life? A new purpose for living? A new desire for holiness? A new ambition to please God? A new hunger and thirst for righteousness? A new disdain for the world and its ways? If not, do not settle for less. This is what the Holy Spirit always does in the hearts of God's people. If the Spirit hasn't done this in you, don't make excuses. Don't rationalize continuing carnality. Don't explain abiding worldliness. Instead, cry out for help. Plead for grace. Call upon the Lord Christ. Confess your sin and your sins, your evil heart and your evil deeds, your fallen nature and your actual transgressions. Beg God to forgive you in Christ and transform your heart, that you might no longer be characterized by the deeds of the flesh, but by the fruit of the Spirit.

26

The Fruit of the Spirit

Galatians 5:22–23

The gospel is essentially about two things: the forgiveness of sins and changed lives. Through faith in Christ I am justified, all my sins are forgiven, I am reconciled to God, and receive the gift of eternal life. But it doesn't stop there. In Christ I am a new person. A Christian is one who has been crucified with Christ. He no longer lives, but Christ lives in him. He no longer lives in the old ways reflecting the old values and old motivations. He has been transformed. The life he now lives he lives by faith in the Son of God. He has received the Spirit into his heart, and walks by the Spirit, and is led by the Spirit (2:20; 3:2; 4:6; 5:16, 18). It is impossible for him to 'practice' the 'deeds of the flesh' (5:19–21). He can fall into sin on occasion. He can stumble periodically. He is not sinless. In fact, the conviction that he still sins is one of the signs that he is a genuine Christian (1 John 1:8–9). But he cannot and will not habitually, or characteristically indulge the flesh.

Now we will see more clearly why this is so. The Spirit who is in the Christian's heart, by whom he walks, and by whom he is led, inevitably produces His 'fruit' in the Christian's life. Just as it is impossible for the Christian to carry out the deeds of the flesh, so it is impossible for the Spirit not to manifest His fruit in a true believer. Paul used three verses to describe what a Christian *cannot* be (5:19–21). Now he'll take two verses to describe what a Christian *cannot but* be.

These verses are full of encouragement for us. The Apostle of Christ is telling us what the Spirit invariably does in the lives of Christians. He utterly transforms us. He takes selfish, self-centered, prideful, lustful, critical, miserable people, and puts love, joy, and peace in our hearts, patience, kindness, goodness, into our relationships, and faithfulness, gentleness, and self-control into our backbone that is, our wills. Do you wish to be a new person? Christ can change us! Are you tired of looking back at the end of the day at a day filled with harsh, mean, selfish behavior? Do you know that your heart must be changed? Then look to the Spirit of Christ, who not only can, but will bear His fruit in us. First we'll look at the fruit itself, then at each fruit individually.

The Fruit in General

> But the fruit of the Spirit is… (v. 22)

We notice first that he speaks of *'the fruit of the Spirit,'* not *'the deeds of the Spirit,'* as we might otherwise have expected. Rather than contrasting the 'deeds' of the 'flesh' with the 'deeds' of the 'Spirit,' he instead changes the term. He speaks of 'fruit' rather than 'deeds.' Why? Probably because 'deeds' would have created the wrong impression. Deeds, or 'works' (*erga* in both cases), is an altogether negative term in this epistle, representing autonomous, meritorious human exertions, the 'works of the law' (eg 2:16; 3:2, 5, 10; cf. 5:19). Some might have been misled into thinking that these are the 'deeds' that the Spirit enables believers to do. While there is an element of truth in that, he wishes to place the emphasis elsewhere. His emphasis is on the Spirit's sole agency in transforming the believer. These are the Spirit's fruit. He produces them. He grows them. Like fruit, they develop naturally as a result of the Spirit's presence in the heart of a believer. They are 'the organic, spontaneous product of the Spirit,' says Hendriksen,[153] the 'natural product of a vital relation between the Christian and the Spirit,' says Burton.[154] Thus the contrast is heightened. 'Deeds' stimulates images of strain and effort, of the wasting, exhausting effects of sin. 'Fruit,' however, grows naturally over time. One thinks of the process of growth, maturation, and completeness. A tree doesn't struggle to produce fruit. The natural effect of the Spirit's presence is godly character. He sanctifies, He cleanses, He purifies, He illuminates, He gives wisdom, He gives insight. Godliness cannot but follow as one grows and matures in Christ. Christian character is the inevitable and invariable effect of the Spirit's presence in a believer's life.

Second, he speaks of the *'fruit' (singular)* not *'fruits' (plural)*. This, too, is intentional, and is freighted with meaning.

1. It means that *the fruit is singular; it cannot be divided*. They are 'different facets of the same jewel,' says Fung,[155] a 'cluster' says Morris.[156] They are either all present and developing, or they are not present at all. Of course some counterfeits may be present, and that may lead to self-deception. One might be by natural disposition a kind or patient person. But if you have no self-control, then it is unlikely that the Spirit is present in your life. The Spirit is growing the fruit, all together, all at once. Consequently I cannot content myself with doing well (as I might perceive it) in seven or eight out of nine categories. I can't say, 'I'm doing quite well at being kind and good, but failing at self-control.' No, the fruit rise and fall together. Though this may not be immediately obvious, a moment's reflection, I think, will reveal its truth.

Say, for example, one has eight of nine, but the one missing is love. Can one truly say that any of the others are truly present if love is not? To cite an obvious example, can I be kind and not have love? Can I be good? Can I be gentle? Can I have all the fruit except self-control? How long will I be patient if I don't have self-control? or have peace? or be faithful? The fruit is integrated one with the other. We can separate them in order to talk about them, but in life, in people, they cannot be divided. They are all of a piece.

2. Similarly, it means that *all the fruit is present in all believers*. Unlike the 'gifts' (*charismata)* or 'manifestation' (*phanerosis)* of the Spirit, which are present in some believers and not in others (1 Cor. 12:4–11), the fruit is present in all. The singular indicates that Paul 'is referring to a cluster, such that *all* these qualities are to be manifested in *each* believer,' says Morris (my emphasis).[157] The lack of overlap with 1 Corinthians 12 is noteworthy. Paul wishes that we measure the presence of the Spirit in a person's life not by the external gifts, not by miracles, gifts of healing, prophesy, tongues, interpretation of tongues listed there, but by character. Paul includes in this passage 'ethical

qualities and spiritual experiences which are not popularly thought of as evidences of the Spirit's presence,' says Burton.[158] What are the signs of the Spirit's presence in a person's life? Is it an ability to talk about spiritual things? Some can talk long and eloquently about spiritual things. Like Talkative in *Pilgrim's Progress*, they can discuss all the fine points of Christian experience and doctrine. But that is not the test. Even if 'I speak with the tongues of men and of angels,' it's not the test (1 Cor. 13:1). What about a bold, public profession of Christ, such as makes known one's Christian commitments to all of the community? No, many shall say, 'Lord, Lord,' who professed Christ, but never knew Him. Some may even be martyred, delivering their bodies to be burned, and yet not be genuine (1 Cor. 13:3). Some may even be like the Pharisees who 'travel about on sea and land to make one convert' and yet are hypocrites (Matt. 23:15). What about the working of miracles? works of wonder? spectacular signs? No. As Jesus said,

> Many will say to Me on that day, 'Lord, Lord, did we not prophesy in Your name, and in Your name cast out demons, and in Your name perform many miracles?' And then I will declare to them, 'I never knew you; depart from Me, you who practice lawlessness.' (Matt. 7:22–3)

Finally, the test of the Holy Spirit's presence in a person's life is not what you *say* or what you *know* or even what you can *do*. I can give all my possessions to feed the poor and still be nothing (1 Cor. 13:3). I can be like Judas, who complained that the expensive ointment used to anoint Jesus for burial should have been sold and the money given to the poor, 'not because he was concerned about the poor, but because he was a thief' (John 12:5–6). The test is not doctrinal purity, not evangelistic zeal, not miraculous faculties, and not social compassion. All of these can be counterfeited. Finally, the test of the Spirit's presence is what you *are*. In the end the test is *character*. Ultimately what counts is godliness. The sign of the Spirit's presence in a person's life is the fruit of His presence, the character qualities of verses 22, 23. Wherever the Spirit goes there results transformation of character.

Organization

What about the organization of this list of fruit? It is difficult to categorize the fruit, and even to separate them. As we have seen, they are the fruit, not the fruit*s*. Because they are one they overlap considerably. Even so, perhaps we can discern the following outline.

1. love, joy and peace - the Spirit's transformation of our disposition
2. patience, kindness, goodness - the Spirit's transformation of our conduct
3. gentleness, faithfulness, self-control - the Spirit's transformation of our character

The first triad has to do with the *disposition of my heart*. The Spirit brings love, joy, and peace to me. The three middle fruit have especially to do with my *attitude and conduct toward others*. I treat others with patience, kindness, and goodness. The last three have to do with *character*. The Spirit makes me meek, faithful, and enables me to exercise self-control.

Finally, a word about the distinction between the Beatitudes and the fruit of the Spirit (Matt. 5:3 ff.). The two passages are similar in that they both record lists of virtues. But aside from 'meekness,' they do not overlap. It seems to me that they are focused on different categories of virtues. The difference, I would argue, is this.

The Beatitudes deal with those virtues which God esteems and blesses, but the world hates. The world despises poverty of spirit, mourning for sin, meekness, purity, peacemaking, and so on. On the other hand, the fruit of the Spirit are virtues, similarly esteemed and blessed by God, but which the worlds seeks but counterfeits. The world wants love, joy, peace, and so on, but won't go to God to get them. Instead, it offers the same through seductive counterfeits.

Let us conclude our introduction by recognizing that this is a tremendously encouraging passage. Perhaps I am one who in my more reflective, thoughtful moments realizes my defects, and bitterly laments them. I am like the publican who dared not lift his eyes to heaven. I know my selfishness. I know my pride. I know my tongue is out of control. I know of my betrayals. I look back over years of hurting people, of crushing whoever dared to get into my way. I look in the mirror and I don't like what I see. Here is what the gospel has to say to us. First it offers us forgiveness. If we will confess our sins and surrender to Christ as Savior and Lord, we will be saved. This is the primary thing. Our guilt must be taken away. In Christ Jesus the full and complete forgiveness of our sins is offered, no matter what might be the degree of your guilt. The murderer can be forgiven. The adulterer can be forgiven. The thief, the liar, the wife-beater, the child-abuser—all—whosoever—the chief of sinners, even the foremost of all. The gospel says to Rahab the harlot, 'You are forgiven.' The gospel says to Ruth the idolater, you are forgiven. It says to David the adulterer, David the murderer, David the deceiver, you are forgiven. It says to the woman caught in adultery, Peter the denier of Christ, the thief on the cross, Paul the blasphemer and persecutor of the church, you are forgiven. This is the 'good news.' 'Whoever shall call upon the name of the Lord shall be saved' (Rom. 10:13). And whoever means whoever. I don't know what you have done? It doesn't matter. Whatever you have done, forgiveness is offered to you if you will but repent and turn to God in Christ.

But beyond this the gospel offers us a new life. The old you becomes a thing of the past. This is what it means to be 'born of the Spirit,' or to be 'born again' (John 3:1ff.). Great as the forgiveness of sins is the gospel does not stop there. It promises transformation. When we truly understand the gospel we'll come to realize what greedy, lecherous, selfish, perverse people we are. We will realize that we are far worse than we ever imagined. But it does not leave us there. It forgives our sins and promises to change us. It takes out the hate and replaces it with love; it takes out the misery and replaces it with joy; anxiety is replaced with peace; impatience with patience; meanness with goodness and kindness; pride and high-handedness with gentleness; inconsistency with faithfulness; self-indulgence with self-control. We become a different person.

This is the key to not only our problems, but the world's problems. The problem with the world is that it is full of people—fallen, corrupt, sinful people. Can the world be changed? Not by the world's methods. It is imagined that if man's environment is changed, then he can be changed. We expect that if we can eliminate poverty through redistributing wealth, or ignorance through education, or lack of opportunity through affirmative action, and so on, that we can change the world. Eliminate sinful social structures and usher in Utopia, the Marxist dreamers said. But these efforts, however much they may or may not reduce some measure of human suffering, cannot ultimately help. We end up merely trading ignorant wretches for educated ones, poor wretches for rich ones. External or environmental changes will not solve our problems. The heart must change, and only the Spirit of Christ can change the heart. The answer to your problems, as well as the world's, is the gospel of Jesus Christ. The church has always insisted that He is the Savior, not of one or two nations here or there, but the 'Savior of the World.' He can and He will save the world and save you (from yourself!) by His Spirit, through transforming hearts one at a time.

Many of you will have seen the diet or exercise ads that have before and after pictures. The old Charles Atlas ads were still in the comic books when I was a young boy. The "before" picture was a scrawny ninety-pound weakling. The "after" an Arnold Schwarzenegger. This is what we have, in effect, in our passage. "Before" you were characterized by the "deeds of the flesh." That is what you were. But now, you have been transformed. Look at what the Spirit does, he is saying. Now you are characterized by the "fruit of the Spirit." Let us then look at the fruit, and begin to paint a picture of what a Christian looks like.

27

The Fruit of the Spirit is Love

Galatians 5:22–23

Love is the most important of the fruit and the most comprehensive. Burton thinks that it is probably even 'thought of as the source from which all the rest flow.'[159] Lenski calls it 'the mother of all other Christian virtues.'[160] It is the fundamental Christian virtue and greatest of the Christian virtues (1 Cor. 13:13). How do you know who is a Christian? A Christian is one who loves. The Apostle John writes,

> Beloved, let us love one another, for love is from God; and everyone who loves is born of God and knows God. The one who does not love does not know God, for God is love. (1 John 4:7–8)

Because 'God is love,' all who know God love. All that we do is done in love. We are to be 'rooted and grounded in love' (Eph. 3:17). We are to 'speak the truth in love' (Eph. 4:15). We are to 'walk in love' (Eph. 5:2). The church is 'knit together in love' (Col. 2:2). 'The love of Christ controls us,' Paul writes (2 Cor. 5:14). 'Let all that you do be done in love' (1 Cor. 16:14). When we receive the Holy Spirit, He removes hatred and bitterness and replaces it with love. He cleanses us of selfishness and preoccupation with self, and sets us about the work of sacrificial service for others.

But what do we mean by love? We have already hinted at the two essential elements of love. We will now make them explicit.

Sacrifice

Love is not primarily an emotion. Love means sacrificial service for others. How do we know that? After all, love as the term is commonly used is not an unambiguous word. What Hollywood means is not likely to be the same thing that the Bible means. Paul had five Greek words at his disposal, each with nuanced meanings. He could have used *storge*, typically used of family love; *epithumia*, used of passion; *eros*, used of romantic love; or *philia*, which overlaps considerably with *agape* (e.g. John 3:35 and 5:20). He used *agape*, perhaps because as a noun it was virtually unused in classical Greek and so he could fill it with Christian meaning. Most typically it is used of God's love for man, which then forms the pattern for man's love in response.[161] Let me cite some examples.

> For God so loved the world, that He gave His only begotten Son, that whoever believes in Him should not perish, but have eternal life. (John 3:16)

God so loved the world that He did what? He gave. Love does what? Love gives. This is its essential meaning. It denotes selfless giving.

> In this is love, not that we loved God, but that He loved us and sent His Son to be the propitiation for our sins. (1 John 4:10)

Here it is again. 'In this is love,' he says. Here is an example of what true love looks like. Here is what real love does. So what did God do? He 'sent His Son to be the propitiation for our sins.' If one loves, one sacrifices. Paul had already used the word in this sense, in this very epistle.

> I have been crucified with Christ; and it is no longer I who live, but Christ lives in me; and the life which I now live in the flesh I live by faith in the Son of God, who loved me, and delivered Himself up for me. (Gal. 2:20)

He 'loved me,' Paul says. So what did He do? He 'delivered Himself up for me,' that's what He did. Love means costly sacrificial service on behalf of the objects of one's love. The long description of love in 1 Corinthians 13 never once mentions feeling. It only describes what love does: it is patient, kind, not jealous, doesn't brag, isn't arrogant, and so on. Love is what love does, not what it feels. If you are in a position where you are trying to determine if someone loves you then ask yourself, do I see self-less sacrifice? Are they primarily interested in using me or helping me? Real love serves the interests and needs of other.

Doing Right

Love then is not to be confused with the romantic or the erotic. Neither is it to be confused with fuzzy feelings. Love means doing the right thing. Consider the following silly sentiment: I love my children, consequently I never want them to suffer, consequently I never spank them. Is that love? No, the parent who will not discipline his child hates him, the Proverbs warn (13:24). 'Whom the Lord loves He disciplines, and he scourges every son whom He receives' (Prov. 3:12, Heb. 12:6). Family discipline, church discipline, national discipline (in the form of legal punishments), and God's discipline are not incompatible with love. Love requires that we do the right thing, even if it is difficult, even if it costs us something, even if judgments have to be made. As the proverbial father says to his son, 'This hurts me more than it hurts you.' Likewise, a loving church disciplines because it must defend the weak and innocent, guard their reputations, and identify and punish the guilty.

Francis Schaeffer once told a parable to illustrate this point. He said imagine that you are walking down the street, and you came upon a man who is beating up an elderly woman. He hits her. He knocks her down. He kicks her over and over again. What is the loving thing to do in this instance? What does it mean to love my neighbor in these circumstances? Doesn't it mean that I use whatever force that is necessary to stop the assailant? Doesn't love mean defending the innocent and punishing evil? Yes it does, and don't ever let anyone accuse you of being 'unloving' because you believe in discipline, be it in the home, at church or in our nation. Real love is tough love. The same Apostle Paul who said love 'bears all things, believes all things, hopes all things, endures all things,' also in the *same* epistle chastised the Corinthians for failing to deal with public sin, and demanded that they 'remove the wicked man from among (them)selves' (1 Cor. 13:7; 5:9–13). He then turned around and said that 'sufficient' punishment had been inflicted, resulting in repentance, and consequently they were to 'reaffirm (their) love for him' (2 Cor. 2:6–8). Paul relates this almost incidentally. Love had been rightly withdrawn. Punishment had been inflicted. Now love was to be reaffirmed. The fruit of the Spirit in no small part consists in knowing how this most comprehensive of Christian virtues applies in a given set of circumstances. Do I love the assailant by leaving him alone, or by stopping him? The Spirit gives us the wisdom that keeps love on track, that keeps it from becoming a spineless sentimentalism. The most unloving thing a person or church or society can do is leave self-destructive behavior unaddressed. Shall we just stand by and say nothing and do nothing as a person destroys himself and his family? Is that love? The Spirit helps us to discern that true love means punishing wayward children lest they harm themselves. It means disciplining church members who are so blinded by selfishness or pride that they may destroy themselves if they are ignored. It even means punishing criminal activity in society. Love means doing the right thing, not just the 'feel good' thing, not just what the wayward think they want.

Sympathy

We need to clarify. Love also means sympathetic affections. Sometimes the discussions of the sacrificial dimension of love have overlooked the emotional element altogether. But, after all, Paul could have used words such as 'service' (*latreia*), or 'sacrifice' (*thusia*), or 'obedience' (*hupakoe*). He could have said, 'the fruit of the Spirit is service' or 'the fruit of the Spirit is sacrifice.' If he had, he would have been saying something that is true. The fruit or result of the Spirit's work in a person's life is service, sacrifice, and obedience. But he didn't. He had something more to say. He looked for a word which also conveys emotional content. Why? Because he had in mind both the service and the affection that motivates the service. These two elements together, then, are what the Holy Spirit puts in our hearts. The love of God that is 'shed abroad in our hearts through the Holy Spirit' fills our hearts with sympathetic affections for others resulting in sacrificial service on their behalf (Rom. 5:5).

Transformed

Love also means transformed relationships with God and man. In relation to God this means that the old bitterness and hatred towards Him is removed. We are born 'haters of God,' 'haters of the light' and 'lovers of darkness' (Rom. 1:32; John 3:19–20). We were 'formerly alienated and hostile in mind, engaged in evil deeds' (Col. 1:21). This meant that we tended to blame God for everything that went wrong. We were constantly angry with God. We bitterly resented any affliction. We hated Him for our suffering and pain. We resisted any claim upon our time or money or allegiance. We railed against His omniscience and omnipotence. We hated His scrutinizing our every thought, word and deed. We were rebels against His authority. We insisted on our autonomy, refusing to be told what to do, refusing to honor God as God, and refusing to offer to Him the worship of which he is due. That is where we were. But then the Holy Spirit took up residence in us. He renewed our minds and utterly transformed our attitudes towards God (Rom. 12:1–2). Now we love the light and hate the darkness. Now we delight in God and His works. We admire His creative hand, and the power and wisdom and craftsmanship represented in all that is around us. We no longer blame God when things go wrong, but trust God. We are no longer embittered by affliction, but accept it as the will of our loving Father (Heb. 12:5–13). We gladly surrender to His authority, and conform our behavior to His will. We delight in gathering in worship and rendering to Him the honor of which He is due. We are overwhelmed by His grace to us in Christ Jesus, that 'while we were enemies we were reconciled to God through the death of His Son' (Rom. 5:10). We don't have to be brow beaten into attending church on Sunday, or tithing our income, or keeping the Sabbath. We delight in these things, and are pleased to serve God in any way that we can. While we, with Peter, might hesitate to answer directly the question, 'Do you love me?' (John 21:15–17), we nevertheless are growing daily in the love and knowledge of Christ.

The best illustration of this that I can find is found in Luke 7. The stage is set in verses 36–9.

> Now one of the Pharisees was requesting Him to dine with him. And He entered the Pharisee's house, and reclined at the table. And behold, there was a woman in the city who was a sinner; and when she learned that He was reclining at the table in the Pharisee's house, she brought an alabaster vial of perfume, and standing behind Him at His feet, weeping, she began to wet His feet with her tears, and kept wiping them with the hair of her head, and kissing His feet, and anointing them with the perfume. Now when the Pharisee who had invited Him saw this, he said to himself, 'If this man were a prophet He would know who and what sort of person this woman is who is touching Him, that she is a sinner.'

This uninhibited display of love for Jesus by this immoral woman resulted in an indignant response by a Pharisee named Simon. Jesus answered him with the parable of the two debtors.

> And Jesus answered and said to him, 'Simon, I have something to say to you.' And he replied, 'Say it, Teacher.' 'A certain moneylender had two debtors: one owed five hundred denarii, and the other fifty. When they were unable to repay, he graciously forgave them both. Which of them therefore will love him more?' Simon answered and said, 'I suppose the one whom he forgave more.' And He said to him, 'You have judged correctly.' (Luke 7:40–3)

The parable clinches the point that Jesus wishes to make. Then Jesus makes the application.

> And turning toward the woman, He said to Simon, 'Do you see this woman? I entered your house; you gave Me no water for My feet, but she has wet My feet with her tears, and wiped them with her hair. You gave Me no kiss; but she, since the time I came in, has not ceased to kiss My feet. You did not anoint My feet with perfume. For this reason I say to you, her sins, which are many, have been forgiven, for she loved much; but he who is forgiven little, loves little.' (Luke 7:44–7)

The woman has responded to the grace of Christ with grateful, loving service. Love obviously means affection for Christ. She is aware of how much she had been given. Her heart overflows with gratitude and love. But that affection results in costly service. She washed His feet with her tears. She wiped His feet with her hair. She affectionately kissed those feet. She anointed His feet with costly perfume. Because she was forgiven much, she loved much. Likewise this will be our response to the gospel. Because we have been forgiven much we will love much, resulting in willing, spontaneous, loving service.

Are our hearts moved in this way? Do we know at what cost our sins have been forgiven? Do we know what sacrifice was made on our behalf? Do we know what we deserved? Our hearts should be profoundly moved like this woman's. What love we ought to feel! What gratitude! And what willing service ought to follow.

Likewise the Spirit has removed the old bitterness, anger, and hatred towards others. Once we blamed the world for everything. We were embittered by this perceived wrong or that. We were angry, miserable people. We hated this individual and that, this group and that. These dark feelings were harbored, even nursed. Some of us were capable of erupting at the slightest provocation. Others of us manifested our hatred by snobbish rejection of others, or by arrogant condescension. Similarly we were paralyzed by self-centeredness. We didn't care about anyone but number one. We were utterly preoccupied with self, with our own pleasure, our own fun, our own prosperity. Oh, we might dust a few crumbs in the direction of others, but only a few, and then for sake of public relations, so that we might be seen as generous.

But the Holy Spirit has come and taken away the old hatred and the old selfishness, and replaced it with a selfless, sacrificial love for others. Our love 'covers a multitude of sins,' (1 Pet. 4:8), and so we are able to look past offenses and love people anyway. The petty things that used to upset us no longer do. We have freely received, so we freely give. We have been forgiven much, and so we love much. We're not angry at the world anymore. We don't nurse our resentments anymore. We love our enemies. We pray for those who despitefully use us. The old bondage of selfishness is broken. We are able to love one another, to pray for one another, to bear one another's burdens. Before I might have said, 'I don't want anything to do with those poor people,' or rich people, or old people, or young people as the case may apply. But I can't ignore them anymore. Now I love them. Now I am ready to serve them.

Again there is a parable that illustrates the point found in Matthew 18:21–35. Peter asks about forgiveness, and Jesus answers with a story about a man who owed his king ten thousand talents of silver, or the equivalent of multiple millions of dollars. Jesus said,

> But since he did not have the means to repay, his lord commanded him to be sold, along with his wife and children and all that he had, and repayment to be made. The slave therefore falling down, prostrated himself before him, saying, 'Have patience with me, and I will repay you everything.' And the lord of that slave felt compassion and released him and forgave him the debt.(Matt. 18:25–7)

The word love is not used in the parable. But similar terms are: the king felt 'compassion,' he 'released' the slave from his obligations, and 'forgave him the debt.' Having been forgiven much by His superior, an obligation to be similarly compassionate and forgiving is implied. But this is not what happens in this case.

> But that slave went out and found one of his fellow slaves who owed him a hundred denarii, and he seized him and began to choke him, saying, 'Pay back what you owe.' So his fellow slave fell down and began to entreat him, saying, 'Have patience with me and I will repay you.' He was unwilling however, but went and threw him in prison until he should pay back what was owed. (Matt. 18:28–30)

The incongruity of this is what stands out. How could one so forgiven not be forgiving? The experience of being forgiven is transforming, resulting in a forgiving outlook towards others. Jesus goes on to conclude the story,

> So when his fellow slaves saw what had happened, they were deeply greived and came and reported to their lord all that had happened. Then summoning him, his lord said to him, 'you wicked slave, I forgave you all that debt because you entreated me. Should you not also have had mercy on your fellow slave, even as I had mercy on you?' And his lord, moved with anger, handed him over to the torturers until he should repay all that was owed him. So shall my heavenly Father also do to you, if each of you does not forgive his brother from your heart. (Matt. 18:31–5)

One who has been forgiven forgives. One who has been shown mercy, shows mercy. John says similar things.

> We know love by this, that He laid down His life for us; and we ought to lay down our lives for the brethren. (1 John 3:16)

You have received sacrificial love, and so you give sacrificial love in return. And this means more than nice thoughts:

> But whoever has the world's goods, and beholds his brother in need and closes his heart against him, how does the love of God abide in him? Little children, let us not love with word or with tongue, but in deed and truth. (1 John 3:17–18).

This is what the Holy Spirit does in real believers. He plants the seed of love in their hearts and it grows into this kind of sacrificial care. What a community results! Listen to these ideals:

> Be devoted to one another in brotherly love; give preference to one another in honor; (Rom. 12:10)

> . . . and walk in love just as Christ also loved you, and gave Himself up for us, an offering and a sacrifice to God as a fragrant aroma. (Eph. 5:2)

> In this is love, not that we loved God, but that He loved us and sent His Son to be the propitiation for our sins. Beloved, if God so loved us, we also ought to love one another. (1 John 4:10–11)

We are not able to love in this way on our own. This love is not cheap sentimentalism. This love is giving, caring, helping, compassionate, involved love. It is self-sacrificing love. It is love that lays down its life for another. It is Christ-like love.

It is also primarily covenantal love. Almost without exception the commands to love are concerned with love for the brethren. 'Love *one another*,' we are repeatedly told (John 13:35; 15:12, 17; 21:7–16; Rom. 12:10; 13:8; Gal. 5:13; 1 Thess. 3:12; 4:9; 1 Pet. 1:22; 1 John 3:11; 3:23; 4:7; 4:11; 2 John 5). The Bible won't allow us to indulge a Charlie Brown type of humanitarianism: 'Humanity I love, it's people I can't stand.' The Holy Spirit works into our hearts a love for the people within the covenant community, i.e. the members of the church. This love, which is the primary mark of the true Christian, is not theoretical. It is real love for real people, with all their flaws, all their failure, all their quirks, all their deficiencies, all their differences from myself. The Holy Spirit will not let me say, 'I don't like those people.' He won't let me say, 'Those people at the church are strange.' He won't permit me to become arrogant or condescending because they are unlike myself. He won't allow me to stand apart or aloof. These are all the excuses that we are tempted to use as we refuse to love. We are tempted to dismiss people, to brush them aside, to withdraw and ignore their needs. We are tempted to isolate ourselves in our own little cocoons of self-interest and social comfort. But the reason why our rationalizations of selfishness won't wash is because the church has always been made up of people who are difficult to love. It has always been the case. *We're commanded to love not because it's easy, but because it isn't.* The commands assume our reluctance and unwillingness, but insist upon it anyway. This is the love that turns the world upside down. Do you want to be this kind of person? Of course you do and so do I. How does it happen? By the work of the Holy Spirit. This kind of love is the fruit of His presence in the life of a believer. He will make you a loving person. He will obliterate the selfishness and pride that keep getting in the way. He will transform your heart and fill it with compassion, charity, grace, and genuine care. This is the promise of the gospel.

28

The Fruit of the Spirit is Joy

Galatians 5:22–23

'Thou hast conquered, O pale Galilean; the world has grown grey from Thy breath.' Thus spoke the English skeptic Charles Swinburne in 1866, summarizing what is often the unbeliever's view of the Christian religion. Christianity takes all of the spice out of life, they think. Would you like to be a bore? Would you like to empty your world of color? Do you want to live a life devoid of pleasure and passion? Then become a Christian. Contrast this with the testimony of C.S. Lewis, who in 1955 entitled his account of his spiritual pilgrimage, *Surprised by Joy*. Life for him, up to that point, had been a dreary, colorless existence. He didn't know joy *until* he found Christ. D. L. Moody said of the day that he was converted that the sky was bluer, the trees were greener, the sun was brighter. Life was immeasurably better. Nearly every Christian would say the same. They too would say that they never knew happiness until they found Christ.

If this is true, then why have so many pagans shared Swinburne's perspective? Why does the perception persist that Christians are a joyless bunch? This is especially noteworthy since the world doesn't mind conceding that real Christians have peace. They'll acknowledge that. They'll admit that real Christians have patience, that they are kind, that they have self-control, and so on. They'll even admire all those qualities. But joy? Never. Why is this? I believe it is because the world fails to understand what real joy is. They have this idea of what it takes to enjoy life, coupled with what Christians have and don't have, what they can do and can't do, and can't imagine that devout Christians could be anything but miserable. You can't do any of the fun stuff, and have to do lots of boring stuff, they think. This is bondage to the world. 'Let us tear their fetters apart, and cast away their cords from us,' say the kings of the earth against the Lord and His anointed (Ps. 2:2–3). God's law is 'fetters,' chains, slavery to them. What do they want? Let's look then at what the world offers, and then that of which true joy consists.

False Joy

We may have to concede that perhaps the worldlings have encountered one too many joyless Christians. Perhaps the world hasn't seen our joy. Perhaps all they see are dreary, gloomy, depressed, somber believers. 'Those church people,' they say, 'are a bunch of negative, unhappy, defeated, complaining, griping, bores!' This they contrast with the excitement and stimulation of the world. They can't imagine giving up the pleasures of the flesh for the chains of 'God's' law. 'They are surprised that you do not run with them into the same excess of dissipation, and they malign you,' says Peter (1 Pet. 4:4). It is unimaginable that one would not 'carry out the desire of the Gentiles' and pursue a 'course of sensuality, lusts, drunkenness, carousals, drinking parties and abominable idolatries' (1 Pet. 4:3). Give all that up for the life of the monastery? Never!

There may be an element of truth in the pagan critique presented here. It may be that there have been and now are some Christians who are overly dull, even unnecessarily dull. But I wouldn't want to give too much credence to the critics for two reasons. First, dull, boring Christians are not the norm. Moreover, the perverted norms of the world are not to be the criteria by which we determine what is boring and what is not. Second, as for the world itself, there is no joy in Mudville. Oh, yes, there is plenty of excitement, fun, revelry, pleasure. But it is fleeting. It is happiness that lasts for a season. Hebrews speaks of 'the passing pleasures of sin' (Heb. 11:25). Worldly pleasure is all vanity and striving after the wind (Ecc. 2:11). Look at the faces of the most worldly of the worldlings—the media stars, the models, the athletes. Are they a happy group? Recently we heard that the heroin look was in. Hollow, sunken eyes, malnourished—you've seen them.

This is to say that the world, by and large, misunderstands what joy is. Both joy and the subsequent fruit, peace, are closely related to one another. They both indicate a positive state of mind. If we were to identify peace with contentment, with a settled sense of well-being, we might also identify joy with what the world calls happiness, though at a much deeper level. True joy is a deep, constant, abiding quality that combines peace, contentment, well-being, and delight. Yet it is compatible with seriousness, with suffering, and with sorrow. It remains present and constant in every circumstance of life. True joy is much deeper than mere happiness. It doesn't change with circumstances as does happiness. Our joy is 'in the Lord,' and because He doesn't change, neither does it.

Confusion with respect to joy has also been caused by the Christian community as well. Some have given the impression that the Christian life is an endless string of pleasantries. They have refused to acknowledge that there is an appropriate and unavoidable seriousness about life. Life is not one big party. Life is not all happiness and smiles. When I encounter people who are always bubbling with enthusiasm the warning lights flash. Granted, some folks have been blessed with especially optimistic personalities, and some with especially positive circumstances. Everything for them has gone well so far. But, basically, when I see someone 'happy' all the time, I figure that they just don't understand what is going on in the world. Poor thing, I think. Don't you understand the degree of human need, the suffering, poverty, hunger and spiritual sickness that is in the world? The Apostle Paul ponders unbelief with 'great sorrow and unceasing grief' (Rom. 9:2). 'His spirit was being provoked within him' by the sight of the idols that he encountered in Athens (Acts 17:16). Beyond the human condition generally, don't you understand your own sinfulness, I have wondered? How can you be so happy all the time? Why are you smiling all the time?

My first period of rapid Christian growth occurred as an undergraduate in college, and was accompanied with deep conviction of sin and dissatisfaction with myself. Yet there we were in our college Bible studies singing,

> Happy, happy, happy, happy,
> Happy are the people whose God is the Lord .
> Where does this happy feeling come from?
> This happy feeling comes from Jesus,
> Every day he more than pleases,
> That's where this happy feeling comes from.

Never sung that one? How about this:

> At the cross, at the cross, where I first saw the light,
> And the burden of my heart rolled away.
> It was there by faith I received my sight,
> And now I am happy all the day.

Well I didn't have such a happy feeling. I wasn't 'happy all the day.' I was struggling. The Christian life was a fight for me. I was discouraged and depressed. The transition from indifferent church goer who fit in with everyone, to committed Christian who offended many, was difficult for me. I grieved the loss of friends. I suffered as I was socially displaced. Rejection cost me a great deal emotionally. The concept of the Christian life which was assumed by my fellow Christians had no place for such. One was to be happy. If one wasn't, I was told by well-meaning but misinformed brethren, one was being a bad witness. But I was heartened by the words of Jesus who anticipated this in saying, 'Blessed are those who mourn, for they shall be comforted' (Matt. 5:4). Jesus, one may note, anticipated that there would be circumstances worthy of mourning and that His people would mourn. The idea that Christians should be smiling all the time reveals a very unrealistic and superficial view of life. We work by the sweat of the brow, don't we? We struggle to live. We face the constant reality of sickness, disease, tragedy, and death. Jesus is called a 'man of sorrows acquainted with grief' (Isa. 53:3). Paul spoke of the 'sorrow upon sorrow' he would have experienced if his friend Epaphroditus had not been spared (Phil. 1:27). The Ephesian elders 'wept aloud' when Paul left them, announcing that they should 'see his face no more' (Acts 20:37). The early church wept with 'loud lamentation' at the death of Stephen (Acts 8:2). Christians are not spared the common trials of humanity. Our suffering and pain is not diminished in the least by the cross. Indeed, as I heard John MacArthur say many years ago, for many Christians their trouble just begins when they become Christians. Up to that point they were swimming with the tide. They were partying-up with all the rest. But now they have the world to fight. Now they have friends who have turned on them. Now they struggle with the flesh. Now the devil is giving them fits.

Yet, and here is the point, there is in all of this *the abiding reality of joy*. Like Paul we are 'sorrowful, yet always rejoicing' (2 Cor. 6:10). This is incomprehensible to the world. How can one be 'sorrowful' and yet 'always rejoicing'? How can Paul in the same epistle admit to 'sorrow upon sorrow,' and yet also require that we 'rejoice always?' (Phil. 1:27; 4:4, 1 Thess. 5:16). Yet it is the fruit of the Spirit's presence in our lives. We have in all of our circumstances a 'joy unspeakable and full of glory' (1 Pet. 1:8). This is not a trouble free life. Rather it is what one widow who deeply grieved the loss of her husband called 'a zest for life.' The Spirit, not by preventing difficulties but by transforming our perception of those difficulties, maintains in us an energy, a vitality, and purpose for living. He fills us with peace, with contentment, with a sense of well-being, with delight, with what Karl Barth called 'a defiant nevertheless.' How is this possible?

True Joy

True joy is found only in the Lord. Our chief delight is in the Lord. We rejoice 'in the Lord' (Phil. 3:1; 4:4). Our joy is 'of the Holy Spirit' (1 Thess. 1:6; cf. Rom. 15:13). 'Our heart rejoices in Him, because we trust in His holy name' (Ps. 33:21; cf. Pss. 5:11; 40:16). We may make further distinctions which may prove helpful.

First, our joy is in the Lord Himself. Think of the human analogy, say a loved one who is the 'apple of your eye,' one in whom you delight. Perhaps it may be your child, or another family member. As you watch them, or hear them speak, or see them work or play, your heart delights in them. Your heart is flooded with joy. This is how we become about God. We rejoice in His work and ways. Our joy is anchored in that which is good, beautiful, gracious, just, and immutably so. It is in the light of His unchanging reality that we view our circumstances and problems. However bad things may get, we may 'delight (our)selves in the Lord,' because He is ever one who is delightful (Ps. 37:4). We find joy both in His person and in His works. Begin with His person, that is, God's nature, or attributes. There is so much in God which feeds our soul and in which we may rejoice. Read books such as *Knowing God,* by J.I. Packer, or *The Attributes of God,* by A.W. Pink. 'Plunge yourself in the Godhead's deepest sea,' as C.H. Spurgeon said.

Let me give some practical examples. God is immutable, as we've just mentioned. Yet we live in a world of *Future Shock*, a world in which everything changes at whirlwind speed. People change, morals and manners change, customs change, fashions change. Nothing remains the same. Nothing can be relied upon. The corner grocer closes down. The milk man stops delivering. The schools quit teaching. The government can't be trusted. This is all unsettling. We feel that we have no reference points, no fixed principles, no dependable institutions, no reliable people. Everything is in flux. In the midst we ponder an unchanging God. He is our anchor in the sea-change of life. We rejoice with Jeremiah,

> The Lord's loving kindnesses indeed never cease, for His compassions never fail. They are new every morning; great is Thy faithfulness. (Lam. 3:22–3)

We sing with the hymn-writer,

> Great is thy faithfulness, O God my Father;
> There is no shadow of turning with thee;
> Thou changest not, thy compassions, they fail not;
> As thou hast been thou forever wilt be.
> Great is thy faithfulness! Great is thy faithfulness!
> Morning by morning new mercies I see:
> All I have needed thy hand hath provided—
> Great is thy faithfulness, Lord, unto me!

As we are battered by the changes of life, we rejoice in our unchanging and utterly reliable, completely dependable Lord.

Or we could ponder God's providence. Many people encounter terrible accidents, tragic diseases, and natural disasters, and conclude that they are the result of arbitrary, random, or chance forces. If they are, then the only possible response to such is despair. If they are chance events, they are devoid of meaning. They have no purpose. But if God is sovereign and if His control over all things is total, then my view of the events of life is transformed. If He has even numbered the numbers of hairs upon my head and if not even a sparrow falls from the tree apart from His will, then I am able to rejoice even in the midst of great trials knowing that what I experience, I experience by the hand of God. The great biblical example of this is Joseph. At the end of his life he was able to say to his brothers regarding their wicked act in selling him into slavery, that though they meant it for evil, 'God meant it for good' (Gen. 50:20). God meant it! This is a source of great comfort and joy for the people of God. We delight in His sovereign rule.

Then again we could contemplate the love of God. We live in a harsh, cruel world. We live in a world where every man is out for himself. We are taught to look out for number one. Yet the Bible teaches that God is love. He is love itself. When I've reached the bottom, when I'm feeling low, when I'm feeling rejected or defeated, I can remember that at least God loves me and delight myself in his tender mercies.

Not only do I delight in His person, but I also delight in His works. The psalmist says,

> I will sing for joy at the works of Thy hand, how great are thy works O Lord. (Ps. 92:4–5)

As we study creation we are amazed at the wisdom and the power of God. As we study God's works of redemption we are astonished at His great mercy and grace and patience and goodness and kindness and love. There is so much cause for joy as we study the person and works of our triune God, Father, Son and the Holy Spirit. When the world would rob us of our joy, lift up our eyes from the things of the earth and contemplate the depths of the Almighty.

Second, we rejoice in our salvation. Our joy is anchored not only in theology but also in eschatology. We can all agree, I assume, that the most important question in this life is where we'll spend the next. 'What does it profit a man,' said Jesus, 'if he should gain the whole world and lose his own soul?' (Matt. 16:26). I can lose my house and my wealth. I can lose my car, my friends and my family. But I cannot lose my joy. Why? Because this world is passing away and the next world has been taken care of. Consequently everything in this life, with regard to circumstances, is relative. So we can say with the apostle Paul,

> For I consider that the sufferings of this present time are not worthy to be compared with the glory that is to be revealed to us. (Rom. 8:18)

We can see the suffering of this world as 'momentary, light affliction' (2 Cor. 4:17). The letter to the Hebrews speaks of those who

> Accept joyfully the seizure of your property, knowing that you have for yourself a better possession, an abiding one. (Heb. 10:34)

For us the big question has been resolved. Consequently, we can rejoice in whatever circumstances we might find ourselves. Yes, there are serious trials in this world, but because this world is short and eternity is long, the serious problems of this world are not *that* serious. When we grieve, it is not 'as do the rest who have no hope' (1 Thess. 4:13). If I didn't know God, if I were ignorant of my eternal destiny; if I were facing death without certainty; if I were vague about my salvation, then nothing in all the world could give me joy. But because I do know God, and I do know my eternal destiny, and I am facing death with certainty of eternal salvation, then there is nothing in all the world that can rob me of my joy. Our problem is that we are too tied to the things of this world. We are wedded to material things, and people, and jobs, and status. We are in love with the things of this world. Consequently when we lose the things of this world, we are devastated by it and our joy evaporates and we collapse in depression and sorrow. A loved one dies, and we're devastated and we're not able to cope with it. We experience employment reversals, and we are devastated by it, and we can't cope with it. Friends abandon and forsake us, and we're crushed by it. What is the problem? We need to adopt the eternal perspective and sit loose to the things of this world. Jesus says, 'rejoice …that your names are recorded in heaven' (Luke 10:20). He said,

> Blessed are you when men cast insults at you, and persecute you, and say all kinds of evil against you falsely, on account of Me. Rejoice, and be glad, for your reward in heaven is great, for so they persecuted the prophets who were before you. (Matt. 5:11–12)

Jesus is saying that persecution doesn't matter if your reward in heaven is great. If your reward in heaven is great then you are still able to rejoice, and even be glad, even though you are persecuted and rejected in this world. So when the world would rob us of our joy, let us lift our eyes from the present and gaze into eternity. Remember the eternal destiny of our souls, and in that perspective view the small and relatively insignificant losses of this world.

Third, we rejoice in the progress of the gospel. Our joy is wrapped up in the advance of the kingdom of God rather than in our own circumstances and well-being. Among the best biblical examples of this is found in Philippians 1:12–20. There we read of the Apostle Paul writing from prison after years of glorious ministry. Now from a filthy Roman prison cell he is attacked by his fellow Christians. Apparently they were accusing the Apostle Paul of being a jail-bird of some sort, clearly out of the favor of God and so suffering the consequences of disobedience or sin. The Apostle says of them that they were preaching Christ 'even from envy and strife' (1:15). He says they proclaimed Christ 'out of selfish ambition, rather than from pure motives thinking to cause me distress in my imprisonment' (Phil. 1:17). Paul knew their motives. He knew that they preached from 'envy and strife' and from 'selfish ambition' and in order to cause him 'distress.' His remarkable conclusion?

> What then? Only that in every way, whether in pretense or in truth, Christ is proclaimed; and in this I rejoice, yes, and I will rejoice. (Phil. 1:18)

The Apostle Paul figures that if Christ is proclaimed and the gospel is progressing, he'll rejoice even from the prison cell as he is being attacked by hypocrites. If we let them, people will rob us of our joy. As was the case in the Apostle Paul's life, they may attack us out of envy, they may do evil against us from evil motives, they may try to manipulate and control us. These kinds of things may even go on in the context of the church and through the actions of Christian people. There is nothing more disillusioning than the attacks of those that we once regarded as our friends. There is nothing so discouraging as being rejected by those who ought to know better. Should we then collapse in a heap of joyless protoplasm? No, like the Apostle Paul we should be asking ourselves the question, is Christ being proclaimed? Is the kingdom of God advancing? If that is the case, then we can rejoice even in the midst of our discouragement, rejection and persecution. The question is not, am I being recognized? The question is not, are things going my way? The question is not, did I get the credit? The church is not a business, the church is not a social organization. The question is, am I able to contribute to the unity and fruitfulness of the kingdom of God? If I can, then I can rejoice in whatever circumstances I am. The problem for many of us is that our horizons are too small. Our joy or our happiness is dependent upon our own personal circumstances. That is too limiting. We all need a bigger cause than our own little empires. Seek first Christ's kingdom and you will rejoice as you see the gospel progressing, souls being won to Christ, saints being built up in the knowledge and love of Christ.

So it is that true joy, true happiness, is a gift of the Holy Spirit. God gives us his Holy Spirit, and the Spirit transforms our hearts so that our chief love and delight in life is Christ and His kingdom. Our joy is to know Him. Our delight is to see His kingdom advancing. The unchanging realities of Christ, our salvation, and His kingdom provide for us a foundation of joy that cannot be shaken, that remains constant whatever our circumstances might be.

29

The Fruit of the Spirit is Peace

Galatians 5:22–23

Those in whom the gospel has taken root, in whom the Spirit is at work, will be characterized by an all pervasive peace. They will have peace of mind. They will be calm in the midst of life's storms. They will not panic in times of stress or crisis. They will not be anxious in times of trial or temptation. The Spirit will keep them in a state of peace. They will even have peace in their relationships. Indeed, because they have peace in their hearts, they will be peacemakers among their fellows.

Who wants this peace? Everyone does. Years ago Francis Schaeffer said that one could do anything to the American people so long as one could guarantee personal peace and affluence. Indeed much of the behavior around us today can be understood as attempts to find peace apart from the 'Prince of Peace' and His 'gospel of peace' (Isa. 9:6; Eph. 2:7). All such attempts are doomed. They will never work, and here's why.

The Bible teaches that we are all born apart from God, and yet we all know that He is there and that He has a law. Even the atheist, in spite of his denials, is aware of the existence of God and the law by which he will be judged. The problem of unbelief, says the Bible, is not a problem of a lack of information, but of the suppression of information. The problem is that both the atheist and the false religionist 'suppress the truth in unrighteousness.' God has made Himself evident 'within them' and 'to them;' 'His eternal power and divine nature have been *clearly seen*, being understood through what has been made, so that they are without excuse' (Rom. 1:18–20). The problem is not a lack of knowledge. Paul continues,

> For even though they knew God, they did not honor Him as God, or give thanks; but they became futile in their speculations, and their foolish heart was darkened. Professing to be wise, they became fools, and exchanged the glory of the incorruptible God for an image in the form of corruptible man and of birds and four-footed animals and crawling creatures... For they exchanged the truth of God for a lie, and worshiped and served the creature rather than the Creator, who is blessed forever! Amen. (Rom. 1:21–3, 25)

Regarding the law of God, Paul lists various sins and concludes,

> and, although they know the ordinance of God, that those who practice such things are worthy

> of death, they not only do the same, but also give hearty approval to those who practice them. (Rom. 1:32)

Further, he says of non-Jews who were not given the Scriptures,

> in that they show the work of the Law written in their hearts, their conscience bearing witness, and their thoughts alternately accusing or else defending them. (Rom. 2:15)

The psychology of unbelief is a psychology of *angst*. The unbeliever knows of God and His law, and yet is not reconciled to God. He lives with a conscience that accuses and condemns him. He knows that there is a coming day of reckoning for which he is not prepared, and though he is not willing to give up his toys in order to get right with God, that awareness fills him with dread. Isaiah says 'there is no peace for the wicked,' likening their experience to 'the tossing sea, for it cannot be quiet, and its waters toss up refuse and mud' (Isa. 57:21). So what does the unbeliever do? He seeks out substitutes. He turns to false gods, to idols, and various counterfeits, all of which promise, as did the false prophets of old, 'peace, peace, where there is no peace' (Jer. 6:14; 8:11). Where does he turn? There are really only two alternatives.

False Peace

The world offers a number of seductive *counterfeits* of true peace.

First, he can join the race away from God. Why is life lived at such a hectic pace these days? Why is so much of what keeps us busy mindless or escapist? Study human behavior. Up we jump in the morning, rush out the door, work all day, home for a quick change, and out again for an evening of entertainment, or even to just plop down in front of the TV. We are always moving, always doing, always watching something, always listening to something, always going somewhere. Why? Because if we keep going we'll never have to stop to reflect on life. We'll never have to consider the value of what we're doing. We'll never have to think of the great issues of life, death, and eternity. So we keep running. This is unmistakably a hallmark of the modern world, and it is unhealthy and destructive of family life, education, and personal piety. And yet, Christian people get caught up in it. We too get swept up in the whirlwind of contemporary culture. We, too, are running all over town, chauffeuring our children here, there, and everywhere, unable to gather the family for a meal, unable to rest. What drives all this? A massive flight from God all around us. What should we do? Resist! Slow down. Pause. Reflect. Think. We were watching an old episode of 'Andy Griffith' the other day. It was fascinating to watch him and his friends just sit on the porch and rock. Granted it presents an idealized and romanticized view of life in a small town. Granted also that they did not discuss great themes together. Yet the pace made significant thought and deep relationship possible, which for the most they are not today. We repeat: the pace of life today is driven by a massive flight from God, as man seeks peace apart from his Maker

Second, he can join the crowd. He can seek peace and safety in numbers. He can join the mass, join the herd. I remember back when I was in junior high the obsessive concern I had with the length of my pants. It had to be just so, probably within an eighth of an inch of the desired length. Why? Because I had to fit in. I had to match what the other boys were wearing. Our children become slaves of their peers at an early age, a problem to which premature institutionalization probably contributes.

But the problem is not just one of childish peer-dependency, but adult as well. Notice the trend toward centralization over the past 70 years. Greater and greater concentrations of people and power are found in the government, in corporations, and in metropolitan areas. What drives us together? Fear. The quest for security and safety, as in the days of the tower of Babel (Gen 11:1 ff.). We have become a nation of sheep. We all follow the fashions in clothes, cars, homes. There is a sense in which even the most non-conforming of today's college students conform to a highly stylized non-conformity. We were once sitting behind a large group of high school boys at a University of Miami football game, each of whom was wearing a hat. No two of them had the hat on in the same way. One was wearing it conventionally, another with the bill up, another backward, another backward with the bill up, another sidewards, and so on. They were expressing their individuality, right? Wrong. They were conforming to non-conformity. *They each had a hat!*

The worst of all the manifestations of 'mass man' is in the area of thought. Solzhenitsyn complained, in his famous Harvard Commencement Address of 1978, of the 'idols of prevailing fad,' and of censorship administered not by the state, as in the Soviet Union, but censorship 'dictated by fashion.'[162] One pays a steep price in this society for challenging the accepted wisdom, for, in effect, disturbing the peace. That is how I think we should see the trouble that the church finds herself in. As long as no one is challenging the status quo, all are at peace. Sinners feel safe in the herd. But when a gospel believing church preaches the law of God, the fornicators, adulterers, and homosexuals react. When we preach repentance, the liars and cheaters and thieves resent it. The world gets stirred up. How dare you disturb our peace, they say. Fall into line, they insist. Go back into your church and don't lift your voice again. This is why Christian people adopt the world's fashions, whether clothing or thoughts. The world's fads are driven by the same massive flight from God as activism is. I am amazed when I see Christians repeating the same hackneyed phrases as the world uses, or racing to buy the latest thing. Don't join the herd. Realize where this comes from. The world may mock us as old fashioned and out-of-date, but deep down, they all know better. In their few quiet moments, they know that all is not well. The safety of the crowd is no safety at all.

Third, he can join the party. We are a nation that is *Amusing Ourselves to Death*, as Neil Postman entitled his amazingly insightful book. We are the most self-indulgent, hedonistic, pleasure seeking society in at least a thousand years. Hours and hours and hours are spent each week entertaining ourselves. Four to six hours a day are spent in front of the television. The average high school student is said to spend five hours a day listening to music. The sexual revolution is completely out of control, with 40% of America's teenage girls becoming pregnant before they are out of high school, or one in ten *each year*! We all know the dreary statistics on drug and alcohol consumption. Love of sports has reached idolatrous proportions. What is happening here? We are seeking peace on a playground, peace in a bottle, or peace in a pill. We are seeking relief from a dreary, meaningless existence through sensual pleasure and excitement. We want to withdraw for a while from life's unsolvable problems and relax. We watch sports to escape. We plop down in front of a television and escape. Isn't this even the language that we use?

Ironically, as we get older the pendulum swings away from following the crowd, and we build our cabin in the woods, so that we can *escape*. We run now in order to *hide*. We have to get away from it all. But does it work? Do we finally find our peace and rest in retirement heaven? No, not there either. Instead, as each year passes we feel eternity pressing harder and harder upon us. Death is knocking. We feel its approach. Fear gnaws at our souls, so we run out for another round of golf, another game of tennis, a night out on the town.

But it can't work. None of it works. Not even religion works. We have witnessed the growth of exotic eastern religions, especially amongst the entertainment elite. They have it all, and have found that it doesn't work. They've had unlimited resources with which to have 'fun,' and like Solomon before them have found that it is all 'vanity and striving after the wind.' They have tried it all and done it all in massive quantities and still they are empty. Still they have no peace. So finally they turn to religion. This is good because religions are designed to deal with the problem of our guilt. The single profound insight of religion is that people feel guilty and need a means of removing their guilt, of appeasing the gods. Religion is universal because guilt is universal. So they prescribe sacrifices, either in the form of animal sacrifices, or of ascetic practices, such as prayer, fasting, or poverty, or sacrifices in the form of moral conduct. This is how one removes one's guilt and gets right with God. One performs religious works or moral works and thus appeases the deity. But does it work? Of course not. Why not? Well, it is obvious why not. It doesn't work because one can never do enough. There is always another sin for which one must appease the deity. Religion makes slaves of people. They live in fear that their sacrifice is inadequate. They must always do more. More is demanded by the priest or witch doctor. Guilt drives them on and on. It never ends. They can never rest. They can never know peace. Nothing that the world offers works. Nothing.

True Peace

True, deep, lasting peace can only be found in God, and God can only be known in Christ Jesus. Jesus is the source of real, permanent peace.

This is so not because Jesus is some sort of ultimate trip. At the time of the 'Jesus Movement', t-shirts appeared on the scene that said, 'get high on Christ.' This is to reduce the gospel to a subjective experience that some might find to be superior to all the rest, but, on the other hand, others might not. No, the gospel brings peace because of things that happened outside of myself, in history, in time and space, not just in the realm of thought and experience. True peace, lasting peace, is a gift of the Holy Spirit, and is only to be found in the Holy Spirit, for the following reasons.

First, in Christ we have peace with God. The peace we have with God is an objective peace. It is not peaceful feeling, but an end to actual conflict with the One who has been our Enemy (Rom. 5:10). At the cross Christ bore our sins in His body, thereby removing our guilt (again, actual guilt, as in a guilty verdict, not at this point guilt feelings), and reconciling us with God. Paul writes,

> ...it was the Father's good pleasure ...to reconcile all things to Himself (through Christ), having made peace through the blood of the cross ...

> although you were formerly alienated and hostile in mind. (Col. 1:19–21)

Even more simply he writes,

> Therefore having been justified by faith, we have peace with God through our Lord Jesus Christ. (Rom. 5:1)

What we all sense is true. We are separated and guilty. The solution is not activism, collectivism, self-indulgence, or religion. The solution is faith in Jesus Christ, the Savior of the world. He removes the guilt that brings the wrath. God is no longer against us. We no longer face His anger. We are no longer under His judgment. Like two formerly warring nations who have ceased hostilities, a state of peace exists between us. The war is over. This can be so for you. You can be right with God through Jesus. You can have peace with God. Jesus has removed the source of provocation. All you need to is come to Him by faith.

Second, through the Holy Spirit we have peace in our hearts. It is the task of the Spirit to apply the work of Christ to our hearts, working faith in us, and then convincing us that it is so. Have you even seen an actual acquittal on television? The moment that the accused hears the verdict of 'not guilty,' he is overwhelmed with a sense of relief. Joy floods his heart. Those who are acquitted sometimes even collapse in emotional release. Similarly, this is how it is for those who have faith in Christ. They have heard the verdict of 'not guilty,' and they are overwhelmed with relief. They realize that the big issues of life have been settled.

Let me use another, though mundane, illustration. Back in my junior high days there was this bad boy named Jimmy Meyers. One day he got real angry at me about something, and said he was going to fight me the next day after school when we got off the bus. I went to prayer meeting that night. That whole night and all the next day I was extremely upset, to the point of making myself sick. How I was dreading the end of the school day, boarding the bus with Jimmy, knowing that when we got off my life would be over! Finally the bell rang ending seventh period. We boarded the bus. There was Jimmy in the back. We drove home on our Crown-built 'Freeway Flyer,' speeding along the San Diego Freeway at sixty-five miles per hour. My bus stop was the first. We turned the corner and stopped. The door opened. I got off and stood waiting. The door closed. No Jimmy. The bus drove off. I looked around. I had survived! Hurray! I ran home, filled with joy. The day of reckoning had passed, and I had lived to tell about it. But then the thought crossed my mind, maybe he meant tomorrow? Oh no, I thought, and dread filled my heart once more. It went on this way for probably two months. Every day I thought the day of reckoning had come. Every day I breathed a great sigh of relief. I even went to the church's mid-week prayer meeting a couple of times. We never did have the fight. Apparently Jimmy was as scared as I was. I trust that God will forgive the comparison with Jimmy, but this for me illustrates the psychology of unbelief. We know that there is a day of reckoning. We dread its approach. The writer to the Hebrews speaks of 'those who through fear of death were subject to slavery all their lives' (Heb. 2:15). But when through Christ the day passes we are freed from the fear of death and judgment. One can see in the faces of adult converts a visible change come over them. They have in Christ a 'peace that passes comprehension' (Phil. 4:6). The Holy Spirit convinces us of the certainty of these things. He 'bears witness with our spirit that we are children of God.' Paul writes,

> For you have not received a spirit of slavery leading to fear again, but you have received a spirit of adoption as sons by which we cry out, 'Abba! Father!' (Rom. 8:15)

Why do we have peace? Because the big issues are resolved. We have been reconciled to God. We have been adopted into the family of God. We are His children. He is our Father. I have a whole new outlook. I have nothing to be concerned about in time and eternity. He is my shield and fortress. He is my refuge and strength. He is my help in need. He will never leave me or forsake me. We have a foundation of peace that cannot be shaken. Jesus said,

> Peace I leave with you; My peace I give to you; not as the world gives, do I give to you. Let not your heart be troubled, nor let it be fearful. (John 14:27)

Again He said,

> These things I have spoken to you, that in Me you may have peace. In the world you have tribulation, but take courage; I have overcome the world. (John 16:33)

Clearly this does not mean a trouble-free life. Jesus says, 'in the world you have tribulation.' We will continue to suffer physical ailments. We will continue to struggle with the issues of life—feeding, clothing, and housing our families. We will continue to die. Some of us may be martyred. All of us, to a greater or lesser extent, will suffer rejection by a world that hates us because it hated Jesus. But through it all there is profound contentment. Through it all we can say with the Scriptures, 'If God is for us who is against us?' (Rom. 8:31). We see ourselves primarily as children of God, of brethren with Christ, and so we have adopted an eternal perspective. We say with the Apostle (in the same Romans 8 passage emphasizing adoption that was cited above),

> For I consider that the sufferings of this present time are not worthy to be compared with the glory that is to be revealed to us. (Rom. 8:18)

Life is short, eternity is long, and so we can do without and go without if this is the will of my Father in heaven. I can endure material deprivation. I can survive the loss of friends and even have withdrawn from me the love of family members. Listen to that great Christian the Apostle Paul:

> Not that I speak from want; for I have learned to be content in whatever circumstances I am. I know how to get along with humble means, and I also know how to live in prosperity; in any and every circumstance I have learned the secret of being filled and going hungry, both of having abundance and suffering need. I can do all things through Him who strengthens me. (Phil. 4:11–13)

The Holy Spirit works this deep, enduring contentment into our hearts. We don't have to race like mad men through life as the world does. We don't have to slavishly follow the crowd and all the trends. We don't have to drown our sorrows in physical or chemical pleasures. We are at peace with God. We are at peace with our circumstances. We are at peace with ourselves.

Third, through the Holy Spirit we have peace with others. Let's go back to Jimmy. When I was fretting about him I was of no use to others. I was completely preoccupied with my trials. My anxiety kept me in turmoil. But peace in the heart opens the door to helping others. Peace with God (objective peace) which brings peace in my heart (subjective peace) frees me to love others and be a 'peacemaker' (relational peace; Matt. 5:9). The peace of the Spirit has a pervasive effect upon me, which then has a settling and calming effect upon others. Surely you have seen this. The Holy Spirit gives to His people both the wisdom and calming peace to inspire confidence in warring factions, and to spread peace among them. He makes peacemakers of us. We make peace in our own relationships, so that so far as it depends on us we are at peace with all men. We don't take revenge. We don't pay back evil for evil, but overcome evil with good (Rom. 12:17 ff.).

Ask yourself, what am I known for? Am I the first to reconcile? The first to forgive? The first to make peace? Or does the other guy always have to take the initiative? I am amazed at how long standing feuds are allowed to persist in the church. Are you a peacemaker? Then make peace. Bud Leonard, father of John Leonard (formerly missionary to the Arabs in France, and faculty member of Westminster Theological Seminary in Philadelphia), an elder of the Granada Presbyterian Church, and a native Savannahian, was tragically injured in a car accident that left him paralyzed from the neck down. I was an assistant minister at the time and was splitting pulpit duty, including Sunday morning, with the other assistant, Danny Levi. One day we went together to visit Bud. There he was, lying on his bed, unable to move, nearly dead, hardly able to speak. He whispered out, 'James 3:16.' It took several tries for us to understand. Finally we got it and turned to it. It says,

> For where jealousy and selfish ambition exist, there is disorder and every evil thing. (James 3:16)

The other assistant, Danny, looked knowingly at me and softly chuckled. I didn't understand. I thought he had the wrong reference. Danny whispered, 'He's worried about us.' I thought about it for a moment, and then was overwhelmed. Ol' Bud is dying here on this bed, can't move, can't read, can hardly speak, and he's worrying about Danny and me getting along with each other. Bud was a peace maker. Paul exhorts us to treat one another with humility, gentleness, patience, forbearance, 'being diligent to preserve the unity of the Spirit in the bond of peace' (Eph. 4:3).

Is peace characteristic of our lives? If the Holy Spirit is present in our hearts, it must be. If it isn't, I should ask myself, have I made peace with God? Have I, in other words, repented of my sin, and turned to Christ as Savior and Lord? Do I have peace in my heart? Knowing that I have made peace with God, do I have the assurance, the confidence that the Spirit gives that I am a child of God, and the consequent contentment which follows? Am I a peacemaker, or a trouble maker? Am I able to bring people together, to reconcile those who are in conflict? Peace is the fruit of the Spirit. He is the source from which true peace flows.

30

The Fruit of the Spirit is Patience, Kindness, Goodness

Galatians 5:22–23

We move along now to the middle triad, patience, kindness, and goodness, or those fruit having to do with conduct towards others. We note the main point: the Holy Spirit transforms the way that I look at and treat other people. The Spirit works in such a way that I come to view others with understanding, sympathy, forbearance, and generosity. I can no longer dismiss them with the wave of the hand. No longer can I 'blow up' because of perceived or real deficiencies in them. I now am patient, kind, and good to all. If there is a single key to how the Spirit does this in us, that key is *humility*. We come to look with sympathy towards others because the Spirit has shown us our own weaknesses and our own consequent need of the patience, kindness, and goodness of others.

Transformed Conduct

We begin to look at the Apostle's specific language. *First, the Apostle Paul writes of 'patience.'* The Greek word, *makrothumia* is a compound word which means long-suffering. It is the opposite of what we mean when we speak of someone being *short*-tempered. One who is patient is '*long*-tempered.' It particularly has application in circumstances in which one is provoked, and might otherwise be inclined to erupt against the source of provocation.

For example, we are at times provoked by *people*. We are angered by their attacks or slights. We become frustrated by their quirks and habits and inabilities. Why does he always leave his socks on the floor? Why doesn't she ever squeeze the toothpaste tube from the end? We can grow impatient and intolerant of them. Further, we grow impatient of those whose ability, knowledge, or performance is not up to par. Athletes are impatient of the uncoordinated, the experienced of the inexperienced, the knowledgeable of the ignorant, the initiated of the uninitiated. Have you ever tried to teach someone to drive? Then you have struggled with patience. I spent a number of summers working for Bekins moving company. The summer college boys were put on trucks with veteran drivers. Typically they would verbally abuse the rookies because they didn't know exactly how to move furniture—as though one ought to roll out of the womb knowing the techniques, presumably just as they did. They had no patience whatsoever with those who did not know what they knew, or could not do what they could do.

Through the Spirit, we become patient of others, even when provoked. In order to better understand what patience means, look at the following texts and note the words with which it is combined.

> …walk in a manner worthy of the calling with which you have been called, with all humility and gentleness, with patience, showing forbearance to one another in love. (Eph. 4:1–2)

> …walk in a manner worthy of the Lord, to please Him in all respects...strengthened with all power, according to His glorious might, for the attaining of all steadfastness and patience …(Col. 1:10–11)

> And so, as those who have been chosen of God, holy and beloved, put on a heart of compassion, kindness, humility, gentleness and patience; bearing with one another, and forgiving each other, whoever has a complaint against anyone; just as the Lord forgave you, so also should you. (Col. 3:12–13)

> And we urge you, brethren, admonish the unruly, encourage the fainthearted, help the weak, be patient with all men. See that no one repays another with evil for evil, but always seek after that which is good for one another and for all men (1 Thess. 5:14–15)

Patience is spoken of in connection with humility, gentleness, forbearance, steadfastness, 'bearing with one another, and forgiving each other,' not repaying 'evil for evil,' but instead seeking 'that which is good for one another and for all men.' In the parable of forgiveness the slave who owes the unpayable debt pleads, 'Have patience with me…' Similarly, the fellow slave who owes him a few cents pleads, 'Have patience with me' (Matt. 18:26, 29). In both cases patience would mean looking with sympathy at the debtor's plight, giving him additional time to repay the debt. It means compassion and tolerance. One might be frustrated by the failure of the debtee to repay up to that point, but the godly response is to have 'patience,' and relax the strict requirements of the contract.

Not only people but *circumstances* can also provoke rash responses from us. As an undergraduate at the University of Southern California reporting for my first day of work at an upscale restaurant in Marina Del Rey (Los Angeles), I got stuck on a metered on-ramp of the Santa Monica freeway. I could see before long that I'd never get there on time. I was so frustrated that I pounded the steering wheel. Then I punched the windshield. Crack, it went. We grow impatient in frustrating circumstances. We are exhorted to be patient in the contexts of persecution requiring endurance (2 Tim. 3:10), unfulfilled promises from God requiring faith, (Heb. 6:12–15), suffering requiring waiting for deliverance (James 5:7–10). The meaning of patience is 'don't give up.' Persevere. Remain faithful. Be steadfast. Endure. Keep going. Don't give in to the temptation to doubt, to disobey, and to give-up, to quit. Even as in the days of Noah, despite extraordinary provocation, 'the patience of God kept waiting,' so you too must keep waiting (1 Pet. 3:20). This patience, both with people and circumstances, is a fruit of the Holy Spirit's presence in a believer's life.

Second, the Apostle Paul speaks of 'kindness'. Chrestotes means being charitable in our assessment and treatment of others. It means showing sympathy, understanding, and generosity toward others, especially the undeserving. This is illustrated in Luke 6:27–36.

> But I say to you who hear, love your enemies, do good to those who hate you, bless those who curse you, pray for those who mistreat you. Whoever hits you on the cheek, offer him the other also; and whoever takes away your coat, do not withhold your shirt from him either. Give to everyone who asks of you, and whoever takes away what is yours, do not demand it back. And just as you want people to treat you, treat them in the same way. And if you love those who love you, what credit is that to you? For even sinners love those who love them. And if you do good to those who do good to you, what credit is that to you? For even sinners do the same. And if you lend to those from whom you expect to receive, what credit is that to you? Even sinners lend to sinners, in order to receive back the same amount. But love your enemies, and do good, and lend, expecting nothing in return; and your reward will be great, and you will be sons of the Most High; for He Himself is kind to ungrateful and evil men. Be merciful, just as your Father is merciful.

Here kindness, the kindness of God that we are to emulate, is associated with loving, doing good, blessing, turning the other cheek, giving, lending, and showing mercy. It is extended to those who don't love you back, who aren't good, who can't pay back, who are enemies, who mistreat you, who take your coat and are ungrateful and evil. This is what kindness is. It is associated with compassion, humility, gentleness, and patience in Colossians 3:12–13, with grace in Ephesians 2:7, and is contrasted with severity in Romans 11:22. Lightfoot defines *chrestotes* with 'a kindly disposition toward one's neighbor;'[163] Hendriksen as 'mildness, benignity;'[164] Plummer as 'sweetness of temper which puts others at ease, and shrinks from giving pain;'[165] Eadie as 'gentleness, affability...the soft answer...a serene, loving, and sympathizing temper.'[166]

This then takes us a step beyond patience. Kindness is not merely enduring the foolishness and failure of others. Kindness is not content to merely tolerate. It is not content with merely putting up with another. It must actually return acts of love. It refuses to be *un*kind. It refuses to return evil for evil. It will not be rude. It will not insult. It will not degrade. It is courteous to enemies. It is helpful to critics. It is good to those who hate it, it blesses those who curse, it prays for those who mistreat.

There was a man in Miami who deeply and cruelly wounded me during my years as an assistant. Years later he called me to ask my advice about what to do for his back problem. He remembered that I had tried almost everything to avoid surgery. I never tried acupuncture. But I tried everything else. I was very surprised to hear his voice, to say the least. The thought crossed my mind that this was a moment for sweet revenge. I could tell him that I was busy and to call 911 if he needed help. A split second later I decided to help him, and patiently led him through the options that I had explored. I attributed this right response to the Holy Spirit. The Spirit inspires kindness from us. He moves a Louis Zamperini to return to Japan after World War II to minister to his former captors and tormentors. He inspires a Corrie Ten Boom to find her former S.S. guards and forgive and love them.

Third, the Apostle Paul writes of 'goodness.' Agathosyne is almost synonymous with 'kindness,' and often used interchangeably with it. But it can have one difference. It too indicates a generous spirit, but also carries the sense of the good which the good man does. Goodness is doing the good thing, meaning the right thing, the necessary and proper thing. For example, Jesus, when he cleansed the Temple, driving out the moneychangers with a whip, could not be said to be doing a *kind* thing. But He was doing a *good* thing. When Jesus denounced the Pharisees as a brood of vipers, he was not being kind, but he was being good. It was the right thing to do. Trench explains:

> A man might display his agathosyne, his zeal for goodness and truth in rebuking, correcting, chastising...but we could not say that his chrestotes was shown in these acts of righteous indignation.[167] (*NT Synonyms*, p 235).

'Goodness' indicates that which is generous, merciful, and forbearing. But it also designates doing the right thing. When facing evil, goodness will confront, exhort, discipline. These initiatives may not be what is wanted, but they are at times what is needed, what is necessary. Look again at 1 Thessalonians 5:14–15. In the same sentence in which he says 'be patient with all men,' he also says 'admonish the unruly.' He continues, 'always seek after that which is good for one another and for all men.' Goodness is what Joseph demonstrated when he refused the advances of Potipher's wife (Gen. 39:8). In doing so he might have hurt her feelings and even insulted her, but it was the right thing to do. Goodness is what John the Baptist did in denouncing Herod's marriage to his brother's wife (Mark 6:18). Goodness is what Paul demanded when he commanded the Corinthians to 'remove the wicked man' from among them (1 Cor. 5:11). These were not 'nice' things to do or say. But they were the right things to do and say. The Holy Spirit gives us the wisdom, the sensitivity and the courage to do good, even if it means being tough.

The Heart of Transformation

These three, patience, kindness, goodness, are the fruit of the Spirit. The Spirit transforms our hearts so that we look at people differently. We can't look at them the same way any longer. What then is the difference? How does the Spirit change the way that we look at others? By making us humble.

First, the Spirit gives to me a more humble outlook on the irritating habits, qualities, and views of others. How so? He helps me to see my pride. I am frustrated with them, and consequently impatient and unkind, because I see my self as superior to them. They, you see, are uncoordinated, forgetful, sloppy, irrational, and tasteless. Of course I get frustrated with them. I, on the other hand, am none of the above. I, on the other hand, am 'poetry in motion,' graceful, brilliant, and cultured. This is not only the problem of an inflated self-assessment, but also a form of arrogance against God. Most of what is wrong with others has to do with the way that God has made them. They are uncoordinated, unintelligent, and so on, because that is how God made them. Ultimately I am displeased with God. Ultimately I am saying, 'I would not have made such a person as they are.' The Spirit helps me to see this for what it is, and see me for what I am. I too am loaded with annoying quirks. I too need the patience and kindness of others.

Second, the Spirit gives me a more humble outlook on trying circumstances. Years ago I drove to downtown Boston to shop at noon. The inevitable happened. I drove around and around and could not find a place to park. After about thirty-five minutes of that I was blind with rage. I pounded my steering wheel. I hated Boston. I was in a state! The most unkind things were coming out of my mouth. What were my expectations? I was expecting that there should have been a parking spot for me. I was expecting, in effect, that I should not have to experience that which the mass of humanity has to experience.

What was I anticipating at noon in Boston? It is the same every noon. Should I expect God to disrupt cause and effect in order to open up a parking spot for me?

What about traffic? Should I not have to wait in traffic? Should God part the cars like He did the Red Sea and allow me to pass through? Should I not get a flat tire? Should I not suffer computer failures like everyone else. 'Why me?' we ask. The real question is, 'Why not me?' The truth is, we don't much like how God is running the show. He should have arranged things differently. His timetable is off. It was the wrong time for the light to turn red. It was the wrong time for me to get sick. It was the wrong time for mechanical failure to occur. We want our way now. This is why single people sometimes grow impatient and marry an inappropriate person. They want results now. They want action now. When they don't get it, they take things into their own hands. I'm reminded of the British soldier during the Second World War who was overheard saying, 'If I only were in charge of the universe for five minutes I'd set it all right.' In other words, God is doing a poor job of governing the world, and Private Joe Bloggs could do better. This is arrogant. We wander to the kitchen in the middle of the night. We trip over a chair that we don't see. Frustrated, we turn and kick the chair! Is there anything more irrational than that? At whom is our impatience ultimately directed?

Sometimes, as in this last example, our anger is directed at ourselves. But this is a manifestation of pride as well. We walk through life with unreasonable expectations. I'm in the driveway shooting baskets. The longer I shoot, the more frustrated I become. One of the children comes out, and I snap at him. I miss again. I'm angry. Why am I angry? Because of pride. Why is this pride? Because I always miss. What is unusual about missing? Where does this expectation of perfection come from? The same is true at the typewriter or word processor. I'm making mistakes. The longer I type, the more impatient I grow. But the fact is, I always make typing mistakes. I have unreasonable, proud, inflated expectations of my capabilities. The boneheaded reality is that our lives are riddled with mistakes. So why get worked up about it? Why get excited about losing the keys? You lose the keys every day. You lose them every time you sit down! Pride drives our inflated self-assessment. The Spirit helps us to look honestly at the real us, and to accept ourselves and our circumstances as God has ordered them.

Third, the Spirit gives me a more sympathetic view of the sins, failures, weaknesses, and needs of others. This moves us beyond impatience with quirks to impatience with moral defects. If I know my own heart, I will not be too hard on others as they fail and fall. As Paul put it,

> Therefore let him who thinks he stands take heed lest he fall. (1 Cor. 10:12)

Addressing Roman Gentiles who were beginning to look arrogantly at Israel's apostasy, Paul warns,

> They were broken off for their unbelief, and you stand only by your faith. Do not be conceited, but fear. (Rom. 11:20)

They have fallen and you stand. Why do you stand? Only 'by your faith.' Consequently 'do not be conceited,' as though you were somehow superior, 'but fear.' The Spirit humbles us so that we see our common frailties. I too am vulnerable. I too fail. I too am weak. As the national poet of Scotland, Robert Burns (1759–1796), wrote,

> O would the Power the giver give us
> To see ourselves as others see us.

Our tendency is to see *your* sins as obvious and serious, and *mine* as minor and subtle, or even non-existent. Paul writes,

> And so, as those who have been chosen of God, holy and beloved, put on a heart of compassion, kindness, humility, gentleness and patience; (Col. 3:12)

Patience, kindness, gentleness, and humility and compassion are lumped together here and elsewhere (Eph. 4:2). Because we are what we are only by the grace of God (1 Cor. 15:10), only because we 'have been chosen by God,' we ought to be patient, forbearing, and forgiving of one another. Well you say, you don't know what I deal with trying to handle so and so. No, you don't know what so and so has to deal with in trying to handle you! God has been patient and kind and good to us when we didn't deserve it. So also we ought to be to one another.

This is not to sentimentalize what is required. Again we cite Paul,

> And we urge you, brethren, admonish the unruly, encourage the fainthearted, help the weak, be patient with all men. (1 Thess. 5:14)

The fainthearted are to be encouraged, the weak are to be helped, all are to receive patience, yet still the unruly are to be admonished. For all our sympathy, we still do the right thing. For all our understanding and compassion, our patience and forbearance, our kindness and tenderness, we still must do what is right and good and best for all, and that at times will include saying some hard things and taking some drastic steps. Still, we view the sin, the failure, the weaknesses, and needs of others with sympathy. We show them patience. We are kind. We do them good.

Frankly, as we have repeatedly suggested, we in the Christian community are still too tough on each other. We are too quick to condemn, too quick to judge. Ironically, it is often those who oppose the official, public judgments of the church through its court (the session) who are the harshest critics of all. They oppose church discipline, even while they inflict personal discipline through censorious private opinions. We are all quick to become intolerant and unkind toward any opinion but our own. We judge and condemn with a minimum of knowledge. We assign ourselves the roles of judge, jury, and executioner.

You don't like this about yourself and I don't like it about me. Thankfully these things don't have to be. Through the Holy Spirit our handling of others will be characterized by patience, kindness, and goodness. Through the Holy Spirit we become patient, kind, and good.

31

The Fruit of the Spirit is Faithfulness

Galatians 5:22–23

We arrive now at the first character quality found in the last triad of fruit, organized according to the following categories:

1. the *disposition* of the Christian - love, joy, peace
2. the *conduct* of the Christian - patience, kindness, goodness
3. the *character* of the Christian - faithfulness, meekness, self-control

To make fruit fit so neatly together we have placed love in the first group, even though it is more comprehensive than just 'disposition.' We also should understand that there is overlap between fruit, and even between categories of fruit. Even so, they seem to fall out along these lines, and it is not surprising that they should. The Apostle Paul's mind seems to work in organized ways, and rather than pitching out the 'deeds of the flesh' or the fruit randomly, he presents them in such a fashion that they relate to one another.

What then is faithfulness? The word *pistis* usually means simply 'faith,' but in the context of a list of virtues takes on the nuance of trustworthiness, fidelity, honesty, loyalty. If goodness means doing what is right, then faithfulness means continuing to do what is right. It is closely related to endurance and steadfastness. The faithful person is one who at all costs continues to do the right thing. If he makes a promise he keeps it. 'He swears to his own hurt,' the Psalmist says, 'and does not change' (Ps. 15:4). His yes is yes and his no is no. He is dependable, reliable, consistent. He honors his commitments. He sticks by his convictions. He resists the temptation to compromise his principles.

The Proverbs pose an important question for us today. They say,

> Many a man proclaims his own loyalty, but who can find a trustworthy man? (Prov. 20:6).

To say that there is need for faithfulness is to state the obvious. As the Christian memory of our civilization dims, we are increasingly paying the price for the fading of this Christian virtue. For generations our culture was shaped by the Puritan fathers and their precisionist ethic of absolute and inflexible integrity. You may know the oft repeated answer of the English Puritan John Rogers to the pejorative question, 'Why must you be so precise?' 'O Sir,' he answered, 'I serve a precise God!' Thus spoke Puritanism.

They made famous the Protestant work ethic: honest work for honest wages. We are indebted to them for many of our ideals for the Christian family such as priestly fathers, godly mothers, and carefully nurtured children. They were devoted church members. By any reasonable standard, they were men and women of heroic proportions. Yet our age mocks them as hard, cold legalists, and elevates anti-heroes in their place. Indeed as some commentators have pointed out, true heroes have disappeared from the scene and been replaced by celebrities, an altogether different entity. The rich and famous can have no virtue at all. They can be as obscene as a Madonna, as vulgar as a Rosanne, and as bizarre as a Dennis Rodman. These are the kinds of people that our culture elevates. They are richly rewarded for their decadence. They are given influence and a public voice. The faithful husband and father, working eight to five to support his family, is seen as boring and unimaginative. The godly mother who sacrifices much to care for her children is seen as passé. Our anti-heroes are almost never married, drink heavily, are promiscuous, have unusual jobs or no job. They are conventionally unconventional. Of course they 'hear the beat of a different drummer.' They can't be tied down. They are pleasure-seeking nomads. Self-sacrificing, hard working fathers and mothers are not to be seen on the television or in the movies.

So we have sown the wind of unfaithfulness and have reaped the whirlwind of social chaos. In our generation we have witnessed the collapse of virtues that were normative for centuries. Employers all across this country complain of the death of the work ethic. You can't depend on people any more. You can't count on employees to give you an honest day's labor. They loaf on the job. They stretch their breaks. They report late and leave early. You can't count on the quality of the work once it is finally completed. Shoddy workmanship has become the norm.

Nowhere is this more apparent than in the realm of marriage. The institution of marriage is in a state of collapse in our day, with fifty-percent of all new marriages ending in divorce, with thirty-percent of all children being born out of wedlock, and with seventy-five percent of all children spending some part of their years growing up with a single parent. Back in 1979 Armand Nicholi II, of Harvard University, wrote in *Christianity Today* in an article entitled 'The Fractured Family: Following It into the Future,' that 'Social scientists warn us the family is disintegrating and may not survive this century.'[168] At the heart of this national tragedy is men and women who have not been faithful to their vows. How has it become so easy to dishonor one's word? Why can promises so easily be cast aside? It is harder to break a business contract in most states in this country than to end a marriage.

Where is the faithful man? Woman? Where is the honest neighbor, the reliable friend, the hardworking employee, the faithful spouse? Why are we overrun with vandalism, with shoplifting, with conventional robbery, with white collar crime, with faulty checks, with credit card fraud? Even the best of us pale in comparison with the ethical integrity of previous generations. Our ethics are sloppy. We excuse partial obedience. We rationalize disobedience. We fully comply only as it is convenient. We cut corners, we compromise quality, we indulge 'white lies,' and amazingly, think nothing of it. We are *Losing Our Virtue*, as David Wells so aptly put it in the title of his book.[169]

We want to have integrity, don't we? We want to be reliable. We want to be dependable. We want to be consistent and precise. How can we become such? Not by merely trying hard. Faithfulness is a 'fruit' of the Holy Spirit. Only Christ can make us faithful. He is 'faithful and true' (Rev. 3:14; 19:11). 'He was faithful to Him who appointed Him' (Heb. 3:2). He is 'a merciful and faithful High Priest' (Heb. 2:17; cf. 2 Thess. 3:3). He asked His accusers, 'can any of you prove me guilty of sin?' (John 8:26). Of course, none could. He was above reproach. He was beyond accusation both in word and deed. He continues to be utterly reliable. Our God is a faithful God (1 Cor. 1:9; 10:13; 2 Cor. 1:18; 1 Thess. 5:24; 2 Thess. 3:3; 2 Tim. 2:13; Heb. 10:23; 11:11; 1 Pet. 4:19; 1 John 1:9). His word is faithful and true (1 Tim. 1:15; 3:1; 4:9; 2 Tim. 2:11). We can depend upon Him and all that He says.

Faithfulness is the 'fruit' of the presence of the Holy Spirit in a believer's life. He conforms us to His image. He makes us like He is. We become faithful because He is faithful. Would you like to be known as a person of irreproachable honesty, integrity, reliability, dependability? The Holy Spirit makes such of His people. We can trace this in two directions.

Faithfulness to God

When the Holy Spirit comes to dwell in our hearts He begins immediately to create in us a burden to be faithful to all that our God is and all that He requires of us. We want to hear on judgment day the words, 'Well done, good and faithful servant' (Matt. 25:21). Our great ambition is to be pleasing to Him (2 Cor. 5:9). Faithfulness to God requires two things of us.

First, faithfulness to God is found in believing all that He says. I am faithful to God as I believe all that God says about Himself and His gospel in His word. Christians have always faced the awful temptation to pick and choose what they will believe according to where society is registering its disapproval. Today, even as we speak, there are Christians all over the world who are being persecuted for their beliefs. Coptic Christians in Egypt, Christians throughout the Middle East, in China, in Africa, Protestants in Latin America, Catholics in Cuba, and so on. Tens of millions of Christians were martyred in the last century and the pace continues. Some observers note that there have been more Christians killed for their faith in the twentieth century than in all previous centuries combined. An estimated 150,000 Christians are martyred each year today. In the West we face a different kind of pressure, but pressure nonetheless. There is a price to pay when one confesses Christ. Faithfulness to God means responding to the pressure to compromise, to affirm 90% of what the Bible teaches and dodge the persecution attached to the 10%, to pick and choose doctrines, with unflinching orthodoxy, 'holding fast the word of life' (Titus 1:9). This is a major concern of Paul throughout the Pastoral Epistles. 'Guard what has been entrusted to you,' Paul tells Timothy (1 Tim. 6:20). 'Retain the standard of sound words which you have heard from me …Guard through the Holy Spirit who dwells in us, the treasure which has been entrusted to you.' Though others have turned away, such as Phygelus and Hermogenes, 'be strong' and 'entrust to faithful men' the things 'which you have heard from me.' 'Suffer hardship with me, as a good soldier of Christ Jesus' (2 Tim. 1:13–15; 2:1–3). We are warned,

> If we endure, we shall also reign with Him; If we deny Him, He also will deny us. (2 Tim. 2:12–13)

We are warned again, 'all who desire to live godly in Christ Jesus will be persecuted' (3:12). Though evil men and imposters come to deceive (and compromise the integrity of the gospel),

> You, however, continue in the things you have learned and become convinced of, knowing from whom you have learned them. (2 Tim. 3:14; cf. 4:1–5)

This is also a major concern (*the* major concern?) of the Book of Hebrews. Those who are tempted to fall back into Judaism, a protected religion of the Roman Empire, are warned in verse after verse to resist that temptation. We must 'hold fast,' he tells them (3:6). Sternly they are warned,

> Take care, brethren lest there should be in any one of you an evil, unbelieving heart, in falling away from the living God. (Heb. 3:12; cf. 4:11; 6:1–6; 10:19–31; 11:12)

They are urged, 'Let us hold fast the confession of our hope without wavering, for He who promised is faithful.' 'Do not throw away your confidence ...you have need of endurance ...we are not of those who shrink back to destruction, but of those who have faith to the preserving of the soul' (Heb. 10:23, 35, 36, 39).

The story is told of the Huguenot woman who was imprisoned for her faith in the fortress prison at Aiguesmortes for thirty-seven years. The dragoons seized her at her wedding reception. When she was finally released she was an invalid, and had to be carried out by her husband. He had moved soon after her imprisonment to close proximity and had waited patiently for *thirty-seven years* for the occasion of their reunion. She left behind etched in stone the word, 'resist.' Resist! When the higher critics attack the infallibility of Scripture, resist. When the evolutionists attack the doctrine of creation, resist. When those who wish to discard inconvenient life through abortion and euthanasia, compromising the doctrine of the sanctity of human life, resist. When those who spout liberal optimism or see sin as sickness rather than rebellion against God and so compromise the doctrine of sin, resist. When American pluralism compromises the doctrine of the uniqueness of Christ and denies that He is 'the Way the Truth and the Life,' positing instead that there are many saviors and many ways, resist. When the Hedonists, the Libertines and the Antinomians say 'all things are lawful' and so compromise the doctrine of the Christian life, resist. In each of these cases we are tempted to fit in, to conform to the party line, to only say that which is fashionable. We are tempted to avoid the appearance of being unlearned or backward or ignorant. Yet faithfulness to God means loyalty to the gospel, even if it means that we offend our friends, lose the respect of the world or are thought of as odd. Biblical authority is probably the number one issue facing the church today, and the number one issue we face in our personal lives. Whether or not we will send missionaries to 'the lost' depends upon whether or not we believe the Bible. Whether or not we will live lives of moral purity depends upon whether or not we believe that the Bible is true. Only if we are faithful to all that God says will the Scriptures remain for us the 'rule of faith and practice.'

Second, faithfulness to God means obeying all that God commands. This means obeying not just in the areas with which I am comfortable and am in agreement. If I only obey God in the areas with which I already agree and reject the rest, then I am not really obeying God at all. Then I am only doing what *I* want, and on occasion it happens to correspond to what God says. Faithfulness to God means obeying in all areas in which He speaks, and over the long haul, whether I want to or not or feel like it or not. God commands that we honor and protect life. When one of our young women gets pregnant out of marriage, faithfulness requires that we resist the temptation to get an abortion. It means that even though I may be unhappy in my marriage, that I honor my vows. It means that though I may be desperate for money, I resist the temptation to steal or cheat. Though I am in a bind, I resist the temptation to lie. Faithfulness to God means that I obey Him whatever the cost. I don't misrepresent the facts. I don't shade the truth. I don't cut corners.

At times, this is going to mean ridicule. The world will look at our tight ethical system, our moral strictness and laugh and scoff. They'll wonder why we're not joining in the party. They'll wonder why we're missing out on all the fun. At times, faithfulness to God will mean inconvenience for us. There are things we cannot do that others do. There are things that we miss out on that others are able to participate in. There are movies that our children won't see because, by Christian moral standards, they are inappropriate. There are activities in which we will not participate because they violate the sanctity of the Lord's day. There are burdens that we will bear because we will not end life prematurely. But a man or woman of integrity will obey no matter what. They will bear the cost. They will endure the hardship. John writes, 'I have no greater joy than this, to hear of my children walking in the truth.' Then he adds, 'Beloved, you are acting faithfully in whatever you accomplish for the brethren' (3 John 5–6). 'Walking in the truth' spells faithfulness. The work of the Holy Spirit will result in faithful conformity to the law of God. It will result in faithful love for the brethren. It will result in obedience to the Great Commission. It will result in us conforming our lives to all that God requires of us. God sent His Son, condemning sin in the flesh, Paul writes,

> in order that the requirement of the Law might be fulfilled in us, who do not walk according to the flesh, but according to the Spirit. (Rom. 8:4)

As we walk according to the Spirit, we fulfill, or carry out, the requirements of the Law. We will love God and our neighbor. We will hallow the Christian Sabbath. We will honor our parents and others in authority. We will faithfully defend innocent life. We will remain loyal to our marriages for our entire lives. We will never steal, cheat, lie, or twist the truth. The spirit of covetousness will give way to contentedness. We will boldly proclaim Christ and fulfill the Great Commission.

It is this Spirit, then, that motivated Athanasius to defend the doctrine of the Trinity *contra mundum*, standing alone against the world. It is this spirit which inspired Martin Luther to defend the doctrine of justification by faith alone, boldly declaring at Worms, even with his life on the line, 'Here I stand. I cannot do otherwise. God help me. Amen.' It is this Spirit which enabled John Bunyan to spend years and years in prison for his faith, which he would not compromise. It is this Spirit which drove J. Gresham Machen to oppose the liberals in the 1920s and 30s, and in the process suffer loss of the social status bequeathed to him by his family and suffer the reproach of the world. 'And what more shall I say? For time will fail me if I tell of Gideon, Barak, Samson, Jephthah, of David and Samuel and the prophets,' and of all the rest of the saints (Heb. 11:32–3). These were 'faithful unto death' (Rev. 2:10), words engraved on Machen's tomb, 'men of whom the world was not worthy' (Heb. 11:38).

Faithfulness to Others

As we are seeing, in being faithful to God's commands, I will of necessity be faithful in my relations with others. God, after all, requires that I love my neighbor, that I not murder, commit adultery against, steal from, lie to, or covet my neighbor. We can break these in two categories.

First, faithfulness in relation to others means being true to my word. A faithful person is one whose word is reliable. He means what he says. He is dependable to a fault. He is utterly honest. He avoids exaggeration, embellishment, and distortion. This is not to say that there is not room for hyperbole, irony, and figures of speech. The Bible uses all of these forms. 'All the country' went out to see John the Baptist (Mark 1:5). Of course all did not go. It is hyperbole. The key is that it is understood as such and does not lead to misrepresentation in the minds of the readers. Neither should our statements misrepresent.

If the faithful man is late for work, he doesn't claim that it was the traffic if it wasn't. His yes is yes and his no is no (Matt. 5:37). If he makes a promise, he keeps it. If he makes a pledge, he honors it. Sometimes circumstances change and plans also have to change. We planned to give, but then there was a death in the family. In such circumstances one is released from one's promise. If I get in a wreck on the way to church next Sunday morning, though I said I would be here, I am released from the promise because of the changing circumstances. Still, excepting extraordinary events, I must be utterly faithful in fulfilling my promises. I ought to be known as one who will do what he says he is going to do.

Ask yourself if you find yourself constantly having to tack 'really' on to your sentences in order to get people to believe you. Why is that? Are your words not otherwise reliable? Is this an admission of dishonesty? Do you teach people not to believe you through your constant embellishments? Do people mistrust you because they periodically catch you shading the truth? Do you teach others to be skeptical of your promises because you so frequently fail to keep them?

The Holy Spirit causes us to care about the truth. Consequently we are zealous to be accurate in all that we say. I must be a 'reliable source.' This means that I not only speak truth, but that I avoid untruth. Everything that I repeat I should be able to document. Years ago Bubble Yum bubble gum nearly went out of business because a rumor spread that its gum was laced with spider eggs and caused cancer. How do such rumors spread? Because people are not careful about what they repeat. As a public person about whom things get said, I can tell you that it is amazing how distorted the information can be. I remember when the word around town was that IPC's new minister was a charismatic! A charsimatic! Only verifiable truth should ever leave our mouths.

A faithful man is a man of integrity. If he says he is going to be somewhere at 7:30, he'll be there. The Proverbs say,

> Like a bad tooth and an unsteady foot is confidence in a faithless man in time of trouble. (Prov. 25:19)

When I returned to California after two years in England, I remember being amazed at how people would fail to do what they said they would do. They would tell you that they were coming to your dinner party, but if something better came along at the last minute, they'd drop it. Of all people, we Christians ought to be dependable. Ask yourself, what are you known for? When people think of you do they think of someone who is on time, prepared, reliable, true to their word? Or do they think of someone who is late, unprepared, unreliable, and undependable? The Spirit creates a people who are true to their word.

Second, faithfulness in relation to others means being true to my responsibilities. The Spirit makes me keenly aware of the tasks to which I have been called, all of them, and inspired in me a zeal to be faithful to them all. Let me make this as tangible as I can.

With respect to my family, am I the father or mother that I ought to be? Does the clock bear that out? Do I spend both quantity time and quantitative time with my children? The former can never substitute for the latter. Our children need us to be there, a lot. Do I provide for my children according to their emotional, social, financial, and spiritual needs? Many parents do well in one or two categories and are content to do no more. But we cannot be faithful to our responsibilities as parents to provide for our children, and only provide materially and not emotionally and spiritually as well. Similarly, am I the son or daughter, and brother and sister that I ought to be? We are commanded to honor and obey our parents. Do I, or am I their chief critic? Do I blame them for all of my problems? Do I slash their reputations in the presence of others?

With respect to work, am I honest in my work? As an employee, do I work hard? Do I provide my employer with an honest day's work? If I might put a feather in the cap of Bob Jones University, their graduates are often sought by leading corporations for this very reason—they are honest, and they do an honest day's work. This should be true of all of us. If my work is that of studenting, do I work hard? Am I honest, or cheating along with the majority?

With respect to the church, am I a faithful citizen of the kingdom of God? Am I regular in my attendance at the Sunday services? Am I giving proportionately (i.e. at least tithing)? Am I behaving in a manner that is godly, supportive, and exemplary? Am I consistent in my devotional life and in family worship? Am I, in other words, true to the vows that I took as members and officers? This too is a matter of integrity.

With respect to the community, am I a responsible part of my community? Am I politically informed? Do I care? Am I involved? In all of this, I should check my calendar and check stubs. Do they reflect the faithful fulfillment of your responsibilities? Do they reflect right priorities?

Finally, with respect to all of these responsibilities, do I remain loyal to those for whom I am responsible? Or, do I 'head for the tall grass' as soon as trouble starts? When David fled Jerusalem at the time of Absalom's bid for the throne, Ittai the Gittite, a man from Gath, a foreigner, who had served with David for just one day, was urged by David to return home. Why should he stay? Ittai answered,

> As the Lord lives, and as my lord the king lives, surely wherever my lord the king may be, whether for death or for life, there also your servant will be. (2 Sam. 15:21)

A faithful person is one who perseveres over the long haul in his responsibilities, and can be counted upon in thick and thin. Can your spouse count on your loyalty? Can your employer? Can the church officers? Will you persevere with them? The Holy Spirit works in such a way in the hearts of His people that they are characteristically faithful, people who can be counted on, people who can be relied upon, time and time again.

32

The Fruit of the Spirit is Gentleness or Meekness

Galatians 5:22–23

The commentators labor to find an English word that corresponds to the Greek *praus*, *prautes*. 'Meekness,' as in a 'meek little man,' communicates weakness, or a lack of energy and vigor. 'Gentleness' does not seem to capture it all either. The word combines both gentleness and strength.[170] Toward God, it indicates a submissive, teachable, pliable spirit. Toward others, it indicates 'humility, patience, and forbearance.'[171] It means humble submission to God, and humble consideration of others. It is used in combination with a 'quiet spirit' in 1 Peter 3:4, with the 'lowly of heart' in Matthew 11:29, with wisdom that is pure, peaceable, reasonable, full of mercy and good fruits in James 3:17, where is it also contrasted with jealously and selfish ambition. It is combined with reverence when Peter speaks of the manner in which Christians are to defend the faith (1 Pet. 3:15–16), with forbearance (2 Cor. 10:1), with humility and forbearance (Eph. 4:2), with kindness, humility, long-suffering, forgiveness and forbearance, as qualities that the Christian is to 'put on' (Col. 3:12), with righteousness, godliness, faith, love and perseverance as those qualities that the Christian is to 'pursue' (1 Tim. 6:11), with patience as one corrects the opposition (2 Tim. 2:24–5), with maligning no one, being uncontentious, and showing consideration (1 Tim. 3:2–3). It is humble, quiet, controlled strength, and resembles the last of the fruit, self-control. But whereas the latter is more concerned with external control of behavior, the former focuses on internal control of the heart.

Meekness was not a virtue in the ancient world, and is not one today either. The ancients, like the moderns, admire the strong, the proud, the powerful, the assertive. Even with the extensive feminization of our society we still award our prizes to those who fight their way to the top and who crush the opposition in the process. In fact, mass media's feminine ideal is a tough, aggressive, take-no-prisoners kind of woman. Athletics perhaps serves as a parable of life. The fans love the power dunk, the power back, the power hitter, the powerful left hook. As one brought up in the 1960s in Los Angeles, where our sports heroes were the painfully shy, almost apologetic Jerry West and Sandy Koufax, today's in your face, bragging, trash-talking, taunting athlete comes as shock. But the fans love it. Humility has vanished. Don't just defeat your foe, destroy him. Don't just win, humiliate him. Promote yourself. Broadcast your achievements. Like Cassius Clay, you're not just the greatest, you're the double greatest. Sell yourself. If you've got it, flaunt it.

The Bible, however, stands this ethic on its head. Greatness, as God measures greatness, is found not in self-assertive domination, but in the quiet strength that is meekness. The two most important men in the Bible are called meek. It is said of Moses, the greatest of all the Old Testament characters, at a time when his leadership was being challenged,

> Now the man Moses was very humble, more than any man who was on the face of the earth. (Num. 12:3)

The word 'humble' as translated in the LXX, is the same used in Psalm 37:11 and quoted in Matthew 5:5, *prautes*, meekness. Likewise the greatest Man who ever lived said of Himself,

> Come to Me, all who are weary and heavy-laden, and I will give you rest. Take My yoke upon you, and learn from Me, for I am gentle and humble in heart; and you shall find rest for your souls. For My yoke is easy, and My load is light. (Matt. 11:28–30)

The word translated 'gentle' is our word 'meek' again. Both Moses and Jesus were meek. They were plenty strong, even as the world counts strength. But their power was governed by gentleness and humility, by quietness of spirit and peace.

Ironically, Jesus said, it is the meek, quoting, as we mentioned, the 37th Psalm, who shall inherit the earth (Matt. 5:5). For all the proud self-assertiveness of the great ones of the earth, in the end, the meek win. They 'inherit the earth.' 'Fret not yourself because of him who prospers in his way, because of him who carries out wicked schemes …for evildoers will be cut off, but those who wait for the Lord, they will inherit the land' (i.e. earth). It only looks like the wicked get away with their oppression, with their lying, cheating and stealing, as they trample on others in order to get ahead. Who finally will enjoy the beauty, the resources, the fruit, the good things of this world? Not the wicked who currently prosper. Not the proud, not the oppressive, not the wicked, but the humble, meek, righteous people of God.

Keys to Meekness

The Apostle Paul exhorts us 'by the meekness and gentleness of Christ' (2 Cor. 10:1). What is the key to our acquiring such meekness? The key is a true knowledge of ourselves that comes through the illumination of the Holy Spirit. The Spirit humbles us by showing us the truth about ourselves, our identity, and our destiny. This can be seen in the life of Moses, as described by the letter to the Hebrews. There we find that meekness is based upon the following.

First, we must understand our true identity. We read in Hebrews,

> By faith Moses, when he had grown up, refused to be called the son of Pharaoh's daughter. (Heb. 11:24)

Many of our proud distinctions are based on pedigree. I may be proud and unapproachable, demanding, overbearing, condescending because of my family, my class, my clan, or heritage. Because you are of a lower class, I may not wish to associate with you, or indeed have anything to do with you. Yet Moses was raised as a grandchild of the great Pharaoh. He was a member of the royal family, the most powerful, wealthy, and important family in all the world. Why should he wish to mingle with a slave people? Because he realized his true identity. He may have been 'the son of Pharaoh's daughter,' but he was also (and more importantly) a member of the enslaved people of God. Moses knows who he is.

So who is Moses? Moses is but a man among men. What is man? Pharaoh thinks that he is a god. The ancient Egyptians believed the pharaoh was divine. But Moses knows that he is but a man, and man is but dust. He will one day return to dust (Gen. 3:19). Thankfully God is 'mindful that we are but dust' (Ps. 103:14). He takes it into account in His dealings with us. But we too should take it into account in our dealings with God and with one another. Abraham timidly, yet boldly, intercedes for Sodom saying,

> Now behold, I have ventured to speak to the Lord, although I am but dust and ashes. (Gen. 18:27)

How dare I speak, he says. God is God and I am but 'dust and ashes.' A true understanding of his identity results in humility before God. Spurgeon tells the story of a man who identified himself in prayer as, 'Thy dust,' and his children as, 'Thy dust's dust.' That may be pushing the point a bit, but the insight is essentially accurate. What becomes of pride, of ego when this sinks in? How can we think we're something great in light of our creatureliness? Paul applies the point in this way, humbling the proud Corinthians as he asks,

> For who regards you as superior? And what do you have that you did not receive? But if you did receive it, why do you boast as if you had not received it? (1 Cor. 4:7)

Everything that we have has been given to us by God. It is a gift. How then can we put on airs? How can we imagine ourselves superior to the rest? Your exceptional strength, intelligence, wisdom, or beauty are merely superiorly arranged dust, and God did the arranging! The proud self-made man? He lives a fantasy. His achievements are to be respected. Yet they are not a source of pride. Where exactly would Mr. Self-Made be were it not for the moment-by-moment blessing of God? To whom does he owe his health, strength, intelligence, beauty, and opportunities? Where would he be if God were to take one or more of these away? What if he had all of his current capabilities but lived in Outer Mongolia? Then what would he have accomplished? The Holy Spirit helps us to see this about ourselves, and removes this source of pride. We are but dust.

Beyond this, the Spirit shows us our identity as sinners. The slavery of Egypt is a biblical metaphor of slavery to sin. Moses knows that though he serves in Pharaoh's courts, he is a slave. Similarly, the Spirit shows us that we are sinners. Perhaps once you thought that you were something. Once you were self-righteous, you had a high opinion of yourself and of your moral and religious accomplishments. This allowed you to look down your nose at those you saw as being less moral, or less religious, or less loving, depending on which was your source of pride. But the Spirit helps us to see ourselves as we truly are, and we never forget it. Paul once thought of himself as 'blameless' as measured by the law. He had a basis for 'confidence in the flesh' (Phil. 3:4–6). But then the law, particularly the 10th commandment, showed him the true condition of his heart. He came to realize that 'nothing good dwells in me, that is, in my flesh' (Rom. 7:18, cf. 7:7–11).

If nothing good dwells in us naturally, then of what do we have to be proud? Paul saw himself in this light for the rest of his life. 'Worm' theology is disparaged in some circles these days as harmful to healthy self-esteem. Isaac Watts didn't mind singing of 'such a worm as I,' but today we worry about the effect of such sentiments on self-image. Be that as it may, knowing that one is a moral worm has a wonderful effect on Christian character, particularly meekness. We see it when the Apostle Paul instructs 'spiritual' ones to help those who have fallen into sin.

> Brethren, even if a man is caught in any trespass, you who are spiritual, restore such a one in a spirit of gentleness; each one looking to yourself, lest you too be tempted. (Gal. 6:1)

Restore the fallen with 'gentleness' (meekness), knowing your own weakness, knowing your own vulnerability, 'lest you too be tempted.' There is no room for spiritual pride. Paul continues to refer to himself as 'a nobody,' as 'the very least of all the saints' as 'the least of the apostles who am not fit to be called an apostle' (2 Cor. 12:11; Eph. 3:18; 1 Cor. 15:9). 'Christ Jesus came into the world to save sinners,' he says, 'among whom I am foremost of all' (1 Tim. 1:15). The great apostle sees himself not as the chief of all the saints, but the chief of all the sinners. He sees himself not as the foremost of all Christians, but as the least of all. This is his identity. So how can he be anything but quiet, reserved, humble, and meek? How can we be anything but quiet, reserved, humble, and meek? With Paul we say, 'By the grace of God I am what I am' (1 Cor. 15:10). There's no place for pride. There's no room for boasting. When I realize who I am and what I've done, I put my hand over my mouth, like Job, lest I blaspheme. I fall silent. I grow more and more reserved.

The story is told about a young Scottish minister who preached his heart out one Sunday morning, to the acclaim of the congregation. An older woman shook his hand at the door and told him how wonderful he was. 'It was the Lord! It was the Lord!' said the young man, feigning modesty. 'I didn't say it was *that* good,' snapped the woman in reply. Meekness is not false modesty or forced self-deprecation. The Apostle says we're to have a 'sober estimate' of ourselves.

> For through the grace given to me I say to every man among you not to think more highly of himself than he ought to think; but to think so as to have sound judgment, as God has allotted to each a measure of faith. (Rom. 12:3)

Such a judgment of ourselves may honestly recognize our abilities. Yet we should recognize that insofar as such are present, they are a gift of God, leaving no room for an attitude of superiority.

Second, we must understand our true calling and destiny. What are we called to do? To suffer hardship as servants of Christ. Look at Moses,

> choosing rather to endure ill-treatment with the people of God, than to enjoy the passing pleasures of sin. (Heb. 11:25)

Moses was called to leave Pharaoh's palace and the 'passing pleasures of sin' for Jethro's pasture and the 'reproach of Christ' (v. 26). For forty years he tended another man's sheep. One might have asked, 'Isn't he over-qualified for that?' Couldn't he more effectively serve as a positive influence within Pharaoh's court, like Joseph did? Couldn't he make better use of his gifts and abilities there? He shouldn't go out into the fields, should he? God's answer was, yes he should. Why? Because after tending another man's sheep for 40 years he'd finally be ready to tend God's sheep and lead them to greener pastures in the Promised Land. Jesus said (Matt. 16:24),

> If anyone wishes to come after Me, let him deny himself, and take up his cross, and follow Me.

When we became Christians, we lost our lives. We no longer live (Gal. 2:20). Consequently, there is no job too menial, and no task too low, that we cannot perform it. We have no turf to protect, no prerogatives to assert. The Holy Spirit gives us joy in serving, whatever the service might be. Our service may involve suffering. We may endure 'the reproach of Christ,' understood as 'abuse suffered for Christ' by P. E. Hughes (Heb. 11:26).[172] If we live for Christ, there is a price to pay. 'If they persecuted me, they'll persecute you,' Jesus said (John 15:20). We're not to be surprised by this (1 Pet. 4:3, 4, 12). We've been destined for this (1 Thess. 3:3). We could be martyred for Christ. Our name and memory could be disgraced, but the Holy Spirit gives us the capacity to accept this. Our symbol, after all, is a cross! Suffering is our calling. Humbly we submit. We accept the lowly place without resentment. This is meekness.

In the midst of this, the Holy Spirit enables us to see our eternal reward. Consequently, we are able to defer or delay gratification now and meekly endure. People grab for all the toys because 'now' is all that there is for them. This is what drives the acquisitive spirit. This is what is behind our consumeristic, materialistic age. We get pushy and demanding because we want it all now. We demand our own way and our rights and trample on others in the process. But the Spirit convinces us that 'the meek shall inherit the earth' (Matt. 5:5). Paul writes, 'If we endure, we shall also reign with him' (2 Tim. 2:12). Peter writes,

> Humble yourselves, therefore, under the mighty hand of God, that He may exalt you at the proper time. (1 Pet. 5:6)

I don't have to promote myself and grab all the prizes now. I don't have to step on everyone else as I climb to the top. If I know that a banquet is soon to come, I can forego snacks. I don't need the *hor d'oeuvres*. I can endure deprivation with calm, with quiet, with strength and without anger and envy. Remember Jesus,

> the author and perfecter of faith, who for the joy set before Him endured the cross, despising the shame, and has sat down at the right hand of the throne of God. (Heb. 12:2)

Because, Jesus says, 'of the joy set before Him,' He was able to endure a cross whose 'shame' He despised. The apostle Paul also writes,

> For I consider that the sufferings of this present time are not worthy to be compared with the glory that is to be revealed to us. (Rom. 8:18)

Because there is a 'glory' to be revealed, our outlook on our present suffering is transformed. It is as nothing to us. We are able meekly to endure. We are able patiently to suffer. It is but 'momentary, light affliction' that produces 'an eternal weight of glory for beyond all comparison' (2 Cor. 4:18).

The result of knowing my true *identity* and my true *calling and destiny* is meekness. When I know who I truly am, and what I am called to do, I am humbled. I cannot be proud. I cannot regard myself as superior to others, or better than all the rest. And I have nothing to prove. God is my judge. I can wait for eternity and its rewards.

Tests of meekness

Test yourself by asking of yourself the following questions.

First, am I teachable? Jesus writes,

> Therefore putting aside all filthiness and all that remains of wickedness, in humility receive the word implanted, which is able to save your souls. (James 1:21)

The word translated 'humility' is our word 'meekness.' The receiving of and submitting to the word requires humility. It takes meekness to have your views changed by the Bible. It takes meekness to have your values reordered. If one thinks that one already knows everything, or at least that one's opinions are superior to everyone else's, then one will never learn and never grow. Many of us are people with firm convictions. We believe what we believe strongly! Certainly our core convictions, summarized in the early Creeds, are not subject to revision. We are not open to rethinking the doctrine of the Trinity or the dual nature of Christ, for example. But strong core convictions need not mitigate against learning. The church historians say that Calvin's theology never changed. He got it right the first time. But for most of us failure to change is a sign of intellectual death. If we've quit revising, we've quit thinking. Ask yourself if you have learned anything new in the last fifteen years. Have you had any new insight or fresh understanding in the last decade? If we are truly meek, we will be constantly learning, constantly revising, constantly expanding our knowledge. God's 'compassions' are 'new every morning' said Jeremiah (Lam. 3:23). There is always something heretofore unseen to appreciate in God. Our problem is that our egos can become so wrapped up in our opinions that our views can never change without devastating our whole self-concept. Martyn Lloyd-Jones (1899–1981), in his book on the Sermon on the Mount, says,

> we (should) have such a poor opinion of ourselves and our capacities that we are ready to listen to others.[173]

Cromwell said to his divided brethren, 'consider in the bowels of Christ that you might be wrong.' The overwhelming impression that I had at the end of a year of seminary was how little I knew. The one thing I knew was that I knew nothing. The more that time passes the more convinced I become that that is true. Last year I read books about the Christian view of art and architecture. A whole new, hitherto unexplored, world opened up. This year it has been a Christian critique of literature. Again, an unexpected world lies before me.

Those areas are relatively easy for me to be meek about because I know that I know nothing. However, we each have our areas in which we see ourselves as experts, and our identity is wrapped up in our certainty. Even in these areas, the meek one knows his own weakness, foolishness, and ignorance, and so is teachable.

Second, can I take correction? Or, am I always on the defensive? If someone lovingly identifies a flaw or a fault, do you receive it and take corrective action? Or do you become a martyr? Do you become mad or hurt? Do you think, 'They don't understand me. They don't understand my circumstances.' Do you make excuses and explain away your failings? Do you attack the messenger as one who doesn't love you or is out to hurt you? Again Lloyd-Jones says,

> the man who is truly meek is the one who is amazed that God and man can think of him as well as they do and treat him as well as they do.[174]

Young people, do you receive your parents' correction joyfully and endeavor to follow their wishes? Employees, do you thankfully receive the correction of your supervisors and endeavor to improve your job performance? Husbands and wives, are you able to receive the complaints of your spouses and improve your respective performances in the home? Or are you defensive? Or do you counter-attack? The meek are able to receive a corrective exhortation because they know that in many areas they fail and are blind to their failure. They know that they need help. They are eager to do better. They are pleased that others care enough to confront.

Third, am I gentle with others? In particular, am I gentle with those with whom I differ? The lowly orientation of the meek results in gentleness in the treatment of others. The proud show no such understanding. They live in such a settled state of perfection that they are able to self-righteously grumble and complain about every flawed institution, every imperfect leader, and every defective program. They are not able to look with sympathy and understanding at human frailties. They are not able to see in the weakness of others their own weakness. All they can see is how they would have done things differently or better, given their superior intelligence and moral character. But as Isaiah prophesied of the Messiah, whose words Matthew applied to Jesus,

> a battered reed He will not break off, and a smoldering wick He will not put off. (Matt. 12:20; cf. Isa. 42:3)

The Puritan Richard Sibbes (1577–1635) preached one of the greatest sermons ever preached on this text, drawing out from it the extraordinary tenderness of meek Jesus, who doesn't break the almost broken 'bruised reed' and doesn't quench the barely lit 'smoking flax.' He treats with gentleness the weak of faith, the struggling and discouraged, encouraging, helping, and strengthening them. Looking at the ignorant masses, 'He had compassion on them because they were as sheep not having a shepherd' (Mark 6:14; 8:2; 9:36). Those who are Christ-like do the same. When dealing with opponents, they 'must not be quarrelsome, but be kind to all … patient when wronged,' says Paul,

> with gentleness correcting those who are in opposition, if perhaps God may grant them repentance leading to the knowledge of the truth. (2 Tim. 2:25)

When arguing with unbelievers, always be ready, says Peter,

> to make a defense to everyone who asks you to give an account for the hope that is in you, yet with gentleness and reverence; (1 Pet. 3:15)

When restoring one who was 'caught in any trespass,' the spiritual ones are not to be self-righteous and condemning, but,

> restore such a one in a spirit of gentleness; each one looking to your self, lest you too be tempted. (Gal. 6:1)

Meek is not weak. It is the quiet, humble strength of those who know their true *identity*, *calling*, and *destiny*, and therefore are gentle in their dealings with others.

33

The Fruit of the Spirit is Self-Control

Galatians 5:22–23

We come now to the last of the fruit, and the one upon which the others particularly depend. 'Self-control' is a compound word made of *ego*, I, and *krateo*, to hold, take, restrain. Self-control is the ability to control one's impulses, passions, and desires, and to resist temptation. Scripture requires of elders that they have 'self-control' (Titus 1:8). The Apostle Paul uses the term of athletes who must exercise self-control, that is, must be disciplined 'in all things' (1 Cor. 9:25). He also exhorts those who are unmarried and do not have 'self-control,' that is, who cannot control their sexual passions, to marry, 'for it is better to marry than to burn' (1 Cor. 7:9).

When the Apostle was summoned to appear before Felix they discussed 'righteousness, self-control, and the judgment to come' (Acts 24:25). If we take these as God's claim upon us, man's response, and God's evaluation, then we have some insight into how comprehensive this last of the fruit can be. Our response to all that God requires of us can be summarized as a matter of self-control. In other words, will you control your own selfish desires, buckle down, and do what God commands? As this relates to the fruit, I may want to be loving, joyful, peaceful, patient, kind, and so on, but I never will be if I cannot restrain my passions. For example, if I cannot control my temper, then I will lack the inward graces of love, joy, and peace, I will not treat others with patience, kindness, and goodness, and I will lack the character qualities of faithfulness and gentleness. I will blow up in unworthy circumstances, putting my soul in a state of unrest, insulting those around me, and violating Christ's commands. Love is the most comprehensive of the fruit, but in some ways, self-control is the most critical, for all the above reasons.

As we have seen so often in this study of the fruit, this puts us at odds with our culture. The propaganda of the past 30 years has been, 'if it feels good, do it.' Nike's fabulously effective sales pitch, 'Just do it,' is the more recent version of the same. Life has no context. Existence has no meaning. Actions have no consequences. There is no right or wrong. There are no standards. If you feel like it, do it. If you have an itch, scratch it. If you have a lust, feed it. If you have a desire, fulfill it. Don't worry. Don't think about it. Only immediate self-gratification matters. Pleasure is all that counts.

A whole generation has been brought up this way. Armand Nicholi II argued,

> Society seems to have given up on its traditional civilizing task of controlling aggressive and sexual impulses. The deep moral confusion we have observed over the past decade seems to have lifted all restraint. During the past ten years, I have noticed a marked change in the type of problems that bring people to a psychiatrist. Previously, a great many came because of their inability to express impulses and feelings. Today, the majority come because of an inability to control their impulses. (People in my field relate this lack of control to the declining influence of the father in the home).[175]

The effect of all this is a society that is out of control. Where is this evident, you might ask? Where is it not evident, I would respond? I led a youth group to Jamaica a few years back. I'll never forget how one evening one of the boys poured a bowl of cereal about fifteen minutes before supper. He was hungry. He ate. It was that simple. He couldn't wait. He had to satisfy his hunger right then and there. This is the way that many, if not most, children have been brought up since World War II. Their tantrums were tolerated as children. Every desire was instantly met. They were encouraged to express every impulse that ever came over them. Suppression of such, it was thought, is positively harmful. Just do it. You want to say something? Just say it. The result: the most foul-mouthed generation in living memory. Many others cannot control their gossip, their sarcasm, or their criticism. Frustrated? Go ahead and blow up. Never mind the epidemic of 'crimes of passion,' which account by the way, for most of the murders, rapes, physical assaults, and physical abuse in our nation. Burning with sensual passion? Why wait for marriage? Why not have an epidemic of illegitimacy, of venereal disease, of abortion, and of burned out, cynical victims? A few years back a *U.S. News and World Report* cover story (May 19, 1997) argued that while teenage promiscuity is a problem, the larger problem is adults. Promiscuous adults are responsible for much more of all of the above than teenagers—more out-of-wedlock children, more disease, and more abortions. Amazingly these same adults report overwhelmingly conservative beliefs, viewing sexual relations outside of monogamous, heterosexual marriage as always or almost always wrong. The problem? No self-control. But let's keep moving. Want to party? Then go ahead and drink yourself into oblivion. Drink to get drunk, and do it frequently. It's fun. It makes you feel good. Why not? If it impairs judgment, destroys families, and kills thousands on the roads each year, so be it. Finally, if you're hungry, go ahead and eat now, eat all you want, and eat whatever you want. For all our talk of exercise and good nutrition, we are still the most overweight nation in the world. According to recent statistics, one third of all Americans are obese. Back in the 1980s (December 22, 1980), *U.S. News and World Report* reported that there was 2.3 trillion pounds of excess fat stored in American bodies (14.3 lbs/adult over 18), containing enough energy to fuel 900,000 automobiles for 12,000 miles. Since then obesity has come to be seen as an epidemic. Just do it! No context. No restraint. No consequences. No control.

Then to top it all off, when any individual's conduct becomes not only compulsive and habitual, but also destructive, we then absolve him or her of responsibility for their actions by labeling it an 'addiction.' The drunk is addicted to alcohol, the pervert to perversion, the smoker to tobacco, the criminal to violence, the glutton to food, and so on. Lack of self-control is no longer considered moral failure deserving society's reproach, but a disease evoking society's sympathy.

My point in rehearsing again the grim statistics and society's inadequate response is to remind us of how completely hostile to Christian purposes society has become. Do nothing and say nothing, merely drift along with popular culture, enjoy the music, the shows, the movies, and the advertisements, and you will be overwhelmed by the 'just do it' propaganda. I have often said that it is almost impossible to communicate the gospel to those in their teens and early twenties because they are typically so immersed, and consequently seduced by popular culture. Not until they marry and have their first child do they finally calm down enough to listen. They finally begin to ask serious questions about life and eternity around the time that they bring their first baby home. Many of our converts are in that category. But we also notice that some who thus respond remain there only for about a decade. Then they begin again to question, this time if they really want to live under the constraints of the gospel. The world and the flesh begin to look appealing to them again. The temptations are enormous. 'Just do it' is an alluring, if counterfeit, alternative. If we are to have self-control in this civilization, we must fight back. And we need help. We cannot survive on our own. What is the key to self-control? The power of the Holy Spirit. Self-control is *the fruit of the Holy Spirit*. How does He do it? By strengthening our minds, wills, and emotions.

Renewed Minds

The transformation of Christian conduct is the consequence of the renewing of our minds (Rom. 12:1–2). The first problem in sin is the way that we look at things. Where does evil originate? From within. Jesus said,

> That which proceeds out of the man, that is what defiles the man. For from within, out of the heart of men, proceed the evil thoughts, fornications, thefts, murders, adulteries, deeds of coveting and wickedness, as well as deceit, sensuality, envy, slander, pride and foolishness. All these evil things proceed from within and defile the man. (Mark 7:20–3)

The problem is our hearts, and what we like and what we want. It's the way we look at things and how we view them. The Proverbs say of man,

> For as he thinks within himself, so he is. (Prov. 23:7)

We are what we think? If we are to change, our hearts must change, and with our hearts our thinking. This is exactly what the Holy Spirit does and only the Holy Spirit can do. He regenerates us. He causes us to be born again (John 3:7). We become new creatures (2 Cor. 5:17). In this way, the Spirit enables us to see the evil of our action and to hate it. The things with which we once toyed and flirted are now odious to us. We come to 'abhor what is evil; cling to what is good' (Rom. 12:9). We come to see through the seductive images of the world and perceive what they really represent and what they would have us do. One drunken spree or one passionate fling are what? Do they represent a wonderful time, great fun, excitement, air-brushed romance? No, that is not reality. Reality is offending the God who made us and saved us, grieving the Holy Spirit, ruining your reputation, bringing reproach to the name of Christ, possibly destroying your marriage, losing your family, and maybe, in the case of the fling, bringing an illegitimate child into the world. Is that fun? Is it glamorous? Is it exciting? Romantic? In the fantasy-land of Hollywood it may be. But in the real world, sin has severely destructive consequences. Think of how gratifying it can be to express the impulse of anger by beating or shooting someone. Hollywood indulges that desire all the time, often in humorous ways. We even derive vicarious pleasure when a Stalone or Schwarzneggar smashes in someone's face. But in the real world such indulgence destroys lives, not the least of which is the life of the one expressing the anger. What would sin have you do? The Holy Spirit changes our outlook on these things, and creates in our hearts holy hatred for evil in all its forms. We see through the world, with its 'lust of the flesh, the lust of the eyes and the boastful pride of life.' We see the futility of it all. We see that 'the world is passing away, and also its lusts' (1 John 2:16–17). This is where the Holy Spirit first begins to change us. Sin loses the enslaving power of its appeal. We no longer love darkness and hate the light but rather the reverse (John 3:19–21).

We then begin to *purge our thinking* environment. These altered perceptions and desires then become the basis for controlling ungodly input. The old nature is subdued in Christ, even dealt a mortal blow (Rom. 6). But the flesh continues to war against the Spirit, the Spirit against the flesh (Gal. 5:17). Obviously it's no good trying to live a holy life while subscribing to pornographic magazines. It is futile to exhort your children in the paths of purity if they are being bombarded by soap operas, sit-coms, and pop music. As they used to say in the computer industry, 'garbage-in, garbage-out.' Paul exhorts us in this way,

> Finally, brethren, whatever is true, whatever is honorable, whatever is right, whatever is pure, whatever is lovely, whatever is of good repute, if there is any excellence and if anything worthy of praise, let your mind dwell on these things. (Phil. 4:8)

The Spirit leads us to purify the environment in which we live. We remove the garbage and only let our minds 'dwell' on 'these things.' Even this is the work of the Holy Spirit. There are forms of entertainment which once amused us, but no longer do. The old jokes are not funny to us anymore. The 'unfunny joke,' as my childhood preacher called it, the 'funny' drunk, the off-color comment, no longer strike us as humorous. The songs that celebrate promiscuity, drugs, and violence aren't enjoyable now. We want nothing to do with them. We don't miss them. They have no appeal. They are crude. They depict an ugly and tragic side of life. They undermine chastity. The sanctified heart, washed clean by the Holy Spirit, abominates the whole scene. The disciplined life of the mind becomes a natural part of the life of the believer, as the working of the Holy Spirit transforms his thinking and desires.

Strengthened Wills

Flowing from our corrected thinking and transformed desires comes the renewed will. There is irony in the inclusion of *self*-control in a list of the fruit *of the Holy Spirit*. Is control of our behavior a result of the Spirit's efforts or ours? The answer is both. The Spirit works to enable us to get in control of ourselves. The Bible is always beautifully balanced as it avoids the extremes of deism (which says God does nothing, we do it all) and fatalism (which says the God does everything and we do nothing). The Apostle Paul expresses the balance in several of his other letters.

> So then, my beloved, just as you have always obeyed, not as in my presence only, but now much more in my absence, work out your salvation with fear and trembling; for it is God who is at work in you both to will and to work for His good pleasure. (Phil. 2:12–13)

Because God is 'at work,' we 'work out' our salvation. The Spirit's work guarantees the success of ours; it is not an excuse for laziness or irresponsibility. Because He is at work we work and win.

> for if you are living according to the flesh, you must die; but if by the Spirit you are putting to death the deeds of the body, you will live. (Rom. 8:13)

There again is the balance. 'If *by the Spirit,*' by the illumination of the Spirit, by the power of the Spirit, '*you* are putting to death the deeds of the body...' Who puts sin to death? We do. How do we accomplish such a monumental task? By the Spirit. He enables. He inspires. He empowers. The Apostle reminds the Colossians that they have died with Christ and been raised up with Him, and that their life is now 'hidden with Christ in God' (3:3). So he exhorts them,

> Put to death, therefore, whatever belongs to your earthly nature: sexual immorality, impurity, lust, evil desires and greed, which is idolatry. (Col. 3:5 NIV)

The NASV translation is weak at this point. The word is not 'consider as dead,' but 'put to death.' We put to death our sinful desires and acts. The passive formula of 'let go and let God' is woefully inadequate. Self-control, like sanctification, requires vigorous personal exertion. Look again at 1 Corinthians 9, where Christ's Apostle uses a series of athletic metaphors.

> Do you not know that those who run in a race all run, but only one receives the prize? Run in such a way that you may win. And everyone who competes in the games exercises self-control in all things. They then do it to receive a perishable wreath, but we an imperishable. Therefore I run in such a way, as not without aim; I box in such a way, as not beating the air; but I buffet my body and make it my slave, lest possibly, after I have preached to others, I myself should be disqualified. (1 Cor. 9:24–7)

The Christian life is like a race. 'Run in such a way that you may win.' As we've seen, it is like the life of an athlete in training, who 'exercises self-control in all things.' It is like the boxer who swings 'not without aim.' In 1 Timothy Paul likens Christian ministry to military service, athletics, the 'hard working farmer,' the workman, and the slave (2:1–26). He speaks of suffering, disentanglement from the affairs of everyday life, and hard work. In Ephesians he again uses the metaphor of warfare, as he exhorts,

> Finally, be strong in the Lord, and in the strength of His might. Put on the full armor of God, that you may be able to stand firm against the schemes of the devil. (Eph. 6:10–11)

Your strength, he says, is 'in the Lord.' Yet you must 'put on' the armor and stand firm. This is not a popular message, but the fact is that self-control, indeed the successful living of the Christian life, requires discipline, discipline, discipline. Self-denial is a central fact of our calling (Matt. 16:24–6). A thousand times a day and in a thousand different ways we say no to ourselves in order to say yes to God. You do so as a parent, in your vocation, and as a church member. When you change that diaper, when you drive the car pool, when you send a check to 'Junior' off at college, when you nurse an elderly loved one, self must be denied. After all, we'd all rather be lounging around a pool. We'd all rather be out on a yacht. We'd all rather take a nap. But the Holy Spirit strengthens our will so that we do the right thing.

The same is true of all of life. Self-control requires a disciplined use of the public and private means of grace. Christ has given to us His word, His sacrament, prayer, and his people to build and strengthen us. When Sunday morning rolls around, the flesh would, frankly, rather sleep-in. Sunday evening, the flesh is just too tired. Or too interested in recreation. Or too caught up in entertainment. Thankfully the Spirit changes our hearts so that we love His word, and love His worship, and love His people. 'We know that we have passed out of death into life, because we love the brethren,' says the Apostle John (1 John 3:14). But still, because the flesh would rather lie in bed all day and be waited on by a team of servants, we must have the personal discipline to get up each day, read our Bibles, pray and go about our daily tasks. Over the long haul the Spirit uses the word, sacraments, prayer, and saints to build us into the kind of people for whom self-control comes instinctively.

Then as we face temptation, we will have learned to say no to ourselves and to turn away from seductive opportunities. This requires brutal honesty and tough decisions. Paul says that we're to 'put on the Lord Jesus Christ, and make no provision for the flesh in regard to its lusts' (Rom. 13:14). Make *no* provision. Provide no opportunities for the indulgence of the flesh. Put distance between yourself and sin. Face reality with respect to your weaknesses. We can trace this out along the following lines.

1. *Total abstinence* of that which is inherently evil. We must have total control of that which is evil of itself in any amount, such as murder, extra-marital sex, theft, falsehoods, coveting.

2. *Moderation* in all that is permitted and evil only in its abuse. We must be careful not to be more strict than the Bible. Eating, drinking, recreation and a host of other things are permitted so long as they don't reach idolatrous proportions.

3. *Avoidance* of all which inevitably or even generally leads to sin for you. Do you tend to overeat? Then avoid occasions and contexts in which you will tend to do so. Do you tend to lose your temper? Where and when? Avoid such occasions. Does drink lead to drunkenness for you? Then abstain. Does the beach lead to lust? Then stay away. The principle here is 'flee immorality' (1 Cor. 6:18; 1 Tim. 6:11; 2 Tim. 2:22). We are not to test how close we can come to crossing the line into sin. Stay far, far away from it. As we do so, practicing self-discipline, self-denial, and self-control, all in the context of dependence on the Holy Spirit, we will grow in godliness.

Disciplined Emotions

If this degree of self-control sounds impossibly difficult and unattractive to you, realize that the emotions do eventually follow the mind and will. We've seen this already as we've discussed how we come to see sin in a different light. The Spirit changes our heart so that we hate the sin, and even feel deeply that hatred. The Holy Spirit reminds us of sin's misery and arms us with a zeal to avoid it. So initially that gorgeous piece of pie may still look good, and you may feel like eating it. In time, as you do what is right, shunning gluttony and embracing self-control, you will begin to look at that pie differently. We will come to hate sinful passions and their consequences, be they anger, fornication, drunkenness, or gluttony. This holy hatred is perhaps the key to self-control. We are not in control of our impulses until we absolutely hate the sin to which the impulse will lead. One may even reach a point where one would rather die than commit that offense, where even the thought of such is abhorrent to one.

Then, on the other side, we come to love what is good and right. We want nothing more than to seek first the kingdom of God and his righteousness (Matt. 6:33). We want nothing more than to know God and Jesus Christ whom He sent (John 17:3). We no longer wish to live for ourselves but for Him who died and was raised (2 Cor. 5:15). Our ambition is to be pleasing to Him (2 Cor. 5:9). We come to the place where we can say with the Psalmist,

> For a day in Thy courts is better than a thousand outside. I would rather stand at the threshold of the house of my God, than dwell in the tents of wickedness. (Ps. 84:10)

The nearness of God is our good (Ps. 73:28). Beside Him we desire nothing on earth (Ps. 73:25). He becomes our chief aim, our chief end, our chief delight, and the world, a fading memory.

Finally, the Apostle Paul writes,

> ...against such things there is no law. (Gal. 5:23b)

This statement seems to mean that 'there is no law against these things,' i.e. that the fruit are consistent with the law so revered by the Judaizers. Morris sees this as a 'masterly understatement,'[176] whose intention, according to Burton is for 'rhetorical effect.' This 'mild assertion,' he says, 'has the effect of an emphatic assertion that these things fully meet the requirements of the law.'[177] The Apostle Paul is saying to his critics 'your law is not against any of this, is it? There is no conflict between law and gospel.' He is saying essentially what he teaches in Romans 8:4, that the requirements of the law are fulfilled 'in those who walk according to the Spirit and not according to the flesh.' The work of the Spirit in producing these fruit at the same time shapes character which fully conforms with the teaching of the law. A people who are characterized by the fruit of the Spirit are not saved by law-keeping, but are in the end living consistently with the moral law of God, and it is just such a people that we are called to be.

34

Those Who Belong to Christ

Galatians 5:24–26

As we come to the end of Galatians 5, we remind ourselves that the Apostle Paul is combating two commonly repeated errors. The first is that of the 'legalists,' who insist that one is saved by faith in Christ *plus* moral and religious works. From 2:16–5:12 he refutes them summarizing his message, for example, in 2:16 as,

> nevertheless knowing that a man is not justified by the works of the Law but through faith in Christ Jesus, even we have believed in Christ Jesus, that we may be justified by faith in Christ, and not by the works of the Law; since by the works of the Law shall no flesh be justified. (Gal. 2:16)

The second error is that of the 'libertines,' or antinomians. From 5:13–26 he swings his guns around 180° as he refutes those who use the doctrines of grace as an excuse for sin. Yes we are justified by faith alone apart from works, he says. Yet those who are so justified are not thereby handed a license to sin. They may not turn their 'freedom' into 'an opportunity for the flesh' (5:13). The flesh wars against the Spirit and the Spirit against the flesh (5:16–17). Those who 'practice' the 'deeds of the flesh,' such as immorality, idolatry, jealousy, and drunkenness, cannot be real Christians and 'shall not inherit the Kingdom of God' (5:19–21). Where the Spirit is present so also is the fruit of the Spirit.

The flesh and Spirit are mortal enemies. These two, the 'flesh,' meaning fallen human nature and the sinful actions that proceed from it, and the 'Spirit,' God's Holy Spirit and those who are led by Him, are polar opposites. They are mutually exclusive. They are utterly incompatible. They cannot and do not intersect. This is the point that Paul drives home as he describes the true Christian in verses 24–6.

Belongs to Christ

True Christians are those who 'belong to Christ.'

> Now those who belong to Christ Jesus have crucified the flesh with its passions and desires. (Gal. 5:24)

What is a Christian? A Christian is one who belongs to Christ. He designates them naturally as 'those who belong to Christ.' We are His. We belong to Him. We are His property. We are His children. This implies His care for us (because we are His), His provision, and His protection. But his main thought is ethical, not devotional. Because we belong to Christ we 'have crucified the flesh.' His point is that our life is not our own. It belongs to Christ because we belong to Christ. In a similar way, Paul asks the Corinthians, 'Do you not know …that you are not your own? For you have been bought with a price' (1 Cor. 6:19–20). He already told the Galatians 'it is no longer I who live' (Gal. 2:20). If you are a Christian, you don't have a life of your own. 'He died for all,' the Apostle tells the Corinthians, 'that they who live should no longer live for themselves, but for Him who died and rose again on their behalf' (2 Cor. 5:15). We don't have our own life. But don't worry, we never did. We *thought* we did. Yes indeed! We thought that we were the captain of our own ships, calling our own shots, doing our own thing. But that was an illusion. We weren't really. The Apostle tells the Romans there are only two options. One is a slave 'either of sin resulting in death, or of obedience resulting in righteousness' (Rom. 6:16). He exhorts them,

> For just as you presented your members as slaves to impurity and to lawlessness, resulting in further lawlessness, so now present your members as slaves to righteousness, resulting in sanctification. (Rom. 6:19)

Here is what we were doing before we came to Christ. We 'presented (our) bodies as slaves to impurity and lawlessness.' He is as matter-of-fact about this as he could be. '(We) were slaves of sin,' he tells us six different ways in Romans 6:16–20. We only thought that we were 'our own man.' We, along with the rest of the 'whole world,' as John says, 'lie in the power of the evil one' (1 John 5:19). We, along with the rest of the world, 'formerly walked according to the course of this world, according to the prince of the power of the air, of the spirit that is now working in the sons of disobedience' (Eph. 2:1–2). This needs to be kept in mind when the demands of Christian discipleship are considered. Those who appear the most free, who do whatever they please, rejecting God, living for themselves, are actually slaves of sin and the devil. Their freedom is slavery. Their freedom, their autonomy, is a myth, an illusion, a sham. They are in bondage. The stars and starlets who flaunt their freedom are actually in chains, oppressed by the tyrannical power of sin. The question of Christian commitment is, do you want to be a slave of Christ and righteousness and be free from the oppressive power of sin, or a slave of sin and free from the demands of God?

Having said this, we are Christ's slaves. He is our master. We belong to Him. We are under His rule and authority. Our life is not our own. In practical terms this means that our basic question in life is, 'What would Christ have me do?' Just as the slave goes to his master, we go to our Lord and ask for our instructions. Our principles for life, our values of right and wrong, our ethical standards, are those which He gives to us in His word. Our vocational decisions, whether we shall work as house servants or in the fields (as we might put it) are up to Him. We don't have any business going out and making these decisions on our own. We don't run our own life. We belong to Him. As we decide about marriage and family, we ask the One to whom we belong what He wants. I am not to decide that I want person 'A' to be my spouse and not 'B' for my own selfish reasons. I don't choose this job over that just because it is what *I* want. When I plan the ideal size of my family, I am not to say '*My* will not

Thy will be done.' Here too, as in *every area of life*, I am not my own. I belong to Him. Whatever His will, whether it be the mission field working with Stone Age tribes or luxury suites on Manhattan, I am ready to do it. But I might not be happy, one might say. What if I'm not fulfilled? I might not be comfortable doing that. The answer is, that is entirely a secondary issue. We are not our own. We belong to Christ.

Crucifies the Flesh

'Now those who belong to Christ Jesus,' he says, 'have crucified the flesh with its passions and desires.' Notice the active voice. Elsewhere Christians are said to have been crucified with Christ, the passive voice indicating something being done to them (e.g. Rom. 6:6; Gal. 2:20). Here the voice is active, indicating that this is something that the believer does. He has 'crucified' the flesh with all its 'passions' (*pathemasin* denoting the outward expressions of sin) and its 'desires' (*epithumiais* denoting the inner directive force of sin). The aorist tense indicates once-for-all, decisive, and here violent action. The believer has decisively acted to put the flesh to death so that 'not only its outward fruits are destroyed,' says Burton 'but its very dispositions and desires are put to death.'[178] The idea here is that the old sinful nature is an enemy. It is a menace to your soul, wicked, destructive, and harmful. It is like a dangerous criminal against whom extreme measures must be taken. Immediate, radical steps are necessary. We cannot deal with the flesh by throwing a bucket of cold water upon it. We cannot settle for locking it in the back room. We can't tell it to go sit in the corner. Scolding and lecturing won't do. Neither will spanking or flogging while saying 'No, No!' The flesh is like a rampaging maniac trying to break into our houses in order to get at our spouse or children. Nothing will restrain it. It must be put to death. We must crucify it.

Paul uses this violent, decisive language because the root causes of both legalism and libertinism are the same. Both overestimate human ability to resist sin and underestimate sin's power to deceive and enslave. If progress in grace is to be made, we must get past this kind of naiveté. The dangerous, destructive nature of sin must be understood. Otherwise we may end up like the children of Israel, longing for the leeks and melons of Egypt while we forget the harsh reality of slavery. Sin is not a thing to underestimate. It is dangerous to become overconfident about it, and so begin to relax, to drop one's guard, then to flirt with, toy with, joke about, and then gaze longingly at. Get to that place, and it'll come back to get us! Give carnality or worldliness just a few crumbs from our table, and we may soon find that we are feeding a beast that has grown too big to control. It will overwhelm us. Our lust, our thirst for drink, our hunger for excessive food, may overpower us again. Become overconfident, take lesser measures because of pride in our own strength or confidence in our ability to control ourselves, and we may find ourselves ignoring the caution signs and plunging ourselves and our families into ruin. Live life with an inflated sense of our moral backbone and wisdom, and we may fall into huge errors. Like 'Casey at the Bat,' our pride may be our downfall, as we overvalue our ability and undervalue the strength of our enemy. No, the flesh must be crucified. Extreme, radical measures are the only areas that hold back the 'deeds of the flesh' found in verses 19–21. Crucify lust. Crucify pride. Crucify self-righteousness. Crucify jealousy. Crucify bad temper. Crucify drunkenness. The flesh must be put to death!

Walks by the Spirit

> If we live by the Spirit, let us also walk by the Spirit. (Gal. 5:25)

We 'live by the Spirit,' the Apostle Paul says. We 'live' in that we have been raised from spiritual death and given life by the Spirit. We also are empowered by the Spirit, and so enabled by the Spirit to live the Christian life. Since these things are so, since these great indicatives are true, then the imperatives must follow. 'If we live by the Spirit, *let us also walk by the Spirit.*' The word 'walk' is *stoichein,* rather than the more usual *peripatein,* because it indicates not just walking, but walking in a row, or marching in a line. The present tense indicates (as usual) 'habitual practice,' says Morris.[179] It means to behave according to a standard. 'Let us keep in step with the Spirit,' the NIV renders it. March with the Spirit. Keep in line with the Spirit. If we will do this, then the problems of verse 26 will be avoided. We'll avoid the deeds of the flesh and be characterized by the fruit of the Spirit.

> Let us not become boastful, challenging one another, envying one another. (Gal. 5:26)

Burton defines becoming 'boastful,' rendered 'conceited' by the NIV, as 'glorying in vain things,' as 'setting value on things not really valuable.'[180] Bruce labels it as 'mere pretentiousness,' as boasting 'where there is nothing to boast about.'[181] This pride manifests itself further in 'challenging' one another, a word used of athletic and military contests where the aim is to establish one's superiority over another, and 'envying' one another. Fail to crucify the flesh and fleshly pride manifests itself in conceit, and envy. This is where uncrucified flesh manifests itself, especially in churches where sin is taken seriously. We tend to hide obvious sins. But pride tends to erupt into conceit, boasting, arrogance, feelings of superiority, attempts to challenge and thereby cut down others, promotion of one's self, resentment of others for what they have. But this will not happen (at least for long) amongst real Christians. Why not? Because they know that they belong to Christ, and so are not out for themselves. They have crucified the flesh with its passions and desires. They are living by the Spirit and walking by the Spirit. The flesh is suppressed. Pride is buried. Envy is mortified. The fruit of the Spirit is manifest.

Where are we in the scheme of things? Do we belong to Christ? Have we crucified the flesh, and are we walking by the Spirit? Or are we still aggressively provoking some, and envying others? Are we characterized by the deeds of the flesh or the fruit of the Spirit? Are we still in the power of the evil one, or do we 'belong to Christ?'

35

The Nuances of Burden Bearing

Galatians 6:1–5

Do I consider myself a spiritually mature, or spiritually carnal, person? 'I don't make such judgments about myself,' one might say. 'I wouldn't want to brag, after all.' Sorry, this is just the first of several judgments that this passage requires. It asks us to determine if someone is 'caught in any trespass,' if we are 'spiritual,' and that if so, we get involved restoring the fallen brother. The whole scene envisioned by the Apostle is unimaginable by today's standards. Verses like these that remind us periodically of how far we have drifted from biblical and apostolic practice, and of the degree to which we have been infected by the spirit of the age.

The contrast between the Spirit and the flesh that dominated the last half of Galatians 5 continues in Galatians 6. Christians are people who have been justified by faith. That was the burden of the first three-fourths of this Epistle (chapters 1–5:12). Christians are also people, who having been justified by faith in Christ, walk by the Spirit, are led by the Spirit, and bear the fruit of the Spirit (5:13–26). What does this mean? What is the effect of the Spirit's presence in a person's life? Answer: the evidence of the presence of the Spirit in a person's life is found not in mystical experience or in miraculous powers, but in transformed character and conduct. The deeds of the flesh are not practiced. The fruit of the Spirit ripens. Our lives are characterized by love, joy, peace, and so on. We will not become 'boastful' and envious (5:26). Our relationships will not be characterized by rivalry. We will not be saying, 'I'm better than you and I'll prove it.' We will not be thinking, 'You're better than me and I resent it' (these two examples were given by Stott). We will seek the good of others. Our attitude will be, 'You are a person of value in your own right and I want to serve you.'

So these are the tests of the Spirit. Now the Apostle Paul will present another. What does a Spirit-controlled Christian do when he encounters sin in the life of another believer? The Apostle envisions a very real and not infrequent situation. One Christian learns that another believer is trapped in some sin. What is one to do? Some would say that the spiritually mature thing to do is to overlook it. Look the other way. Ignore it. Mind your own business. Don't be Pharisees, they would argue. Don't be judgmental. Just love them. Just forgive and forget. That is the only sensitive, loving, Christian thing to do.

Others might say that the spiritually mature thing to do is to expose it. Make the tough call. Take the strong stand against sin by publicly denouncing it and putting as much distance between oneself (or the church as a whole) as is possible. Otherwise one might be found condoning sin. One might be encouraging future sin. Yet between these two extremes, the Apostle presents another way.

Responding to the Sin of Others

First, the Apostle of Christ requires that we *gently confront* the sins of others.

> Brethren, even if a man is caught in any trespass, you who are spiritual, restore such a one in a spirit of gentleness; each one looking to yourself, lest you too be tempted. (Gal. 6:1)

'Brethren,' he says, reminding us of our responsibilities as members of a spiritual family. 'Even if,' in spite of my preceding exhortations to walk in the Spirit, a 'man,' meaning any member, falls into sin, you have duties to fulfill. The verb 'is caught,' refers not to being caught by others in the act of sinning, but being overtaken or entrapped by sin. It 'seems to imply that the brother is not intentionally doing wrong; he is 'caught' by the sin and goes astray,' says Morris.[182] The word 'trespass' (*paraptoma*) also 'contains the idea of falling,' continues Ridderbos. 'It is not the deliberate, the planned, aspect of sin that is stressed here, but rather the unwitting element. Mistake rather than misdeed is the force of the word, though without absolution of responsibility.'[183] Bruce sees it as 'an isolated action' rather than 'a settled course of action.'[184] However it is used synonymously with 'sin' (*hamartia*) in Romans 5:20, and the Apostle Paul speaks of 'some' or 'any' trespass, and consequently the situation envisioned cannot be limited to the accidental. 'Caught,' then, envisions sin as bondage, a snare, rather than a free and rational choice.

When such happens, what is one to do? Ignore it? Expose it? The spiritually mature are to gently 'restore' such a one. 'You who are spiritual,' those who are spiritually minded and controlled by the Spirit, will gently confront and restore the fallen brother. Am I a spiritual rather than a carnal Christian? If so, then I will confront. I will do so with 'a spirit of gentleness.' I will do so humbly, 'looking to (my)self.' Yet, no amount of super-spiritualizing can absolve us of the responsibility to do so. We cannot make love an excuse for inaction. We cannot make the accusation of insensitivity an excuse. We cannot make minding our own business an excuse. We cannot make acceptance and non-judgmentalism an excuse. This is a God-given responsibility placed upon each one of us. We can't even make spiritual immaturity an excuse, claiming that 'I am not 'spiritual.'' If such is the case, that is an argument for a renewed seriousness about the things of God, not excuse for doing nothing. When a fellow believer, particularly a fellow church member, is overtaken by sin, we must get involved. We cannot avert our gaze.

Some years ago 0% of our elders' time in Session meetings was taken up with matters of pastoral oversight and church discipline. Now maybe one quarter of our time is. Frankly, there is nothing that I dislike more and nothing that I would rather avoid than the time, trouble, grief, heartache involved in confronting public sin. How I would like to turn my back on all of it! But can we? Of course not, not without disobeying Christ. When a member is becoming caught up in some sinful pattern of life, they are like one of the lost sheep that we are obligated to pursue and find. Love requires it. Leave them alone and they may destroy themselves. This one is about to destroy his family through an affair. That one is destroying his life through alcohol. Another is being crushed by debt brought on by undisciplined spending habits. We cannot stand by silently while they ruin their lives and damn their souls.

But aren't we being judgmental? Yes. The problem is that a great deal of sloppy thinking goes on in the discussion of judgmentalism. All judgments are not forbidden. Many judgments are required. The same Jesus who says, 'judge not,' turns around in the next verse and says, 'do not cast your pearls before swine' (Matt. 7:1–6). When a church picks a pastor, shouldn't it make judgments? When members pick officers, aren't they required to judge their relative character and gifts for the role? When we pick a husband or wife, aren't judgments made? Shouldn't they be? Harsh judgments are forbidden. Judgments based on ignorance are forbidden, as when one judges on the basis of hearing one side of a story or judges the motives of others (1 Cor. 4:4). But judgments of character and conduct are not. They are required in many circumstances. Failure to make judgments in many situations is not a manifestation of love, but moral failure. We shouldn't call a segregationist to be our pastor. I shouldn't marry a child molester. I shouldn't elect as officers men who are fiscally irresponsible. So it is necessary for all Spirit-controlled Christians to make these sorts of 'judgments,' and gently confront those who fall into sin.

Second, we are to *confront so as to restore*. The whole point of confrontation is not to prove our moral superiority, or to humiliate the offender, but remediation. 'Restore' is a word used of setting a fractured or dislocated bone, and means to return to former condition. It is used of the disciples 'mending' their nets in Mark 1:19. They are to be restored to full membership in the church, subject to all the rights and privileges thereof, including the personal acceptance of all the members without exception. Morris, citing the work of E.A. Judge, points out that 'gentleness' was originally a disposition of the powerful toward those in lower stations. If that is the case, the Apostle Paul may especially have the church leaders in mind. They are to correct, and thereby assist the fallen one. We may not stand by and pretend that it is none of our business. Neither are we to gloat or condemn and say, 'he had it coming,' or 'I knew it would happen.' Nor are we to gossip. The details of the procedure for confrontation and restoration may be found in Matthew 18:15–17, though they are not detailed here. There He says,

> And if your brother sins, go and reprove him in private; if he listens to you, you have won your brother. (Matt. 18:15)

The winning of the brother is the goal of the confrontation that he describes. 'If he listens to you,' with respect to his sin, 'you have won your brother.' Sometimes, however, it doesn't turn out that way. Sometimes he won't listen. Sometimes he resents the confrontation and becomes angry. Then the confrontations must continue.

> But if he does not listen to you, take one or two more with you, so that by the mouth of two or three witnesses every fact may be confirmed. (Matt. 18:16)

The group that goes to him also seeks to 'win' the brother. And if he still refuses to part with his sin?

> And if he refuses to listen to them, tell it to the church; and if he refuses to listen even to the church, let him be to you as a Gentile and a tax-gatherer. (Matt. 18:17)

Finally the 'church,' meaning either the elected representatives of the church or the congregation as a whole, must be told and the individual removed from membership, made to be to them as a 'Gentile and a tax-gatherer,' that is, outside of the covenant community. Sometimes members must be removed, as in 1 Corinthians 5:13. 'Remove the wicked man from among you,' says the Apostle Paul in the strongest terms. Sometimes members must be shunned, as in 2 John 10–11, and 2 Thessalonians 3:6, 14. If the Bible is our rule of faith and practice, then these passages cannot simply be explained away or ignored. This is clearly the response to sin that Jesus requires of the church, and that the early church practiced. A congregation that truly loves those who have fallen will practice confrontation, excommunications, and shunning because it is the God-ordained means of winning the fallen brother. But it seems so cruel, so mean, so heartless, some might say. He is my friend. Yes, but if you love your friend you'll follow the God-appointed means of restoring that friend, rather than behaving as though you were more wise than he.

Even so, these are extreme cases. The hope in all stages is that the fallen one will be restored. The goal is to win the fallen member back into the fold. This was the case in 2 Corinthians 2, where Paul directed the church to 'reaffirm (its) love for him,' that is, for one upon whom 'punishment' had been inflicted resulting in repentance (2 Cor. 2:4–8). The goal of confrontation and discipline in the church is no different than the same in the family, or for that matter, in the professions. Good parents don't confront their children because they hate them and wish to humiliate and destroy them. The goal is correction and restoration. The medical profession doesn't discipline it members because it delights in humiliating them, but so as to correct malpractice and restore public confidence in the profession as a whole. Loving, gentle confrontation aims at the repentance and restoration of the fallen one.

But the spiritual ones are not to see themselves as superior. They must never assume that they could not do the same, or something equally as bad. We'll say more about this later. 'Looking to yourselves,' he says, 'lest you too be tempted.' Such judgments are made with the deep conviction of one's own weakness and vulnerability, and therefore with sympathy for the fallen one rather than contempt for them and pride in oneself.

Third, we are to *help bear the burden of sin*.

> Bear one another's burdens, and thus fulfill the law of Christ. (Gal. 6:2)

Our response to the sins of others is not to judge and stand aloof, but to 'bear one another's burdens.' Paul uses the present imperative, indicating a way of life. We are to live lives that are helpful to others. It also indicates, as one commentator puts it, 'sharing the pain of failure.'[185] This is a far cry from the 'live-and-let-live' attitude of today. The current mood is, mind your own business. The attitude of the past, and even the present in some circles, is condemnatory aloofness. Neither is right. God requires of us loving involvement. This, he says, fulfills the 'law of Christ,' a phrase found only here in the New Testament (though see the similar 'law of faith' [Rom. 3:27]; 'law of the Spirit of life in Christ Jesus' [Rom. 8:2]; 'under the law [*ennomos*] of Christ' [1 Cor. 9:21]). Stott points out that 'love our neighbor,' 'bear one another's burdens,' and 'fulfill the law' are equivalent expressions (Gal. 5:14). The same Christ who offers grace and forgiveness also requires wholehearted, lowly obedience (Matt. 20:25–7). Generally the test of discipleship is not a spectacular act of service, but the mundane. We are to be burden-bearers, whether the burden be emotional, spiritual, financial, or otherwise. We are to get down and get dirty in helping others with their burdens. Notice as well that it is assumed that we have burdens and that we need help in bearing them. We are not stoics, who pretend to be able to bear their own loads. Neither are we the superspiritual, who pretend that Christ bears all their burdens without human assistance. He uses people to meet our needs, even as He did in sending Titus to Paul in the midst of a great trial (2 Cor. 7:5–6). We want to be Titus-like, comforting, encouraging, assisting others in their troubles. This is our calling, though there is significance to our doing so.

Notice how beautifully the text answers all our natural objections to confronting those who are caught in sin. We say it sounds harsh, the Apostle Paul says do so with 'a spirit of gentleness.' We say it sounds self-righteous, the Apostle says we're to look to ourselves, 'lest (we) too be tempted.' We say it sounds unloving. The Apostle Paul says it fulfills the law of Christ. We say it sounds judgmental. He helps us to distinguish between being judgmental and judgmentalism.

Barriers to Burden-bearing

Still these are barriers to confrontational and restorative burden bearing. The Apostle brings two of them to our attention. They are not exhaustive. Many others could have been discussed, no doubt. But these two closely related barriers he presents for our consideration now.

> For if anyone thinks he is something when he is nothing, he deceives himself. (Gal. 6:3)

The first barrier to service is *conceit*. The problem that the Apostle Paul is addressing is that of being self-deceived about our own importance. We may think that we are 'something,' that is, above the obligations of burden bearing for one reason or other. We're too good. We're too busy. Conceit interferes with our service of others. As Stott puts it, 'our conduct to *others* is governed by our opinion of *ourselves*.'[186] But the gospel teaches that we are 'nothing,' and as such, owe all that we are to Christ. We are nothing but lost sinners. We do not earn our salvation. We do not deserve it. We can do nothing to secure it. We can do nothing to retain it. Every step that we take as Christians is enabled by the Spirit. Our dependence upon Him is absolute. The world may think that we are something. Within certain earthly circles we may be highly regarded. But where it counts, in the sight of God, we are nothing. How does the Apostle Paul combat conceit? By reminding us that we are 'nothing.'

One can see that the true gospel psychology flies in the face of the secular variety. Pop psychology is obsessed with telling us that we are wonderful. It seeks to bolster our self-esteem, our self-image, and our self-worth. The gospel, however, tells us that you are 'nothing.' The Apostle does not hesitate to say 'nothing good dwells in me' (Rom. 7:18). A few years back some Christian counselors jumped on the 'self,' bandwagon and began to say that Jesus taught us to love ourselves since he said that we are to love our neighbors *as ourselves*. First we must be able to love ourselves, they said, then we will be able to love others. That bit of exegesis qualifies for the 'top ten' bogus interpretations of the centuries, standing the meaning of the statement on its head.

Jesus, after all, assumes that we selfish sinners *already* love ourselves, and that that is a *problem* to be corrected, not a virtue to be *pursued.* Other Christian pop psychologists began to talk about how good we could feel about ourselves since we were so worthy that Christ died for us. Imagine, they said, what worth we must have if Christ died for us! This stands alongside the defective exegesis mentioned above as one of the top ten defective theological formulations, since it stands grace on its head, grace being that doctrine that says that Christ died for us though we were *not* worthy of His sacrifice. Biblical theology has fallen on hard times in recent years even among its friends.

Ironically, true gospel psychology leads to true psychological freedom through fully acknowledging our total depravity and worthlessness. In this respect I was disappointed to find that even the *Trinity Hymnal* changed the words to 'Beneath the Cross of Jesus' from the original:

> Two wonders I confess,
> The wonders of redeeming love
> And my own worthlessness.

The editors got squeamish about this in this age of feel-goodism and changed the words to,

> Two wonders I confess,
> The wonders of redeeming love
> And my unworthiness.

It is a slight change, but no doubt inspired by the self-esteem propaganda. Other evangelical hymnals changed the words of 'Alas and Did My Savior Bleed' from,

> Would he devote that sacred head
> For such a worm as I!

They weren't happy with calling people worms. So out went the worm, and in came,

> Would he devote that sacred head
> For sinners such as I!

There, that softens the blow, doesn't it? Never mind that the Psalmist calls himself a worm in Psalm 22:6, and that God calls Israel a worm in Isaiah 41:14. This is thought to be bad psychologically, leading to poor self images and depression. But it shows a complete lack of understanding of the psychology of grace. The Apostle could repeatedly boast, even exult, in being the 'chief of sinners' (1 Tim. 1:15). Full confession is liberating. Nothing so magnifies the grace of Christ (which is the source of all our joy) so much as realizing how utterly degraded and unworthy we are apart from Him. When the Apostle Paul says, 'I am the least of the apostles, who am not fit to be called an apostle,' he immediately adds, 'But by the grace of God I am what I am' (1 Cor. 15:9–10). When he says he is 'the very least of all saints,' he immediately speaks of the grace given to him to preach 'the unfathomable riches of Christ' (Eph. 3:8). This is gospel psychology (2 Cor. 12:11). Similarly, nothing so frees one to serve others as realizing ones worthlessness. Why should I not sweep the floors? Why should I not deliver a meal? Why should I not move chairs and set up tables? What could be too lowly for lowly me? What could be beneath the dignity of the undignified me? What could be too mundane for ordinary me? The doctrines of grace knock the socks off pride—pride which puffs up, pride which separates, pride which insulates us from others. Grace is the great leveler. I have to say with Paul, 'the least of all the apostles, who am not fit to be called an apostle,' that 'by the grace of God I am what I am'

(1 Cor. 15:10). No one of us is superior to the rest. Some are more gifted than others. But where do the gifts come from? This is the way that the Apostle Paul puts it to the Corinthians:

> For who regards you as superior? And what do you have that you did not receive? But if you did receive it, why do you boast as if you had not received it? (1 Cor. 4:7)

The great leveling question of the gospel is, 'What do you have that you didn't receive?' The answer is, nothing. Then the follow up, then why do you boast? What is there left to boast about? Pride is demolished. Arrogance is obliterated. Feelings of superiority are banished. We all stand on level ground at the foot of the cross. We are 'nothing.' No longer may pride be a barrier to burden-bearing.

Consequently we're not worrying about what others are thinking. What keeps people from confronting sin? Why do they get upset when their church confronts sin? Pride. What will the neighbors think. What will they say about us at the club? What will they say about us at the bowling alley? Oh no, they'll talk bad about us! So we fret. Why? Because we want to be something. Relax, realize we're nothing and do the right thing.

The second barrier to burden-bearing is *comparing ourselves with others.*

> But let each one examine his own work, and then he will have reason for boasting in regard to himself alone, and not in regard to another. (Gal. 6:4)

We are to 'examine (our) own work,' and not compare it with others so as to establish our fancied superiority. We are to do the best that we can with respect to our own work. If we are doing our best to correct the imperfections of our own work, then we are unlikely to be critical of the accomplishments (or lack thereof) of others. Then we will have 'reason for boasting,' not that he is commending boasting (he is not). What he is commending is living in such a way that praiseworthy characteristics emerge. This is work that is praiseworthy 'not in regard to another,' not in comparison to others, but 'in regard to (oneself) alone.' We must not imagine that we are 'doing well because of a fancied comparison with someone else,' as Morris puts it.[187]

> For each one shall bear his own load. (Gal. 6:5)

At first glance this verse seems to contradict verse 2. There he says we are to 'bear one another's burdens;' here he says 'each one shall bear his own load.' How do we reconcile these two statements? First, we should note that a different word for burdens is used in verse 5 (*bare* vs. *phortion*). Whereas the former generally indicates a burdensome load, this one usually indicates a normal load, as in a normal work load. There he is concerned that we help others. Here he is still concerned with comparing ourselves with others. The 'burden' here is probably the burden of sin and guilt, as well as obedience and service. We are to bear this, deal with it ourselves, rather than grow complacent by comparing ourselves with others. We all have our own relative responsibilities. As J. B. Phillips puts it, 'every man must 'shoulder his own pack.'' We often have very different sized packs, relative to our gifts, abilities, opportunities, and failures. This is why comparisons are futile, and even harmful. We stand alone before God on judgment day. No two people are exactly alike and no two set of circumstances are exactly alike. Consequently comparisons are meaningless.

Yet, much harm is done by comparing ourselves with others. And it cuts in both directions. I might compare his squalor with the relative suffering of others, and conclude no one is so badly off as I am. No one suffers as I do. No one has less than I. Consequently, I am not obligated to do anything for anybody. After all, I am at the bottom. I have the least amount of time. I have the least amount of money. How could I possibly help others? How could I possibly bear the burdens of others when I can hardly bear my own? Then another says, I do more than anyone else. I give more time. I give more money. They do nothing and I do everything. No more! I quit! Perhaps another writes a check and says, that is more than most do, and is content to go home and put up his feet. The problem in each of these cases is that the comparisons are utterly irrelevant. No, I've understated the case. They are completely, totally, and absolutely irrelevant. We are judged in relation to our own work alone. To whom much is given much is expected (Luke 12:48). If little is given, whether monetarily or in time or giftedness, then little is expected. But what is required is determined by what is given to each one, without respect to what others are doing with what they have.

Yet, as worthless as such comparisons are, yet we indulge them all the time, and they are the source of much bitterness, pride, envy, and lethargy. Don't worry about what someone else is doing. Don't presume to judge them. We are not in their shoes. We can't know whether they are pulling their own load and we shouldn't care. We should do what before God we are able. When a situation of need arises, we are to do what we can to help bear that burden and leave the judgments to God. Don't fret about what others are failing to do. Don't worry about what others are going to think about us. Don't be guilt driven in your motivation. As we often have said, we do the best we can with what we've got. Is there a sin that must be confronted? Is there a burden that must be borne? Each of us is to 'examine' our work. Scrutinize it carefully. Am I doing what I should? Am I as involved in the life of the church as I ought to be? Am I bearing the burdens of others? Am I fulfilling the law of Christ?

36

Sharing All Good Things

Galatians 6:6

The subject of today's text is an awkward one for preachers: the compensation of ministers. This is not a subject that we would choose to preach on. Yet because we are committed to preaching verse-by-verse through the Bible, on occasion we find ourselves confronting texts which are difficult for one reason or another. This is one such occasion. No matter what the preacher says he is quite vulnerable to being misunderstood.

Let us then say at the outset that there is no hidden agenda in what follows. We merely do here what we have done for the previous five chapters and five verses, which is, explain without bias the Apostle Paul's text. What does he say? What are the implications for us today? Should preachers be paid? Some churches rely wholly upon lay preachers. Should we? If preachers are paid, how much should they be paid? Should they be kept "humble and poor," or should they be well paid, or somewhere in between?

Paid

The Apostle Paul writes,

> And let the one who is taught the word share all good things with him who teaches. (Gal. 6:6)

It is remarkable how early the practice of setting aside certain men for the teaching of the word as a full-time, compensated role, was established in the church. In the earliest decades of the church, unlike today, there was probably no established way to ensure regular provision for the teachers of the church. With many of the church's early converts coming straight from paganism into the Christian community, the task of instruction was crucial. The young converts had to be taught respecting God, man, Christ, salvation, Christian living. These teachers taught at great personal sacrifice. So the Apostle Paul introduces a general principle—the one taught is to share 'all good things' with the one who teaches. Exactly what this sharing entailed is not spelt out. It probably included food, lodging, clothing, and so on. Take good care of your teachers, he essentially is telling them. Provide for the material needs of those who devote their lives to full-time preaching and teaching. 'The laborer is worthy of his hire,' said Jesus as he sent out the seventy to preach (Luke 10:7).

This theme is developed most fully in Paul's first letter to the Corinthians. Paul's right to the title of 'apostle' was being challenged, as well as his right to 'eat and drink,' to take along with him 'a believing wife,' and his 'right to refrain from working' (1 Cor. 9:1–5). He asks the following questions:

> Who at any time serves as a soldier at his own expense? Who plants a vineyard, and does not eat the fruit of it? Or who tends a flock and does not use the milk of the flock? (1 Cor. 9:7)

His obvious point—if they, soldiers, farmers, and shepherds, share in the fruit of their labor, so ought preachers. Then he moves from what might be considered 'common sense' arguments, those 'according to human judgment,' to the requirements of the law. He is not arguing merely on the basis of common human practice, but ultimately on the basis of Scripture.

> I am not speaking these things according to human judgment, am I? Or does not the Law also say these things? For it is written in the Law of Moses, 'You shall not muzzle the ox while he is threshing.' God is not concerned about oxen, is He? Or is He speaking altogether for our sake? Yes, for our sake it was written, because the plowman ought to plow in hope, and the thresher to thresh in hope of sharing the crops. (1 Cor. 9:8–10)

The lesson to be drawn from both common human experience and the law?

> If we sowed spiritual things in you, is it too much if we should reap material things from you? (1 Cor. 9:11)

Again he cites Old Testament precedence.

> Do you not know that those who perform sacred services eat the food of the temple, and those who attend regularly to the altar have their share with the altar? (1 Cor. 9:13)

Finally he invokes the command of Christ in addition to common sense and the Law:

> So also the Lord directed those who proclaim the gospel to get their living from the gospel. (1 Cor. 9:14)

The same things are taught in 1 Timothy 5:17–18, Paul saying of those who labor at preaching and teaching that they are especially worthy of 'double honor,' that they, like the ox, are not to be muzzled while threshing, and that 'the laborer is worthy of his wages.' That the early church compensated its preachers seems beyond dispute. But let us delve into this further and answer why this might be so.

First, because preaching the word is a full time job. It can be done on a part-time basis. But ordinarily, it cannot be done well with anything less than the full-time attention of the one called and gifted to preach. This is clearly what lies behind the apostolic injunctions and practice. Why is this so?

1. There is the matter of the *preparation of the preacher*. Preaching is not just a matter of standing up and giving a speech. It requires moral and spiritual readiness. Such requires time spent in the word and prayer each day, as well as other reading which prepares the heart for the task. It is not just a matter of throwing together a talk. The preacher must spend considerable time preparing his heart. There must be time for thought, for meditation, for reflection. I suspect nearly everyone says that one reason why preaching is on the decline is that the pace of life in the modern world allows little time for reflection. One of the great things for me about vacations is that there is extended time to think. Finally we slow down enough to weigh, to ponder, to reflect. This 'full-time' time for preparing the preacher is

vital if he is to be anointed with spiritual power, and not just delivering religious talks.

2. There is the matter of *preparing the sermon*. Preaching requires careful study. Years are set apart for intensive study of Scripture, doctrine, church history, and pastoral theology. Hours of hard, tedious work goes into reading the original languages, reading the commentaries of the learned men that God has given to the church. This is merely the prelude to writing or outlining an exposition of Scripture. Then there is preparation of the sermon itself. Hours must be spent organizing one's thoughts into a coherent whole. Those thoughts must be enlivened by illustration, elaboration, and application. The sermon must be rehearsed (at least mentally) so that one commences preaching thoroughly familiar with what one has planned to say. This all takes time. I have heard tapes of the late Martyn Lloyd-Jones in which he laments the unspoken assumptions of so called lay-preaching, that is, that preaching is something that can be done on the side. It can't. Not ordinarily. He apparently had been chastised by lay preachers who disparaged the full-timers for being a burden to the church while they (the lay preachers) found it easy to preach in their spare time. It's easy, they said, or at least implied. It's no problem at all. What is wrong with you ministers? they seemed to say.

No doubt there are preachers who don't do enough. Some are lazy and don't prepare adequately. Some don't have the necessary gifts. But it is not 'easy,' even for those who have gifts in abundance. That's why the Apostle Paul says that 'the Lord directed,' not just Paul, who might be accused of special pleading, that those who proclaim the gospel are 'to get their living from the gospel' (1 Cor. 9:14). They are to be supported so that they are able to concentrate on preaching full time. As Luther put it, 'It is impossible for one man both to labour day and night to get a living, and at the same time to give himself to the study of sacred learning as the preaching office requireth.'[188]

Second, pastoring a church is a full-time job. In spite of all that we've just discussed, preachers will sometimes claim that they don't get paid to preach. With the Apostle they say, 'I am under compulsion; for woe is me if I do not preach the gospel' (1 Cor. 9:16). We're going to preach somewhere whether we get paid or not. What we really get paid for is to take care of everything else that goes with pastoring a church—leadership, administration, hospital visitation, pastoral calls, counseling, correspondence, phone calls, denominational responsibilities, meetings, and so on. I was told before I entered the ministry that 90% of one's time in the ministry was taken up with things other than preaching and teaching and preparing to do such. I didn't believe it then. Now I do. That figure is about right, or at least 75-80% is. I spend most of Monday working on sermons. Rarely, if ever, do I find *even one minute* in the day for preaching and teaching from Tuesday to Thursday. Not one! Typically, I sneak in on Friday morning to get three to four hours of preparation completed. What am I doing Tuesday through Thursday? I wouldn't typify it as busy work. Rightly seen, it amounts to the application of the word of God to every aspect of the church's life. Because life refuses to divide up neatly into secular and spiritual realms, the role of the ministers in the decision making process is indispensable. In our case six-hundred in-town members and their one-hundred and fifty covenant children are calling upon three ministers day and night. This is not a complaint. That is what we are there for. I am merely pointing out why the pastorate is not a part-time job. Once a church reaches fifty adult members with a couple of dozen covenant children, the pastoral burden alone is beyond the scope of a man fully employed elsewhere. Never been more true than it is today. The Rev. Donald Hoke, a good friend of this congregation, told me a few years back that back in the mid-to-late 1950s, when he first entered the ministry, he never was called upon for counseling. Never. Now we probably spend ten hours a week among us in counseling situations. What is the difference between then and now? The collapse of the family and other supportive institutions. In the 1950s the schools, the family, and the church were all working together, communicating messages which were compatible with each other. Since then the public schools have all but collapsed, the churches have lost their nerve, and the family is in ruins. Hours and hours must be spent in marriage counseling. More hours are spent in premarital counseling, pre-baptismal counseling, child-rearing training, and so on. Where has pastoral visitation gone, you might have wondered? It has gone to the counseling bench, that's where. The destruction of the primary institutions in our civilization have put a tremendous strain on faithful churches. We have wonderful opportunities as a consequence, but only if we recognize that circumstances are significantly different than they were forty years ago. If we wish we would return to the old days when churches with 500 members had only one minister and no youth workers, then we may fundamentally fail to recognize the different world in which we now live. Now more than ever the ministry is a full-time job, and full-time for not just one, but several men.

Compensation Levels

The question that then arises is, how much should a minister be paid? The Apostle Paul gives us some guidance here as well. But we should acknowledge at the outset how relative money is. Let's consider a church which is searching for a minister. The search committee meets and seeks to set appropriate compensation levels. They ask themselves, what did we pay our previous ministers? What do other churches pay in our community? In our denomination? That are similar to us? The same in size and in structure? What are people in other professions paid who have similar levels of education? All of these factors influence the church, and to some degree should. But they underscore how relative money is. I know of Presbyterian ministers who are paid just under $200,000 in salary and benefits. I know of many, many others who get paid very little. My point is that compensation is relative to many factors. I doubt if the basis should be 'what the market can bear,' as it is in other professions. The most important principles are as follows.

First, he wants those who minister the word not to be subject to a standard of living significantly different from that of the people to whom he ministers. The members are to share 'all good things' with their teachers. What they (the members) enjoy, he should enjoy. What they possess, he should possess. What they are able to do, he should be able to do. But that itself is a problem, because there is a wide range of living standards in any given church. Some have a lot, some have a little. Should the 'all good things' be those of the wealthiest or of the poorest members, or somewhere in between? I think the latter of those options. He should, all things being equal, fit in. He should not be the best paid. He should not be the worst. He should live about like everyone else is living.

Second, he should be compensated enough to free him from concerns for material provision so that he can concentrate completely on serving the church. Where do I get this principle? It is the point of compensating ministers at all. The whole point of compensation is to relieve the preachers of the word of secular employments and concerns. What it takes to do so is going to vary according to the circumstances of the minister and the community. When I was first ordained in 1983 my compensation was $14,000 per year, where it stayed for a couple of years. I'm not talking about the dark ages. This was just a few years back. But as a single man, it was more than enough to free me from material concerns. I saved enough in three years to get married. But then as a married man, more is needed. A lot more. Then with each child, still more is needed, if one is to be free from 'worldly concerns,' using the language used in the official call of Presbyterian ministers. Typically churches have thought that they should provide medical insurance and retirement funds if they are to free their ministers from worldly concerns. If the church has convictions about Christian education, it might provide for the education of the minister's children. If it thinks that the minister's wife should be a stay-at-home mom, then this too would need to be taken into account. None of this has as its objective outbidding another church, or of appealing to the flesh of the minister in trying to persuade him to come or to stay. Neither should the withholding of such be used as leverage to force a minister out of a position. All of these factors should be considered only in terms of making it possible for the minister to 'get (his) living from the gospel,' and not need to take another job or send his wife to work. If a church cannot afford a minister with a large family, then it looks for one it can afford, perhaps with a smaller family. If it cannot afford to support a married man, then it looks for a single man.

Some churches are confused about this. There may be a tendency on the part of churches to neglect appropriate compensation. This is summed up in the old joke, 'You keep him humble, Lord, and we'll keep him poor.' Strangely, some Evangelical churches seem to have confused Protestant pastors for medieval monks. Ministers do not take vows of poverty. They should be paid well. I say this not because I am a minister. I have always believed this. When I was in college I saved all of my tithe money one summer (a practice of which I no longer approve –the tithe belongs to the church), and used it to fund a very large Bible study that met on the Fraternity Row. We arranged for an evangelistic singing group to come for special outreach meetings. They didn't expect to get paid. Instead I handed them a check for twice what they normally received. Why? A worker is worthy of his hire. They came at great inconvenience. I knew that they were struggling to make ends meet. We should not be asking ourselves about how cheaply we can get by when we bring in outside speakers or pay youth workers or anyone else involved in Christian ministry. If the going rate is $X, pay them $2X. By secular standards, even that rate is scandalously low. If the company for whom you work brings in an outside speaker, it will pay extraordinary amounts of money to tie him up for several days. Christian ministry comes relatively cheap.

I don't know any ministers getting rich off of the ministry. I do know hundreds of them who were smart enough to have gone to any professional school and made triple what they now are, but instead made the choice to serve God in the ministry. Almost without exception they barely get by. Almost without exception they work long hours. Almost without exception their families suffer. Almost without exception the ministry is frustrating, spiritually exhausting, emotionally stressful, and thankless. Let me again issue a disclaimer—I am not talking about myself.

Our church is a wonderful place to minister the gospel. Our congregation takes good care of us. What I would like for us to appreciate is the lot of the vast majority of pastors. Few, if any, men in the ministry suffer from having too much. Many do suffer from having too little. Don't be afraid of overpaying those who minister the word to you. Don't make it your objective to pay as little as you can and still qualify as having freed the ministers from 'worldly concern,' if just barely. Share 'all good things.' But maybe he can't handle a large salary, one might say. Maybe he'll become materialistic if he gets too much money. If so, then you've got the wrong minister. Any minister mature enough to minister the word to you is mature enough to handle his compensation, at whatever level.

There may also be a tendency on the part of members to envy or begrudge the compensation of its ministers. No doubt this tendency is exactly what Paul is responding to in 1 Corinthians 9, and it may lie in the background of Galatians 6:6 as well. Some see it as an easy job compared with manual labor. Some mistake the flexibility of hours, a true advantage, with number of hours. I wouldn't care to compare the ministry with other kinds of work. Lots of people work long and hard. I can just say that most of the ministers that I know do essentially nothing but take care of their families and the work of the ministry. They are either reading, or are studying, preparing, or on the phone, or on the road basically all the time. They eat, drink, and sleep the ministry. Ministers are considered 'self-employed,' and no doubt some have abused the freedom that comes with being such. There are some lazy ministers. But not many. Most work long and hard. And along with the normal emotional and physical stress, there is the spiritual as well. Ministers are on the front lines, as it were. The devil saves his sharpest darts for them. They face his most savage attacks. I am amazed and disheartened by the number of ministers who commit suicide, who fall into adultery, who struggle with depression. The ministry is spiritually tough. It is not for the fainthearted.

Let me now sum up. The church's responsibility to financially support those who minister the word with 'all good things' is not a burden that must be borne, but a 'sharing,' a fellowship in which it is privileged to participate. The goal of this 'sharing' is that of relieving those who teach of secular or material concerns so that they are better able to concentrate on the ministry of the word. The amount of compensation is relative, aiming at equality with the membership generally, and yet being affected by numerous variables, which either increase or decrease the amount required to truly relieve your teachers of material concerns. For most ministers the ministry is not about money, nor should it be. No amount of money could bring us to a given church, and no amount could lure us away.

Let us then support the proclamation of the word, sharing 'all good things' with those called to full-time ministry.

And let us remember that verse 6 is connected to verse 7.

> Do not be deceived, God is not mocked; for whatever a man sows, this he will also reap. (Gal. 6:7)

While what has been called 'the law of sowing and reaping' has much broader application than just compensating ministers, its first application does have to do with the compensation of ministers. Boice argues respecting the ministers that,

> …if congregations refuse to support them and so forfeit good teaching, preferring to spend their money on themselves, the results will be corruption. But if, on the other hand, they support good teachers, a spiritual harvest will result.[189]

Pray for your ministers. And 'share all good things' with them. The law of sowing and reaping, presented in the next verse, may mean, in connection with this verse, that if we as a church fail to provide adequately for our ministers, we are like the one who sows to the flesh and reaps corruption. Sow good seed, and all good things to those who shoulder the load full-time, so that the church might reap a full harvest. Pinch-pennies here, balance the budget on the backs of the employees, and we may undermine the effectiveness of our ministers, and in the long run undermine the budget as well. Don't be 'penny-wise' and 'pound foolish,' as the old saying goes. Be generous, and God will abundantly bless.

37

The Law of Sowing and Reaping

Galatians 6:7–8

The words of the Apostle Paul are ominous, fearsome, sobering, and strengthening, as he says,

> Do not be deceived, God is not mocked; for whatever a man sows, this he will also reap. (Gal. 6:7)

When I was a young boy, the Baptist minister under whose ministry I sat between the ages of 10 and 20, preached a sermon on this text that made a crucial difference on how I handled my teenage years. I was at a stage when I was just beginning to question whether I wasn't foolishly being a 'goody-two-shoes.' After all, here I sit in church and the party is *out there*. Not only are they having all the fun, but they are pointing their fingers at me and laughing. I am missing out. Is it worth it? Galatians 6:7–8 answers this with a resounding yes!

As we saw last time, the first application of this text has to do with the compensating of ministers. Verse 7 is connected to verse 6:

> And let the one who is taught the word share all good things with him who teaches. (Gal. 6:6)

But let's move on now and look at the principle more broadly. What is true of a church's care of its ministers is true as well of all life. We will reap what we sow.

The principle

'Do not be deceived,' introduces an undeniable truth. 'This is an immutable law of God, which the phrase 'God is not mocked' emphasizes,' says Boice.[190] God may not be 'treated with contempt,' or 'outwitted.' Don't think that you 'can ignore the commands God has given and go (your) own way with impunity,' as Morris puts it.[191] 'For whatever a man sows, this he will also reap.' Don't be fooled about this, he is saying. Don't deny for a moment that there is an inseparable connection between actions and consequences. If we sow corn, we will not reap wheat. This is a truism of agriculture. But the principle also applies to life generally. You will reap what you sow. What you sow is what you will harvest. What we do will determine what we will become and where we go. What we put in is what we will get out. In the end, over the long haul, justice is served, we get what we deserve. We become what we do. We cannot expect 'to reap the *fruit* of the Spirit if we do not sow in the *field* of the Spirit,' Stott maintains.[192] The adage put it like this: 'Sow a thought, reap an act; sow an act, reap a habit; sow a habit, reap a character; sow a character, reap a destiny.'

The Apostle Paul now applies the principle in two directions: sowing the flesh and reaping corruption, and sowing the Spirit and reaping eternal life. Why do some Christians not grow in holiness? Because holiness is a harvest. It depends on what one sows.

Sowing the Flesh

> For the one who sows to his own flesh shall from the flesh reap corruption, but the one who sows to the Spirit shall from the Spirit reap eternal life. (Gal. 6:8)

If one sows the 'flesh,' that is, who lives for the here and now, lives to satisfy temporal desires, who lives as though this world were all there is, will in the end reap 'corruption.' 'To 'sow to the flesh' is to pander to it, to cosset, cuddle and stroke it, instead of crucifying it,' says Stott.

> Every time we allow our mind to harbour a grudge, nurse a grievance, entertain an impure fantasy, or wallow in self-pity, we are sowing to the flesh. Every time we linger in bad company whose insidious influence we know we cannot resist, every time we lie in bed when we ought to be up and praying, every time we read pornographic literature, every time we take a risk which strains our self-control, we are sowing, sowing, sowing to the flesh.[193]

We deceive ourselves. We con ourselves by calling our lies 'little white lies.' But one small lie makes a second, larger lie easier. We indulge in just a little hateful gossip. But the next time, more gossip and worse gossip is easier. We entertain a lustful image or action, and the next time, we go further. The flesh, we must remember, is *pleasurable* and *progressive.* It always wants more. It is never satisfied. With what result? We become not just one who once lied, but liars. We become hateful gossips. We become adulterers. We become what we do. We reap what we sow. We become dishonest, twisted, unfaithful souls, selfishly manipulating life to our own ends. All that we are and all that we accumulate ultimately proves to be vanity and striving after the wind (Ecc. 2:11), amounts to nothing, will be consumed by the moth and rust (Matt. 6:19–21), and will be destroyed in the fires of judgment by so much wood, hay, and stubble (1 Cor. 3:12). This is not just true of the notorious sinner, who is more obviously living to fulfill bodily appetites. Yes, the philanderer and the glutton are living for the flesh. They are living for sensual pleasure. All they seem to care about is bodily pleasure. But it is also true of the moral person who lives a clean and upright life, but whose whole attention is on accumulating the gadgets, the comforts, the accomplishments, the prestige to be found in this world, and who gives no attention to his soul. His body will die and return to the dust. All his material possessions are destined ultimately to return to the dust. Sow the flesh, focus on the here and now, on the present, and one inevitably will reap 'corruption' or 'destruction' (NIV). While this word can be understood in a number of ways, as Morris points out, 'here it surely points to ultimate loss; it is the opposite of eternal life.'[194]

Sowing the Spirit

But if one 'sows to the Spirit,' one will 'from the Spirit reap eternal life.' To 'sow to the Spirit' means to concentrate on the things of the Spirit, to devote oneself to the things which feed the soul, such as public worship, prayer, Bible reading, and selfless service. It means to focus not on this present world, which is passing away, but on eternity, on knowing, pleasing, and serving God. It is to set one's mind on the Spirit and walk by the Spirit (Rom. 8:6; Gal. 5:16, 25). It is to seek the things that are above (Col. 3:1), not earthly things (Phil. 3:19). As was true of sowing the flesh, so also with the Spirit, it is the little things that add up. As one exercises discipline in small things—turning off a lewd television show, getting up a little earlier to have time for prayer and Bible reading, setting aside 15 minutes a day for family devotions, saying no to an extra helping of food, controlling and restraining the tongue on occasions when you want to lash out so badly, making the effort to get yourself to church each week, giving back excess change to a clerk who has returned too much, telling the truth even when it hurts—one reaps a harvest of godliness. Note that there are two kinds of sowing and two resulting harvests. What the Apostle Paul says makes perfect sense. It is only logical. Sow the flesh and you'll reap corruption. The 'process of moral decay will set in,' says Stott, and 'we shall go from bad to worse until we finally perish.' Do the opposite, sow the Spirit, and 'a process of moral and spiritual growth will begin,' leading to external life.[195]

Making the Application

As I mentioned, these verses had a hugely important impact on me as a schoolboy. The Baptist minister under whose ministry I grew up emphasized this verse one Sunday morning, and I never forgot it. Sow immorality, sow drunkedness, sow drug abuse, sow dishonesty, and you will reap an awful harvest. It may not happen today or tomorrow. But do not be deceived. God is not mocked. You are not getting away with anything. He sees. He knows. He will visit upon you the judgments that your sins deserve. Scripture proves this over and over again, whether in the lives of Lot, Isaac, Jacob, Samson, Eli, Samuel, or Solomon. But never is this more clear than in the life of David. David had his moment. He saw Bathsheba, sent for her, committed adultery, and sent her away. He seemed to have gotten away with it. People often do seem to get away with their sin. But God is not mocked. Bathsheba sent word that she was expecting. So David sent for her husband, one of David's elite soldiers, and brought him home from the front lines. But Uriah refused to sleep with his wife at a time when his fellow soldiers were enduring hardship out-of-doors. So he had Uriah murdered, and then married Bathsheba. She bore him a son. Again, he seemed to have gotten away with it. But the Scripture says, 'but the thing that David had done was evil in the sight of the Lord' (2 Sam. 11:27). Having sown the flesh, David reaped the flesh for the rest of his life. First the child died, then his son Amnon raped his half-sister Tamar, then Absalom her full-brother murdered Amnon, then Absalom led a rebellion against his father David, plunging the nation into civil war, culminating in the death of Absalom. Then Sheba led a second rebellion against David. There was no end to it. David's sins were passed on to his children. He indulged sexual sin. They indulged it. The propensity was passed down to Solomon, whose foreign wives and concubines were his undoing, on down through the Davidic line. Was it just a little harmless fun? No, it did what it always does—it destroyed lives. It tore apart families, it led to violence, it almost destroyed a nation. Sow the wind, and one will reap the whirlwind (Hosea 8:7).

If one might identify 'the big lie,' of all the lies of our popular culture, it is that one can sin with impunity. Rarely are there any consequences for sin. The drunks are all funny drunks. They are the life of the party, beloved by all. They don't seem to get in wrecks and kill people, like they do in real life. They don't fail on their jobs and get fired, like in real life. They don't turn their homes into hell-holes. The immorality is all romantic, glamorous, exciting, air-brushed fun. Teenagers don't get pregnant, like in the real world. No one gets a venereal disease, like in the real world. Single mothers don't live in abject poverty. Adultery doesn't lead to divorce and heartbroken children. If there is a divorce, it is happy for all. If there is an abortion, there are no regrets. Life is painless. Sin has no consequences. The whole culture screams at our youth, do what you feel like doing. If you have an itch, scratch it. If you have a desire, fulfill it. But listen to what God says: don't be deceived. God is not mocked. You will reap what you sow.

Our neighbors, by and large, tend to live for the present. Even if they are not grossly immoral they are consumed with the temporal. They too are sowing the flesh. They give no thought to eternity. They pay no attention to their souls. They live for the present. They surround themselves with all the creature comforts and forms of entertainment that they can afford. They go from meal to ballgame to a weekend away to new car to new clothes. This is what popular culture encourages as well. The people on TV and in the movies don't go to church. They don't read the Bible. They don't contemplate or discuss the eternal destiny of their souls. They are all, almost without exception, happy atheists. They live like there is no God. And there are no consequences. The message is: who needs God? One can be happy, fulfilled, satisfied from this world alone. One does not need the Bread of Life. One does not need Living Water. This world alone fulfills us. There is no empty space in the heart. There is no troubling sense of meaninglessness.

But what will they *really* reap from a lifetime of sowing this world? In this life, a deep, profound angst, an unrelieved sense of purposelessness, a troubling sense that surely there is something more to life. In the next world they will reap corruption and the opposite of eternal life, destruction. Wake up, dear people. Wake up to what is going on all around us. We are 'amusing ourselves to death,' as Neil Postman would say. This world is merely a preparation for the next. Sow the spirit, not the flesh. Concentrate on believing and obeying God, in cultivating the fruit of the Spirit. Remember that there is no profit in gaining the whole world, with all its prestige, power, pleasure, if you lose you own soul in the process (Matt. 16:26). 'Paul is reminding the Galatians that they should get their priorities right and give time and energy to that which concerns ultimate issues,' says Morris, 'and not merely the passing things of here and now.'[196]

Similarly we might ask, why do some Christians grow in holiness while others do not? Because holiness is a harvest. It depends on what one sows. Do you want to grow in spiritual maturity? Do you look around you and see strong, knowledgeable, zealous Christians and wish you were more like they? Well, what are you doing about it? What you sow you will reap. What are you sowing? You are sowing something. What is it? You will harvest exactly what you are sowing. If you do not sow spiritual commitments how can you expect a spiritual harvest? If you are not regular in public worship; if you do not spend time daily in the word and prayer; if you do not practice tithing and sacrificial giving; if you do not practice the other disciplines of the Christian life such as Sabbath observance; if you do not practice sacrificial service, how can you expect to harvest the fruit of the Spirit? How can you become Christ-like if you don't feed on the Bread of life? You will reap what you sow. It is that simple.

Yet for all that we've said so far, a real Christian is tremendously encouraged by this passage. Why? Because it guarantees that his sacrifices pay off in the end. What sacrifices? Let me summarize them again.

First, there are the sacrifices of missed pleasures. He's missed the party. He has not indulged the flesh. He has missed out. He might be tempted to regret that he didn't join in the 'fun.' But this passage is a sobering dose of reality for him. It takes him behind the appearances to reality—the reality that they will reap corruption and destruction, and he will not. Ultimately, he has missed nothing at all. An 'abundant life' is found only in Christ. The 'fullness of joy' and true 'pleasures' are found only in the presence of God (Ps. 16).

Second, there are the sacrifices of Christian disciplines. There is time spent in worship, in private devotions, in tithing, in observing the Sabbath, in serving others *that might have been spent on oneself.* I could have been out having fun instead of sitting in church, one might be tempted to think. I might have gone to the ballgame, or to the party, or to the movie, and instead, here I sit. These verses promise that we are not wasting our time. It is worth it. When we are tempted to doubt they strongly remind us that God is not mocked! Persevere! Press on! The Lord will reward your diligence. He will transform you. He will ultimately glorify you. It is worth it! 'All these things shall be added unto you' (Matt. 6:33). Peter raised the issue,

> Behold, we have left everything and followed You. (Mark 10:28)

Jesus answered,

> Truly I say to you, there is no one who has left house or brothers or sisters or mother or father or children or farms, for My sake and for the gospel's sake, but that he shall receive a hundred times as much now in the present age, houses and brothers and sisters and mothers and children and farms, along with persecutions; and in the age to come, eternal life. (Mark 10:29–30)

A hundred times as much shall be received 'in the present age,' Jesus says!

Finally, there are the sacrifices of *persecution and rejection*. Real Christians have a hard time fitting in these days. They are absolutists in a day of relativism. They are particularists in a day of pluralism. They believe in right and wrong. They believe in truth and error. For much of the world this makes us Neanderthals. Worldlings are shocked at our closed-mindedness. They are horrified at our judgmentalism. They are disgusted by our narrowness. This means that many 'nice' and 'fun' people will not like us. This means that we may be socially ostracized and rejected. There are organizations which we may never be asked to join. There are parties that we may never be asked to attend. We may feel isolated. We may have our feelings hurt. We may hurt for our children, who don't understand and suffer the consequences of our convictions. Is it worth it? Yes it is. How do we know? Because God promises that we will reap what we sow. Our obedience, our faithfulness will pay huge dividends that those who sow the flesh will never see.

My uncle Abe visited our family at the time of my grandmother's death in 1966. At the time he boasted of having bought a drawer full of stock in a Japanese photography company. He said it was called 'Fuji Foto.' He bought it for pennies, he said. We laughed and laughed. That was the funniest name we ever heard. 'Fuji Foto.' Uncle Abe had the last laugh. Little more than a decade later those little green boxes of 'Fugi Foto' were everywhere. The world is like what we were. Worldlings cannot see the value of living by the Spirit. All that they can see is the flesh. They laugh and laugh at us. But come harvest time, come time to collect the profits of a lifetime of investing, they will reap nothing but corruption, but we will reap eternal life.

38

In Due Time We Shall Reap

Galatians 6:9–10

Why is it that people don't believe the law of sowing and reaping? Why do they think that they can get away with evil, that they can sin with impunity? Because of one thing—the lag time between actions and consequences. A columnist recently observed that the popular moral gurus in the United States of the 1970s and 80s were talk-show hosts Phil Donahue and Dr Ruth. Today the most popular radio programs in the nation are Rush Limbaugh and Dr. Laura Schlessinger, commentators who, for the most part, affirm traditional morals. Why? Lag time. The moral revolution of the 1960s that said that we needed to break with the old traditions, liberate ourselves from bondage to guilt, give ourselves 'permission,' as Donahue liked to put it, to indulge our fantasies and so on, didn't fully go to seed until the late 1980s. Only then did the onslaught of illegitimacy, adultery, divorce, abortion, single-parent households, unsupervised and out-of control youth reach epidemic proportions. The party lasted a long time. It seemed like it would never end. It always does. But finally God's judgments begin to fall, though many still refuse to see it. Peter characterized the pagans of his day as 'mockers … following after their own lusts,' who ask,

> Where is the promise of His coming? For ever since the fathers fell asleep, all continues just as it was from the beginning of creation. (2 Pet. 3:4)

They think that they can sin without consequence because of the lag time. God's threat remains unfulfilled. 'All continues just as it was from the beginning of creation,' they say. Peter promises,

> But do not let this one fact escape your notice, beloved, that with the Lord one day is as a thousand years, and a thousand years as one day. The Lord is not slow about His promise, as some count slowness, but is patient toward you, not wishing for any to perish but for all to come to repentance. (2 Pet. 3:8–9)

The lag in time between promise of judgment and actual judgment is a matter of the patience of a God who is 'not wishing for any to perish but for all to come to repentance.' But the day will come, 'like a thief,' he says,

> But the day of the Lord will come like a thief, in which the heavens will pass away with a roar and the elements will be destroyed with intense heat, and the earth and its works will be burned up.

> Since all these things are to be destroyed in this way, what sort of people ought you to be in holy conduct and godliness, (2 Pet. 3:10–11)

Lag time is also behind the tendency among the people of God to become demoralized and give up. Last time we looked primarily at the warning, the emphasis in verses 7–8. Now we will look at the promise that 'we shall reap,' and how it relates to our perseverance in obedience.

The Problem

> And let us not lose heart in doing good, for in due time we shall reap if we do not grow weary. (Gal. 6:9)

Don't 'lose heart,' he says. Press on. Keep on 'doing good.' Why might they lose heart? Because of the very thing that we are acknowledging. There is lag time between planting and harvesting, between sowing and reaping. He says, 'in due time we shall reap,' recognizing that at any given time we may not be reaping. There is a time for reaping, and it might not be right now. Typically there is a four month lapse between planting and harvesting (John 4:35). That time would come, but it was not yet. In the meantime, the righteous go unrewarded, and the wicked seem to be getting away with their wickedness. This is the struggle of the Psalmist in Psalm 73. The wicked are prospering. The righteous are suffering. Why bother to obey? Why pay the price? Why deprive ourselves of the fleshly pleasures? Why work so hard at denying the flesh?

In addition, we grow tired of the struggle. We let down our guard and allow selfishness to creep in again. He warns us first not to 'lose heart' (*enkakeo*), rendered 'become weary' in the NIV. It seems to have a range of meaning from becoming demoralized (Luke 18:1; 2 Cor. 4:1; Eph. 3:13) to becoming exhausted (2 Thess. 3:13). 'Let us not lose heart in doing good,' the Apostle Paul says, 'for in due time we shall reap if we do not grow weary.' He warns us again not to 'grow weary' (*ekluo*) or 'give up,' (NIV), or 'slacken our efforts' (NEB). If there is a progression here, it is from 'slackening of the mind (giving up) …to weakening of bodily functions (growing faint),' says Fung.[197] Doing good requires continuous effort. 'If the farmer tires of sowing and leaves half his field unsown, he will reap only half a crop,' Stott points out.[198] Like the farmer, we must be patient (James 5:7). The Scotsman John Brown complains, 'Christians frequently act like children in reference to this harvest. They would sow and reap in the same day.'[199]

So in practical terms, here is the situation. We offer help to people. We do so repeatedly. Perhaps the help is financial. Perhaps it is spiritual counsel. But we see no results. There are no changes. We see no improvement. We get discouraged. We 'lose heart.' We are tempted to give up on them. Demoralized, we 'grow weary.' We lose the motivation to help not only this one person, but feeling 'burned,' anyone at all.

Or perhaps our area of concern is that of personal spiritual growth. We have been seeking Christ diligently in the means of grace for a number of months. We have been getting up early every morning for prayer and Bible reading. We have been pleading with God that we might get in control of our tongue. We have been consistent in public worship, sitting week by week under the ministry of the word, prayer, and sacrament. We have been hallowing the Sabbath, committing it entirely to worship, rest, and works of mercy. Yet, we see no progress. We are not in control of our tongues. We do not seem to be growing in holiness. So we get discouraged. We are disheartened. We lose the will and energy to maintain the disciplines. We give up. We slacken.

Maybe our problem is that of Christian witness in an age of license. This is the problem of missing the party. We have struggled and sacrificed to walk in obedience. But we have been ostracized by our old buddies. We miss the drinking parties. We miss the fulfilling of our lusts. We miss the life of conspicuous consumption lived by our friends. We miss the leeks and melons of Egypt. Is it worth it? we ask ourselves. We get discouraged, demoralized, depressed, and lose the energy to keep up the fight. We give in.

The time lag is a problem for us as well as for out-in-out pagans. We too wrestle with it.

The Solution

The solution is so simple that many miss it. It comes down to this. Finally we must believe the promises and threats of God. Here is why we should not 'lose heart in doing good.' Here is why we should not 'grow weary.' 'For,' he says, indicating purpose or reason, 'in due time we shall reap.' There it is. Not now, but 'in due time,' we will harvest the fruit of what we have labored so long to plant. Do you believe it? Or are you unbelieving? God is saying, you will reap at the time of His choosing, a 'due time,' His time. It is true. It is infallibly certain. You will reap. Our labor will be rewarded. Our efforts do not escape the notice of the Almighty. All our tears He has collected in His bottle (Ps. 56:8). He sees them. He remembers them. We will harvest abundantly. We can take it to the bank. We can count on it.

The critical matter is believing. Finally the Christian faith is a matter of faith! Do we believe the word of God. If we do, we will persevere in doing what is good and right. We will act as though what the Bible says is true. If we don't believe it, then we will ignore its threats and promises and do what we want. The critical thing in the Christian life is faith. We must believe God concerning all that He says about Himself, His Son, and what He requires of us. Don't believe the threats? Then go on and do what you want. Don't believe the promises? Then ignore them. But if we really believe them, then we will take them to heart and conform our lives to them. A person who believes that the weather report warning of a hurricane is true gets out of the way of the hurricane. As he believes he acts. We will reap, he says. Believe it! If we do, we will 'do good to all men.' We will persevere.

> So then, while we have opportunity, let us do good to all men, and especially to those who are of the household of the faith. (Gal. 6:10)

We have a responsibility to do good to all, Christian and non-Christian. In addition, 'all men' means both those who are able to reciprocate and those who are not. Don't become discouraged by a lack of response. Keep on doing good to all. But our good-doing has a covenantal priority. We are 'especially' to do good to 'the household of faith,' or 'the family of believers' (NIV). This is to be done 'while we have opportunity' (*kairos*=the right time, the opportune moment). In due 'time' we harvest. In the meantime, let us persevere in doing good.

Outlook

Thus the sowing and reaping principle applies in three directions: God's word, sown in the hearts of the people (6:6); godliness, worked out in our own hearts (6:7–8); and in the community, by doing good to all (6:9–10). The outlook demanded by these verses is that of perseverance over the long haul. We have no promise of immediate harvest. This means we must walk by faith and not by sight (2 Cor. 5:7). The connection between action and consequence is often not apparent. The response of faith is keep on doing what is right and good despite appearances.

Here's how it sometimes works for me. You may have similar thoughts respecting your own situation. Sometimes ministers get discouraged. I've been at a place for ten years. What do I have to show for it? I might ask. Not as much as I had hoped in a number of areas. There have been big disappointments. There are times when I think it has all been for naught. I have been wasting my breath. But the basic commitment that I bring to a ministry is that which I think the Bible requires of us in all of the Christian life. That is, a commitment to the long haul. I think that we have to think in terms of decades, of generations, of not just our children, but our grandchildren. When I first came to Savannah Dr. J. I. Packer, my theology teacher, mentor, and hero, told me that I needed to stay at least ten years if I were to do any good. That way of thinking is foreign to the way that most people look at life today. Ours is a culture that encourages instant results and instant gratification. The menu at the typical fast-food store may be a symbol of that, as it offers to you exactly what you want to scratch whatever itch of our appetites that we may be feeling. The TV remote control may be another. With a satellite dish providing more than one hundred stations from which to choose, one need not go more than a moment without finding exactly what one wishes to be entertained by. It is all right there at one's fingertips. The Bible encourages us to look at life not in terms of the immediate, but in terms of generations. What impact will today's decisions have upon our children's children? Doesn't the Bible continually threaten us with what might be the impact upon our grandchildren? The covenant is made with Abraham and his descendants (Gen. 17:7). The Second Commandment threatens those who violate it with punishment to the 'third and fourth generation' (Exod. 20:5). The Psalms are full of promises and exhortations regarding our children and our children's children. Teach your children, so that they will teach their children to put their trust in God (Ps. 78:5–7). The blessing of God upon those who keep His covenant extends to their children's children (Ps. 103:17–18), and makes it possible for the faithful to see their children's children (Ps. 128:6; cf. 102:28; 112; 113; 127). God promises through Isaiah:

> 'And as for Me, this is My covenant with them,' says the Lord: 'My Spirit which is upon you, and My words which I have put in your mouth, shall not depart from your mouth, nor from the mouth of your offspring, nor from the mouth of your offspring's offspring,' says the Lord, 'from now and forever.' (Isa. 59:21)

The Bible encourages the long view. When it comes to the ministry of the church, think not of what will fill the church tomorrow or the day after. Instead, ask what kind of ministry will endure for two hundred years? Upon what foundation must the church rest if it is to endure for generation after generation? It may mean a different kind of ministry if it must do something more than stir up a lot of excitement at the present moment. This, by the way, is exactly why we focus on systematic expository preaching. It is not as popular as topical preaching, but it uncovers the 'whole counsel of God,' and it will endure. This is why we sing Psalms and great hymns. There is a good deal of fluffy stuff that is a lot more popular. But it lacks the biblical content that must be present if it is to build character. And it won't be around in fifty years. It will not endure, whereas the church will still be singing 'Holy, Holy, Holy' and Psalm 23 two-hundred years from today. This is why we teach our children substantial hymns and Psalms rather than kids stuff. This is why we teach them the Children's and Shorter Catechisms. This is why we emphasize Sabbath observance. This is why we practice spiritual, non-sensuous worship. This is why we practice church discipline. These are culture-shaping ordinances. These are the foundations upon which an enduring church will be built. Take any of these commitments away, and we are left with a weaker, softer church, a church less likely to survive the battle with secular paganism. The first question is not what will keep my kid coming to the junior high group. It is not what will appeal to my neighbor Joe Pagan. The first question is: What is the foundation upon which a church must be built if it is to serve the generations? We may not have had the impact on our city that we might have hoped for. But in due time we will reap! We are faithfully striving to be all that God wants His church to be. We will reap! Maybe not today, maybe not tomorrow, maybe not the next day. But we will reap.

Apply all this to personal holiness. You're getting no where, you say. The disciplines through which you are seeking Christ are not bearing fruit. What is the answer? All things being equal, press on. In due time you shall reap if we do not lose heart. The harvest has not yet come. But keep at it. Make sure to be in public worship every Sunday, morning and evening, without fail, under the ministry of the word, engaged in the ministry of prayer, receiving the sacraments, enjoying the fellowship of the saints. Keep at it. We will reap. Get up every morning without fail. Spend twenty minutes each day reading Scripture for half of the time, and spending the other half praising, thanking God, confessing your sins, searching your souls, and offering your petitions. Persevere! Conduct family worship every day even though it is difficult, even though it seems that everything gets in the way of it. Press on! We will reap! Take the long view. These disciplines, consisting of a few minutes each day and a few hours each week, will over the long haul, will over months and years and decades, make of you a pillar of spiritual strength. Don't lose heart! Believe the promises of God! Trust the divinely given means of grace. Harvest will come.

Apply this also to the service of others. Keep on helping. Keep on loving. Keep on caring. Persevere in doing good over the long haul. Change will come! We must not confuse this with sentimentalism. We must preserve room for 'tough love.' This, in fact, is just what we mean. Keep on working, trying, disciplining, praying! In due time we shall reap.

This is the way that we must look at all of life. Don't take short cuts. Do what you do well. Seek out quality and substance. Dig deep wells. Don't settle for the superficial. Ours is a junk culture which demands instant results. So we throw up junk buildings, write junk novels (and read them), compose junk music (and listen to it), enjoy junk entertainment, and eat junk food from the junk food store. Don't fall into this way of thinking. Remember the seed that was cast upon the rocky (i.e. shallow) soil. Its springs up immediately but cannot endure the scorching heat of persecution (Matt. 13:1–23). This may be a parable of our age. Modern, popular culture tempts us to compromise. It tries to persuade us to ignore truth and seek 'success.' But we must not lose heart as we seek to understand 'lag-time.' We must not faint, but press on, and in due time, we shall reap.

39

The Christian's Boast

Galatians 6:11–15

As we draw to the close of the Apostle Paul's letter to the Galatians, we can be thankful that he concludes with a review of the central themes with which he has been concerned. He has had much to say. Some of what he has said has been difficult to understand. Like good authors even today, he provides a summary at the end.

> See with what large letters I am writing to you with my own hand. (Gal. 6:11)

The Apostle probably at this point took pen in hand and began to write, having dictated the letter up to this point. 'I am writing,' he says, 'with my own hand.' This seems to have been his practice, and was a common practice in the ancient world (2 Thess. 3:17). This way an author confirmed the authenticity of a document as his own, even as our signature does today. The other possibility is that he wrote the whole letter in his own hand, but this seems less likely. The 'large letters' he used would have contrasted with the small characters of a professional scribe. He also may have been using large letters for the sake of emphasis, as we might use all caps or bold or italics. Some have suggested that he wrote with large letters because his eyesight was bad, but we have no way of knowing if that is the case or not. Rather, what he seems to be doing is emphasizing the main points of his letter *in his own handwriting*, giving emphasis and authenticity to what he has written through a scribe up to this point. Let us then look at his summary together.

The Errors of the False Teachers

By uncovering the true motives of the Judaizers in verses 12 and 13, the Apostle Paul distinguishes their externalizing of religion with the internal requirements of true Christianity.

> Those who desire to make a good showing in the flesh try to compel you to be circumcised, simply that they may not be persecuted for the cross of Christ. (Gal. 6:12)

First, Paul attacks their pride. The false teachers were more concerned with impressions than with souls. They wish to 'make a good showing in the flesh.' Boice suggests that the verb translated 'make a good showing' in the NASV and 'make a good impression' in the NIV (*euprosopesai*) 'carries overtones of insincerity.'[200] They want acceptance. They want praise. They want recognition within their circle of companions. The physical, fleshly act of circumcision corresponds to the fleshly motivations of the false teachers. 'Compel' means force, it means that to them 'it was necessary for true Christian initiation,' and not merely 'a helpful rite for people who chose to accept it,' says Morris.[201] In verse 13 he repeats the charge. They 'desire to have you circumcised,' he says, '*that they may not boast in your flesh.*' Why then do they insist upon it? They want converts. They want notches in their Bibles. They want to be able to impress other Judaizing brethren with how many Gentile Christians they have been able to persuade to adopt the ceremonial and cultural laws of Israel. They are obsessed with what Alan Cole called, 'ecclesiastical statistics,' as we might be with baptisms, and 'decisions.' Why? So that they might boast in them. They seek 'bragging rights.' They want to boast about how many converts that they have been able to talk into being circumcised. Obsession with numbers and appearances did not begin in the twenty-first century. It has always been with us. Some people come to church *just to be seen*. Some do volunteer work *just for the sake of acknowledgment*. Some evangelize and recruit *just so that they might boast*. We have to continually search our own motives. Why do we want the church to grow? So that our reputation will be enhanced? So that people might think that we're wonderful? or clever? Some churches are so concerned about nickels, noses, and noise that they'll compromise anything and everything to get them. Like the Judaizers, they'll water down the message. They'll compromise the cross. Or they'll corrupt the worship. Why? To be known and admired. Whole denominations have compromised the Bible's tougher doctrines, warming to other religions, for example, cooling the fires of hell, and relaxing Christian morals so that they might be more *socially acceptable*. How many formerly Christian colleges and seminaries have abandoned Christian commitments for the sake of *academic respectability*? The road to religious ruin is paved with concern for one's reputation. Until we are ready to accept rejection by the great ones of the earth, and say 'we are fools for Christ's sake,' we are vulnerable to this, the pressures to which the Judaizers succumbed (1 Cor. 4:10). Paul is dealing with a pride problem, even as we are today.

Second, he attacks their cowardice. Not only do they preach 'circumcision' for the sake of their own reputation, but so that they 'may not be persecuted for the cross of Christ' (v. 13). The 'persecution' that they could escape would be both Roman and Jewish. Identify with Judaism through circumcision, and Christianity would have official Roman sanction (as did Judaism), and avoid persecution at the hands of the Roman state. At the same time, adopting circumcision would remove the major obstacle to Jewish acceptance as well. So there was a great temptation to say what the world wanted to hear. And it wouldn't involve denying everything that the gospel taught. One could still preach Christ and the cross. It just meant adding works and the law to the gospel. Just do that, just do that little thing, and the persecution evaporates. One can still preach the fall, sin, the atonement, the resurrection, the ascension, and the return of Christ. All that! Just modify the doctrine of justification by faith. Just add works. Just say we are saved by Christ plus keeping the ceremonial law. Then everything will be all right.

What is this but cowardice? That's what it is, pure and simple. Look at it clearly. It is merely a tactic whereby one might escape persecution. The church has dealt with this in every age. The world will always be offended by the gospel. In any particular age there will be some particular manifestation of that offense. That is the point at which we are tempted to flinch. We are pressured to adapt the message. All the religions of the world do. They are all syncretistic to some degree or other. But Christianity is absolutistic. It claims to be the final truth. It cannot compromise, not without losing its message altogether. The world today says, 'It is okay for you to believe in Jesus, but just believe that other religions are valid as well.' 'Just don't say that you are right and everyone else is wrong.' Our absolutism is what the world cannot stand in our day. Consequently many have compromised the gospel. They are now saying that Jesus is one way, even the best way, but not the only way.

Luther said that if we believe the whole gospel except at that point at which the world is attacking, then we in fact are denying Christ. It may be that what we think we believe we only continue to affirm because we have not been challenged at that point. Why then do we compromise? To avoid rejection and ridicule. To avoid pain and suffering. To avoid the scorn and mockery of the world. To avoid persecution. We compromise because we are afraid. We compromise because of cowardice.

My Old Testament teacher in England, Rev. J. A. Motyer, used to warn us as we labored to do our Hebrew declensions, 'Don't lose your nerve.' That is a word for the church today. Don't lose your nerve! Conflict with the world is absolutely unavoidable. 'If they hated Me they'll hate you. If they persecuted Me they'll persecute you,' Jesus warned (John 15:18–21). 'All who desire to live godly in Christ Jesus will be persecuted (2 Tim. 3:12). It cannot be avoided if we are to be faithful. 'In the world you will have tribulation,' Jesus said (John 16:33). So don't lose your nerve!

Third, he attacks their hypocrisy. Paul points out the hypocrisy of requiring circumcision, which for Paul and the Judaizers functions as a symbol of the whole law.

> For those who are circumcised do not even keep the Law themselves, but they desire to have you circumcised, that they may boast in your flesh. (Gal. 6:13)

Those who were insisting that one be circumcised, or in other words, were insisting that one keep the whole ceremonial law in order to be saved, were 'not even able to keep the Law themselves.' Circumcision represents for Paul a legal approach to God. Yet those who were the legalists were not able to fulfill the legal requirements. This is the way it always is. The legalists cannot keep the law because no one is able to keep the law. Jesus said of the Pharisees that 'they say things, and do not do them.'

> And they tie up heavy loads, and lay them on men's shoulders; but they themselves are unwilling to move them with so much as a finger. (Matt. 23:4)

Paul likewise accused his countrymen of hypocrisy saying,

> you, therefore, who teach another, do you not teach yourself? You who preach that one should not steal, do you steal? You who say that one should not commit adultery, do you commit adultery? You who abhor idols, do you rob temples? You who boast in the Law, through your breaking the Law, do you dishonor God? (Rom. 2:21–3)

Even this is not different from what we have today. You who say that one has only to be sincere in order to go to heaven, are you sincere? You who say that one has only to be good in order to go to heaven, are you good? Are you able to fulfill even these minimum requirements? Of course not. No one is good, Jesus said, except God alone (Mark 10:18). There is none who does good, says Paul (Rom. 3:10).

The error that sums up these three errors is that of settling for an externalized religion. They were concerned with appearances, with ritual, with circumcision with ceremony. They failed to understand their deeper heart problems of self-righteousness, pride, cowardice, selfishness, and hypocrisy. They were settling for the superficial. This has always been a great problem of the people of God. The prophets were always warning of empty ritualism, of settling for correct form and ignoring the deeper heart issues. God warned through Isaiah,

> this people draw near with their words and honor Me with their lip service, but they remove their hearts far from Me, and their reverence for Me consists of tradition learned by rote. (Isa. 29:13)

Jesus repeated this warning to the Pharisees in Mark 7:6–7. The warning has needed repeating ever since. The Christian life requires various disciplines if it is to be successfully lived. But don't mistake the disciplines for personal trust in and love for Christ. Don't settle for just showing up in church each week, as though there were some virtue in placing your body in the pew. There is none, if your heart is far from God. The true Christian faith is a matter of the heart. It consists of looking to, relying upon, depending upon the cross of our Lord Jesus Christ. Let us not repeat the errors of the externalists. God wants our hearts. He wants humble, sincere faith.

How can we identify false versions of Christianity? There is a sense in which the true and false may both be identified by that in which they 'boast.' False teachers may be identified by their concern for reputation and appearances, by their flight from persecution, by their denial of the graciousness of the cross, and their hypocrisy. Their concerns are self-centered. In sum, they boast in *themselves*. This is what we saw in verses 12–13. Now we move on to examine true Christianity, as Paul continues his summary of his teaching on Galatians. In what does the real Christian boast? What is the true Christian outlook?

The True Christian Outlook

What then is the true Christian outlook?

First, it is to boast in the cross.

> But may it never be that I should boast, except in the cross of our Lord Jesus Christ, through which the world has been crucified to me, and I to the world. (Gal. 6:14)

Crosses, we may be reminded, were not shiny little jewel-studded medallions. Morris points out what a shock these words would have been in the first century. The cross was a brutal instrument of death. It was a symbol of shame. It represented the ultimate in public disgrace. The word 'cross' (*crux*) would not have been even mentioned 'in polite Roman society,' says Bruce.[202] Further, to pagan Greeks the cross of the Christian faith represented 'foolishness,' and to the Jews it was a 'stumbling block' (1 Cor. 1:18–23). But the Apostle Paul not only mentions it, he glories or 'boasts' in it. Thus the Apostle's outlook contrasts sharply with the pride of the Judaizers. They are concerned for reputation, for appearances, for image. They preached circumcision so that they might avoid persecution 'for the cross of Christ' (v. 12). Paul, almost defiantly, is concerned with that which was a symbol of shame. He glories in the cross. His whole life is the cross. Let's focus first on what he means by the 'cross,' and then on what it means to boast in it.

By the 'cross' the Apostle means the gospel of the cross, the gospel for sinners who need a Savior. The cross was not an unfortunate incident in the life of their leader. It was not an unpleasant setback for their burgeoning movement, concerning which the rank and file would rather not be reminded. It is for the Apostle Paul nothing less than the whole gospel. The cross, then, is a reminder that he is a sinner who is unacceptable to God, who could do nothing to save himself, who is utterly dependent upon the grace of God. It represents the kind provision of God for him, who so loved the world that He sent His only begotten to die and suffer. It represents blood atonement, apart from which there can be no forgiveness of sins. The cross is the opposite of salvation by works or ceremony or by religious ritual. The cross represents the doctrines of the free grace of God in Christ. These were the truths that led him to repent of his sins and devote himself entirely to Christ. These are the truths that delivered him from bondage to lust and covetousness and pride and selfishness and guilt, and brought him peace of mind and conscience, security, and assurance. The cross represents the peace that passes understanding, and that joy that is inexpressible before the throne of grace. It represents not shame, but his salvation. Consequently for him these are the most wonderful truths in all the world. He boasts in them. He revels in them. He glories in them. The cross is his pride.

This is baffling to the world. Most people boast in their accomplishments, especially as they relate to their wealth or athletic feats or intellectual prowess. Not Christ's Apostle. Because of the cross he understands the truth about himself. 'I am a nobody,' he will say (2 Cor. 12:11). 'Nothing good dwells in me' (Rom. 7:18). He tells the proud Corinthians, 'By His doing you are in Christ Jesus' (1 Cor. 1:30–1). You have absolutely nothing about which to boast. Are you wise? Christ is our wisdom. Are you righteous? Christ is our righteousness. Are you sanctified? Christ is our sanctification. Are you redeemed? Christ is our redemption. Paul's conclusion: 'Let him who boasts, boast in the Lord' (1 Cor. 1:31). We can claim nothing for ourselves. Apart from him we can do nothing (John 15:5). All that we have and all that we are we owe to Him. 'By the grace of God I am what I am,' the Apostle Paul says, and we all say with him (1 Cor. 15:10). What do you have that you didn't receive? Don't limit the consideration to 'religious' things. Do you boast in your family? Who gave you that family? Do you boast in your intelligence? Who gave you that intelligence? Do you boast in your wealth? Who gave you that wealth? Do you boast in your athletic ability? Who gave you that athletic ability? Let the Apostle ask us again,

> For who regards you as superior? And what do you have that you did not receive? But if you did receive it, why do you boast as if you had not received it? (1 Cor. 4:7)

We have absolutely nothing, no, let me say it stronger—we have *absolutely*, absolutely nothing about which to boast in ourselves. Our only boast is 'in the Lord.' Our boast is in the cross of Jesus Christ. Jeremiah put it this way:

> Thus says the Lord, 'Let not a wise man boast of his wisdom, and let not the mighty man boast of his

> might, let not a rich man boast of his riches; but let him who boasts boast of this, that he understands and knows Me, that I am the Lord who exercises lovingkindness, justice, and righteousness on earth; for I delight in these things,' declares the Lord. (Jer. 9:23–4)

Second, it is to die to the world. The consequence of Paul's embracing of the cross was that the 'world' was now dead to the Apostle Paul. 'The world has been crucified to me,' he says. Dead things, of course, have no appeal to us. He doesn't care about the world. It is dead. It is road-kill. It can offer him nothing. This is what he understands now. The world offers only death. All that it promises is doomed to vanish with the passing of time. It will succumb to rust and corrosion. The moth will consume it. It will all deteriorate and vanish. Our lovely new clothes and shoes—what will they look like in ten years? That beautiful shiny new car—how will it perform in fifteen years? What will become of that gorgeous home in 100 years? What becomes of our vacation once it's over? The food once it's eaten? This is why Jesus said,

> Do not lay up for yourselves treasures upon earth, where moth and rust destroy, and where thieves break in and steal. But lay up for yourselves treasures in heaven, where neither moth nor rust destroys, and where thieves do not break in or steal; for where your treasure is, there will your heart be also. (Matt. 6:19–21)

The world is dying. It cannot endure. Nothing lasts. Look at the ruins of the ancient civilizations—the pyramids of the Egyptians, the temples of the Greeks, the arenas of the Romans. Everywhere one sees death. This is why John writes,

> Do not love the world, nor the things in the world. If anyone loves the world, the love of the Father is not in him. For all that is in the world, the lust of the flesh and the lust of the eyes and the boastful pride of life, is not from the Father, but is from the world. And the world is passing away, and also its lusts; but the one who does the will of God abides forever. (1 John 2:15–17)

The world has been crucified. It is dead. It is 'passing away.' It has no appeal any longer.

Not only is the world dead to the Apostle Paul, but also 'I to the world,' he says. The world could evoke no reaction from him. As the world parades its wares past him, it is as though it were dealing with a corpse. It does not tempt him. It does not provoke him. It does not seduce. He is dead to the world. Unlike the false prophets, he is not concerned with his reputation with the world. He doesn't care about appearances. He is not trying to impress them. Similarly he is not concerned with the world's threats of persecution. Nor is he concerned with the opposite, the world's promises of peace and prosperity if one will conform, if one will 'play the game.' No, he is dead to the world. So he lives a life of blissful detachment from the things about which most people are concerned. I remember a few years ago hearing about the person who lied about the cemetery in which a loved one was being buried. Does concern for the world get any more silly than that? Is it not obvious that once we die we are past concern for burial in a prestigious plot? May we all with the Apostle gracefully die to the world and its concerns.

Third, it is to look to the supernatural.

> For neither is circumcision anything, nor uncircumcision, but a new creation. (Gal. 6:15)

Neither the observance nor the non-observance of this rite has anything to do with salvation. He will not hypocritically insist upon it because it isn't 'anything.' There were circumstances when Paul was willing to see it practiced, for cultural reasons (Acts 16:3). But never where it was being claimed it was necessary for salvation. In itself, circumcision neither contributes nor detracts from salvation. What matters is being 'a new creation.' This then is the basic point Paul is making regarding the true Christian outlook. Is the Christian religion a human or divine work? Is Christian discipleship a supernatural work wrought by the Holy Spirit, or a natural work wrought by us? Is the Christian faith one inaugurated by circumcision and maintained by the works of the law? Or is it an internal, supernatural work of the Spirit, who causes us to be born again, who further enables us walk in a manner that is pleasing to God?

This is what the false teachers then and now failed to realize. To be a Christian one must be born again. It is not a matter of us gritting our teeth and doing our best. No, we must be regenerated by the Holy Spirit of God. A Christian is a new creation. Paul writes,

> For the flesh sets its desire against the Spirit, and the Spirit against the flesh; for these are in opposition to one another, so that you may not do the things that you please. (2 Cor. 5:17)

We become Christians when we are transformed by the Spirit of Christ. He changes our hearts. He causes the 'old things,' the old lusts, the old desires, the old priorities, the old perspectives on life all to 'pass away.' In Christ, 'new things have come.' This is the wonder of the gospel and the heart of the gospel. Everywhere the religions of the world say we must try harder. Do good, more good, more and more good, and we might be saved. Christianity says, we must be born again by a sovereign work of God. We won't be saved by our works. Neither will we become better by our works. He makes us new people in Christ. He cleans out all the old filth and scrubs us fresh and clean. The old way of religion says, get circumcised, keep the law, do good, be religious, and maybe we'll be acceptable. The new way of the gospel says, forget it, we can't be good enough. But God will save us in Christ, and He will transform and change us. We don't have to be what we were. We don't have to wallow in the gutter. We don't have to be slaves of our lusts, or tongues, or tempers. We can be changed. We can be born again. We can, and we will, be made new in Christ Jesus.

This is the true Christian outlook and the Christian's boast: we boast not in ourselves but in Christ. We are concerned not about ourselves but about His cross. Our confidence is not in ourselves, but in His grace alone. May it never be, he says, that we should boast, except in the cross of our Lord Jesus Christ.

40

Mercy, Peace and Grace

Galatians 6:16–18

We come now to the end of our study of the Apostle Paul's Epistle to the Galatians. Galatia, we may remember, is the southern region of present day Asia Minor, or Turkey, and the location of the churches which the Apostle had founded in Pisidian Antioch, Lystra, Derbe, and Iconium, the record of which is found in Acts 13; 14. He has been battling the 'Judaizing' party, those who taught that Gentile believers must become practicing Jews as well as Christians if they were to enjoy full membership in the community of God's people. Jewish traditions and customs, such as dietary and cleansing ordinances (Gal. 2:11–14), religious holidays (4:10), and, supremely, circumcision were being made obligatory. Luke reports that some were teaching that, 'Unless you are circumcised according to the custom of Moses, you cannot be saved' (Acts 15:1). The Apostle Paul has been defending himself and his gospel from one end of this epistle to the other from the attacks of those who sought to undermine its graciousness. Now he defends the doctrines of grace one last time, exhorts them one last time, and blesses them as he brings his letter to a close.

The Christian's rule

> And those who will walk by this rule, peace and mercy be upon them, and upon the Israel of God. (Gal. 6:16)

'Walk' is a typical New Testament way of speaking of one's manner of living. Those who will 'walk' according to 'this rule,' that is, this standard, this gospel, will be blessed with peace and mercy. 'Mercy' and 'grace' are nearly synonymous, the difference being 'mercy' is grace considered from the perspective of the recipient, whereas 'grace' is more particularly the disposition of favor in God that results in His showing mercy. 'Peace' is the state of being that flows from God's grace—peace with God, and peace in the heart, and peace in relationships.

Given his criticism of the false prophets and their rules, his description of the Christian way as a 'rule' (*kanon*) is interesting. It is a word used of a measuring rule or rod used by a carpenter or surveyor. Which 'rule' or 'way' are we to follow if we should receive the mercy and peace of God? The rule he has just described in verses 14–15, the way of the cross, of boasting only in the cross, of crucifying the flesh and its passions, and of life as a 'new creation' (Gal. 5:24; 6:14–15). The church's rule or 'canon' is the gospel. It is a 'rule' which eschews justification by works and works-righteousness, and protects the graciousness of the gospel. To all who believe and practice such comes the 'mercy' of God, and through it, 'peace.' The blessing is promised for all who will 'take this principle for their guide' (NIV).

The concluding phrase, 'the Israel of God,' is an unusual one, found only here in the New Testament. The 'and' (*kai*) should be translated 'even' (NIV), or omitted altogether (as in the RSV), notes Stott. In other words, those who walk by the 'rule,' and those who make up the 'Israel of God,' are one and the same. Does he call the church 'Israel'? The alternative, to imagine that the Apostle Paul now divides the people of God into two groups, Jews and Gentile, when he has labored for six chapters to prove the opposite, that we are 'all one in Christ Jesus,' seems an impossible argument to make, or at least highly unlikely, and contrary to all expectation. Similarly, elsewhere Christian believers are called 'The true circumcision,' and 'Abraham's offspring' (Gal. 3:29; Phil. 3:3). Likewise Peter applies a number of Israel's Old Testament titles to the church, calling it 'a chosen race, a royal priesthood, a holy nation, a people for God's own possession' (1 Pet. 2:9). This is the apostolic practice. By the phrase 'the Israel of God,' Paul is designating the whole people of God , the true Israel, the spiritual Israel, as contrasted with the false Israel to whom a false peace is offered by the false Judaizing prophets. Mercy and peace come to 'the Israel of God,' the Christian church, through the 'rule' of grace and faith in Christ. This expression, says Lightfoot, 'stands here not for the faithful converts from the circumcision alone, but for the spiritual Israel generally, the whole body of believers whether Jew or Gentile.'[203] A number of mistakes have been made by those who confuse the present day secular state in Palestine with the 'Israel of God,' not the least of which has been at times a blanket endorsement of everything done by that state. The church is Israel. We are the heirs of the promises of God made to His people.

The Blessing of God

That 'peace and mercy' are to be found by walking according to the gospel 'rule' has important implications for us. Boice comments, 'It is sometimes said that those who are concerned with the essence of the gospel and with true doctrine are the disrupters of the church, but Paul says the opposite. The truth is that the gospel is the real promoter of peace and is the channel of God's mercy.'[204] In every era of the church there are those who wish to compromise the integrity of the gospel for one reason or another. The Judaizers had their reasons. Others since them have had their reasons. When faced with such, the church is tempted to respond to their demands with compromise, all in the name of 'peace.' A faction grows up in the church that is offended with some element in the gospel message. Typically in the last one hundred years or so it has had to do with either the exclusive claims of Christ, the moral demands of the gospel, or the 'negative' side of the gospel having to do with sin, judgment, and the cross. Notice, all three areas have to do with how one is perceived in a pluralistic society. Whether we are at the country club or the stock car race, we don't want to be put in the position of having to say that Jesus is the only way to heaven, or that some of our neighbor's lifestyle choices are immoral, or for our neighbor to think that our religion is gloomy. So the church is pressured to water-down these distinctives of the gospel. For the sake of peace, many churches do. In fact, when the gospel is watered down, a semblance of peace is restored. The faction is placated. But what the Apostle Paul is saying is that real peace and mercy are only possible when we walk by the canon or rule of the gospel. One can artificially create a superficial peace. The church can reach an equilibrium of sorts, where each of the factions tolerate each other. But the price is the silencing of the real gospel. Compromise gospel standards, and you destroy the graciousness of the gospel, lose the gospel, and lose peace as well. Real peace, peace with God, peace in our hearts, and peace in our relationships is the fruit of an uncompromised gospel, the full gospel, with all its offensiveness. Do not lose it for the sake of expediency.

The real troublemakers in the church are those who seek compromise. It often doesn't seem this way because compromisers are by definition moderate. They are merely trying not to offend. They are trying to respond to the feelings of others who are not at one with the church's historic convictions. They cloak themselves in the garb of sensitivity and reasonableness. But the truth is that departures from the 'rule' undermine the peace of the church because they undermine the gospel upon which it stands.

All of this is to say that there is a connection between doctrine and experience that is not always obvious. The Christian faith can be described as a 'rule.' It is a given body of doctrine and practices. Yet it is a 'relationship with Christ.' It is also a 'form of teaching' to which we commit ourselves (Rom. 6:17). The mercy of God is to be found in believing and practicing all that the gospel teaches us and requires of us. The peace of God likewise results when we are faithful to the gospel walk and 'rule.' Neither the mercy of God nor the peace of God drop on us out of heaven. Only those who 'walk by this rule' receive the blessings of peace and mercy.

The Church's Responsibility

> From now on let no one cause trouble for me, for I bear on my body the brand-marks of Jesus. (Gal. 6:17)

'Now that I've set the record straight,' the Apostle Paul is saying, 'let me hear of these false teachings no more.' Why? 'For,' he goes on, 'I bear on my body the brand-marks (*stigmata*) of Jesus.' In other words, he has suffered enough. Some of the details of the Apostle's suffering may be found in 2 Corinthians 11:23–5. Five times he had received thirty-nine lashes, three times beaten with rods, and once stoned. The stoning took place in Lystra, one of the Galatians cities (Acts 14:19). They would have known of it. This is a plea for the churches to handle these problems themselves, and endure whatever persecution might arise as a result. He is not appealing to the Judaizers not to trouble him. That would be futile. He is not telling the church not to let him know if there is trouble, as though he would want to be left in the dark. Rather, he is exhorting the church to resist the false teachers, correct them, and if need be, silence them. 'It would be far better if the churches he founded at such cost would assume their own share of suffering,' says Boice, 'above all by resisting the kind of teaching that the legalizers upheld and therefore, if necessary, by enduring whatever persecution might follow.'[205] The church has a responsibility to maintain purity of doctrine and practice, and to purge the church of whatever corruptions might seep in.

There are several New Testament examples of this being urged upon the church. The Apostle Paul warns Titus of 'rebellious men, empty talkers and deceivers, especially those of the circumcision, *who must be silenced* because they are upsetting whole families, teaching things they should not teach, for the sake of sordid gain' (Titus 1:10-11). Similarly the Apostle John warns of one who denies fundamental doctrines of Christ. He says,

> If anyone comes to you and does not bring this teaching, do not receive him into your house,

> and do not give him a greeting; for the one who gives him a greeting participates in his evil deeds. (2 John 10–11)

Will separation from error mean trouble for the church? Will it result in at least some measure of persecution? Of course it will. Imagine for a moment what would happen if we removed a Sunday School class teacher from his class for teaching false doctrine. All hell, one might say, would break loose. His family, friends, maybe even his class, would be banging on our doors and ringing the elder's phones off the hook. Does that mean that we can shirk the responsibility to do so? No, of course not. Why not? Because the gospel is at stake. We cannot allow a little thing like personal feelings to get in the way of preserving the gospel. Why do you think that the Apostle Paul has to repeat over and over to Timothy, saying the same thing in a variety of ways, guard the gospel? (1 Tim. 6:20; 2 Tim. 1:13–14). He does so because our tendency is to wink at doctrinal error, to let it pass, to shrug our shoulders.

Let me suggest another scenario. What if your senior minister began to get a little off track, and after a while a little more, and then a little more? What if while this was happening the church continued to grow and maintained the appearance of health? What if he were confronted by the Session and he absolutely resisted any correction from them? Imagine what would happen if they tried to remove him, and he was unwilling to go. Imagine what would happen if they called for a congregational meeting for the purpose of dissolving the pastoral relationship with him, and he was intent on fighting to preserve his position. The fight, the carnage, would be dreadful. The sad thing is that he would have his defenders. Some would defend him by attacking the church for being judgmental. Others would seek a 'do nothing' policy, and would protest the failure to 'let sleeping dogs lie.' Does that absolve the church of the responsibility of making the tough call, of making the difficult decision? Whatever the cost it must be done. Why? Because the gospel is more important than our desire for peace and quiet. These difficult decisions must be made. That is essentially what the Apostle is saying to the Galatian churches. Don't 'trouble' me with this any longer. Handle it. Do the right thing. Confront and remove heresy. Guard the gospel from error. Endure the 'trouble.' But people might think that we are harsh. They'll think that we are unloving. They'll think that we are extremists! Radicals! Yes, they will. But if we are to be faithful we still must do it.

> The grace of our Lord Jesus Christ be with your spirit, brethren. Amen. (Gal. 6:18)

The Apostle Paul always concludes his letters with a prayer for grace for his readers. Often the greeting will invoke the three persons of the Trinity. But here he concentrates on the Savior. 'Spirit' emphasizes the spiritual nature of the blessing being invoked. 'Brethren' shows that for all their conflict, Paul still regards them as members of the family of God. 'Amen' gives to the letter 'a devotional tone,' says Morris.[206] This closing punches home the theme of the whole letter—grace. How are we saved? Not by faith in Christ plus certain moral and religious works. Not by keeping the Ten Commandments, observing religious holidays, and doing enough good things. We are saved by faith in Christ plus nothing. We are saved, says the epistle of the Galatians and the whole Bible, only by the grace of God in Christ.

Endnotes

1 J. M. Boice, 'Galatians,' in *The Expositor's Bible Commentary* (Vol. 10, ed. F. E. Gaebelein. Grand Rapids: Zondervan, 1976), 409.
2 J.B. Lightfoot, *Saint Paul's Epistle to the Galatians* (1890, London: Macmillan, 1986), 27.
3 J. G. Machen, *Machen's Notes on Galatians*, ed. J. H. Skilton (Nutley, NJ: Presbyterian & Reformed, 1977), 15.
4 F. F. Bruce, *The Epistle to the Galatians* (Grand Rapids: Eerdmans, 1982), 19.
5 Boice, 'Galatians,' in *The Expositor's Bible Commentary*, 425.
6 Ibid.
7 Ibid.
8 R. Y. K. Fung, *The Epistle to the Galatians* (Grand Rapids: Eerdmans, 1988), 38.
9 J. R. W. Stott, *The Message of Galatians* (Downers Grove, IL: Inter-Varsity, 1968), 12.
10 Boice, 426.
11 E. deW. Burton, *A Critical and Exegetical Commentary on the Epistle to the Galatians* (ICC. Edinburgh: T&T Clark, 1921), 18–19.
12 Richard N. Longenecker, 'Galatians,' *Word Biblical Commentary*, Vol. 41 (Dallas: Word Books, 1990), 16.
13 Stott, 23.
14 Longenecker, 16.
15 Stott, 25.
16 Max Zerwick and Mary Grosvenor, *A Grammatical Analysis of the Greek New Testament, Vol. II* (Rome: Biblical Institute Press, 1974), 565.
17 Longenecker, 23.
18 Stott, 31.
19 Longenecker, 30.
20 Longenecker, 32.
21 Ibid., 33.
22 See Stott, 34.
23 Ibid., 40.
24 Ibid., 42.
25 Fung, 86.
26 Stott, 41.
27 Fung, 94.
28 Ibid., 95.
29 Stott, 45.
30 Ibid., 47.
31 Ibid., 50.
32 Bruce, 131.
33 Stott, 52.
34 Ibid., 51.
35 Bruce, 133.
36 Stott, 54.
37 John Calvin, *Institutes of the Christian Religion*, Vol. 1 & 2, The Library of Christian Classics, Vols. XX & XXI (Philadelphia: The Westminster Press, 1960), III, 9.1.
38 From Luther's commentary on Galatians, 101, as quoted in Stott, 59–60.
39 Quoted in Stott, 60.
40 Ibid.
41 Boice, 448,4 49.
42 Fung, 113.
43 Boice, 448.
44 Boice, 449.
45 Boice, 449.
46 See Fung, 122.
47 Stott, 65.
48 Boice, 449.
49 Stott, 65.
50 Ibid.
51 Fung, 124.
52 Leon Morris, *Galatians: Paul's Charter of Christian Freedom* (Downers Grove, Illinois: IVP, 1996), 92.

53 Ibid.
54 Ibid., 93, n3.
55 Boice, 435.
56 Bruce, 148.
57 Morris, 93.
58 Ibid.
59 Machen, 165.
60 Stott, 70.
61 Bruce, 149.
62 Ibid.
63 Morris, 96.
64 Morris, 99.
65 Ibid., 100.
66 Morris, 101.
67 Ibid., 103.
68 Boice, 459.
69 Morris, 104.
70 Ibid., 105.
71 Ibid.
72 Stott, 83.
73 The LXX (70) is the Septuagint, the Greek version of the Hebrew Bible, named for the 70 scholars who are alleged to have translated it.
74 Morris, 112.
75 Stott, 88.
76 Ibid.
77 Morris, 113.
78 Fung, 159.
79 Boice, 465.
80 Morris, 113.
81 Ibid.
82 Stott, 89.
83 Morris, 115.
84 Ibid., 117.
85 Boice, 467.
86 John Calvin, *The Epistles of Paul the Apostle to the Galatians, Ephesians, Philippians, and Colossians*. Tr. T. H. L. Parker in *Calvin's New Testament Commentaries*, ed. D. W. Torrance and T. F. Torrance, Vol. 11 (Grand Rapids: Eerdmans, 1965), 66,67.
87 Morris, 121.
88 Boice, 468.
89 Stott, 100.
90 Ibid.
91 Stott, 102.
92 Stott, 103.
93 Stott, 106.
94 Morris, 129, n9.
95 Boice, 472.
96 James Stewart, *The Life and Teaching of Jesus Christ* (Nashville: Abingdon Press, n.d.), 17.
97 Boice, 472.
98 Stewart, 15,16.
99 Ibid., 15.
100 Morris, 128.
101 Ibid., 129.
102 Ibid., 130.
103 Ibid., 131.
104 Stott, 107.
105 Boice, 476.
106 Quoted in Morris, 134, n. 26.
107 Morris, 135.
108 Fung, 193.
109 Stott, 108.
110 Stott, 111.
111 Morris, 137.
112 Stott, 112.
113 Morris, 140.
114 Morris, 140.
115 Ibid., 142.
116 Morris, 145.
117 Ibid., 146.
118 Ibid., 148.
119 Boice, 484.
120 Stott, 127.
121 Morris, 153.
122 Stott, 132.
123 Stott, 133.
124 Ibid.
125 Morris, 157.
126 Morris, 157.
127 Ibid.
128 Fung, 228.
129 Morris, 158.
130 Morris, 159.
131 Morris, 160.
132 Morris, 162.
133 Stott, 140.
134 Lightfoot, 208.
135 Ibid., 209.
136 Burton, 297.
137 Lightfoot, 209.
138 Burton, 303.
139 Burton, 303.

140 Lightfoot, 210.
141 William Hendrikson, *Galatians and Ephesians*, New Testament Commentary (Grand Rapids, Michigan: Baker Book House, 1979) 219.
142 Morris, 170.
143 Lightfoot, 210.
144 Ibid.
145 Bruce, 247.
146 Fung, 256.
147 Burton, 307.
148 Fung, 258.
149 Burton, 309.
150 Boice, 496.
151 Lightfoot, 211.
152 Boice, 497.
153 Hendrikson, 223.
154 Burton, 313.
155 Fung, 262.
156 Morris, 173.
157 Ibid.
158 Burton, 313.
159 Burton, 314.
160 R.C.H. Lenski, *The Interpretation of St. Paul's Epistles to the Galatians, to the Ephesians, and to the Philippians* (1961, Minneapolis, Minnesota: Augsburg Publishing House, 1962), 290.
161 Though this is not its exclusive use. *Agapaō* is used in 2 Timothy 4:10 of love of the world. In 2 Samuel 13 (LXX) both the verb *agapao* and the noun *agape* are used of Amnon's incestuous rape of his half-sister Tamar (2 Sam. 13:15, LXX) (see D. A. Carson, *Exegetical Fallacies* [Grand Rapids: Baker Book Company, 1984)] 30, 51–4).
162 Alexander I. Solzhenitsyn, *A World Split Apart: Commencement Address Delivered at Harvard University, June 8, 1978* (New York: Harper & Row), 29.
163 Lightfoot, 213.
164 Hendriksen, 224.
165 Cited in Ian Barclay, *Living and Enjoying the Fruit of the Spirit* (Chicago, Moody Press, 1975), 54.
166 Quoted in Geoffrey B. Wilson, *Galatians: A Digest of Reformed Comment* (Carlisle, PA: The Banner of Truth Trust, 1973), 110.
167 Richard C. Trench, *Trench's Synonyms of the New Testament* (Peabody, Mass.: Hendrickson Publsihers, 2000), 235.
168 Armand Nicholi, II, 'The Fractured Family: Following It Into the Future,' *Christianity Today*, May 1979.
169 David F. Wells, *Losing Our Virtue: Why the Church Must Recover Its Moral Vision* (Grand Rapids, Michigan: Wm. B. Eerdmans Publishing Co., 1998)
170 See Fung, 269.
171 Ibid., 270.
172 P.E. Hughes, *A Commentary on the Epistle to the Hebrews* (Grand Rapids, Michigan: Wm. B. Eerdmans Publishing Co., 1977), 495.
173 Martyn Lloyd-Jones, *Studies in the Sermon on the Mount, Vol. 1* (1959, London: Inter-Varsity Fellowship, 1962), 70.
174 Ibid., 69.
175 Nicholi, 'The Fractured Family,' *Christianity Today*, 25 May 1979.
176 Morris, 175.
177 Burton, 318.
178 Burton, 319.
179 Morris, 176, n. 58.
180 Burton, 324.
181 Bruce, 257; cf. Phil. 2:3
182 Morris, 177.
183 H. N. Ridderbos, *The Epistle of Paul to the Churches of Galatia.*Tr. H. Zylstra, NICNT (Grand Rapids: Eerdmans, 1953), 212n2.
184 Bruce, 260.
185 Cited in Morris, 178, n5.
186 Stott, 159.
187 Morris, 180.
188 In Stott, 168.
189 Boice, 504.
190 Boice, 504.
191 Morris, 182.
192 Stott, 170.
193 Ibid.
194 Morris, 183.
195 Stott, 171.
196 Morris, 183.
197 Fung, 297.
198 Stott, 171.
199 In Stott, 172.
200 Boice, 506.
201 Morris, 187.
202 Bruce, 271.
203 In Morris, 190.
204 Boice, 507.
205 Boice, 508.
206 Morris, 191.

Bibliography

Barclay, Ian. *Living and Enjoying the Fruit of the Spirit*. Chicago: Moody Press, 1975.

Barclay, W. *The Letters to the Galatians and Ephesians*. Daily Study Bible. Rev. ed. Edinburgh: St. Andrew Press, 1976.

Boice, J. M. 'Galatians.' In *The Expositor's Bible Commentary*, Vol. 10, ed. F. E. Gaebelein. Grand Rapids: Zondervan, 1976.

Bruce, F. F. *The Epistle to the Galatians*. NIGNTC. Grand Rapids: Eerdmans, 1982.

Burton, E. deW. *A Critical and Exegetical Commentary on the Epistle to the Galatians*. ICC. Edinburgh: T. & T. Clark, 1921.

Calvin, J. *The Epistles of Paul the Apostle to the Galatians, Ephesians, Philippians, and Colossians*. Tr. T. H. L. Parker in *Calvin's New Testament Commentaries*, ed. D. W. Torrance and T. F. Torrance, Vol. 11. Grand Rapids: Eerdmans, 1965.

________. *Institutes of the Christian Religion—Vol. 1 & 2*, in John T. McNeill (ed.) The Library of Christian Classics, Volume XXI (Philadelphia: The Westminster Press, 1960).

Cole, R. A. *The Episle of Paul to the Galatians*. TNTC. Grand Rapids, Eerdmans, 1965.

Fung, R. Y. K. *The Epistle to the Galatians*. NICNT. Grand Rapids: Eerdmans, 1988.

Guthrie, D. *Galatians*. NCB. London: Marshall, Morgan & Scott, 1973.

Hendriksen, William. *Galatians and Ephesians*, New Testament Commentary. Grand Rapids, Michigan: Baker Book House, 1979.

Hughes, P. E. *A Commentary on the Epistle to the Hebrews*. Grand Rapids, Michigan: Wm. B. Eerdmans Publishing Co., 1977.

Lenski, R.C.H. *The Interpretation of St. Paul's Epistles to the Galatians, to the Ephesians, and to the Philippians*. 1961, Minneapolis, Minnesota: Augsburg Publishing House, 1962.

Lightfoot, J. B. *Saint Paul's Epistle to the*

Galatians. 10th ed. 1890; repr; London: Macmillan, 1986.

Longenecker, Richard N. 'Galatians.' *Word Biblical Commentary*, Vol. 41. Dallas: Word Books, 1990.

Lloyd-Jones, Martyn. *Studies in the Sermon on the Mount, Vol. 1.* 1959, London: Inter-Varsity Fellowship, 1962.

Luther, Martin. *A Commentary on St. Pauls' Epistle to the Galatians.* Tr. P. S. Watson, based on the Middleton edition of the English version of 1575. London: James Clark, 1953.

Machen, J. G. *Machen's Notes on Galatians*, ed. J. H. Skilton. Nutley, NJ: Presbyterian & Reformed, 1977.

Morris, Leon. *Galatians: Paul's Charter of Christian Freedom*, Downers Grove, Illinois: Inter-Varsity Press, 1996.

Nicholi, Armand, II. 'The Fractured Family: Following It into the Future,' *Christianity Today*. 25 May 1979.

Ridderbos, H. N. *The Epistle of Paul to the Churches of Galatia.* Tr. H. Zylstra. NICNT. Grand Rapids: Eerdmans, 1953.

Sanderson, John S. *The Fruit of the Spirit*. 1972, Grand Rapids, Michigan: Zondervan Publishing House, 1976.

Solzhenitsyn, Alexander I. *A World Split Apart: Commencement Address Delivered at Harvard University, June 8, 1978*. New York: Harper & Row.

Stewart, James. *The Life & Teaching of Jesus Christ*. Nashville: Abingdon Press, n.d.

Stott, J. R. W. *The Message of Galatians*. Downers Grove, IL: Inter-Varsity, 1968.

Trench, Richard C. *Trench's Synonyms of the New Testament*. Peabody, Mass.: Hendrickson Publsihers, 2000.

Zerwick, Max and Mary Grosvenor. *A Grammatical Analysis of the Greek New Testament*, Vol. II, Rome: Biblical Institute Press, 1974.

Wells, David F. *Losing Our Virtue*. Grand Rapids: Eerdmans, 1998.

Wilson, Geoffrey B. *Galatians: A Digest of Reformed Comment*. Carlisle, PA: The Banner of Truth Trust, 1973.

Westminster Confession of Faith.

Subject Index

Scripture Index

Galatians

God's Proclamation of Liberty

Joseph A. Pipa, Jr

ISBN 978-1-84550-558-5

Joseph A. Pipa, Jr. has been both a church pastor and theological professor. He is President and Professor of Historical and Systematic Theology at Greenville Presbyterian Theological Seminary in South Carolina and exercises a worldwide expositional ministry.

The glorious doctrine of justification by faith far exceeds even the great charters of freedom and liberty which we have seen throughout history. This doctrine is expounded by the apostle Paul whose letter this is and in it we see the key themes of his theology expounded. Joseph Pipa, an able Biblical expositor committed to the inerrancy of Scripture, brings this important letter with practical lessons for the church of every age alive for us.

> Here is a clear, succinct, and powerful exposition of a key Pauline letter. Pipa writes pastorally, an apt reflection of Paul's own desire to inform and edify. He writes learnedly, aware of challenges to Paul's gospel from Federal Vision and New Perspective quarters.
>
> Robert W. Yarbrough,
> Professor of New Testament,
> Covenant Theological Seminary, St Louis, Missouri

> Martin Luther once called the Epistle to the Galatians "my Katie von Bora" – this letter was as dear to the Reformer as his own wife. In Galatians, Joseph Pipa has given the church a clear, stirring, and accessible exposition of this beloved letter.
>
> Guy Waters,
> Associate Professor of New Testament,
> Reformed Theological Seminary, Jackson, Mississippi

Galatians

A Mentor Commentary

David McWilliams

ISBN 978-1-84550-452-6

David McWilliams has been the senior pastor at Covenant Presbyterian Church, Lakeland, Florida for 20 years.

While Dr. McWilliams' exposition of Galatians keeps in mind the various mischaracterizations of Paul's epistle that have become dominant, his purpose is not primarily polemical. The author sees Paul's paramount concern to be acceptance with God through the work of Christ. McWilliams affirms: 'everywhere in every way Paul's concern is with the gospel; he is concerned with the personal salvation of sinners.' Written principally, though not exclusively as an aid to preachers, Galatians is an exposition that is scholarly yet readable, combining the rare qualities of depth and brevity.

Written against the background and reflecting a knowledgeable grasp of the scholarly debates, past and present, the author largely steers clear of those debates and remains focused throughout on tracing and expounding the apostle's argument for its own sake and with an eye to preaching. Having had the opportunity of reading this clear and gracefully written book during its production, I commend it most highly.

Richard Gaffin,
Professor of Biblical and Systematic Theology, Emeritus,
Westminster Theological Seminary, Philadelphia

Timely, lucid, and reliable, this is an excellent commentary for preachers, Bible study leaders and others. McWilliams admirably succeeds in his aim for brevitas and claritas, the two qualities in commentators that Calvin most commended. He distils a great deal of scholarship into uncluttered and readable prose.

Robert Letham,
Senior Tutor, Systematic & Historicial Theology,
Wales Evangelical School of Theology, Bridgend, Wales

The Parables of Jesus

Entering, Growing, Living and Finishing in God's Kingdom

TERRY JOHNSON

ISBN 978-1-84550-292-8

Jesus spoke to the people in parables – not only that, he seemed to think in parables, acted out parables – he was a walking parable. Parables are almost unknown elsewhere in Scripture, yet they comprise a huge proportion of Jesus' teaching to those around him, and through them, to us. He always intended his parables to have life-changing implications: in fact he defined them as being what determined those who were alive to his message, and those who were not. So, what impact have Jesus' parables had on your life. Have they changed yet? Terry Johnston will help you make sure that is so.

> ...the expositor we have all been waiting for... a statement of Christian ethics as profound as it is readable. He is as faithful in bruising as in uplifting, but, being a true pastor, even his bruises have a velvet and healing touch.

ALEC MOTYER,
Well known Bible expositor and commentary writer

> The work of Terry Johnson is to be commended because it comes from one of the leading young pastors of America. What is refreshing is that the ministry of Terry Johnson has not only historical integrity but it has a very definite appeal to young people, proving once again that the genuinely classic is of interest to all, both the old and the young

HUGHES OLIPHANT OLD,
John H. Leith Professor of Reformed Theology and Worship,
Erskine Theological Seminary, Due West, South Carolina

The Family Worship Book
A Resource Book for Family Devotions
Terry Johnson

ISBN 978-1-85792-401-5

Do you struggle to provide enjoyable, meaningful and spiritual times of family devotions? Do you avoid the whole subject but have the nagging thought that you should be doing something?

Let Terry and Family Worship equip you for leading your family in worship with the help of some key questions: What is family worship? What have other people done? Why should I do it? How can I start? A valuable resource which you will not exhaust in years.

> Terry Johnson has provided us a superb resource for family religion. Johnson provides a brief but compelling argument for the importance of family worship, but then takes those he has convinced in theory to the next step: actually putting it into practice! In a day and age when family worship is a rarity, and in which parents who are called to lead in it are not likely to have had personal experience of it in their own upbringing, Johnson's book will prove to be an invaluable aid. May the Lord use this book to bring about a revival of family worship in our land."

Ligon Duncan,
Senior Minister,
First Presbyterian Church, Jackson, Mississippi

> A great service to parents who desire to revive the practice of family worship. Johnson's book provides many practical resources and ideas for actually putting this into practice...an excellent resource for christian families.

Ray Van Neste,
Director, R. C. Ryan Center for Biblical Studies,
Union University, Jackson, Tennessee

When Grace Comes Home

How the 'Doctrines of Grace' Change your Life

TERRY JOHNSON

ISBN 978-1-85792-539-5

Terry Johnson has provided a splendid work on how right theology bears upon our worship, character, suffering and growth in the Christian life.

JAMES MONTGOMERY BOICE,
Late pastor of Tenth Presbyterian Church,
Pennsylvania, Philadelphia

Rarely can the vitamin content of sweet, strong, classic pastoral Calvinism have been made so plain and palatable as it is here.

J I PACKER,
Board of Governors' Professor of Theology,
Regent College, Vancouver, Canada

He manages to make theology what it ought always to be: God honouring and rigorously practical....at the same time this book urges Christians to grow in grace. A book we have needed for some time. I cannot recommend it highly enough.

DEREK THOMAS,
Minister of Preaching and Teaching,
First Presbyterian Church, Columbia, South Carolina

The fine book proves for Christians something that they should already know, but often miss: theology matters!

W. ROBERT GODFREY,
President, Westminster Seminary in California,
Escondido, California

When Grace Transforms

The Character of Christ's Disciples put forward in the Beatitudes

Terry Johnson

ISBN 978-1-85792-770-2

The Beatitudes are Jesus' handbook to living a fuller life. This better, more contented and satisfying life is only for the people who believe in him, because, as Terry demonstrates, the Sermon on the Mount was preached to the disciples and not to the general population.

He explains the beatitudes, showing both what they don't mean, and opening up what they do. His conclusions are strong, challenging, and immensely practical.

You will be engaged in the impact of Jesus' words as you never have before.

> My "Sermon on the Mount' note book is now crammed with Johnsonisms – pithy one-liners that get to the heart of what Jesus meant by adorning the righteousness of the kingdom of God. This is where preaching and teaching needs to go. A marvelous book which I cannot recommend too highly.
>
> Derek Thomas,
> Minister of Preaching and Teaching,
> First Presbyterian Church, Columbia, South Carolina

> Terry Johnson has done it again. ...he shows us here a picture of what transforming grace looks like in the life of a believer... What a timely emphasis for a generation long on license and short on character.
>
> Ligon Duncan,
> Senior Minister, First Presbyterian Church,
> Jackson, Mississippi

When Grace Comes Alive

Living Through the Lord's Prayer

Terry Johnson

ISBN 978-1-85792-882-2

Terry reveals the spiritual depth of the Lord's prayer. Each subject is covered in depth – 'Actively praying for' – includes contrition, God's will to be accomplished, removing temptation etc. 'Attitude in prayer' – includes arguing our case before God, keeping an eternal perspective, the prayer covenant, pleasing God, reverence, etc.

This is a profoundly accessible book, one that cleverly combines the theology of the Lord's Prayer with down-to- earth application. Terry teaches us not only how we should pray but also how we should live.

> I am delighted with Terry Johnson's *When Grace Comes Alive,* specifically because it could serve as a clarion call to humble and believing prayer in thousands of churches across the world. ....I found his discussion of 'praying without ceasing' to be sensible and hopeful for us ordinary Christian folk. ...If this book blesses others as it has me, great good for the Kingdom of God will come from it!

Douglas F. Kelly,
Richard Jordan Professor of Theology,
Reformed Theological Seminary,
Charlotte, North Carolina

> What is refreshing is that the ministry of Terry Johnson has not only historical integrity but it has a very definite appeal to young people, proving once again that the genuinely classic is of interest to all, both the old and the young.

Hughes Oliphant Old,
John H. Leith Professor of Reformed Theology and Worship,
Erskine Theological Seminary, Due West, South Carolina

New Testament Theology

A New Study of the Thematic Structure of the New Testament

J. Julius Scott Jr

ISBN 978-1-84550-256-0

James Julius Scott Jr is Emeritus Professor of Biblical and Historical Studies at Wheaton College Graduate School. His doctorate is from the University of Manchester where he studied under F. F. Bruce.

Julius Scott has a passion for the New Testament but he thinks that most people read it without seeing half that is going on! He carefully unfolds 7 themes in the New Testament by answering these 7 questions.

1. Who is Jesus?
2. What must I do to be saved?
3. How should a Christian live?
4. What is the Church?
5. What is the church's relation to society?
6. How shall it end?
7. What does the New Testament teach us about God?

These are vital questions for all Christians, indeed the answers to them will inform and influence every aspect of our lives. Dr. Scott carefully brings together all the evidence from the New Testament to help us do just that.

> This book is a labor of love – for the Scriptures, for readers, for learning, for teaching, and for God himself. The author takes up each topic in a wise, thorough, probing, and reverent manner. Readers will gain fresh insight into the history of New Testament times, the convictions of the biblical writers, and the implications of the age-old yet ever new Christian message for today. Readers will also glimpse the work of major New Testament scholars as their research has unfolded over recent decades. This is an excellent intermediate survey for college students, as well as for laypersons eager to move to new levels of biblical understanding.
>
> Robert W Yarbrough,
> Professor of New Testament,
> Covenant Theological Seminary, St. Louis, Missouri

New Testament Background Commentary

A New Dictionary of Words, Phrases and Situations in Bible Order

W. Harold Mare

ISBN 978-1-85792-955-3

W. Harold Mare (1918-2004) served as Professor of New Testament at Covenant Theological Seminary, St Louis, Missouri until his retirement in 1984. After his retirement, Dr. Mare continued to teach as an emeritus professor at Covenant until his death in 2004 while doing archaeological excavations in Jordan.

The New Testament is a fascinating collection of documents that illuminate the life and ministry of Jesus of Nazareth. It contains an amazing number of details in its texts that can easily be lost on the modern mind. This means that the full impact can pass by the reader, yet sometimes that snippet of information has major consequences for the meaning of the passage.

Commentaries are of some use, they cannot always pause long enough to develop the detail as they explain the main teaching of the passage. Bible dictionaries are helpful, but they are more interested in expressing the meaning of words rather than the significance of situations.

Harold Mare has helped the modern reader by combing the best elements of both in his New Testament Background Commentary. It is both a commentary and a dictionary of words, phrases and situations that shed light on the point the writer is trying to make. He accomplishes this by placing the explanations in Bible order so that it is easy to access the background comments of this book as you read through the Bible passage.

It is an invaluable companion to any reading of the New Testament. It is such a helpful tool you will wonder how you managed without one before!

Revelation

A Mentor Expository Commentary

DOUGLAS F. KELLY

ISBN 978-1-85792-688-9

Douglas F Kelly is the Richard Jordan Professor of Theology, Reformed Theological Seminary, Charlotte, North Carolina.

A compelling presentation of Paul's theology enriched There is so much in the past, present and future that we do not understand. The book of Revelation helps us understand who is in full and sovereign There is so much in the past, present and future that we do not understand. The book of Revelation helps us understand who is in full and sovereign control, the victorious lamb on his throne. And what a great unveiling of the glorious saviour is revealed in this apocalyptic book! In 65 expositional chapters, Douglas Kelly draws our attention to the central theme of this profound book; the Lord Jesus Christ himself.

Written from a semi-preterist point of view, Dr. Kelly provides both theological and pastoral insights of great consequence to John's apocalyptic vision that often puzzles its readers. Highly recommended.

DEREK THOMAS,
Minister of Preaching and Teaching,
First Presbyterian Church, Columbia, South Carolina

The Church, including the Western church and the global South in the global Eastern Church, need to read the book of Revelation now more than ever. Let Douglas Kelly be your guide.

MICHAEL A. MILTON,
Chancellor/CEO elect,
The James M. Baird Jr. Professor of Pastoral Theology,
Reformed Theological Seminary

Christian Focus Publications

publishes books for all ages

Our mission statement –

STAYING FAITHFUL

In dependence upon God we seek to impact the world through literature faithful to His infallible Word, the Bible. Our aim is to ensure that the Lord Jesus Christ is presented as the only hope to obtain forgiveness of sin, live a useful life and look forward to heaven with Him.

REACHING OUT

Christ's last command requires us to reach out to our world with His gospel. We seek to help fulfil that by publishing books that point people towards Jesus and help them develop a Christ-like maturity. We aim to equip all levels of readers for life, work, ministry and mission.

Books in our adult range are published in three imprints:

Christian Focus contains popular works including biographies, commentaries, basic doctrine and Christian living. Our children's books are also published in this imprint.

Mentor focuses on books written at a level suitable for Bible College and seminary students, pastors, and other serious readers. The imprint includes commentaries, doctrinal studies, examination of current issues and church history.

Christian Heritage contains classic writings from the past.

Christian Focus Publications Ltd,
Geanies House, Fearn, Ross-shire,
IV20 1TW, Scotland, United Kingdom.
www.christianfocus.com